HOMEOWNERS ASSOCIATIONS

*A How-To Guide for Leadership
and
Effective Participation*

By

John Paul Hanna

and

Grace Morioka

Palo Alto, California

Published by Hanna Press

All rights reserved.

Copyright © 1999 by Hanna Press.

No part of this book may be reproduced or transmitted in any form or by any means, electronic or mechanical, including photocopying, recording, or by any information storage and retrieval system without written permission from the publisher, except for the inclusion of brief quotations in a review.

First printing 1988.
Revised Edition 1999.

Printed in the United States of America.

Cover Design by Michael A. Rogondino

International Standard Book Number: ISBN-0-9621093-1-2

Library of Congress Catalog Card Number: 98-75300

For
Barbara

and

For
Ken,
Mom and Dad

About the Authors

John Paul Hanna is a practicing attorney and partner in the firm of Hanna & Van Atta in Palo Alto, California.

His firm, Hanna & Van Atta, specializes in real estate law. The firm has created over 1500 property owners associations in the State of California, and actively represents numerous homeowners associations. Mr. Hanna is the author of the California Condominium Handbook and California Condominium Handbook 2d – Law and Practice, Residential and Commercial Common Interest Development, published by West Group. He received his B.A. and J.D. degrees from Stanford University and Stanford Law School.

Mr. Hanna has also co-authored the three-volume work entitled California Common Interest Developments: A Guide to California Common-Interest Development and Community Association Law, published by West Group in 1999 and supplemented annually.

Mr. Hanna has served on the Condominium and Cooperative Housing Committee of the Real Property Section of the California State Bar Association, and is a member of the Real Property Section of the American Bar Association. He has assisted in drafting common interest development legislation in California. He is a member of the American College of Real Estate Lawyers (ACREL), the College of Community Association Lawyers, the Executive Council of Home Owners (ECHO), and the Community Associations Institute (CAI).

Grace H. Morioka is the president and founder of Commoncents Management, an association management firm located in San Jose, California. She received her B.S. in Commerce from the University of Santa Clara, and worked for several years in the accounting field upon graduation. For the past 17 years, Ms. Morioka has worked in the association management industry as a professional association manager and a management consultant who has managed over 50 homeowners associations. She also consults with developers in setting up homeowners associations, and has worked with Mr. Hanna and his partner David Van Atta to establish new common-interest developments in California.

PREFACE
By Grace H. Morioka

I first read the original version of <u>Homeowners Associations: A How-To Guide</u> by industry expert and attorney John Paul Hanna in 1990, six years after I began my career as an Association Manager. From the first guide, I learned more about the property association and common interest development industry than I had from the six previous years in this business! The book became the "bible" that countless Board Members, association managers and I used to avoid the legal pitfalls and operating nightmares that are experienced by less knowledgeable industry professionals and community association boards of directors.

Little did I realize back then that I would someday get the opportunity to work with John in revising and updating this valuable guide. This new, revised version of the "Guide" has been completely updated with a new look, new format, and the latest changes in the laws applicable to community associations. The forms have also been revised. It has been a very long road to making this new Guide a reality, and we both hope that you will find the new book even more valuable and useful than the previous version.

For additional information and references to other materials, please visit our website at www.hannapress.com.

INTRODUCTION
By John Paul Hanna

This book is intended for use by members of real property owners associations, residential and commercial, and is particularly designed to be a guide for officers, directors, and committee members of such associations. This book is national in scope so that it will be useful to the widest possible audience. To achieve that goal, it is necessary to be general, rather than specific, and the reader is cautioned to always seek local legal counsel to be guided by local laws, ordinances and regulations.

The authors would like to acknowledge the assistance and help of Sally Morton and Melissa Wager in preparation of the manuscript, with special thanks to Linda Wadkins Brost for editing and manuscript preparation.

We hope you find this new Guide a practical and helpful "bible" for any community association.

WARNING - DISCLAIMER

This book is designed to provide information in regard to the subject matter covered. It is sold with the understanding that the publisher and authors are not engaged in rendering legal, accounting or other professional services. If legal or other expert assistance is required, the services of a competent professional should be sought.

Every effort has been made to make this book as complete and as accurate as possible. However, there may be mistakes both typographical and in content. Therefore, this text should be used only as a general guide and not as the ultimate source of information. Furthermore, this book contains information on associations only up to the printing date.

The purpose of this book is to educate and entertain. The authors and publisher shall have neither liability nor responsibility to any person or entity with respect to any loss or damage caused or alleged to be caused directly or indirectly by the information contained in this book.

CONTENTS

Chapter 1
The Legal Authority of Associations   1
1. What Creates and Governs the Project   1
2. State Statutes   1
3. Local Ordinances   1
4. Federal Statutes   1
5. Interpretation of Legal Documents   2
6. Enforcement   2
7. Amending Documents   2
8. General Powers, Common Law   3
9. Loans   3
10. Lack of Authority   4
11. Standard of Reasonableness   4

Chapter 2
Duties of the Association   5
1. What Are the Duties of an Association?   5
2. Statutory Duties   5
3. Contractual Duties   5
4. Local Ordinances   6
5. Federal Statutes   6
6. Common Law Duties   6

Chapter 3
Legal Documents and Structure   8
1. Basic Legal Documents   8
2. Members   10
3. Directors   10
4. Officers   10
5. Management   10
6. Committees   11
7. Master Association   11
8. Sister Association   11
9. Common-Interest Ownership   11
10. Formation   12
11. Phased Developments   12
12. Changes in Legal Documents   13
13. Reformation of Documents by Court Order   20
14. Judicial Review and Interpretation of Documents   20

Chapter 4
Membership   21
1. Qualification   21
2. Membership Roster   21
3. Membership Certificates   21
4. Suspension   21
5. Discrimination in Sale or Lease   22
6. Age Restrictions   22
7. Liability   22

8   Tort Liability of Members   22
9   Contractual Liability   22
10   Comparison of Members in Incorporated Association vs. Unincorporated Association   23

Chapter 5

Transfer of Membership   24
1   Transfer of Membership   24
2   Transfer Fees   24
3   Restrictions on Transfer   24
4   Right of First Refusal   25

Chapter 6

Directors   26
1   Eligibility   26
2   Number of Directors   26
3   Term of Office   26
4   Initial Directors   27
5   Nominations   27
6   Election   28
7   Resignation   29
8   Removal of Directors   30
9   Replacement   31
10   Duties of Directors   31
11   Fiduciary Duty   32
12   Business Judgment   33
13   Prudent Person Rule   33
14   Conflicts of Interest   34
15   Delegation   34
16   Compensation   34
17   Liability   35
18   Limits on Liability   36
19   Directors' and Officers' Insurance   37
20   Cost of Defense   37
21   Bonding   37
22   Indemnity   37
23   Board Meetings   38
24   Role of the Board   41
25   Operation of the Board   41
26   Quorum of Directors   42
27   First Organizational Meeting   43
28   Enforcement of Developer's Obligations   44
29   Action Without Meeting   46
30   Telephone Meetings   46
31   Executive Session   46
32   Secret Meetings   46
33   Notices   46
34   Waiver of Notice   47

Chapter 7

Officers   48
1   Eligibility   48
2   Selection of Officers   48
3   Assistant Officers   48

  4 Conflicts of Interest 48
  5 President 49
  6 Vice-President 49
  7 Secretary 49
  8 Treasurer or Chief Financial Officer 50

Chapter 8

Committees 51
  1 Purpose of Committees 51
  2 Committee Membership 51
  3 Delegation 51
  4 List of Committees 52
  5 Committee Reports 55

Chapter 9

Meetings 56
  1 First General Membership Meeting 56
  2 General Membership Meetings 57
  3 Annual Membership Meetings 57
  4 Directors' Meetings 57
  5 Special Meetings 57
  6 Calling Meetings 57
  7 Conduct of General Membership or Annual Meetings 58
  8 Membership Roll 59
  9 Proxies 60
  10 Quorum 60
  11 Developer's Votes 61
  12 Open Meetings 61
  13 Agenda 62
  14 Minutes 62
  15 Resolutions and Motions 63
  16 Documents to Obtain from Developer 63
  17 Adjournment 64

Chapter 10

Conducting a Meeting 65
  1 Robert's Rules of Order 65
  2 Motions 65
  3 Resolutions 65
  4 Seconding Motions 66
  5 Point of Order 66
  6 Obtaining the Floor 67
  7 Calling for the Question 67
  8 Appeals 67
  9 Motions Relating to Nominations 67
  10 Amendments 68
  11 Substitute Motions 68
  12 Privileged Motions 68
  13 Orders of the Day 69
  14 Suspension of the Rules 69
  15 Request for Information 69
  16 To Lay on the Table 69
  17 Reconsider 70
  18 Decorum 70

    19   Voting   70
    20   Recess   71
    21   Adjournment   71
    22   Table of Parliamentary Rules   71

Chapter 11

Voting/Election   73
    1   One Vote Per Owner/Member   73
    2   Weighted Voting   73
    3   Two-Class Voting   73
    4   Voting Register   74
    5   Transfer of Membership   74
    6   Proxies   75
    7   Cumulative Voting   76
    8   Majority   77
    9   Extra Majority   77
    10   Secret Ballot   77
    11   Vote by Mail   77
    12   Developer Votes   77
    13   Nominating Committee   78
    14   Elections   78
    15   Checklist for Elections   81
    16   Ballot   81
    17   Changing the Number of Directors and/or Terms of Office   82
    18   Removal of Directors   83
    19   Vesting of Voting Rights   83
    20   Protecting Minority Interests   83
    21   Notice of Election Meeting   84
    22   Nominations   84
    23   Suspension of Voting Rights   84
    24   Contesting Elections   84
    25   Record-Keeping   84

Chapter 12

Voting Privileges of the Developer   85
    1   Multiple Voting Privileges   85
    2   Creation of Special Voting Privileges   85
    3   Elimination of Special Voting Privileges   85
    4   Extension or Revival of Special Voting Privileges   85
    5   Exercise of Special Voting Privileges   86
    6   Cumulative Voting by Developer   86
    7   Minimum Representation on Board   86
    8   Annexation of Phases   86

Chapter 13

Minutes   87
    1   Minutes of First Board Meeting   87
    2   General Membership Meeting   87
    3   Minutes of Directors' Meetings   88
    4   Action Without a Meeting   88
    5   Telephone and Electronic Meetings   88
    6   Resolutions   88
    7   Minutes Book   89

Chapter 14

Association Records   90
    1   Records to Keep   90
    2   Association Minutes   90
    3   Plans and Specifications   91
    4   Subdivision Maps   91
    5   Condominium Plans   91
    6   Parking Assignments   91
    7   Exclusive Common Area Assignments   91
    8   Membership Roster   91

Chapter 15

Corporate Seal   93

Chapter 16

Association Administration and Operation   94
    1   Association Rules and Regulations   94
    2   Review of Legal Documents and Procedures   94
    3   Adoption of Budget   94
    4   Bank Account   96
    5   Use of Computers   96
    6   Security   97
    7   Start-Up and Initial Organization   97
    8   Attorney for the Association   98
    9   Loans   99
    10   Central Filing System   99
    11   Checklist of Items to be Addressed by Association After First Organizational Meeting   100

Chapter 17

Management   103
    1   General Discussion of Management   103
    2   Management by the Board of Directors or "Self-Management"   103
    3   In-House or On-Site Management   104
    4   Professional Management   104
    5   Management Consultant   105
    6   Selection of Manager   105
    7   Management Contract   107
    8   Termination of Management Contract   108
    9   Handling Member Complaints   109
    10   Site Inspections   109
    11   Delegation   109

Chapter 18

Consultants   110
    1   Attorney   110
    2   Certified Public Accountant, Enrolled Agent or Certified Financial Planner   112
    3   Insurance Broker   113
    4   Manager   114

Chapter 19

Contracts   115
    1   General   115
    2   Authority to Enter Into Contracts   115

3	Types of Contracts and Contract Templates	115
4	Management Contract	116
5	Maintenance Contracts	116
6	Contracts with Consultants	120
7	Capital Improvements	120
8	Remodeling	120

Chapter 20

Maintenance 121

1	Maintenance Responsibility	121
2	Common Area Maintenance	122
3	Maintenance of Restricted Common Areas	122
4	Private Area Maintenance	122
5	Swimming Pools	123
6	Landscaping	123
7	Equipment	124
8	Elevators	124
9	Chimneys	125
10	Streets and Driveways	125
11	Reciprocal Maintenance of Streets and Parking	128
12	Roofs	128
13	Painting	128
14	Maintenance Standards	129
15	Decks, Balconies, and Patios	129
16	Fences	129
17	Carports and Garages	130
18	Storm and Sanitary Sewers	130
19	Windows and Janitorial	130
20	Common Foundations, Walls, and Roofs	130
21	Shingles	131
22	Stucco	131

Chapter 21

Insurance 132

1	Master Policy	132
2	Individual Policies	132
3	Casualty Insurance	133
4	Liability Insurance	133
5	Comprehensive or All-Risk Coverage	134
6	Earthquake Insurance	134
7	Flood Insurance	134
8	Worker's Compensation	135
9	Automobile Insurance	135
10	Non-Owned Automobiles	135
11	Directors' and Officers' Insurance	135
12	Rain Damage	136
13	Auxiliary Structures	136
14	Glass Coverage	136
15	Dram Shop Coverage	136
16	Personal Property	136
17	Boiler and Machinery	136
18	Umbrella Coverage	136
19	Title Insurance	137
20	Property Damage Insurance	137
21	Product Liability Insurance	137

22 "Claims-Made" or "Occurrence" Coverage   137
23 Replacement Cost Endorsement   137
24 Inflation Guard Endorsement   137
25 Nonconforming Building Endorsement   138
26 Waiver of Subrogation   138
27 Co-Insurance   138
28 How to Purchase Insurance   139
29 Cross-Liability Endorsement   139
30 Checklist of Specifications for Insurance Coverage   139
31 General Insurance Discussion   140

Chapter 22
Financial Management   144
1 Budget   144
2 Start-Up Funds   144
3 Original Budget   144
4 First Budget by New Board   145
5 Increases or Decreases in Assessments   145
6 Reserves   145
7 Financial Procedures and Management   145
8 Investing Association Funds   146
9 Estimating Expenses   147
10 Allocating Income and Expense Items   147

Chapter 23
Financial Reports and Accounting   148
1 Financial Reports that are Legally Required   148
2 General Financial Reporting Requirements   148
3 Profit and Loss Statement   148
4 Statement of Assets and Liabilities   148
5 Statement of Reserves   148
6 Annual Statement of Policies   149
7 Distribution of Annual Report   149
8 Accrual vs. Cash Basis Accounting   149
9 Audits   150

Chapter 24
Corporate Reports   152
1 Statutory Reports   152
2 Association Document Requirements   152
3 Disclosure Requirements   152
4 Inspection and Copying of Reports   152
5 Minutes Book   153

Chapter 25
Assessments   154
1 Original Assessments   154
2 Determining the Assessment and Pro-ration   154
3 Regular Assessments   155
4 Special Assessments   155
5 Increases in Annual Assessments   156
6 Decreases in Assessments   156
7 Notice of Assessments   156
8 Commencement   156

    9   Phased Amendments   156
    10   Exemption from Assessments   157
    11   Payment of Assessments   157
    12   Challenging Assessments   157
    13   Accelerating Assessments   158
    14   Billing for Assessments   158

Chapter 26

Collection of Assessments   159
    1   Successful Collections   159
    2   Collection Methods   159
    3   Collection of Assessments from Developers   159
    4   Delinquent Assessments   160
    5   Assessment Liens   160
    6   Costs Incurred in Collecting Assessments   161
    7   One Form of Action Rule   161
    8   Subordination and Priorities   161
    9   Foreclosure   162
    10   Judicial Foreclosure   162
    11   Collection by Suit   162
    12   Personal Liability for Assessments   162
    13   Late Charges and Interest   162
    14   Attorneys' Fees   163
    15   Homestead Exemption   163
    16   Estoppel Certificates   163

Chapter 27

Liens   164
    1   Authority for Liens   164
    2   Notices   164
    3   Enforcement by Foreclosure of Lien   165
    4   Satisfaction, Release and Removal of Liens   165
    5   Use of Liens to Collect Fines   165
    6   Mechanics' Liens   166

Chapter 28

Enforcement of Restrictions   168
    1   Enforcement of Non-Monetary Obligations   168
    2   Authority to Enforce Restrictions   168
    3   Obligation to Enforce   168
    4   Prerequisites to Enforcement   168
    5   Enforcement by Developer   169
    6   Responsibility of Officers and Directors for Enforcement of Restrictions   169
    7   Waiver   169
    8   Discipline of Members   169
    9   Fines   169
    10   Enforcement by Owners   169
    11   Remedies and Defenses   170
    12   Arbitration   170
    13   Mediation   171

Chapter 29

Due Process   172
    1   Due Process Considerations   172

  2 Attorneys 173
  3 Evidence 173
  4 Preservation of Record of Hearing 173
  5 Appeals 173
  6 Delegation to Committees 174

Chapter 30
Legal Action and Lawsuits Against the Association **175**
  1 Actions Against the Association 175
  2 Tort Liability of Associations 175
  3 Contractual Liability of Associations 175
  4 Defense by Insurance Company 176

Chapter 31
Legal Action and Lawsuits by the Association **177**
  1 When Should an Association Bring Suit? 177
  2 Standing to Sue 177
  3 Choice of Court 177
  4 Attorneys' Fees 177
  5 Depositions and Discovery 178
  6 Interrogatories 178
  7 Subpoenas and Summons 178
  8 Alternative Dispute Resolution 178

Chapter 32
Condemnation **179**
  1 Partial Condemnation 179
  2 Taking of an Entire Project 179
  3 Negotiation and Representation 180
  4 Settlement 180
  5 Distribution 181
  6 Condemnation of Condominium 182
  7 Condemnation of Planned Development Project 182
  8 Condemnation of Stock Cooperative Project 182

Chapter 33
Liability Issues **184**
  1 General Discussion of Liability Issues 184
  2 Tort Liability 184
  3 Contractual Liability 185
  4 Limited Liability 185

Chapter 34
Construction or Design Defects **187**
  1 Handling of Construction Defects and Owner Complaints 187
  2 Plans and Specifications 187
  3 Responsibility of Developer 188
  4 Responsibility of Directors 188
  5 Typical Defects 189
  6 Avoidance of Litigation 190
  7 Litigation 191
  8 Statutes of Limitation 192
  9 Alternatives to Litigation 193

Chapter 35
Obligations of Developer   194
    1   Contractual Obligations   194
    2   Statutory Obligations   194
    3   Consumer Protection Laws   194
    4   Common Law-Imposed Obligations   194
    5   Bonded Obligations of Builder/Developer   195
    6   Disclosure   197
    7   Obligations of Developer as Board Member   197

Chapter 36
Warranties   198
    1   Builder Express Warranties   198
    2   Builder-Implied Warranties   198
    3   Condominium Conversions   199
    4   Pick-Up or Warranty Work   199
    5   Appliances   201
    6   Materials and Equipment Warranties   201

Chapter 37
Actions Against the Developer   202
    1   General Liability of Developers   202
    2   Liability of Developer for Failure to Complete Construction or Deliver Promised Facilities   202
    3   Design and Construction Defects   202
    4   Changes by Developer in Design or Unit Mix   203
    5   Promises and Representations by Developer   203
    6   Warranties   204
    7   Suits for Defective Construction   204
    8   Purchaser's Right to Rescind   204
    9   Product Liability Insurance   205
    10   Failure to Enforce Restrictive Covenants   205

Chapter 38
Custodian Unit   207
    1   Authority to Acquire Custodian Unit   207
    2   Assessments Against Custodian Unit   207
    3   Voting Privileges of a Custodian Unit   207
    4   Insurance on Custodian Unit   207
    5   Use of Custodian Unit   207
    6   Sale or Rental of Custodian Unit   208

Chapter 39
Rental of Common Area Office to Developer   209
    1   Rental to Developer   209
    2   Rental to Real Estate Broker   209
    3   Legal Authority   209
    4   Rental Agreement Form   210
    5   Reconversion of Rental Office or Custodian Unit   210

Chapter 40
Destruction or Obsolescence of Project   211
    1   Obsolescence   211
    2   Destruction   211

  3 Insurance Proceeds 213
  4 Distribution of Assets 215

Chapter 41
Extension of Projects; Termination of Projects 216
  1 Extension of Projects 216
  2 Termination of Projects 216

Chapter 42
Taxes 218
  1 Federal Income Taxes 218
  2 State Income Taxes 219
  3 Local Taxes 219
  4 Real Property Taxes 219
  5 Personal Property Taxes 219
  6 Tax Exemptions 219
  7 Application for Exemption 220
  8 Denial of Exemption 220
  9 Mixed-Use Associations 221
  10 Adjusting Income and Expenses to Minimize Tax 221
  11 Switching from Tax-Exempt to Non-Tax-Exempt Status 221
  12 Tax Returns 222
  13 Audits 222
  14 Distribution of Assets on Dissolution 222
  15 Incorporated Compared With Unincorporated Associations 223
  16 Tax Identification Number 223

Chapter 43
Utilities 224
  1 Master Meter 224
  2 Individual Meters 224
  3 Mixed-Use Projects 224
  4 Utility Assessment Adjustments 225

Chapter 44
Public Relations and Communication 226
  1 The Importance of Public Relations 226
  2 Use of Committees 226
  3 Handling of Grievances 226
  4 Newsletters 227

Chapter 45
Exclusive-Use Common Area Rights 228
  1 Authority to Establish Exclusive Common Area Rights 228
  2 Transfer of Exclusive-Use Common Area Rights 228
  3 Use Rights 229
  4 Maintenance 229
  5 Insurance and Liability 230

Chapter 46
Party Walls and Zero-Lot Lines 231
  1 Party Walls 231
  2 Zero-Lot Lines 231
  3 Common Foundations 232

  4 Common Roofs 232

Chapter 47
Association Rules and Regulations   233
  1 Authority to Adopt Rules and Regulations 233
  2 Need for Rules and Regulations 233
  3 Adoption of Rules 233
  4 Subjects to be Addressed by Association Rules 233

Chapter 48
Use Restrictions   235
  1 Use Restrictions in General 235
  2 Population Density Restrictions 235
  3 Age Restrictions 235
  4 Signs 236
  5 Window Coverings 236
  6 Clotheslines 236
  7 Antennas 236
  8 Alterations or Additions 236
  9 Architectural Committee 236
  10 Vehicles and Parking 237
  11 Handicapped Regulations 238
  12 Hobbies 239
  13 Noise Levels 239
  14 Pets 240
  15 Parties 240
  16 Violations of Use Restrictions 241
  17 Unreasonable Restrictions 241
  18 Restrictions Which Are Discriminatory 241
  19 Enforcement 241

Chapter 49
Tenants and Rentals   242
  1 Restrictions on Lease and Occupancy 242
  2 Tenant Relationships 243
  3 Lease Requirements 243
  4 Fees 243
  5 Disciplining Tenants 243
  6 Rental Management Agreement 244

Chapter 50
Fire Safety   245
  1 Fire Alarm Systems 245
  2 Legal Requirements 245
  3 Maintenance Contract 246
  4 Fire Safety Rules 246
  5 Insurance 246

Chapter 51
Toxic Materials   247
  1 Asbestos 247
  2 Proposed Legislation 247
  3 Legal Issues 248
  4 Removal of Asbestos 249
  5 Other Toxic Substances 250

Chapter 52

Pest Control   252
    1   Pest Control Responsibility   252
    2   Repairs   252

Chapter 53

Architectural Control   254
    1   Establishment of Architectural Controls   254
    2   Architectural Control Committee   254
    3   Procedures for Architectural Control Committee   255
    4   Guidelines   255
    5   Enforcement   256
    6   Landscaping   256
    7   Solar Panels   257

Chapter 54

Security   259
    1   Security in General   259
    2   Alarm Systems   260
    3   Guards and Patrols   260
    4   Cooperative Security Systems   260
    5   Security Committee   261

Chapter 55

Resales   262
    1   Rights of First Refusal   262
    2   Signs   262
    3   Transfer Fees   262
    4   Notices to New Members   262
    5   Assessments   262
    6   Statement from Association   263

Chapter 56

Loans and Lenders   264
    1   Authority to Borrow   264
    2   Corporate Resolution   264

Chapter 57

Title and Title Insurance   265
    1   Title Problems in Common-Interest Projects   265
    2   Title to Association Property   265
    3   Title to Restricted Common Area Easements   265

Chapter 58

Multi-Phased Developments   267
    1   Assessments in Phased Developments   267
    2   Phased Budgets   267
    3   Subsidization During Phasing   267
    4   Additional Amenities in Phased Projects   268
    5   Shared Use of Recreational Facilities   268
    6   Insurance on Phased Projects   269
    7   Architectural Control of Phased Projects   269
    8   Promises and Representations by Developer   270

Chapter 59

Master Associations   271
- 1   Master Associations in General   271
- 2   Membership in Master Association   271
- 3   Interaction Between Associations   271
- 4   Use Restrictions   272

Forms

- 1   Annual Meeting Notice   273
- 2   Reminder Notice of Annual Meeting   274
- 3   Sample Agenda   276
- 4   Sample Proxy   277
- 5   Sign-In Sheet   278
- 6   Sample Ballot   279
- 7   Run-Off Ballot   280
- 8   Minutes of First Meeting   281
- 9   Minutes of Special Meeting   283
- 10   Waiver of Notice and Consent   284
- 11   Resolution of Board   285
- 12   Sample Letter of Resignation   286
- 13   Amendment of Articles   287
- 14   Sample First Amendment (of Declaration)   289
- 15   First Amendment to Bylaws   290
- 16   Sample Association Rules   291
- 17   Procedures for Enforcement of Association Rules   295
- 18   Sample Notice of Hearing   300
- 19   Sample Letter to New Owners   301
- 20   Notice of Assessment Increase   302
- 21   Sample Budget Summary   303
- 22   Resolution on Exempt Status   304
- 23   Reminder to Member of Unpaid Assessment   305
- 24   Notice of Delinquent Assessment (Condo)   306
- 25   Notice of Delinquent Assessment (PD)   307
- 26   Notice of Default   308
- 27   Satisfaction and Release of Lien   309
- 28   Sample Management Agreement   310
- 29   Resolution to Adopt Management   324
- 30   Sample Landscape Maintenance Contract   325
- 31   Maintenance Agreement   328
- 32   Lease of Facilities   330

Glossary   332

Index   335

CHAPTER 1
The Legal Authority of Associations

1.1 What Creates and Governs the Project? The legal authority or power of an association is derived from the following various sources, which are commonly referred to as the "legal documents."

Declaration. The declaration, which may be called a "declaration of covenants, conditions and restrictions" (or "CC&Rs" for short), or an "Enabling Declaration," among other things, contains the basic legal structure for the association, and usually defines the purpose and the powers of the association. The declaration is much like the constitution establishing a government, or the charter establishing a city.

Articles of Incorporation. If the association is a corporation, a set of articles of Incorporation will have been executed and filed with the government of the state in which the association is located. Articles tend to vary in length and content. Some contain extensive provisions detailing the duties and the powers of the association.

Bylaws. The bylaws of an association contain the basic rules for governing the association. To some extent the bylaws may duplicate what is found in the articles and in the declaration. The bylaws tend to be more of a working document than either the declaration or the articles of Incorporation. The bylaws are generally easier to amend and are amended more frequently than the articles or the declaration. The bylaws will be slightly different for an incorporated association than they will be for an unincorporated association.

For more information about these documents, see Chapter 3.1.

1.2 State Statutes. Most states have statutory provisions that govern how a property owners association is created, how the land is subdivided into lots or units for purposes of sale, how the lots or units will be offered for sale to the public, and how the associations of owners, which are created to manage the "common interests," are administrated and operated. Officers, directors and other owners responsible for running owners associations will soon learn that most of what they do will be in some way affected by these state statutes.

1.3 Local Ordinances. Local government ordinances may apply to owners associations. Both residential and commercial common interest projects are, of course, subject to zoning regulations, building codes, health and safety ordinances, parking and traffic restrictions and regulations, density control and, sometimes, resale regulations and rent control provisions.

1.4 Federal Statutes. A number of federal statutes and federally regulated entities, such as the Federal National Mortgage Association (FNMA), Federal Home Loan Mortgage Corporation (FHLMC), Federal Housing Administration (FHA) and Veterans Administration (VA), will impact an owners association. For example:

- The Federal Trade Commission regulates disclosure requirements regarding insulation in new dwellings being sold to the public.

- The *Real Estate Settlement Procedures Act* requires certain disclosures and regulates settlement services in connection with the close of escrow on the sale of property financed by federally regulated loans.

- The *Interstate Land Sales Registration Act* applies to the interstate sale of subdivision lots and condominium units in many cases.

- The *National Environmental Policy Act* may apply to the creation and expansion of projects.

- The Securities and Exchange Commission may have regulatory authority over the sale of some types of condominium projects.

- The Internal Revenue Code, of course, applies to the income received by owners associations.

- The *Americans with Disabilities Act* requires compliance with accessibility standards for the areas within a common interest development that are accessible to the public.

- The *Fair Housing Amendments Act* provides for modifications to be made to the common areas, if necessary, to afford access to a unit occupied by a disabled person. The Act also prohibits discrimination against families with children.

These are just a few of the instances where federal laws affect the operation of an owners association. *See Chapter 2.5 for more information.*

1.5 Interpretation of Legal Documents. The board of directors of an association has the primary authority and responsibility to interpret and enforce the provisions in the legal documents. No set of legal documents can anticipate every possible circumstance that will arise, and there will inevitably be times when someone must interpret a particular clause in the project's legal documents. This job is the primary responsibility and function of the board of directors. There are certain rules of interpretation found in state laws. Others are the result of legal decisions by courts and can be found in the appellate reports of cases involving the interpretation of legal documents for a project. The general rule for interpretation is that legal documents for a project should be construed liberally, and the interpretation should be reasonable and based upon the application of common sense and everyday meaning.

1.6 Enforcement. One of the primary powers of an association is to enforce the legal documents, which have created the association and which are the primary source of its power and authority. *See Chapter 28.2.*

1.7 Amending Documents. The authorization to amend a project's legal documents is contained in the documents themselves. There may be certain restrictions on the amendment process, some of which may arise from state laws or regulations. There may also be some restrictions based on local ordinances or on permits granted by the local government. Generally, there will be a reference to such restrictions in the legal documents, although not always.

In states where the state law closely regulates the sale of lots or units in a project with an owners association, there will usually be regulations adopted by the state regulatory agency that limit and control the authority of the board of directors to amend the legal documents of the project during the period that the state regulatory agency has jurisdiction over the project. When the jurisdiction of the state agency has ended, which is generally when the project has been initially sold to individual unit or lot buyers, the control of the state regulatory agency over the form and content of amendments generally terminates. Thereafter, the association has more latitude with respect to the type of amendments that can be adopted by the board of directors and by the required majority of the membership.

See Forms 13, 14 and 15 for forms to be used in amending documents.

1.8 General Powers, Common Law. In addition to the powers derived from its legal documents and from statutory powers and local ordinances, there is a body of common law that has built up over the years that applies to owners associations. That law is contained within the published legal decisions that have arisen out of disputes involving owners associations. Each state has its own body of legal precedents upon which the courts of that state rely. State courts also do take notice of decisions of other state courts and of federal courts and are sometimes persuaded by those decisions from other jurisdictions.

When courts are called upon to examine the action taken by the board of directors of an association to determine whether or not the action should be upheld, the courts will generally apply a test of reasonableness which may take into consideration the following questions:

1. Is the action taken by the association clearly within or reasonably related to the purposes of the association?

2. Is the action taken clearly within or reasonably related to the powers of the association?

3. Is the action taken reasonable in its scope of application to the situation at hand and to other similar circumstances?

4. Has the association acted with reasonable due process in taking the action? *See Chapter 29.*

The courts will review the association's legal documents and, if necessary, applicable statutes, regulations, and ordinances, in order to determine whether the action taken is reasonably related to the purposes and/or is within the power of the association. In determining whether or not the action is reasonable in scope, and whether reasonable due process has been followed, the court will look to appellate court decisions in other cases for guidance.

1.9 Loans. The project legal documents may address the question of whether the association has the power to borrow money, whether the board has the authority to exercise that power to borrow money, and whether the board has the authority to exercise that power on behalf of the association. The state laws governing the creation and the administration of corporations may also include provisions on the authority of associations to borrow money. In cases where it is unclear whether the association has such authority, the lender may require counsel for the association to provide a written legal opinion saying that the board does have the authority to borrow money. Where it is unclear whether the association has the authority to borrow or not, it would be advisable for the membership to adopt an amendment to the legal documents authorizing loans under certain conditions. *See Chapter 56 for more information about loans.*

1.10 Lack of Authority. Where an association and, particularly, a board of directors exceeds its authority, either by violating a provision of the legal documents or a state statute or local ordinance, or by failing to follow due process in taking some action, the member, owner, or other person affected by the action can challenge the authority of the association in a court action and obtain a legal determination of the matter. The result of an unfavorable decision toward the association could be that the rule adopted by the association was void, or the action taken was ineffective, or, possibly, the association would be liable for damages. There is also the possibility that the officers or directors involved in taking the action could be personally liable. *See Chapter 33.2 for more information regarding lack of proper authority.*

1.11 Standard of Reasonableness. Associations are basically quasi-governments, with duties and powers that are similar to, in some respects, but not as extensive as the duties and powers of local municipalities.

The legal requirements and standards of conduct that the courts apply to the actions of a governmental entity should not be the same as tests that are to be applied to the actions taken by non-professional, volunteer officers and directors of a property owners association. The courts will apply a standard of reasonableness to the actions that are taken by the association. Property owners associations are based on the concepts that, to promote the health, happiness, and welfare for the majority of property owners, each must give up a certain degree of freedom of choice that he or she might otherwise enjoy in a separate, privately-owned property. Because owners live in close proximity and use common facilities, each owner must also be willing to accept a certain amount of quasi-governmental interference in his or her private affairs to the extent that they affect other owners or occupants of the project. At the same time, the actions taken by the association in carrying out its duties must be reasonably related to the basic purposes of the association in promoting the health, happiness and welfare of the owners and occupants of the project.

CHAPTER 2
Duties of the Association

2.1 What Are the Duties of an Association? The duties of an owners association are set forth primarily in the basic legal documents, which includes the declaration, articles and bylaws. These duties are also set forth in various federal, state, and local ordinances and statutes. The duties assumed by associations cover a broad spectrum of activities, including:

- The physical maintenance of buildings and grounds
- Establishment of financial policies and procedures
- Adoption of annual operating budgets
- Collection of periodic assessments and payment of bills
- Enforcement of rules and provisions of the legal documents, and the assessment of penalties
- Establishment of rules and regulations, including the procedures for holding hearings
- Selection of consultants, such as attorneys and CPAs
- Employment of managers, contractors, and employees
- Selection and maintenance of adequate insurance
- Enforcement of the rights of the association and its members
- Prosecution and defense of legal actions

2.2 Statutory Duties. State statutes play an important role in defining the duties and obligations of an owners association. There is a wide variation among the states. Some have adopted very specific and detailed statutes regulating the establishment and administration of owners associations. The legal documents that create an association must comply with the laws of the state in which the association is located and does business. The members, officers and directors of the association are subject to and bound by whatever state laws apply to their association. Here the old saying "ignorance of the law is no excuse" is doubly important, because not only must the officers and directors refrain from violating any laws, but they are also responsible for carrying out certain affirmative duties and obligations which are imposed upon them by law. Officers and directors have a responsibility to become familiar with the laws that apply to their association and are responsible for seeing that the laws are observed.

See Chapter 6.10 for more information regarding statutory duties of the association.

2.3 Contractual Duties. Each member of an association who becomes a member by virtue of acquiring ownership of an interest in real property subject to the jurisdiction of the association has, in a sense, entered into a contract with the other members of the association. Under the terms of that contract, each member of the association agrees to be bound by and observe the rules of the association, and further agrees that if he or she does so, that (s)he may be subject to legal action by the association or by any member of the association. There is no effective way to avoid the contractual obligations imposed upon an owner of property who is a member of an association other than by selling the property that will terminate the membership automatically. *See Chapter 4.1 and Chapter 5 for more information.*

2.4 Local Ordinances. Many cities have enacted ordinances that in some way regulate the activities of owners associations. Generally, these ordinances concern certain provisions in the recorded legal documents of the project that establish certain things in which the local municipality has a governmental interest. For example, in a planned development project with a certain density, the local municipality may require that any changes to increase or decrease the open space require the consent of the local planning commission. Another example would be a provision inserted in the legal documents as a condition to approval of the project, that the landscaping in the project as well as the exteriors of the buildings be maintained to a certain standard. Such a provision may provide that if the required level of maintenance is not achieved and/or maintained, the municipality will have some authority to step in and require maintenance to be performed at the owner's expense.

Generally, local ordinances do not directly affect owners associations, although there are exceptions, particularly where cities require staff review of legal documents prior to approval of new projects. In such cases, certain provisions must be inserted in the documents to give the local government authority over certain aspects of the project. These provisions cannot be deleted from the documents without violating the law of the local jurisdiction, which initially required the provisions to be included. Examples of local regulations of the kind that cannot be deleted from the documents are those having to do with site design, safety features (such as installation and inspection of fire safety equipment), aesthetics and architectural design, landscaping, maintenance standards, parking requirements, and discrimination in the use or occupancy of dwellings.

In addition, there may be local regulations on pets and vehicles, particularly recreational vehicles, which may conflict with the provisions of the legal documents, in which case the local ordinance takes precedence if it is more restrictive. Of course, a project may have stricter standards than those imposed by local ordinances, provided that the standards do not discriminate in such a way as to violate civil or constitutional rights. *See Chapter 48.17 for more information.*

2.5 Federal Statutes. A number of federal statutes apply to residential projects. The Federal Trade Law, requiring disclosure of insulation in a new project, is an example of federal regulations that can affect almost every condominium or planned development project where new housing is sold. Also, the offering of a project for sale by mail, radio or television promotion, or some other form of advertising that crosses state lines, is subject to federal regulation. *See Chapter 1.4.*

2.6 Common Law Duties. The appellate decisions of state and federal courts do have an effect upon homeowners associations and their members. In a state that has not adopted extensive statutory rules or regulations concerning the organization and operation of an owners association, the decisions of the appellate courts in that jurisdiction may have far-reaching significance. An example of a court decision that would have such an effect would be one which imposed a certain level of fiduciary responsibility upon officers and directors of an association and found the officers and directors to be personally liable for failure to perform up to that standard.

See Chapter 6.10 for more information about common law duties.

CHAPTER 3
Legal Documents and Structure

3.1 Basic Legal Documents. The basic legal structure of an owners association is contained in the legal documents that are prepared in order to create the association. The declaration is the most important legal document pertaining to an owners association.

The Declaration. The declaration contains the provisions which are required for the creation of an association and for the creation of the restrictive covenants running with the land which must exist in order to create reciprocal obligations among property owners within a project. The term "covenant running with the land" comes from British Common Law, and means an obligation or a restriction which has been placed against a piece of real property by recording a document, such as an easement, or a set of restrictions, usually in the county in which the property is located. Such covenants are usually permanent, and are said to "run with the land" because once they are attached to a piece of property, they automatically follow the property into the hands of the new owner whenever there is transfer of title. Once a covenant running with the land has been created, it continues to affect the property even when title is transferred by deed that omits mention of the covenant. Covenants running with the land can be modified or deleted by a subsequently recorded document, provided the original covenant is of such a nature that its modification or termination is legally permitted.

The declaration starts with a legal description of the project that is usually a "common-interest development." The declaration will define the project, describe it in general terms, describe the owners association and its responsibilities, and set forth the restrictions on the use or enjoyment of the individual lots or units in the project and the common areas. The developer and its attorney, with reference to local, state and federal statutes, make initial decisions about the provisions of a declaration applicable to the project and to the creation of an association. In some cases the declaration will also include provisions which could be found in the articles and in the bylaws.

The Articles of Incorporation. The articles of incorporation is the basic charter document for an incorporated owners association. The association may be incorporated either as a standard private stock corporation or as a nonprofit corporation. It may also be formed as an unincorporated association, in which case there will not be any articles of incorporation, and the legal documents will include just the declaration and the bylaws. Normally the articles are filed with the Secretary of State of the state in which the association is incorporated. In some states, initial directors are named in the articles, and, in others, only the incorporator is named in the original articles. The articles will set forth the name of the corporation, a statement of the purposes of the corporation, and, in most cases, the name and address of a responsible individual who is available to receive service of documents on behalf of the corporation. In addition, normal provisions include a recitation of the tax-exempt nature of the association, and a statement about the disposition of the assets of the corporation in the event of its dissolution. Some articles contain a lengthy recitation of powers and duties of the corporation, a statement about membership, voting rights, and key provisions concerning the board of directors. The tendency under more modern statutes is for the articles to be quite brief, and to have the declaration and the bylaws define the powers of the corporation, the duties of the officers and directors, the number of directors, voting rights, membership rights, and related matters.

The Bylaws. The bylaws contain the rules for administration and operation of the association. The bylaws will usually set forth the number of directors, the term of office of the directors, and the names of the various officers such as president, vice-president, secretary and treasurer or chief financial officer. The bylaws are a working document, and perhaps the most useful document for the members of the board of directors. Questions of voting, membership, procedure, and other administrative issues are normally answered by reviewing the bylaws.

The bylaws will be the most often used and most frequently amended document of the three basic legal documents for a common-interest subdivision. Although the practice varies from one jurisdiction to another, there is not normally a requirement to record the bylaws, and it is easier to amend the bylaws if it is not necessary to record each amendment. Sometimes certain provisions that should have been included in the bylaws were instead included in the declaration or in the articles of incorporation by the initial developer of the project. In such a case, it is always necessary to check the other documents in addition to the bylaws in order to determine what rules are applicable.

The Condominium Plan and Subdivision Map. In the case of a condominium project, the condominium plan is one of the basic legal documents. The condominium plan is normally prepared by a civil engineer, based upon the final architectural plans prepared by the project architect. The condominium plan is a three-dimensional subdivision map. It describes the boundaries of each condominium unit and the boundaries of the "common area."

In the case of a planned unit development where fee-title lots are sold with townhouses or zero-lot line homes, single-family detached homes, patio homes, etc., the project will not have a condominium plan. Instead, there will be a subdivision map that will show each one of the separate fee title lots, together with the common area lot.

In order to create either a condominium project or a planned development project, it is necessary to record a declaration of restrictions, a subdivision map or condominium plan, and at least one deed, deeding out title to the first lot or unit. This deed will contain a reference to the recorded declaration of restrictions, incorporating it by reference into the deed and subjecting that lot or unit and the other lots or units in the project to the declaration.

3.2 Members. The membership in a common interest subdivision project is defined in the declaration, and may also be defined in the bylaws. Membership in the owners association is always mandatory, and is appurtenant to the ownership of a lot or unit in the project. The ownership interest transfers automatically when title to the lot or unit is transferred. Normally a person who owns one lot or unit will have a separate membership for each lot or unit owned. The "definitions" section of the declaration should be reviewed if there are questions about what constitutes an owner, particularly where there may be more than one owner of a lot or unit, or where a lot or unit has been sold under a recorded contract of sale, but title is still of record in the name of the seller.

In some common-interest subdivisions, there are two classes of membership. This is often done so that the developer will have multiple voting rights attached to each of the lots or units that it owns, and can retain control of the board of directors of the association until some percentage of sales of the lots or units, usually 75 percent, is reached. At a specific point in time, or upon the happening of a certain event that is defined in the declaration, the second class of membership will be terminated automatically. Thereafter, there will be only one class that will include the developer with respect to lots/units that it still owns. The terms and conditions of the classes of membership will normally be set forth in the declaration and in the bylaws.

3.3 Directors. A common-interest development must be managed by a board of directors. The members of the board are elected by the membership. The directors are responsible to the membership and normally are members of the association; usually the legal documents will specify whether the directors are required to be members or not. Generally the initial board members who are appointed by the project developer are not owners of lots/units and therefore are not members of the association. Their term on the board is limited in duration. The initial board of directors will be responsible for managing the project until control has passed to the owners (buyers) of lots or units in the project. They are replaced by members of the association who are owners of lots or units in the project at the first annual election. The board of directors is responsible for the establishment of policies governing the operations of the association, for the administration of the project, and for the appointment of the officers who will be responsible for the day-to-day operations of the association. Directors may delegate their responsibilities, but there are limits on the extent to which such responsibilities can be delegated. *See Chapter 6.15.*

3.4 Officers. Usually the officers of the association are elected by the board of directors. They may be members of the board or not, depending upon the requirements of the legal documents. The officers are responsible for carrying out the duties that are prescribed in the project legal documents. It is the responsibility of the board of directors to make policy and it is the responsibility of the officers to execute that policy.

3.5 Management. The appearance of hundreds of thousands of owners associations across the nation has created a growth industry in the association management field. Management consultants offer assistance to owners associations in various ways. Professional managers can handle the burden of administration of the project that would otherwise be performed by the individual members on a volunteer basis. Professional management firms are usually competitive, and the board of directors or the officers of the association can negotiate with two or more professional management outfits in order to obtain the best package of management services to meet the needs of the association.

3.6 Committees. Committees may be appointed by the board of directors to perform a variety of tasks for the board. Committees may or may not be provided for in the project legal documents. The appointment of a committee should be made by the board based on a resolution that contains a full description of the committee's authority as delegated by the Board. There are certain matters that cannot be delegated to a committee, but must be handled by the officers or the board of directors. *See Chapter 6.15 and Chapter 8.3.* The committees that are given specific responsibilities and powers can greatly aid the directors and officers in the carrying out of their duties. Usually committees do not make policy decisions and do not take action, but act as fact-finding or information-gathering agencies, and make recommendations to the board of directors.

3.7 Master Association. In some projects, there may be a two-tiered organizational structure. There may be a number of projects, each with its own owners association, and a master or umbrella association that has authority over each of the individual owners associations. Where a master or umbrella association exists, there will be two different sets of declarations, one for the master association, and another for the subsidiary association.

The master association will have responsibility for maintenance of the common area facilities or recreational amenities that are shared by the subsidiary association. The master association is a device by which the owners of lots or units in various cluster developments may maintain community-wide activities and facilities and provide community-wide services, while at the same time permitting local autonomy among each separate project within the cluster. *See Chapter 59.*

3.8 Sister Association. In some cases, two or more associations may share a contract for goods and services, or may share reciprocal easement areas, or may own or operate or share certain common or recreational facilities. In such cases, the legal documents for the two associations will spell out the inter-relationship of the "sister" associations. There may also be a separate recorded legal document, such as a reciprocal maintenance and easement agreement, which will describe the reciprocal rights of the parties to use certain portions of each other's property, and the responsibilities for the joint maintenance of such facilities.

3.9 Common-Interest Ownership. In a condominium, the common property (which is everything except the interior spaces of the individual units) will be owned by the unit owners on a percentage basis. The percentage of ownership may be set forth in the legal documents for the project, and may also appear on the condominium plan. Generally, each individual unit owner has fee simple title to the unit and will an undivided interest as a tenant-in-common in the common area, along with all other owners. The percentage of ownership may be based upon square footage, may be equal, or may be based upon fair market value. States differ in what they permit with respect to the establishment of percentage interests. Square footage is the most commonly used measure for establishing percentage interests, but it is not always the fairest method of determining percentage interest.

In some condominium projects, the owners of units in a particular building may own undivided interests in only that building; the land beneath that building and beneath other buildings is owned by the owners association. In planned development projects where each owner holds title to a particular lot, the common property (recreational facilities, landscaping, parking, etc.) will usually be owned by the owners association, although in some projects, the common property is owned by the lot owners, as tenants-in-common.

3.10 Formation. Formation of an owners association occurs, in the case of an incorporated association, when the articles of incorporation are filed and/or recorded in the appropriate governmental office having jurisdiction over the formation of corporations. An unincorporated association is created when the bylaws of the association are executed and officially adopted. The bylaws may or may not be recorded. Once the articles (in the case of an incorporated association) are filed and the bylaws are adopted, the association is a legal entity existing separate and independent from the members of the association and separate from the developer of the project.

It is not true that an association remains legally dormant or without existence so long as no lots or units in the project have sold and closed escrow. Even though the project is rented out, or stands vacant, and no units have been sold, once the association has been formed it does have separate, independent legal existence and the officers and directors of the association have certain responsibilities regarding the association.

3.11 Phased Developments. A phased development is one that is planned incrementally to allow for flexibility in the development and sale of the project. The developer may wish to reserve the right to change the design of units in later stages. It may also want to spread out the burden of paying the expenses of running recreational facilities for a large number of owners.

Whenever an association is one of several associations in a large project, there will be more than one set of legal documents to consider. There may be a declaration, articles and bylaws for an umbrella association that has jurisdiction over a number of sub-associations. The officers and directors of a sub-association will be responsible for the relationship between the sub-association and the master association and other sister associations. The legal documents of the sub-association and the master association will describe the details of membership, voting rights and assessments. In some cases, the members of the sub-association may also be members of the umbrella association. In other cases, the sub-association may hold the membership in the umbrella association itself, and in such event the voting rights in the umbrella association may be exercised by the board of directors or by a designated representative of the sub-association. *See Chapter 59.*

3.12 Changes in Legal Documents. When an owner becomes a member of an owners association, he or she becomes subject to a set of legal documents that were prepared by a developer or a developer's attorney for that particular project. Most of the provisions in the legal documents tend to be "boilerplate," which means that the provisions are used repeatedly and will be found in almost all legal documents prepared for owners associations. The form of a particular section may vary from one document to the next, but the substance is very similar. If the documents are well prepared, they will be tailored to the specific needs of a project. However, in many cases, the developer does not make a very thorough effort to tailor the documents to the particular project. Its interest is primarily in getting the project developed and in a position to be sold, and it is not concerned about the details of managing the association.

It is commonly understood that owners of the lots or units in the project, who will eventually take over the management of the owners association, will modify the documents to fit the needs and desires of their project, based upon the experience of the owners living in that project. In addition, there is no set of legal documents that is without flaws. There will almost always be minor corrections necessary in any set of legal documents for a project, no matter how carefully they were drafted.

The interests of the developer in setting up the project will frequently differ from the interests of the owners who take over ownership and possession of the project from the developer. The owners, officers and directors of an association should, therefore, assume that it will be necessary to make a number of amendments in the documents within a relatively short period of time after they take over the administration and operation of the project. The amendment process can be somewhat burdensome, and so it is important to think carefully about amendments, and to minimize the number of amendments. It is advisable for the owners of a new project to live with the legal documents that they have inherited for a time in order to get a "feel" for the project and the way the documents work. Once they understand how the project administration operates and are familiar with the governing documents, then they can intelligently approach the matter of amending the documents to make them conform more precisely to the needs and desires of the owners and members of the association.

The rules and regulations that apply to an association will also be changed from time to time, and this is another reason for amending the legal documents in order to conform to changes in the law.

"Condensing" the Documents. Once the homeowners association is ready to amend their legal documents, in addition to changing provisions to meet the needs of the homeowners, there will commonly be items that can be considered for removal.

State and Regulatory Agency Requirements. In those states that regulate the sale of projects to the public, a substantial number of legal provisions may be required by state regulatory agencies. These provisions may be of value in protecting consumer rights, but may not necessarily be beneficial to the long-term administration of the association after all of the lots or units have been sold to the public. Generally, the jurisdiction of the state regulatory agency charged with consumer protection law enforcement terminates when the final lot or unit has been sold to the public. The reason for the existence of the consumer protection laws no longer exists, and it is at that time possible for the association to amend its legal documents to eliminate some of the unnecessary consumer protection provisions which may make it more cumbersome to manage the association.

Invalid Tax Provisions. A number of associations were created at a time when the tax laws applicable to owners associations did not provide for tax exemption. Although the law now specifically exempts nonprofit homeowners associations from the payment of income taxes on receipt of their assessments from members, the associations may still be operating under a set of legal documents that were drafted prior to the change in the law. Those legal documents may contain some provisions that were inserted in an attempt to qualify the association for exemption from tax under the old Internal Revenue Code sections, which applied to community associations, religious or charitable groups, etc. Consequently, there may be some wording in those old documents requiring that upon dissolution of the association, its assets be distributed to another tax-exempt organization. It is no longer necessary to have such a requirement in the association documents in order to qualify for tax exemption (*see Chapter 42.6*). It is important to amend the documents to remove such provisions so that if the association were to dissolve, the assets would be distributed to the members rather than to some charitable organization. *See Chapter 42.14.*

Provisions Pertaining to Developer Rights. Frequently, legal documents that are prepared by developers of new projects will contain a two-class voting structure. The purpose of such provisions is to give the developer more voting strength so that it can control the board of directors during the period of time that it is actively involved in selling the project to the public. Once those voting rights have terminated, then the two-class voting structure is no longer desirable, and the document should be amended to eliminate all references to the two-class voting structure.

One of the problems with amending documents is that some of them require a two-thirds or three-quarters vote or consent of the total membership in order to amend. It can be very difficult to get that high a percentage of members to actually participate in the voting or approval process. There are different ways of handling that problem (*see Chapter 9.10*), but the short answer is for the association to amend its documents to lower the requirements down to a reasonable level such as 51 percent of the total voting power of the association, or in some cases perhaps even less than that, such as 51 percent of a quorum.

Another provision that frequently causes difficulty is a provision that requires an amending document to actually be signed by all of the owners or a majority of the owners, depending upon what percentage is required in order to adopt an amendment. That can be a burdensome requirement if there are several hundred members. In such cases, it is a good idea to amend the documents to eliminate the requirement of signatures of the owners and to provide that what is required is either their vote or written consent. Written consent can be given separately without a formal meeting and can be solicited and obtained at a time mutually convenient for the owner/member and the representative of the board who is trying to get written approval of a proposed amendment.

Other consumer protection requirements found in the legal documents include provisions regarding quorum, budget, periodic reports, audits and maintenance of reserves. Once the jurisdiction of the consumer protection agency of the state over the project has terminated, the board should study the legal documents and decide what amendments, if any, need to be made to streamline the administration. Quorum requirements could be relaxed, budget requirements could be changed, periodic reports and reporting requirements could be modified, audits could be eliminated or made less expensive, and reserve requirements could be modified to make them either more or less stringent.

The board and the membership need to keep in mind the question of vested owners' rights before making amendments to legal documents. For example, if pets are specifically permitted in the project to begin with, and a majority of the owners get together and vote to exclude pets, this provision, if effective, could cause difficulty for owners who bought into the project with the expectation of being able to live there with their pets. In such cases, the answer is to include a clause in the amendment, which is generally referred to as a "grandfather clause." The effect of a grandfather clause is to make an exception in certain cases from the rules that are created by the amendment process. In the example given where pets were originally permitted and then the legal documents are amended to prohibit pets, a typical grandfather clause would make an exception for those who at the time of the amendment have pets, and would permit them to continue to have their pets in the project so long as they continue to live there and so long as their pets continue to live.

Another legal consideration involved in the amendment process it that of due process. The term "due process" as applied to the administration and operation of an owners association means in general terms that the board of directors, the officers, and the members, in taking action or in amending or adopting provisions in documents, conduct themselves and the association in such a way as will not deprive any member of the "due process of law," which is a basic constitutional right. *For a more detailed discussion of the concept of due process, see Chapter 29.*

Another legal concept relevant to amending documents is that of property rights. For example, a project was set up originally so that the owner of a condominium unit was given the exclusive right to use a particular yard area, and the board of directors decides to change the landscaping design of the project to eliminate private yards. In order to implement this plan, a new plan is presented to the membership which, upon its adoption by a majority vote, will eliminate the private yards; the owner of a unit whose private yard rights are being eliminated has a legitimate complaint that (s)he is being deprived of property rights without his/her consent. In such a case, unless the legal documents specifically permit such a deprivation to occur by majority vote, it could not be done without the consent of the lot/unit owner adversely affected by the amendment.

The officers and directors of the association also need to be concerned with civil rights. If the action or proposed amendment of documents would tend to deprive an owner or occupant of a project of his/her civil rights, the action or the amendment may, if the board is not careful, create a cause of action for violation of civil rights in which not only the association could be held liable, but the directors and officers as individuals might also be held liable. *See Chapter 4.7.*

Procedures for Amending Documents. In deciding to amend documents, there are certain procedures that should be followed. First, it is probably a good idea to appoint a committee to study the matter. The committee could be charged with creating a specific amendment or it could be charged with the job of reviewing one or more legal documents for the project in their entirety and coming up with suggestions for a series of amendments. Either the committee or the board should consult legal counsel for assistance in preparing the amendments and on the legal procedures to be followed in getting the proposed amendments approved by the membership and properly recorded. It is important that the review process include a full examination of the legal documents, not just the portions that are being amended. It is necessary to make sure that the amendment of one section will not affect other sections in the documents, or put the new section into conflict with other provisions of the same document, or provisions of other legal documents governing the project. The legal counsel for the association should be responsible for advising the association that the amendments conform to applicable law, and as to proper adoption and recording procedures.

After the amendment has been proposed by the committee, reviewed by legal counsel, and approved by the board, it then needs to be submitted to the membership for vote. If the legal documents require that amendments be adopted by vote at a meeting, it is necessary to call a meeting in accordance with the association's bylaws and present the amendment for approval, carefully following all of the procedural requirements set forth in the legal documents. If the legal documents permit the amendment to be adopted by written consent as an alternative to a vote, it is not necessary to call a meeting.

A copy of the amendment may be mailed or personally delivered to each owner, and a time limit should be stated in the mailer. The mailer should also include a copy of the proposed amendment, an analysis of the provision that is being amended, statements of the pros and cons of the amendment, and any other information that would be pertinent or helpful to each of the owners in deciding whether to vote for or against the proposed amendment.

Prior to the expiration of the stated time limit, the secretary or other authorized representative should review all of the returned documents, check the signatures against the membership roster (*see Chapter 4.2*) to make sure that the written consents or ballots are legitimate, and tabulate the results.

At times it may be necessary to send out a follow-up letter if the responses are slow. Once the minimum required number of signatures or consents or votes of approval has been obtained, it is not necessary to continue to wait for the rest of the returns, but in a situation where the legal documents permit amendment by a written consent of a majority, the amendment can be declared effective even though returns are still trickling in.

The board can now officially adopt the amendment in the form of a resolution. The resolution should recite that the written consent of the required number of members has been obtained, and that pursuant to the authority granted under the legal documents, the amendment has been adopted. That statement would be included in a document along with the amendment, and the document would be signed by the president and secretary, certified to by the secretary, and then it will either be recorded or filed of record or simply placed into the official book of minutes and resolutions of the association, depending upon what the legal requirements are. If it has to be recorded with the County Recorder or filed with the Secretary of State or similar officer, then those procedures must be followed. Counties vary with respect to their recording requirements. Typically, the original and a copy are delivered to the County Clerk; the clerk stamps both the original and the copy, returns the copy to the association's representative, and records the original. It may take up to several weeks for the Recorder's Office to return the file-stamped original legal document showing the date, book and page and other recording information.

There are also fees that must be paid for filing and recording documents. Fee schedules can be obtained by contacting the Clerk or County Recorder, or the documents can be turned over to the association's legal counsel, who will have the documents filed and recorded, and will bill the association for reimbursement of the fees.

In summary, the amendment process is as follows:

1. Study the legal documents of the project and decide what amendments should be made.
2. Review recent changes in statutes and ordinances to see what impact they have on the association and what amendments need to be made. In this connection, the board should have access to a newsletter or publication of some organization such as the Executive Council of Homeowners (ECHO) or the Community

Associations Institute (CAI). It is a good idea to have a subscription to a local publication to keep current on changes in the law affecting owner's associations. It is also important to check periodically with the attorney advising the association in order to learn what new developments in the law have occurred which require the documents to be reviewed and possibly amended.
3. Appoint a committee to prepare draft amendments. The committee should review all legal documents to be sure no inconsistencies will result from the adoption of the amendments.
4. Submit the draft to the attorney for the association and get his or her approval in writing.
5. Have the board approve the amendments.
6. Have the committee organize a campaign to obtain approval of the amendments and to carry out the mechanics of obtaining the approval.
7. Submit approved amendments to membership (by mail or personal delivery) for written consent, or call a meeting and take a vote.
8. Write follow-up letters, if necessary.
9. Tally votes and/or returns from mailing or personal solicitation.
10. Present results to the board for final action in the form of a resolution signed and certified by the president and secretary.
11. Have the amendments filed in the official minute book of the association. If required, have the original recorded or filed for record with the county or other appropriate governmental agency.
12. Send copies of amendments to all members of the association.

Sample forms to review include:
Amendment to Articles (Form No. 13)
Amendment to Bylaws (Form No. 15)
Amendment to Declaration (Form No. 14)

One of the problems in administering a project is apparent inconsistencies or ambiguities in the legal documents. It is not always possible to anticipate all situations that will arise, and, indeed, those drafting the legal documents make no attempt to create documents that will handle all situations and stand for all time. When a disagreement about the interpretation of a provision of a legal document occurs, the board of directors has several alternatives:

1. The board can read the document, interpret it, and make a ruling. That ruling can stand unless the matter is submitted to a vote of the entire membership at an annual or special meeting.
2. The board can refer the matter to legal counsel for interpretation. Based upon the opinion of counsel, the board can make a ruling, which again will stand unless the board is overruled by the general membership.
3. The legal document can be amended to eliminate the ambiguity or the inconsistency.
4. The issue can be submitted to a court by filing a declaratory relief action. *See Chapter 28.11.*

In order to minimize legal expenses, the board or its committee can do as much drafting of the amendments as it desires. However, the board should not assume it has covered all the issues in directing an attorney to look only at the document that the board has prepared and edit it for form and content. Although the board may not want the attorney to spend time reviewing other provisions of the document or other project legal documents, it is possible that by limiting the attorney's review to just the material prepared by the committee, important points will be missed and some future conflict will arise between the amendment and other sections of the legal documents.

It is also important that the board ensure that it has authority from the membership to expend funds to have counsel prepare and review amendments. The board should not assume that a majority of the members will approve the amendment, and will approve the board spending the funds of the association to pay an attorney to assist the board in preparing amendments.

Manager's Note: *Before drafting any amendment that will alter the enforcement powers of the association (for example, changing the parking rules or the number of allowable pets), the board should hold meetings, open to all members, to solicit the support and opinions of the membership. In obtaining membership support prior to expending funds for counsel to draft and review amendments, the association will ensure that the amendment is quickly approved, and, after approval, will be quickly accepted by the members as part of the association's operating policies.*

If the legal document that is to be amended requires an extraordinary majority such as 75 percent of the total number of members to approve the amendment, it may be impossible to achieve such a high percentage of approval. In some states legislation has been adopted to help an association amend its legal documents to lower the voting requirement. In such cases, the association may be permitted to file an action and to appear in court to ask the judge to supervise the process of amending the documents by the vote of a simple majority. The board should consult its attorney regarding such questions if the association requires more than a majority to amend its legal documents.

The execution of an amendment may require observance of certain statutory provisions. Some statutes require a certificate in writing stating that an amendment has been approved by the required percentage of owners. Some statutes differentiate between a "certified" document and a "verified" document. In some cases, the document must be acknowledged before a notary public. In other cases it may be signed by an officer who, in addition, signs a separate declaration under penalty of perjury certifying that the amendment has been approved by the required percentage of owners.

Still other statutes may require that after an amendment has been recorded or filed, a copy is mailed to each member of the association, together with a statement that the amendment has been recorded. It is important to observe all of the rules for adoption of amendments, whether contained in the legal documents or in statutes or ordinances. The failure to follow the rules may serve as a ground for attacking the validity or the enforceability of the amendment at a later date.

3.13 Reformation of Documents by Court Order. In exceptional circumstances, it may be necessary or advisable to petition the court having jurisdiction over such matters to revise the legal documents. The revision may take the form of bringing the documents up-to-date, or permitting the association to carry out its functions or to take care of a problem that has arisen which is beyond the control of the members, if the documents do not contain the necessary provisions to permit the members to take care of the problem themselves by amending their documents. For example, suppose that documents are prepared for a phased development, and that a lender forecloses upon a portion of the project, so that the complete project is never built. In such a case, the court would have authority, upon request of the members, to reform the legal documents to enable the association to operate effectively and to fairly apportion the burden of assessments based upon the changed configuration of the project.

3.14 Judicial Review and Interpretation of Documents. When courts have been called upon to interpret ambiguity in legal documents, many courts have applied a policy in favor of strict construction of the covenants. That means that any ambiguity is resolved in favor of permitting the maximum unrestricted use of property. Other courts have questioned that policy and have applied a rule which looks to the underlying purpose of the documents and tries to find a way to construe the documents in order to uphold the purpose they were designed to accomplish.

CHAPTER 4
Membership

4.1 Qualification. The project legal documents will often include a definition of "membership," which includes the qualifications for membership in a property owners association. Membership in an association is appurtenant to the interest in the lot or unit, and comes automatically with acquisition of title. Any conveyance of title carries with it membership in the association. Normally, only record owners are entitled to membership; however, if the legal documents so provide, a purchaser under a recorded contract of sale may be considered the owner for purposes of the project legal documents. Where there are several owners in the same lot or unit, and the "one-vote-per-membership" rule applies, the owners have to agree among themselves as to how the vote will be exercised. *See Chapter 11.1.*

4.2 Membership Roster. The secretary of the association or the professional manager should maintain an up-to-date membership roster, including the name and address of each member.

Manager's Note: Although the association's professional manager may keep the records of the association, it is important that the secretary also have an updated list of, at the very least, the names and addresses of each owner/member of the association. One of the easiest methods of keeping track of members is to enter the names and addresses into a spreadsheet computer program. Larger associations—over 100 units—may find a database program to be very helpful in maintaining these important records.

4.3 Membership Certificates. Membership certificates do not have to be issued unless they are required by statute or by the legal documents governing the project. In some states there are statutory requirements which membership certificates must meet if the association elects to issue them. Membership certificates in the form of wallet-sized cards may be useful in gaining entrance through security gates, or for gaining entrance to recreational facilities where membership identification is required for admission. Automatic entry through otherwise locked doors by magnetized keycards is also a good method to control and limit access.

4.4 Suspension. Suspension of membership itself is not possible in an owners association; however, certain membership privileges may be suspended, including the right to vote, the right to use recreational facilities, and the right to use certain common areas or facilities. Before suspension is used as a disciplinary measure, the legal documents should be reviewed to determine if provisions exist that allow suspension to be used. If such a provision is not included, the documents should be so amended. Where suspension is used, there should be notice to the member in advance, with a date, time, and place specified when the owner will have the opportunity to appear and defend himself or herself prior to the suspension.

4.5 Discrimination in Sale or Lease. Discrimination based on race, color, religion, sex, age, physical handicap, marital status, national origin, or ancestry is unlawful under the Federal Civil Rights Act, the Americans with Disabilities Act, and the Fair Housing Amendments Act. It is also probably unlawful under most state statutes or constitutions, and is typically prohibited in most associations' legal documents. An association should consult its legal documents and its attorney when questions of discrimination arise. *See Chapter 48.18.*

4.6 Age Restrictions. Some state statutes and state courts have prohibited discrimination against children or families with children in residential projects. In such states, there may be general exceptions made for projects that qualify as senior citizens' projects. There may be a minimum age requirement such as 55 or older.

A project seeking to qualify as a senior citizens' project and thus be able to limit membership to adults of a minimum age, should have its documents reviewed by its attorney to ensure compliance with the statutory requirements for a senior citizens' project. For a project that is not presently a senior citizens' project but wishes to become so, there may be certain requirements in addition to amending the documents. Some states require that the project be rehabilitated or renovated in order to be put to use as housing for senior citizens before minimum age restrictions can be enforced. In some cases, if the qualifying senior citizen member dies, his/her heirs or successors are permitted to continue to reside in the project for their lifetime or for some other period of time. If an association or its board of directors attempts to enforce age restrictions illegally, they may be held personally liable for damages in a discrimination suit. The federal government also restricts and regulates projects that are limited to certain minimum age groups. The requirements vary, depending upon whether the minimum age is 55 or 62 years. *See Chapter 48.3.*

4.7 Liability. Members of an association are exposed to personal liability in some cases. In a condominium project where unit owners also own common area in undivided interests as tenants-in-common, they have potential personal liability for personal injury or property damage occurring within the common area. *See Chapter 33.1.*

4.8 Tort Liability of Members. Association members may be personally liable for the negligence of other members or officers or directors of the association, if the acts were done with their participation, knowledge or approval. *See Chapter 33.2.*

4.9 Contractual Liability. Members of an incorporated association are not personally liable for the contractual debts or obligations of the association under normal circumstances. Members of an unincorporated association are liable for the debts of the association, but there may be some limited statutory protection in the case of unincorporated nonprofit associations. *See Chapter 33.3.*

4.10 Comparison of Member in Incorporated Association vs. Unincorporated Association. The members of an unincorporated association are somewhat less insulated from liability than are members of an incorporated association. The amount of legal protection provided by being incorporated varies from state to state. Consult your attorney if there is a question. *See Chapter 33.4.*

CHAPTER 5
Transfer of Membership

5.1 Transfer of Membership. Transfer of membership occurs automatically when legal title to a unit or lot is transferred of record. A member cannot transfer membership in an owners association separately from his/her title. Any attempt to resign membership or to transfer ownership without membership, or to transfer membership separately from ownership, is void.

5.2 Transfer Fees. Whenever a unit or lot is transferred, there is some administrative work that must be performed by the association or its manager.

- The membership roster will need to be changed.
- A demand may have to be made upon the escrow company for payment of outstanding or delinquent assessments.
- Photocopies of the project documents need to be made and given to the new owner.
- Records need to be changed to reflect the name, address and phone number of the new owner for billing and for membership roster purposes, newsletters, etc.
- A welcome and/or information letter must be sent to each new owner.
- Billing and collection instructions need to be implemented.
- A key or gate card may have to be issued and a deposit may be required.
- Copies of the budget and financial reports will have to be duplicated and sent to the new owner.

A transfer fee or document charge is appropriate to cover the expenses incurred in performing these duties. Transfer fees that are unreasonably large can be subject to legal challenge.

5.3 Restrictions on Transfer. In certain areas of the country, restrictions on transfer of membership in condominium or stock cooperative projects are commonly used. The rationale for the existence of such restrictions is that the project is a social enclave and that unit owners should be a socially compatible group. While it is arguable that the difficulty of avoiding social contact with one's neighbors in a small residential project justifies the right to approve new members, the negative aspects outweigh the positive ones because of the possibility of discrimination based on race, religion or similar reasons. However, in most states a restriction on transfer in the form of a right of first refusal is permitted, provided it is spelled out appropriately in the legal documents. *See Chapter 5.4.*

Where such restrictions are properly drafted, they require that either the association or the members become involved in the purchase of a lot or unit when an owner wishes to sell. There are practical difficulties in the association exercising a right of first refusal if it does not have the funds to make the down payment on the unit, and does not have the credit to obtain a loan. Further, it may be a problem if no single owner has the ability or is willing to purchase the unit, and the owners, as a group, have difficulty in collectively exercising the right of first refusal.

In a commercial project, restrictions on transfer may be both desirable and enforceable. For example, in a condominium medical office building, an appropriate mix of medical specialties may be mandated by the legal documents, which provide, for example, that an orthopedic surgeon's suite may only be purchased by another orthopedic surgeon in the event the original owner decides to sell.

5.4 Right of First Refusal. Where a right of first refusal is contained in the legal documents, it generally provides that one or more of the owners, or even the association itself, has the right to purchase a lot or unit on the same terms and conditions as contained in an offer made by a third-party purchaser to the owner desiring to sell the lot or unit. In such case, the owner who receives an offer to purchase must give the association and/or the other owners notice of the terms and conditions of the offer and opportunity to purchase on the same terms. If the right of first refusal is not exercised on a timely basis, the owner may make the transfer to the proposed purchaser.

In some states, restrictions on transfer and rights of first refusal may run into conflict with technical rules known as either "the rule against perpetuities" or "the rule against restraints on alienation." The association should consult with its attorney regarding the application of such rules.

CHAPTER 6
Directors

Manager's Note: This entire chapter should be considered a "must-read" chapter for both new and experienced board members.

6.1 Eligibility. The legal documents for the project should provide the eligibility requirements for membership on the Board of Directors. These may be found either in the declaration, the articles, or the by-laws, and sometimes are found in all three documents. Ownership of a lot or unit and membership in the association are normally required, except in the case of the developer and the original directors appointed by the developer, although this is not always the case. Consult your legal documents and state statutes if questions arise concerning eligibility.

6.2 Number of Directors. The project legal documents should specify the number of directors. There may also be statutory requirements for a minimum or maximum number of directors. According to the common-interest development research studies, the majority of all boards have five members, with most others having three or more. Managers and developers prefer smaller boards for their ease in filling vacancies and ensuring a quorum at meetings.

The number of directors may be fixed or variable. Where the number is variable, the legal documents and/or state statutes will provide a minimum and maximum. Some statutes permit a variable number of directors only in cases where a certain minimum number of directors is provided. Selecting the right number of directors for an association depends on balancing several factors, including:

1. The total number of members of the association (the larger the association the bigger the board should be, up to a certain point);
2. The desirability of spreading the workload among a number of members rather than placing it all upon the shoulders of a few;
3. The difficulty of getting a larger number of directors together for meetings;
4. The problem in getting enough members to agree to serve on a board at one time;
5. The requirements of the legal documents, and any applicable statutes.

There should always be an odd number of directors (such as 3, 5 or 7), so that the board does not encounter voting deadlocks. The legal documents may contain provisions governing the changing of the size of the board. *See Chapter 11.17.*

6.3 Term of Office. The legal documents should specify the term of office of the directors. Terms tend to range from one to three years, with one year being the predominant term. Some associations have staggered terms. Some statutes require concurrent terms when the number of directors is less than five. A five-person board with two-year terms might be staggered on a three/two basis (in other words, three board positions are up for reelection one year, and the following year, two board members would be elected). A seven-person board with a similar two-year term might be staggered on a three/four basis; a nine-person board might be staggered five/four, six/three, or, for three-year terms, on a three/three/three basis.

Where terms are staggered, some directors will be elected for one, some for two, and perhaps some for three years. Where terms are concurrent, the members have an opportunity to completely change the administration each year. Staggered terms provide continuity to the management of the board. If an association has concurrent terms, but wishes to switch to staggered terms, it will be necessary to amend all legal documents that contain provisions prescribing the term of office.

6.4 Initial Directors. The developer of the project appoints the initial directors of an association. These directors may be the developer or members of its organization, family or staff. The initial directors serve until the owner/directors who are elected by the association members in the project replace them. The initial directors have the same fiduciary obligations and responsibilities as the directors who eventually replace them, and the initial directors are exposed to the same kind of potential personal liability for their failure to perform their duties as are the directors who are elected to succeed them. *See Chapters 6.10 and 6.11.*

Many states have passed statutes which are intended to protect the interests of the owners who have bought lots or units in the project during the time when the developer still owns a majority of the interests in the project and/or controls the board of directors. A typical minority protection statute will provide for some minimal representation on the board by the owners other than the developer. For example, a statute may require that members other than the developer must elect some percentage, such as 25 percent or one-third, of the board. The laws are designed to ensure that at least one director will represent the minority interests during the time when the developer controls the board and has the power to elect the entire board.

6.5 Nominations. As the time for the annual meeting and the election of the directors nears, certain actions should be taken to prepare for the election of members to the board of directors. Often the association will appoint a nominating committee, whose job it is to review the possible candidates for the board and to come up with the names of those who are to be nominated. This may be done in the form of a slate that corresponds to the exact number of vacancies on the board that are to be filled at the next election. In making its selection, the nominating committee should consider the willingness of the members to serve as directors, and should also consider their business, professional or other relevant qualifications. Evidence of interest in the affairs of the association, such as attendance at meetings or work on committees, is an important indication of the degree of commitment to the project that is desirable for a director to possess.

The nominating committee should start by making a survey of the membership to find out what "talents" exist among the membership. There may be insurance brokers, CPAs, attorneys, bank officers, financial managers, property managers, contractors or builders—all of who can bring their useful, valuable skills and knowledge to the board of directors. Of course it is vital that the people chosen are able and willing to serve and devote the necessary time to attend board meetings and get involved in the operation and management of the project.

The nominating committee should also consider the personalities of potential directors. It is essential that the members of a board work together cooperatively in a positive manner; a divisive influence on the board can be very destructive. Obviously board members do not have to agree with each other all the time, and disagreements at times may be healthy and in the best interests of the association. However, it is very important that the board meetings and the general conduct of the business of the association be done in a friendly, congenial and cooperative atmosphere. If a cantankerous personality is allowed to sit on the board and to turn meetings into ordeals, it may discourage some talented and capable people from serving on the board who would be willing to do so, provided they are not subjected to unnecessarily lengthy or antagonistic proceedings.

At the actual meeting, the nominating committee can be called upon by the president to introduce the slate or the names of persons nominated for the board. After this, members of the association can make nominations from the floor. *See Chapter 11.22.*

The procedures for nomination are as follows: whoever makes the nomination is recognized either by addressing the chairperson, or by raising his/her hand, or by standing. Once recognized, the person making the nomination says: "I move the nomination of *John Doe* for director," or "I move the nomination of the following slate of directors." Nomination motions do not require a "second," and need only be stated to be available for voting when the nominations are closed and the business of the meeting proceeds to the actual balloting or voting. *See Chapter 11.22.*

6.6 Election. When all the nominations have been made, it is customary to have a motion to close the nominations. That motion should be seconded and voted upon by voice vote. A majority of those voting is all that is required to pass that motion. The vote may be taken in various ways:

- A motion can be made to adopt a slate "by white ballot." Such a motion would be made if there were three vacancies on the board and a slate of three names had been presented, or if there were no slate, but only three names were nominated from the floor. A motion for a white ballot would then be in order. The procedure is for someone to move that a white ballot be cast for the three directors who have been nominated. Upon the motion being seconded, the chairperson would call for the vote.
- If the number of directors nominated is exactly the same as the number of vacancies, and a white ballot has been moved, it is only necessary that a majority of those

present and voting (including proxies, if applicable) vote in favor of the motion in order for it to carry.

- If the nominating committee had nominated a slate of three directors, and one more director had been nominated from the floor, and someone were to move a white ballot for the slate of three directors, the vote would have to be unanimous in order to bypass the normal election procedures.
- If there were any dissent from the unanimous vote, then the four names would have to be voted upon.

See Chapter 11 for a discussion of cumulative voting, proxies and secret ballots.

6.7 Resignation. A director may resign office at any time. Normally, it is required that he or she give notice to the president or the secretary of the association, and the resignation is effective either upon the date that such notice is received, or upon such later date as is specified in the notice of resignation. *See Form 12.*

Sometimes a situation arises where one or more directors resign and no volunteers can be found to serve on the board.

<u>What happens when the board does not have the required number of members?</u> A board may serve with less than the full number of members specified in the project legal documents. The remaining members of the board should attempt to fill the vacancy as soon as possible. However, if the vacancy cannot be filled, the board may still continue to operate until the next election.

<u>What happens if all members except one resign?</u> That one member may still continue to manage the project, or at least to perform the duties of the board of directors, until the next election or until his or her resignation.

<u>What if all members resign, or, at the expiration of their terms, no member will agree to serve on the board for the coming year?</u> That, of course, is a very serious situation. Without a board the association has no ability to operate. It cannot enter into contracts. It cannot collect assessments, pay bills, or discharge any of the duties of operating and maintaining the project. The members of the association in such case are not only jeopardizing their economic investment in the project, but they are also potentially subjecting themselves to personal liability for allowing the board to effectively become dissolved or inoperative. Under principles of common law, which in some cases have been codified in the form of statutes, the corporate structure is available to protect shareholders who are members of an incorporated association from liability for the acts or omissions of the corporation or the association. However, this protection of the "corporate veil" is only available so long as the corporation as an entity exists and functions. If all of the board members resign, there is effectively no entity to act and therefore the creditors of the corporation or association are in a position to "pierce the corporate veil" and sue the members directly for the obligations of the corporation or the association. Only uninformed and/or very unintelligent members of an association who are also owners of unit or lots in a project would allow a situation to exist for any length of time

where there was not a board in charge, actively and intelligently managing the affairs of the association.

6.8 Removal of Directors. The project legal documents may contain provisions that describe the process for removal of one or more directors. Most states have adopted laws that impose certain requirements for the removal of a director from a corporation or an association. In situations where cumulative voting is permitted or even required for owners associations (*see Chapter 11.18*), typical statutes will require that no director may be removed (unless the entire board is removed) when a certain minimum number of votes is cast against removal. Sometimes formulas are provided to determine the number of votes that are required to remove a director.

In some cases, the statutes and the legal documents will provide that a director may not be removed from office by vote of the membership if the votes cast against his or her removal would be sufficient to elect that director in an election at which the members voted cumulatively.

For example, suppose that an association has 100 members, with a board of three members, all elected annually, and a motion has been made at a special membership meeting to remove one director from office. A typical formula for determining the number of votes needed to pass the motion would be as follows:

$$X = \frac{S \times D}{N+1} + 1 \text{ (vote)}$$

S equals the number of votes that are voted at the election. D is the number of directors that a voter voting cumulatively desires to elect (in this example, one director who is potentially to be removed). N is the total number of directors to be elected (which would be three in any annual election). X is the number of votes needed in order to elect the number of directors that the party voting cumulatively desires to elect. In this case, the votes sufficient to elect one more director, if the members vote cumulatively would be 26. The calculations are as follows:

$$X = \frac{100 \times 1}{3+1} + 1 \qquad X = \frac{100}{4} + 1$$

Thus, X= 25+1, or X=26. If the votes cast against removal total 26 or more, the director would not be removed. If the votes cast against removal totaled 25 or less, however, the director would be removed.

It may not be necessary to resort to such calculations in order to remove a director. Unless the applicable statutes provide otherwise, the legal documents may simply provide that a director may be removed at any time by a majority vote of the membership. The provisions should be rather specific as to whether that means a majority of the total membership or a majority of those present and voting either in person or by proxy at a special meeting called for the purpose of removing a director.

The entire board of directors may be removed at a special meeting by vote (either in person and/or by proxy), of a majority of the total membership or total voting power of the association. However, if cumulative voting is allowed, when the successor directors are voted upon, it is possible that one or more of the directors who were removed by a majority vote may be reelected in the process of cumulative voting. In some cases where the legal documents or statutory provisions permit, the entire board of directors may be removed at a special meeting called for that purpose, by vote of a majority of the votes represented and voting at a meeting at which a quorum is present, even though the total vote may be less than a majority of the entire membership.

If the legal documents provide that members of a class, where there is more than one class of voters, are entitled to elect one or more directors, a director so elected may be removed only by the applicable vote of members of that particular class. In the case of fraudulent or dishonest acts or gross abuse of authority or discretion, the court may remove a director.

Where the number of the members of a board of directors is reduced by vote of the membership, the reduction in the number of directors does not remove a director prior to the expiration of his or her term of office.

6.9 Replacement. The legal documents for a project and/or applicable statutes normally provide that when there is a vacancy on the board, it may be filled by vote of a majority of the remaining board members. The vacancy may also be filled at any time by vote of the membership at a meeting duly called for the purpose of electing a director to fill the vacancy. The normal election rules would apply at any such special election.

6.10 Duties of Directors. Directors of an owners association have responsibilities similar to those of directors of a business corporation. The legal documents for a project will spell out the duties and obligations of the directors. In addition, the applicable state statutes may contain provisions that describe and define the duties of directors.

In general, the duties of a director are as follows:

1. To remain informed about the association's business at all times;
2. To attend and participate in meetings and to have the secretary indicate the absence of a director from meetings which he or she is unable to attend;
3. To obtain and read minutes of those meetings the director failed to attend;
4. To vote against actions taken or resolutions adopted by the board where the director is in disagreement, and have the minutes reflect his/her dissent;
5. To be knowledgeable about the legal documents governing the affairs of the association;
6. To exercise reasonable diligence in carrying out and following through on responsibilities assumed by or assigned to the director.

A director has an obligation to perform duties that are clearly described in the legal documents or imposed by law, and to perform them in a reasonable and responsible manner. (*See Chapters 6.11 and 6.12.*) For example, the treasurer or chief financial officer of the association is responsible for the association's financial affairs, including the budget. But the accountant or association manager is responsible for preparation of the profit and loss statements, balance sheet, assessment billing and collection, and tax returns. Board members are not expected to be specialists or experts, but are responsible for being familiar with the business, legal and financial aspects of operating the association and to seek and obtain expert advice where needed.

Directors should actively participate in the following:

1. Maintenance of the project.
2. Establishing financial policy and procedures.
3. Compliance with applicable tax laws.
4. Establishing budgets and assessments.
5. Establishing and implementing collections, including taking legal action where necessary to collect delinquent accounts.
6. Establishing and enforcing rules of conduct for owners and occupants.
7. Disciplining members for violation of rules.
8. Prosecuting and defending legal actions for and on behalf of the association.
9. Selecting professionals for the association such as CPAs, auditors and attorneys.
10. Selecting and supervising a management agent or management association.
11. Hiring independent contractors or employees and supervising their actions.
12. Establishing, maintaining and enforcing architectural and environmental standards.
13. Appointing and supervising committees.
14. Establishing and supervising the development of social, recreational, cultural, and other desirable programs for the membership.
15. Procuring and maintaining adequate insurance for the project and for members, including bonds or insurance policies on officers and employees where required, and directors' and officers' errors and omissions and liability insurance where possible.
16. Supervising the processes required by the legal documents, such as giving notice of meetings, notice of assessments, and furnishing annual or periodic reports.
17. Dealing with construction problems with defects in design or construction of the common area improvements.
18. Establishing reserves and ensuring that sufficient assets are available to take care of periodic renovation, reconstruction, replacement and renewal of project improvements.
19. Maintaining adequate books and records of the association and making them available for inspection by members.
20. Periodically reviewing legal documents and making provision for amendment or updating of those documents.

6.11 Fiduciary Duty. Directors are fiduciaries, and as such have a duty of care with respect to the property and affairs of the association and its members. A violation of this duty, which results in an impairment of assets, loss of property, or personal injury, may result in personal liability of an officer or director.

The obligation of a director is to perform his or her duties in good faith, in a manner that (s)he believes to be in the best interests of the association, and with such care, including reasonable inquiry, as a prudent person in a similar position would ordinarily use under similar circumstances. If a director performs his/her duties in good faith, exercising such care as an ordinarily prudent person in like position would use under similar circumstances, relying only on the information, opinions, reports or statements furnished to him/her by those persons, firms or committees that are reliable, competent, expert and merit confidence after reasonable inquiry, then the director should not be liable for a failure to discharge his or her obligations as a director under normal circumstances.

Directors must exercise their powers in good faith and with a view to the interests of the association. Directors may not make decisions for the association that benefit the interests of either the director or of a third party, such as a developer of the project, at the expense of the association and its members. Directors have responsibility not only to refrain from taking action that is against the interests of the association and its members, but also to exercise their sound business judgment and to take action for the benefit of the association when it is required. A director who exercises his/her best judgment in a good-faith manner and takes an action which turns out to be wrong, is less likely to be personally liable than a director who avoids taking the action that a reasonably prudent director would take, and as a result of his/her failure to act, the association is damaged.

6.12 Business Judgment. Directors have a duty to act in good faith and with diligence, care and skill. This applies to both decisions that affect the business and administration of the association, and to decisions of directors and officers such as adopting and enforcing rules, interpreting and applying use restrictions of the declaration, and disciplining members for violations of the rules. The responsibility of a director to his or her association is defined by the "business judgment rule." The business judgment rule requires that officers and directors act in good faith and with a view to the best interests of the association and its members.

6.13 Prudent Person Rule. A so-called prudent person or "prudent man" rule is a rule that applies to, or can be applied to, the acts or omissions of a director. The standard of care imposed upon a director is the "prudent man or prudent person rule"; that includes requirements of actions in good faith and belief in the interests of the association and its members. This standard requires that a director make such inquiries as are reasonable in order to perform his/her duties in good faith and in a reasonable manner.

In performing his/her duties, a prudent director is entitled to rely upon the information, opinions, reports or statements, including financial statements and other financial data prepared by others, including officers and employees of the association, provided that the director believes such persons to be reliable and competent. A director may also rely on lawyers and accountants and other experts with respect to those matters that (s)he believes are within their professional or expert competence. A director may rely on a committee or board upon which (s)he does not serve with respect to matters within the committee's designated authority. (S)he must first make a determination based upon his/her best business judgment with respect to the reliability, competence or expertise of each of those persons, firms or committees before placing reliance on their reports.

6.14 Conflicts of Interest. A director is prohibited from using his or her official position for personal gain. For example, a director who has access to the list of owners and uses it to promote his/her personal business violates this conflict of interest rule. A director who has an undisclosed financial interest in the company that is seeking to obtain a contract with the association also has a conflict of interest. If a director has an employer/employee relationship with the developer which could raise a potential conflict of interest or create dual loyalty problems, the director should make full disclosure of this relationship, and have that disclosure noted in the official minutes of the board meeting. The director should also refrain from voting upon any matter that involves an actual or potential conflict of interest. If a director or an entity in which the director has a material financial interest transacts business with the association, not only must the existence of the relationship and the potential conflict of interest be disclosed, but the transaction must be just and reasonable as to the association. If a situation arises where there is not a sufficient number of disinterested directors without any potential conflicts to vote on a transaction, the interested director who has a potential conflict of interest may vote. However, if that transaction is subsequently challenged by someone asserting that the transaction was not just and reasonable for the association, then the voting director with the conflict of interest may have the burden of establishing that the transaction was just and reasonable at the time the transaction was approved. The basic rule of conduct for directors in order to avoid the problems of conflict of interest is to be, like Caesar's wife, above suspicion.

6.15 Delegation. Officers and directors may delegate some of their duties, but not all of them. Delegation is necessary in some cases to spread out the burden of administration. A director who delegates his or her duties does not avoid responsibility for failure to perform or negligent performance.

There are certain duties that may not be delegated. Delegation of those duties is prohibited either by law or by provisions in the legal documents themselves. Certain limitations on the authority of the board to delegate management responsibilities are imposed by governmental organizations such as FHLMC and FNMA.

Whenever something is delegated by a board or by an officer, the delegation should be done in a clear and unambiguous manner. The duties and responsibilities that are delegated should be in writing, and the fact of that delegation should be recorded in the minutes of the board meeting. The delegation should also include the obligation to follow up, and to ensure that the delegated task was performed in a timely and reasonable fashion.

6.16 Compensation. Officers and directors of owners associations are expected to, and in almost all cases do, serve without any compensation for their services. Most legal documents provide that directors shall not receive compensation for any services rendered to the association, except that directors and officers may be reimbursed for their actual expenses, if reasonable, that are incurred in the performance of their duties. Unless there is a statutory prohibition against it, an association could provide in its basic legal documents for payment of a reasonable salary to officers or directors for services rendered to the association. A director should, of course, refrain from voting on any motion or resolution providing for his or her own compensation. If board members are to be compensated for their services, it should only be pursuant to a resolution adopted by the membership, and not by the board itself.

6.17 Liability. <u>Personal Liability of Officers and Directors</u>. Officers and directors are, in the absence of statutory immunity, potentially personally liable in a number of areas, including:

1. Causing the association to enter into a long-term contract in violation of the legal documents of the project, where the contract turns out not to be in the best interests of the association;
2. Failure to acquire and maintain adequate insurance, or failure to renew an insurance policy on time;
3. Unauthorized entry into a dwelling unit;
4. Failure to adequately maintain the common area, maintain adequate nighttime lighting within the common area, or provide adequate security measures in the common area of the project;
5. Failure to collect assessments, enforce restrictions, or provide adequately for reserves;
6. Failure to file a lawsuit before the statute of limitations has run;
7. Failure to provide adequate safety measures for recreational facilities, particularly where children are involved;
8. Failure to use due care in hiring responsible personnel or in discharging irresponsible personnel;
9. Failure to properly supervise employees;
10. Participating in discriminatory conduct giving rise to a civil rights suit.

Tort Liability of Officers and Directors. Officers and directors can be potentially personally liable for their torts. A director who runs over a pedestrian while driving his car on an errand for the association may be personally liable to the pedestrian in an action for negligence. An officer or director who misuses the funds of the association for personal benefit will be liable in tort.

If a director does not personally participate in some tortious action by the association, (s)he is not necessarily liable simply because (s)he is a director. The director must have been involved either by positive action or by failing to act despite having knowledge of the situation. For example, if a director votes for or approves action that involves the commission of a tort, (s)he will be personally liable even though the act was performed in the name of the association. On the other hand, if a director votes against a tortious action and is on record as being opposed to it, (s)he would not be held personally liable even though all of the directors who voted in favor of the action could be held personally liable. If a certain action was taken under authority of the board which exposed the association and the board of directors to an action for negligence, the individual board members would each have to prove that they did not participate in the vote or that they voted against the action that was approved by a majority of the directors, in order to escape personal liability.

Liability for Contracts. If the owners association is incorporated, neither officers/directors nor members are liable for the contractual obligations (such as business debts) of the association. The same is not true for an unincorporated association, however. Officers, directors and members of a governing body (as well as individual members) of an unincorporated association are at more risk with respect to contractual obligations entered into by the governing body than would be the case if they were directors of an incorporated association.

A director or officer acting on behalf of an association who enters into a written contract in the name of the association, without believing in good faith that (s)he has the authority to do so, may be personally responsible. If the association is not bound to that contract because the director lacked authority from the association to execute the contract, and, as a result, the association was not bound to the contract, the director who signed without authority would be held personally liable.

Failure to Take Action Against Developer. If the board of directors fails to take action against the developer for negligent design or construction, and members of the board were appointed by or are controlled by the developer, the directors could be held personally liable for breach of their obligation to the association and its members, in the absence of statutory immunity. *See Chapter 6.22.*

Failure to Obtain Insurance. Officers and directors could be held personally liable to the association and its members if they were negligent in failing to obtain or to keep in force adequate casualty and liability insurance for the association and its members, in the absence of statutory immunity.

6.18 Limits on Liability. The trend in the law seems to be, at least in some jurisdictions, toward the imposition of greater responsibility and greater liability upon officers and directors of owners associations. In some cases, strict adherence by courts to legal principles has resulted in judgments that are probably not, in the long run, in the best interests of owners associations and their members. For example, in a California case members of a board of directors were held personally liable when they were sued by the owner of a condominium who was assaulted and robbed in her condominium. The assault was carried out by someone who broke in after the board of directors had ordered the owner to remove special security lighting that she had installed on the outside of her unit to illuminate the common area adjacent to her unit at nighttime. The dilemma confronting the board was that the court found, using hindsight, that the removal of the lights was a contributing factor to the break-in and the assault. However, the board had a responsibility to the other members of the association to enforce the restrictions that prohibited anyone from altering or improving the common area without the approval in advance of the architectural control committee and/or the board of directors. The tension that arises between the concerns of the individual and the concerns of the association is a challenge faced by all boards.

The courts tend to overlook the fact that officers and directors of owners associations are volunteers, not businessmen, and that the owners association is not a profit-making business. Different courts apply different standards in such cases, and some courts do not hold officers and directors to the same standards of conduct and responsibility to which officers and directors of private, profit-making corporations are held.

Most well-run projects will provide for indemnity of the officers and directors by the association and its members, so that any liability imposed upon by an officer or director who acted on behalf of the association in good faith would ultimately be paid for by the association and the members.

6.19 Directors' and Officers' Insurance. Insurance protection for officers and directors is almost mandatory in today's litigious society. Most members of an association will refuse to and indeed should refuse to serve their association if they are not adequately protected by insurance against liability for their actions as officers and directors. *See Chapter 21.11.*

6.20 Cost of Defense. If directors or officers are sued for actions taken in their official capacities, the association should provide for the complete cost of defending the officers and/or directors. The association's insurance carrier should, of course, handle the defense. In the event that the carrier denies coverage, or there is no coverage, then the association should pay for the cost of defense when the action involves the conduct of the officer or director in his or her official capacity acting in good faith on behalf of the association.

6.21 Bonding. Bonding of officers and board members, or any member who has access to the funds of the association, is sometimes required in the association's legal documents by state statute and by federal government agencies that guarantee permanent loans on lots or units in a project.

Where bonding is required, adequate bonds should be obtained at reasonable prices, and should be kept in effect as long as required. A bond is similar to an insurance policy. If an officer of an association is bonded, and that officer embezzles funds of the association, the association can seek reimbursement from the bonding company for its losses. The bonding company, in turn, will seek reimbursement of the funds from the embezzling officer or director.

6.22 Indemnity. In order to encourage members of an association to serve as officers and directors, it is necessary that the association indemnify them for claims made as a result of the performance of their duties. Associations have the authority to indemnify officers and directors or other agents acting on behalf of the corporation against liability or expenses, including judgents and fines. The officer, director, or agent being indemnified, however, must have acted in good faith and in a manner that (s)he reasonably believed to be in the best interests of the association. Indemnification should be authorized by the project legal documents, and if they do not contain specific indemnity language, they should be amended to include adequate indemnity provisions.

Officers and directors should be indemnified from personal liability and expenses, including legal expenses, which arise out of legal action in which an officer or board member is made a party because of his/her position with the association. There are exceptions to this principle in the case of willful misconduct or bad faith on the part of the officer or the director, but such cases are rare. Obviously, if the association fails to indemnify its officers and directors in actions brought against them as a result of their performance of official duties, it will soon discourage any member from acting as an officer or director.

6.23 Board Meetings. Meetings of the association's board of directors are held as often as and in the manner prescribed by the project legal documents. Usually the bylaws will require a monthly or quarterly meeting to be held at a specific time and place. The time and place may be stated in the bylaws, and may be changed by action of the board in the form of a resolution contained in minutes of a board meeting.

Some project documents require the meeting of the board to be held within or as close as possible to the project. Some state laws impose a similar requirement, particularly where state regulatory agencies are involved in consumer protection law with respect to the offering for sale of newly developed projects. Although there are exceptions, regular meetings of the board, the time and place of which has been predetermined, do not usually require notice in advance of the meeting. Some state regulations require that notice of time and place of regular meetings be posted in a prominent place within the common area of the project, and that the notice be communicated to the board members a certain number of days in advance of the meeting.

All association members must be allowed to attend a meeting of the board of directors. However, members who are not on the board do not have a right to participate in the discussion unless expressly permitted by vote of a majority of a quorum of the board, or authorized by statute, or by the project legal documents. An association is free to adopt its own rules in this regard, and may, as a policy, permit members to participate freely in discussions at board meetings. The tendency is for board meetings to take much more time than they should, which can discourage busy members from serving on boards. It is important that the chairperson of the meeting maintain control over the proceedings to keep them moving. Allowing non-board members to participate in and interrupt the proceedings will certainly not help the chairperson of the meeting keep the meeting short.

Manager's Note: Allowing a specific time—for example, the beginning of each board meeting—for members to be heard and to address the board of directors with questions, comments, and suggestions will greatly enhance homeowner participation in the association. In addition, homeowner or open forums reduce the incidents of non-board member interference during meetings.

Meetings should be planned in advance by the members of the board of directors or the association manager. The secretary or association manager should prepare an agenda and deliver it to the directors within a reasonable period of time before the date for the meeting. If a director desires to add an item to the agenda, (s)he should notify the secretary or manager before the meeting.

The president must be efficient, fair and decisive in running the meeting. It is up to the president, as the chairperson, to adhere to the agenda, to stop people from discussing extraneous issues, to make sure that all points of view are heard, and to guide the board in the direction of completing the business at hand. S(h)e should have a working knowledge of parliamentary procedure, be able to call for motions when required, and maintain order and decorum.

See Chapter 10 regarding parliamentary procedure.

The board should follow the agenda throughout the meeting. *(See Form 3 for a sample agenda.)* The agenda should call for approval of the minutes of the previous meeting. The minutes should have been mailed or delivered to the directors in advance of the meeting, so that all have read them. The chairperson should ask for approval of the minutes of the previous meeting. A motion should be made, seconded and carried by a majority vote, and the minutes of the meeting should indicate that the minutes were approved. Inaccuracies or omissions in the minutes should be corrected before approval. After the chairperson calls for approval of the minutes, any director who wishes to insert a correction in the minutes may do so simply by requesting that it be done. After all requests for corrections have been heard, the chairperson then calls for a motion approving the minutes as corrected. Upon being made, seconded, and passed by a majority vote of the board, the minutes or corrected minutes become official, and should be inserted into the minutes book. The minutes of the meeting at which the motion is adopted to approve the minutes of the previous meeting (the minutes of which are being corrected) should also be changed, so that the official copy of the minutes is correct.

It is customary, if invitees or guests are present, to introduce them and to structure the agenda so that their business (if they have some business with the board) can be disposed of early in the meeting in order that such individuals may then depart.

Where financial matters are to be considered, the chief financial officer or treasurer of the association should submit a written report in advance of the meeting. (*See Chapters 23.1 and 23.2 for a summary and discussion of financial reporting forms.*) Directors should discuss the financial report, ask questions to clarify any matters that are not understood, and should pass a motion approving or adopting the financial report or requiring it to be modified prior to acceptance.

Committee reports should be in writing. The committee chairperson or person presenting the report should distribute the committee's written report, should give a verbal summary, ask for any questions and be prepared to respond. The system works best if committee reports can be distributed to directors in advance of the meeting, along with the agenda. If the committee is making a recommendation, it should be stated in the written report. The board may accept or reject the committee's report. If it calls for some action, the board may or may not follow the recommendation of the committee. The board may refer the matter back to the committee for further study, or "table" the matter until a later date.

See Chapter 10.16 on motions to "table."

At a regular board meeting, there should be a written report submitted by the association manager, if the association has employed a manager or retained a professional management firm. The board should be prepared to act on recommendations from the manager.

A typical item to appear on the agenda is called "old business." This may consist of a number of matters, such as items that were previously tabled, reports, or items that were on a previous agenda but were not completed. Once an item goes on an agenda, it should stay on all future agendas until final action has been taken and the matter can be removed from the agenda. Items still on the agenda that are from previous meetings would come under the heading of old business.

Another item that frequently appears on an agenda is "new business." This may be an opportunity for directors to bring up matters that are not specifically agendized either because there was not sufficient time to get them on the agenda in advance, or because the director just thought about it during the meeting. Some scheduled items may also appear under new business rather than being scheduled as separate items on the agenda. The rules for meetings are not fixed. Reasonableness and common sense should determine whether to schedule items separately on the agenda, or to schedule them under new business. It is less important how or where something is scheduled on the agenda, than that the meeting proceed expeditiously and efficiently.

It is customary to have a motion to adjourn the meeting. A motion to adjourn is normally not debatable, cannot be amended, must be seconded and requires a majority vote. A meeting can be simply adjourned, or it may be adjourned to another time and place. There are rules concerning the length of time for which a meeting may be adjourned. The rules may require notice be given to directors who were not present at the time of the adjournment. In some cases, the notice of an adjourned meeting must be posted within the common area within a certain period of time after the meeting. The legal documents, state statutes and regulations should be consulted for specifics regarding reconvening adjourned meetings. *See Chapter 10.21 for a more detailed discussion of motions to adjourn.*

As always, the legal effect of the failure to follow rules governing procedures such as noticing meetings or adjourning meetings to another time and place are usually that the holding of the improperly called or noticed meeting may be challenged, and any action taken at that meeting is subject to challenge and may have to be repeated at a properly noticed or held meeting. *For more information, see Chapter 9.6.*

For a discussion of the difference between resolutions and motions, see Chapter 9.15.

Manager's Note: *To increase efficiency of meetings, timed agendas can be used. A timed agenda simply notes the time to be allotted for discussion of each subject on the agenda. For example, review and approval of minutes may take only five minutes, so the timed agenda may show a starting time of 7:00 p.m. and an ending time of 7:05 p.m. A timed agenda is particularly helpful in ensuring that presentations by committees and management are given enough time to be heard, while encouraging everyone to keep the meeting moving.*

6.24 Role of the Board. The owners association is, in a sense, a service-oriented business entity that has the responsibility for maintenance and operation of the project that its members collectively own. An owners association differs, however, from a normal business entity because the officers and directors are volunteers who serve in order to protect and preserve their property interests, and not as part of their business or employment.

The board of directors and the officers have broad powers derived from the legal documents governing the project and from statutory and common law. It is important that the officers and directors understand the purpose of the association, the role of the board, and the responsibility that they bear as officers and directors. Although the members hold the ultimate authority, it is not practical to have an association run by general membership meetings. Therefore, the authority to make policy and the responsibility to manage the association falls to the volunteer officers and directors. Even though they serve as volunteers, officers and directors nevertheless have to exercise a certain degree of care and responsibility in the discharge of their duties. *For more information, see Chapter 6.10.*

6.25 Operation of the Board. The board should hold its meetings in the most convenient place for the benefit of both the members and the board. A meeting room at the project would be the logical place. An alternative would be the home or office of the president or one of the board members. For large meetings, a conference room can be used, or, if necessary, rented. A neighborhood school classroom or auditorium may also serve as a meeting place.

A table and chairs should be provided for the board members. Adequate seating for members and guests expected to attend the meeting should also be provided. For a very large meeting, a sound system and any necessary equipment such as a slide projector or overhead projector or other visual aids should be considered in advance. If smoking is permitted, ashtrays should be provided, and coffee and tea may also be provided.

The president or chairperson should start the meetings on time and keep the business moving as expeditiously as possible. The secretary or association manager should take detailed minutes of the meeting, which should be typed as soon as possible after the meeting with copies distributed to all of the board members. It may be helpful to have a small battery-operated tape recorder and some spare tapes, so that the secretary can listen to the tapes in order to completely and accurately summarize the meeting and to get the exact wording for resolutions. Motions are not always eloquently delivered, and part of the secretary's job is to see that motions and resolutions are properly worded in the minutes.

See Chapter 9.7 for further discussion regarding conducting meetings.

Minutes are not verbatim transcripts, but are records of the motions and resolutions, relevant discussions, and summaries of the actions taken. The detail in the minutes should be complete enough to indicate what topics were discussed, what motions were made, what the vote was on the motion, who opposed the motion, who abstained from voting, the time of commencement and the time of adjournment of the meeting. The minutes should also reflect those in attendance or missing from the meeting. If the secretary or person taking the minutes of the meeting is uncertain as to the exact wording of a motion, it is best to write it out and read it back to the person making the motion and the person seconding the motion before adjournment of the meeting. Good parliamentary procedure calls for the president to repeat the motion prior to "calling for the question" (asking for a vote).

The style of operation of the board depends upon the nature of the association, the size of the project, and the number and personalities of the members serving as officers and directors. The structure of an association is set forth in its legal documents, and may be similar or almost identical for an association having 20 members and one having 200 members. Although two such associations are governed by very similar legal documents, their respective styles or modes of operation could be quite dissimilar. Generally, the larger the association, the more formal will be the structure, rules, and procedures.

6.26 Quorum of Directors. In most project documents a majority of the number of directors authorized in the legal documents constitutes a quorum for the transaction of business and for the holding of a meeting. In some cases it is permissible to have a quorum of less than a majority. Some statutes prohibit a quorum of less than a certain percentage of the number of directors authorized, or less than a certain minimum number, whichever is larger. In a normal owners association that does not have hundreds of members and a large board, it is best to have the quorum be a majority of the authorized directors.

If a quorum is present from the beginning of the meeting, and one or more directors leaves such that there is less than a quorum present, some project legal documents and some statutes permit the board to continue to transact business. In such cases, an action can be taken if approved by at least a majority of the quorum, or whatever greater number is required by law or by the project legal documents. A "majority of a quorum" is the smallest number of votes required to approve actions. Here is how this number is calculated. For a nine-member board, a quorum would be five members. If there were five directors present at the start of the meeting, but one left, there would then be one less than a quorum. However, if a majority of a quorum is required to transact business (which would be the case under most legal documents), three out of the five directors' votes would be necessary to transact business. If one director leaves so that there are only four left, the four directors would still constitute a majority of a quorum, so that business could still be conducted if the legal documents permit it.

6.27 First Organizational Meeting. In a typical owners association, there are really two "first meetings." The absolute first meeting is a meeting of the initial directors who were appointed by the developer of the project. This meeting often tends to be a "paper meeting," meaning that the developer or its attorney prepares a set of minutes reciting the fact that the directors were present, that they adopted the bylaws, set up a bank account, authorized signatures on the bank account and other beginning organizational steps. Minutes of that first meeting are filed in the minute book that is turned over to the board of directors of the association when the new board is elected at the second "first meeting."

This second "first meeting" occurs when the developer turns over control of the association to the purchasers of lots or units in the project at the first election of homeowner representatives to the board of directors. This normally takes place within a certain number of months or days after the sale of the first lot or unit, or after the sale of the lot or unit results in a majority of ownership interests being transferred to the new buyers. The project legal documents, and also perhaps state statutes, prescribe the time within which this second "first meeting" must be held.

At such a meeting the directors would be elected by the membership with or without the votes of the developer being counted. *See Chapter 9.1.* Sometimes the developer will prepare the minutes of that first meeting of the general membership as one of its last acts on behalf of the association. At other times, the newly appointed secretary of the board will be required to take the minutes. The second "first meeting" of the board will follow the first membership meeting at which the new board is elected. If the election occurs at a time other than what is set in the association's bylaws for an annual election, or, in other words, if the terms of the initial directors appointed by the developer have been shortened to less than a year, the developer's directors should submit written resignations, so that vacancies will be created that can then be filled by members of the association.

Once the new "permanent board" has been elected by the members at the initial membership meeting, the new board will then hold its first board meeting to complete organizational steps. The new board will first have to elect new officers. They then have to approve management contracts, approve signature cards for a bank account and perhaps adopt the resolution opening a new bank account.

See Chapter 16.4 and Form 8 for a set of minutes of a first meeting of elected directors, including various resolutions that should be adopted.

At the first meeting the developer will normally turn over to the new board the minute book and original documents including the articles of incorporation, bylaws, declaration, and the minutes of the first meeting.

See Chapter 9.16 for a list of documents that should be obtained from the developer at the first meeting, if possible.

The board should also undertake an inspection of the project to find out if there are any structural or design defects in the project, or any maintenance that is not up to standard, and present to the developer a list of those defects as soon as possible. The members should be asked to cooperate with the board in forwarding any information about construction problems in the project. The board should prepare claims and submit them to the developer as soon as possible after obtaining the information about construction defects in order to defeat any claim that the developer might make of expiration of express or implied warranties. *See Chapter 36.*

6.28 Enforcement of Developer's Obligations. The developer has a number of different obligations to the association and its members. It has contractual obligations under the purchase and sale agreements that are entered into between the developer and the buyers of units or lots in the project. Further obligations are created by statutes applicable to the project. In most cases, the developer will have posted bonds to secure performance of certain improvements in the project.

The developer also has certain obligations by virtue of its control of the board of directors in the initial stages of the project. The failure of the developer to properly carry out the obligations of the board of directors may result in liability of the developer, and perhaps personal liability of the directors appointed to the board by the developer. *See Chapter 6.17.*

In a phased project, the developer may or may not be under obligation to complete subsequent phases, depending upon the requirements in the legal documents. If the developer has promised, either expressly or impliedly, to include subsequent phases, the buyers of units in the earlier phases may sue the developer to either compel it to fulfill its promise and complete the other phases, or to collect the damages they may suffer by reason of its failure to perform.

A developer may agree to subsidize, for a specified period of time, the cost of operating the association, and maintaining the common areas and recreational facilities in order to keep assessments at a reasonable level in the early stages of the project. Rather than have buyers in the first phase pay the entire cost of operating all the common areas and recreational facilities, the developer may have signed a subsidy agreement and posted a bond, if required by the state regulatory agency, to secure its performance under that subsidy agreement. In such case, if the developer fails to pay the subsidy at any time, the association may take action against the bond or the bonding company in order to enforce the obligation for payment of the subsidy. *See Chapter 58.3.*

Manager's Note: *Often, a developer will agree to subsidize the monthly assessments for the first few phases of the development until the number of homes is large enough to cover the operation and maintenance costs of the common area and recreational facilities. For example, if all the recreational facilities—pool, spa and tennis courts—were brought on-line in the first 20-unit phase of a 100-unit complex, each of the 20 units would* *pay almost five times as much per home for the facilities as they would if all 100 homes were built. To prevent the first 20 units from paying significantly higher assessments to cover maintenance and operating costs, the developer will agree to "subsidize" or pay for a portion of each monthly assessment for a specific period of time.*

When the developer has been required to post a bond to ensure completion of common area facilities, and the developer fails to complete the facilities on time, the board of directors of the association should initiate action in the name of the association against the developer in order to enforce the bonded obligations.

In certain jurisdictions, if the board fails to act in such a case, a certain percentage of the membership of the association can petition the board to require a general membership meeting to be held to consider enforcing the bonded obligation of the subdivider. Once the developer has completed the improvements that have been bonded, the board should promptly release the bond. Normally this is done by a statement in writing from the association saying that the improvements have been completed, which statement is delivered to the title company or whatever entity holds the bond so that it can then be released to the subdivider.

In some jurisdictions the developer may also be obligated to post a bond to guarantee payment of assessments for an initial period of months after the close of escrow on the first sale in the project. Normally, the bond would be released and the obligation would terminate after the close of escrow on the sale of a certain percentage of units or lots in the project. When that goal is reached, the bond should be released. If the developer fails to pay its assessments while the bond is still in effect, the association can take action to enforce the bond to collect the delinquent assessments.

If the developer of a phased project decides to change the design, unit mix, or density of units in a subsequent phase, the association and its members may or may not have the right to prevent the developer from making such changes. Whether the developer can do it or not depends on whether it reserved the right to make such changes and whether the changes would materially increase the burden of assessments on the existing owners, or would materially or substantially overburden the existing parking and recreational facilities of the project. A change in unit design may also require approval of the architectural committee, which may be controlled by the members if the buyers have assumed the control of the board. In such cases, the developer would no longer have the right to arbitrarily change the design of units in a subsequent phase. If the developer still controls the architectural committee, and the change in design is so radical that the architectural review committee, which is controlled by the developer, had abused its discretion in approving the design over the objections of the owners of units in the preceding phases, it is possible that the developer would be required to modify its design to fit the design of the existing units.

If the developer has made certain promises or representations to buyers concerning its intentions or plans for future development, the buyers

45

who become members of the association may be able to enlist the support of the court in preventing the developer from changing its plans, or reneging on its promises or representations. For example, if a developer made verbal representations to buyers of lots in a planned development project that a key parcel of land within or close to the project was going to be developed as a park or as open space, and then changed his mind and tried to develop it into a commercial property or tried to sell it to a church, the members might have the right to prevent those things from happening and require the developer to develop it as park or open space land as previously represented.

6.29 Action Without Meeting. If the legal documents permit, and no statutes prohibit, the board may take action without a meeting. The usual requirements are that the written consent of all the board members be filed with the minutes of that meeting. Sometimes an explanation of the action taken is required to be posted at some place within the common area of the project within a certain time after the written consents of all board members have been obtained. See Chapter 13.4.

6.30 Telephone Meetings. In some associations, boards may hold meetings through the use of a conference telephone or similar communications equipment. The usual requirement is that all members participating must be able to hear one another. As is the case when the board takes action without a meeting, an explanation of action taken by telephone meeting may be required to be posted in the common area within a certain time after the telephone meeting has occurred.

6.31 Executive Session. Although board meetings are generally reuired to be open to members (*see Chapter 6.32*), the board may, upon majority vote or majority of a quorum depending upon its rules, adjourn to executive session to discuss personnel matters, litigation matters or matters of a sensitive nature. The nature of the business to be considered in executive session should be announced in the open session before the meeting adjourns to executive session, and should be generally noted in the minutes of the meeting.

6.32 Secret Meetings. In some jurisdictions, the board of directors is prohibited from holding secret meetings, which means meetings that are not noticed, are not open to the membership and are not executive session meetings to which a regular meeting has been adjourned. The effect of holding such a meeting in violation of such statutes would normally be that any action taken at the meeting would be void or voidable at the option of the members or the party concerned by the action taken at that meeting.

Manager's Note: Generally, to encourage participation by and prevent any ill feelings from members, it is good operating procedure for the board to avoid holding any secret meetings even when allowed by the association's legal documents.

6.33 Notices. The project legal documents will normally set forth the requirements for notices which will include the amount of time within which notice must be given and the method by which it may be given. In some cases notice may be given by personal delivery, and in other cases by mail, usually first-class. Some legal documents and some statutes require that notice be posted at a prominent place in the common area in addition to being mailed to all members. The failure to properly notice a meeting can result in all action taken at the meeting being void or voidable.

6.34 Waiver of Notice. Either the project legal documents or state statutes may provide for waiver of notice by board members. If a board member who has not received notice attends a meeting anyway, (s)he is normally considered to have waived notice. There may be an exception if the board member objects at the beginning of the meeting to the transaction of any business because the meeting has not been lawfully called. It is customary for board members to sign written waivers of notice and consent to the holding of meetings wherever notice has not been given in advance.

See Form 10 for a copy of the Waiver of Notice.

CHAPTER 7
Officers

Manager's Note: All the information contained in this chapter should be considered "must-read."

7.1 Eligibility. The project legal documents will normally include the eligibility requirements for officers. Officers usually are required to be members of the association, although there are exceptions to this. They may also be required to be members of the board of directors. It is traditional that at least the president and vice-president be members of the board, but sometimes the secretary and/or the treasurer or chief financial officer may be a member who is not on the board of directors at the time. In the normal situation, the officers are selected by and serve at the pleasure of the board.

7.2 Selection of Officers. Normally, officers are elected by the board. After the annual meeting at which the board is elected, the board convenes for its first meeting. At that time, the first order of business should be the election of officers. The discussion should focus on whether the officers should be selected entirely from among board members, or, if permissible under the legal documents and under state statutes, from outside the board.

7.3 Assistant Officers. The legal documents and state statutes may allow for the appointment of assistant officers. Sometimes, particularly in a large organization, it is helpful to have assistant officers, so that if the secretary is ill or out of town or the treasurer is ill or out of town, an assistant may stand in and serve in the necessary functions. Assistant officers should be authorized by the bylaws, and if the bylaws do not make provision for assistants, the organization wanting to elect assistant officers should amend its bylaws.

7.4 Conflicts of Interest. Directors and officers should at all times avoid placing themselves in a position where they have a conflict of interest. Both the legal documents for the project and state statutes will probably have prohibitions against conflicts of interest.

A conflict does not always exist due to the mere fact that a director has a personal interest, financial or otherwise, in the outcome of a vote on a motion; it is more a question of degree. The interest may be so remote, speculative or unimportant as not to be a factor. In simple terms, the way to avoid conflicts of interest is for officers and directors to be aware at all times of situations which might give the appearance of impropriety. The directors and officers should, in case of any doubt about a conflict, resolve the doubt in favor of the existence of a conflict, and not vote or participate in the vote or discussion on a matter in which they have a personal or financial interest as to the outcome.

The consequences of the existence of a conflict of interest may be that the action taken by the board can be void or voided later if the vote of the director having the conflict was one of the necessary votes to pass the motion. Another consequence is that a director or officer, who achieves some personal gain by reason of a conflict of interest, could be held personally liable to the association for any damages to the association, or for the return of any gain received by the officer or director who profited from such a conflict.

7.5 President. The president acts as the chief executive officer of the board and of the association. (S)he runs the meetings, makes the administrative decisions, fulfills the leadership role, and carries out the policy established by the board of directors. The president should be willing and able to devote sufficient time to the affairs of the association. The president should be chosen based on experience and qualifications.

It is important that the president be familiar enough with parliamentary procedure to run a meeting, and that (s)he be organized and forceful enough to retain control of meetings and to keep the business moving. The president has to be cognizant of Parkinson's Law, which says that the time spent on any item on the agenda will be in inverse proportion to the amount of dollars involved. The required duties of the president should be described in the bylaws and, if necessary, the bylaws should be amended from time to time, so that the description of the president's duties is accurate and up-to-date.

7.6 Vice-President. The vice-president should be chosen carefully, because the vice-president is usually the next in line to be president. The vice-president should be fully capable of taking charge of the board, and running either a board meeting or general membership meeting in the absence of the president. Some boards like to place the vice-president on the nominating committee or in charge of nominations for the board for the coming year. The vice-president is also often a member of the budget committee. In this way, the vice-president, if (s)he is to be the next president, will have some voice in selecting nominees for the board and in preparing the budget to be used in the coming year.

7.7 Secretary. The secretary, like the president and the vice-president, should have duties that are defined in the legal documents. Generally, the secretary keeps the minutes of the meeting, is responsible for sending out notices of meetings, and maintaining the corporate records (except for the financial records that are kept by the treasurer or chief financial officer).

The secretary should work with the president and association manager in preparing the agenda and minutes of the meeting, keeping track of dates for meetings, sending out notices and following up on agenda items and on the implementation of resolutions passed by the board. The importance of diligent record-keeping by the secretary cannot be overemphasized. The secretary is responsible for the creation of records such as minutes, resolutions, correspondence, contacts, and insurance policies. In addition, the secretary is responsible for maintaining a good filing system, so that the documents can be easily found. The secretary should have a basic familiarity with the project legal documents. Like the treasurer or chief financial officer, the position of secretary is one that lends itself to continuity and longevity. Some of the best-run organizations are the ones that have secretaries and chief financial officers who serve for a number of consecutive terms.

Manager's Note: *Most often, an association manager and the management company will perform the duties of the association secretary in taking minutes, writing resolutions, correspondence, notices, and maintaining the files and records of the association.*

7.8 Treasurer or Chief Financial Officer. The treasurer or chief financial officer may or may not have to be a director. Many associations try to achieve stability in the office of the treasurer or chief financial officer by having the same individual serve for more than one year. It is important that the treasurer have some accounting, bookkeeping, banking or financial experience and background. At least one individual on the board or one officer has to be the guardian of the finances of the organization. This job usually falls upon the shoulders of the treasurer. (S)he must constantly be on guard to avoid tendencies of directors and officers to spend outside the budget and put the organization into the red. The treasurer should be prepared to advise and make recommendations to the board on the collection of assessments and the handling of delinquencies. (S)he should administer policy with respect to late fees and penalties.

Manager's Note: *In smaller associations, or associations with limited homeowner participation, it may be difficult to find a qualified homeowner to serve as the treasurer or CFO. If professionally managed, the board of directors may look to its manager, bookkeeper or accountant to provide advice, recommendations and review of the financials, and collection of delinquencies and administration of late charges and penalties.*

CHAPTER 8
Committees

Manager's Note: Before joining a committee, appointing committee members or starting a committee, this is an important chapter to review. Both board members and homeowners should review this information.

8.1 Purpose of Committees. The project legal documents usually provide for the appointment of committees. Committees can be very useful in obtaining greater participation by owners in the administration and operation of the project. They also serve as a good training ground for future directors and officers. The committees serve as an important communication link between the board and the general membership.

The main purpose of committees is to delegate a specific aspect of the responsibility of the board to manage the association to a group of members interested in that particular job. If the board has to get involved in too many of the details of running the association, its members will become over-burdened by the details, and its leadership will be scattered, inefficient, and ineffective.

8.2 Committee Membership. Committees may be composed of two or more directors, or of members who are not directors, or a combination of directors and members. Committee members are appointed by the board of directors.

In order to find potential committee members, questionnaires should be filled out by all members, including incoming members. The questionnaire should call for expression of interest in special committees. It should include the education and work experience of each member, whether or not he or she desires to participate in the association management, a brief description of each committee, and a checklist or series of blanks to be filled in indicating whether that member is interested in serving on one or more committees.

Manager's Note: Another excellent method to solicit interest in committee work is to acknowledge the work of committees at each board meeting, or to have members from committees describe the work they do at a general membership meeting. The association newsletter is also an excellent method to solicit volunteers for committee work.

8.3 Delegation. The board of directors may delegate some, but not all, of its duties. Delegation is a way to spread the burden of administration, so that it falls upon as many shoulders as possible. Officers and directors do not escape responsibility for their duties by delegating them to committees. There are some duties which, either by law or by provisions in the legal documents, cannot be delegated, and others that can be delegated only with approval of the general membership.

FHLMC and FNMA also impose certain limitations on the authority of the board to delegate management responsibilities. For associations interested in preserving the rights of members to participate in FHLMC and FNMA programs, care should be taken not to delegate authority in violation of FHLMC and FNMA regulations.

Sometimes directors run into trouble by relying too heavily upon committees or managers or advisors. The best course of action is to avoid over-delegation, but not to avoid delegation completely, which requires the board to get involved in too many details and may result in the board making decisions without sufficient consideration of all the alternatives and points of view and interests within the association.

8.4 List of Committees.

Architectural Committee. Depending upon the size, type and complexity of the project, the architectural committee may be a very important committee. It is the responsibility of the committee to receive, review and act upon applications for any changes to the exterior of any building, structure, lot or unit in the project, and any change to any part of the common area. This may include landscaping in addition to the structures.

Most association documents have some design control provisions that limit the rights of owners to make alterations in common areas or to the exteriors of any buildings within the project. Some project legal documents contain rather broad provisions controlling the design of a project, including landscaping. The committee's first job would be to carefully review those provisions to see whether these are appropriate for the particular project. Such provisions tend to be "boilerplate," and may need to be tailored to fit the project and the desires of the owners of units or lots within the project.

Generally, the developer of the project appoints the initial architectural committee. The developer may retain control over appointments to the committee until it has sold either all or a certain percentage of the project. The architectural committee should be re-appointed by the new board elected by the owners at the first general membership meeting. The rules for appointment of members to the committee and for the procedures to be followed in submitting, reviewing, and approving or denying plans should also be reviewed carefully by the committee appointed by the board.

It is important that the committee advise owners applying for review of their plans that approval by the committee does not constitute approval by local authorities, and that any proposed improvements will have to comply with all building codes and other local ordinances. If the committee lacks expertise in reading plans and needs the services and assistance of an architect, the association should consider amending the project legal documents to provide for a fee to be paid with an application to the architectural committee for plan review. This fee can then be used to pay the architect for his/her assistance to the committee in reviewing the plans.

Nominations Committee. (*See Chapter 11.13.*) It is a good idea to have a nominations committee, which should be appointed sufficiently far in advance of the annual meeting so that it may make a reasonable survey of the membership to determine who are the best-qualified candidates for election to the board at the annual meeting. A good nominating committee can serve a very valuable function, particularly in a large association, in ensuring that an adequate supply of willing and capable members is available to the board of directors and to the leadership of the organization.

Fiscal or Financial Committee. This committee consists normally of the president, treasurer or chief financial officer, and additional appointed members. Its primary responsibility is to periodically review the financial statements of the association, prepare the annual budget, establish adequate reserves, establish the assessment schedule, and review the insurance program for the project. It should also set policy for collection of assessments, payment of bills, collection of delinquent accounts, and entering into contracts with consultants, managers, and independent contractors.

The fiscal or financial committee should also be responsible for working with the accountant and reviewing the tax status and annual tax or information returns. It should be involved in decisions regarding special assessments, capital improvements, major purchases of personal property, and, in short, everything that concerns the finances of the association. The fiscal committee should also establish policy with respect to investment of the reserves of the association to achieve maximum income consistent with safety.

Personnel. In an association having a very large number of members and responsibility for operation of a large project, there may be a number of on-site employees who work directly for the association, such as landscaping, maintenance, janitorial, security and management personnel. A personnel committee can be a valuable aid to the board of directors in determining policy relating to personnel such as interviews, making recommendations concerning hiring and firing, periodic employee reviews, and employee benefits— including insurance, medical, and related matters.

Property Maintenance and Equipment. This committee should be in charge of the physical maintenance of the project. It should schedule periodic inspections of major systems such as roofs, exterior siding, foundations, heating, ventilating, and air conditioning systems, hot water heaters or boilers, elevators, and solar heating or solar water heating installations. It should coordinate with the landscaping committee with respect to maintenance of common area irrigation equipment. It should also coordinate with the social/recreational committee with respect to maintenance of recreational facilities such as pool, pool pump and filter, spa, sauna, and sport courts.

The maintenance committee should meet with outside contractors who provide such services as painting, pest control, roof maintenance, equipment maintenance, and snow removal. The committee should negotiate contracts and present them with recommendations to the board for action. The committee should also monitor individual lot or unit owners' complaints about the physical condition of the project, and establish a preventative maintenance program.

The committee should periodically check its reserve account to determine if the reserves on hand are adequate and to ensure that the amount set aside for reserves each year is adequate to meet the future maintenance, repair, and replacement requirements of the project.

In a complex project which includes a lot of machinery and equipment, boilers, elevators, etc., it is important that the maintenance committee work with engineering and maintenance staff members or consultants to identify and inventory all the major systems and each piece of equipment. All equipment should be inventoried, inspected and tagged. A maintenance log should be kept which will indicate dates of periodic inspections. Each inspection should be indicated on the tags attached to each piece of equipment that is inspected. The system established should include some kind of "tickler system" which will bring to the attention of the committee the fact that it is time to inspect a particular piece of equipment or that the time for periodic maintenance has arrived.

The maintenance committee also needs to keep a file of all warranties on all equipment to assist it in following up with manufacturers and installers whenever maintenance occurs that is still under warranty.

Owner Relations. This committee should formulate, review and revise house rules and regulations. It should also serve as a public relations vehicle to ensure good communications between the board and the membership. It should review the community rules and establish policy for enforcing the rules. This committee can provide a forum for resolution of disputes between lot or unit owners. It can also act as a forum for resolving disputes between the board or management of the association and individual members. If grievance procedures are to be adopted, they should be formalized with the rules being submitted to all members. All hearings before such a committee should be conducted in accordance with standards of due process. *See Chapter 29.1.*

Social and/or Recreational. This committee should plan and execute social events for the general membership. Where applicable, the members of this committee will work with the other active association committees to publish and distribute the association's newsletter. It should also plan and organize events for new members.

Landscaping. This committee should make periodic inspections of the appearance of the development, including landscaping and planting in common areas, as well as landscaping and planting in private areas or restricted common areas. The maintenance of relatively high and uniform standards of landscaping maintenance throughout a project can be as important as any other one item in keeping the property values and appearance of the project up to par.

The landscaping committee should supervise and make recommendations on the hiring, firing and training of gardeners or landscape personnel. However, direct orders to gardeners or landscape maintenance personnel should be given only under the express authority of the board or of the president of the association or the manager, when such authority has been delegated to the manager. The landscaping committee should also supervise and be responsible for inspections and for the effective operation of the irrigation system for the common area landscaping.

Rules Committee. A special committee may be appointed for the purpose of periodically reviewing the house rules. The rules should be stated as clearly as possible and should be tailored to the needs and desires of the members of the project to which they apply. Where the initial set of rules has been provided by the developer, they will tend to be "boilerplate" and have general applications but will not necessarily have been prepared with the detailed considerations of the likes, dislikes, and personality characteristics of the members who now own the project.

Manager's Note: Like the board of directors, provisions in the legal documents may dictate the size and required membership of the committee. Committees should be kept to small, manageable sizes, and should have an odd number of members (such as 3, 5 or 7), so that decisions among members may not end up in "ties."

8.5 Committee Reports. Committees should report to the board at each board meeting, preferably in writing. Each committee should also be required to prepare an annual report to be presented at the annual membership meeting. Those reports should be filed with the permanent records of the association.

CHAPTER 9
Meetings

9.1 First General Membership Meeting. The first meeting of the general membership will be held at a time prescribed by the project legal documents. In an association subject to statutory regulation, the time for holding the first general membership meeting may be prescribed by statute.

The first general membership meeting is usually a transition time when the developer relinquishes some or all of its control over the board of directors and passes it on to the new owners, the purchasers of lots or units in the development. The first general membership meeting normally will have been organized by the developer or by the community association management firm hired by the developer. The new members of the association should come to the first meeting with the expectation of electing a board that will effectively represent the interests of the new owners.

Although the bylaws may call for staggered terms, a full board should be elected at the first meeting. The directors who have served until that time have been appointed by the developer, and should serve only until the first annual election. In other words, the staggered terms begin for the first time at the election at the first annual membership meeting. How many directors does the developer intend to elect to the board? How many directors are the members entitled to have on the board? Some legal documents and some statutes provide that even though the developer owns a sufficient number of interests in the subdivision to elect the entire board, the members other than the developer are entitled to elect one or more directors.

Has the developer appointed a nominating committee, and has that committee or the developer itself proposed a slate of directors for the board? Is the slate satisfactory, or should additional members be nominated from the floor after nominations have been opened? The following checklist covers the items that should normally be dealt with in planning for the first meeting:

- Prepare and send notice of meeting (see *Chapter 9.6*)
- Prepare financial report and have sufficient copies on hand for distribution
- Prepare agenda and send it out with the notice
- Emphasize the importance of owners attending meetings or sending in proxy
- Obtain report from nominating committee; include slate of names nominated with notice of meeting
- Prepare nomination forms for use at meeting
- Prepare ballots with names of slate and adequate room for additional nominations
- Include information on persons nominated for the board
- Where weighted voting is used, prepare and send out notice of weighted voting designations (see *Chapter 11.2)*

9.2 General Membership Meetings. Meetings of the general membership may be either annual meetings (see Chapter 9.3) or special meetings (see Chapter 9.5). General membership meetings are extremely important. In order for the board of directors and the management of the association to function properly, they need direction and support from the general membership, which they can only obtain in a general meeting in which there is significant participation by the membership.

In some associations, the officers must make substantial efforts to see that general membership meetings are well attended.

9.3 Annual Membership Meetings. An annual membership meeting must be held once a year; usually at approximately the same time each year. The project legal documents will normally specify the time of the annual membership meeting. If an association fails to hold its annual meeting at the required time, some states provide that a court may order a meeting to be held upon the application of a member, after notice to the association, giving it an opportunity to be heard. *See Form 1 for a Notice of Annual Meeting.*

9.4 Directors' Meetings. The board of directors will hold its first meeting immediately following the annual general membership meeting at which the elections to the board occur. Periodic meetings are held by the directors throughout the year at the intervals specified by the project legal documents. *See Chapter 6.23.*

9.5 Special Meetings. Special meetings of the general membership may be called by the board of directors, by certain officers, or by a certain minimum percentage of the members, depending upon the project legal documents and state law. Special meetings always require notice, the requirements for which are contained in the project legal documents and in state law. *See Chapter 9.6.*

The reasons for calling special membership meetings are generally to seek the approval of the membership for an action that the board is considering taking, or to call into question an action that the board has taken, or to deal with an issue that has arisen that requires a vote of the membership.

9.6 Calling Meetings. Membership meetings are usually called by the president, vice-president, secretary, or any two directors. In most cases, meetings may also be called at the request of a certain minimum number or percentage of members. Notices of the meeting are required to be given by first-class mail, although sometimes delivery of notice in person or by telephone or telegraph is permitted. Some project legal documents, statutes and regulations require that the nature of any special business to be considered at the meeting be included in the notice. Some project documents and statutes provide that notice of special meetings be posted in a prominent place within the common area.

Directors should receive notice of special meetings. Directors may waive notice of meetings by signing a written waiver or by attending the meeting.

See Form 1 for a Notice of Annual or General Membership Meeting.

9.7 Conduct of General Membership or Annual Meetings.

Advanced planning for general membership meetings is very important. Every effort should be made to see that the meeting is conducted efficiently and professionally, that all legal requirements are observed, and that the experience is a positive one for the members. The meeting place should be adequate in size, large enough to comfortably accommodate all of the members, and be in a convenient location with adequate heat, light and ventilation. A decision should be made in advance as to whether or not smoking will be permitted, and if so, ashtrays should be provided. If refreshments are to be served, arrangements should be made. Although it is best to hold meetings as close to the project as possible, many associations do not have facilities large enough to hold comfortable meetings. If it is necessary to rent a school classroom, meeting room or auditorium, arrangements (which often include providing the facility with a certificate of insurance) need to be made in advance, and a cleanup crew may have to be provided afterwards.

A sign-in sheet should be kept at the entrance to the meeting. *See Form 5 for a sample Sign-In Sheet.*

If there is an election, ballots should be prepared in advance (s*ee Forms 5-6 for examples)*. Sufficient copies of the agenda, resolutions requiring membership approval, financial reports or other materials to be presented should be available for distribution to all members.

If proxies are to be used, they should be organized, counted and tabulated. The secretary or a representative of the board should be stationed at the door to check in the owners, collect proxies, make a note of which proxies are revoked by attendance, and be prepared to announce to the president or meeting chairperson how many persons are present in person, how many by proxy, and whether there is a quorum.

There are various ways to handle balloting in a large organization. An identification slip can be attached to each ballot with the name, unit or lot number, and number of votes which may be cast by the unit or lot owner. As the ballot is handed to the unit or lot owner, the identification slip could be removed and filed for reference. Another method is for the secretary to have a list of unit or lot owners upon which each owner signs his or her name in the space opposite his/her unit or lot number as a ballot is handed to him/her at the beginning of the meeting.

Ballots should contain names for all nominees and should also have blank spaces for adding names nominated from the floor. There should be a status report from the president somewhere early in the meeting. It is also a good idea to allow time during the meeting for handling questions from members. The president needs to maintain control of the meeting, however, and not let the opportunity for questions turn into a lengthy complaint section. The president has to be experienced enough in parliamentary procedure and in running meetings to be able to maintain control and to keep the business moving. If the president lacks such experience, (s)he should have the assistance of a parliamentarian or someone who can be at his/her side to advise him/her on how to keep the business moving efficiently and in a proper manner.

Where cumulative voting is exercised and secret ballots are used, depending upon the size of the membership, it may take a considerable period of time to count the ballots. (*See Chapter 11.7.*) It is a good idea to schedule the election fairly early in the annual meeting of the members so that the committee or persons appointed by the chairperson to tabulate the ballots can do so while the general meeting continues with the other business of the association.

One of the first items of business at a general membership meeting is to announce that a quorum is present, with a breakdown being given by the secretary as to how many members are present in person, how many are present by proxy, and how many members are ineligible to vote because of suspension of voting privileges.

The chairperson should follow the agenda, which normally calls for approval of the minutes of the previous general membership or annual meeting as one of the first items. When the chairperson calls for approval of the minutes, a motion should be made, seconded, and carried to approve the minutes, unless someone wishes to correct the minutes. Any corrections should be done before the motion to adopt the minutes as approved is made. If the minutes are corrected, the change should be noted by the secretary on the copy of the minutes in the minute book.

The chairperson should introduce invitees and guests.

Committee reports should be on the agenda, should be in writing, and should be delivered by the committee chairperson or spokesperson.

Where a committee makes recommendations, the board should vote upon the recommendation following the committee report.

9.8 Membership Roll. The secretary should keep an up-to-date list of all the members of the association. In a large organization, there should be a cut-off date for voting and for use of proxies. In some very large associations, there may be an established policy regarding a cut-off date. That means that proxies will only be honored if the owner of record as of the cut-off date executes them. It also may mean that new owners who show up at the meeting, who have acquired title after the cut-off date, may not be able to vote or may be able to vote only if they bring with them evidence of their ownership, such as a copy of the deed showing the date of transfer and the date of recordation, which will avoid conflicting proxies or conflicting votes.

Some statutes and some project legal documents provide for a record date for purposes of determining members entitled to notice of or to vote at a meeting. If no such record date is provided for, owners of record as of the close of business on the business date preceding the day upon which the notice is given are entitled to notice. If no record date is fixed for voting, members who are owners on the date of the meeting and are eligible to vote are entitled to vote.

In the case of an adjourned meeting, members on the day of the adjourned meeting who are otherwise eligible to vote are entitled to vote in the absence of provisions setting a record date. The project legal documents or statutes may provide the board with the power to fix a date in advance as the record date for the purpose of determining the members entitled to cast written ballots. While this practice does occur in some jurisdictions, it is not appropriate for a homeowners association to provide a cut-off date for the purpose of exercising the right to vote. The actual legal owner of a unit or lot should be able to vote on matters pertaining to his/her property regardless of considerations of timing. The former owner has no interest in the property or in the affairs of the association and should not be able to cast a vote either in person or by proxy when that vote rightfully belongs to the new owner.

9.9 Proxies. A proxy is a written authorization signed by a member giving another person the power to vote on behalf of such member. The signature is valid whether by manual signature, typewriter, telegraphic transmission, fax, or, in most jurisdictions, by simply marking an "X."

Proxies are good until revoked; however, some project documents and statutes provide for automatic expiration of proxies in 11 months or some other period of time from the date that they are issued unless otherwise provided in the proxy. There may also be a maximum term of years from the date of execution that a proxy is still valid.

Delivering a written revocation to the association can revoke a proxy. It is also revoked by subsequent proxy executed by the same person or by attendance at a meeting and voting in person. If a person who has given a proxy revokes it by attending the meeting and voting, the proxy is not revived if the member then leaves before the meeting is adjourned. In such case, if (s)he wishes the proxy to be effective after (s)he departs, the departing member should re-execute the proxy and deliver it to the proxy holder before leaving. Some statutes provide that a proxy is not revoked by death, termination of membership, or incapacity unless, before the vote is counted, the association receives written notice of such incident.

Certain project documents and statutes provide that a proxy is not valid for voting on certain proposals unless the general nature of the matter to be voted on was described in the proxy. Typical examples of this are votes to remove a director without cause, filling vacancies on the board, amending the articles, selling or otherwise disposing of substantially all of the association's assets, approving a contract between the association and one or more directors, electing to dissolve the association, or approving a plan of distribution of assets. In some large organizations it is required that a form of proxy afford an opportunity to specify choice among approval, or disapproval, or abstention.

There is some uncertainty about whether members of an unincorporated association have proxy rights without a provision to that effect in their project legal documents. The project legal documents should therefore include proxy rights. A proxy must be voted in accordance with its terms. If there is more than one owner of a unit or lot, the proxy should be signed by all unit or lot owners. *See Form 4 for an example of a proxy.*

9.10 Quorum. The number of members who must be present in person or by proxy to constitute a quorum is usually set forth in the legal documents and may also be prescribed by statute. Unless a quorum is present, no business can be conducted. Generally, if a quorum is present, the vote of a majority of the voting power represented at the meeting and entitled to vote constitutes the act of the members, unless either the legal documents or statute require a greater number of votes. Some statutes provide that if the project legal documents authorize a quorum of less than a certain percentage (such as one-third of the total voting power) then only certain matters may be voted upon by less than that minimum percentage of the members, and the general nature of the items voted on may be required to have been included in the notice of the meeting. Consult project legal documents and local statutes.

If a quorum is present at the beginning of a meeting, but members withdraw before adjournment so that there is less than a quorum present, consult project legal documents and statutes to find out whether the meeting can proceed, and if so, what business may be handled.

Some project legal documents provide for a smaller quorum at an adjourned meeting if the normal quorum cannot be obtained at a properly noticed meeting. This is a protective device intended to ensure that the association is not prevented from continuing its operations simply because it cannot obtain a quorum. The effect of taking action at a meeting without a quorum is usually that the action is void or voidable at the option of any member who objects.

9.11 Developer's Votes. The developer in some projects has special voting privileges. *(See Chapter 12.)* The project may be organized with two classes of votes—Class A and Class B memberships. The developer will hold Class B memberships, which may carry more than one vote per membership. Where such provisions exist, the developer's rights usually terminate automatically upon the sale of a certain percentage of interests in the project, or after the passage of a specified period of time. Where the developer is entitled to cast multiple votes, it may choose to do so and to cumulate its votes at a meeting in order to elect a majority of the board of directors. In jurisdictions where this is permitted by law and by the legal documents, it is perfectly valid.

Some developers may have such rights but elect not to exercise them, preferring to let the majority of the members determine who should be on the board rather than impose a board of the developer's choice upon the members. It is important to keep track of the dates and events that cause the developer's extraordinary voting rights to terminate.

9.12 Open Meetings. Members are not normally entitled to participate verbally in directors' meetings unless invited to do so. Some statutes require the board to allow members to speak, but generally such statutes permit the board to establish reasonable time limitations on the members' rights to speak. *See Chapter 6.23.*

Members may participate fully in the discussion and deliberations of a general membership meeting.

"Closed" board meetings or meetings in which members are not allowed to participate or speak breed hostility and should be avoided, if possible. The only exception would be executive sessions of the board, which should only be attended by members of the board of directors and invited participants. *See Chapter 6.31.*

Parliamentary rules should be followed during meetings, and the chair should recognize members before speaking. Members should not interrupt other speakers or otherwise disrupt the orderly conduct of the meeting. Members whose voting privileges have been suspended for failure to pay their assessments are normally entitled to attend meetings and voice their opinions, although they are not allowed to vote so long as their voting privileges have been legally suspended. *See Chapter 28.8.*

9.13 Agenda. An agenda should be prepared in advance of every meeting and should be followed by the chair. To encourage efficient meetings, a timed agenda, which indicates the start and stop times for each item to be discussed during the meeting, can be employed. *See Chapter 9.7.*

9.14 Minutes. Minutes should show the date, time and place of the meeting, the names of officers and directors present, the number of members present in person or by proxy and indicate that a quorum was present. *See Chapters 13.3 and 14.2.*

Minutes should follow the written agenda, assuming that the chairperson follows the agenda. The opening remarks of the chairperson can be summarized. Generally, minutes do not include a verbatim transcript of everything that is said except for the motions that are made. In a large meeting where the secretary is not familiar with the names, members addressing the meeting should state their name and unit/lot number so the secretary can put that information in the minutes. An experienced note-taker can take handwritten notes of the meeting, or a laptop computer can be set up to provide faster note-taking at the meeting. A tape recorder can ensure that minutes of the meeting are accurate and complete.

If there are important legal issues involved, such as disciplining a member, it may be necessary to have a court reporter present for an accurate transcript of the meeting. The chairperson should assist the secretary by restating each motion after it is made, and again prior to the vote. If the chairperson has stated it properly, and the secretary has written it down, the chairperson can ask the secretary to read the motion before the vote is taken.

Minutes should be completed and distributed as soon as possible after the meeting so that they can be reviewed while the events are still relatively recent, in order that corrections can be made if necessary.

Copies of minutes of a board of directors' meeting should be sent to all directors. Copies of minutes of the membership meeting need not be sent to all members unless required by the project legal documents. The original copy of the minutes, signed by the secretary (or the association manager as acting secretary), should be maintained in the official minute book of the association. The minutes of the previous meeting should be read at the beginning of each subsequent meeting. Some associations will mail or deliver copies of the minutes to directors prior to the meeting, so they will have an opportunity to read them prior to coming to the meeting.

Manager's Notes: *To increase accuracy and minimize corrections, minutes of meetings should be typed up as quickly as possible after the conclusion of the meeting. Draft minutes sent a few days after the meeting can be corrected by the board members and sent back to the secretary or association manager prior to the next meeting. The minutes can then be revised, and the board can approve a final, corrected set of minutes at a meeting. See Forms 8 and 9 for examples of minutes.*

9.15 Resolutions and Motions. Motions (as distinguished from resolutions) are all that is usually necessary for routine items. Resolutions are only required where matters of legal or organizational significance are included, such as an amendment to the legal documents, the approval of contracts, authorization for officers to sign signature cards on a bank account, filing lawsuits, or other particularly significant matters. *See Chapter 13.6.*

9.16 Documents to Obtain from Developer. At the initial meeting of the membership, when the developer is still involved in the project, it is important that a number of basic documents be obtained from the developer. These documents should be kept as part of the permanent records of the association. Depending upon the kind of development involved, the documents to obtain might include the following:

1. Minute book, including minutes of initial organizational meeting and all subsequent meetings.
2. Certified copy of articles of incorporation and all certificates of amendment.
3. Original bylaws and all amendments.
4. Original recorded declaration and all amendments.
5. Tax exemption claim forms, if applicable.
6. Tax exemption letter from state taxing authority, if applicable, and copies of previous year's tax returns, federal and state, if applicable.
7. Bank account resolutions.
8. Ledgers.
9. Bank account records.
10. Checkbook and/or passbook for checking and savings accounts.
11. Corporate seal, if available.
12. Membership certificates, if any.
13. Membership register.
14. Original master lease (stock cooperative).
15. Original copies of all leases (stock cooperative).
16. Complete copy of all plans and specifications for the project and the improvements thereon, and as-built architectural drawings, if available.
17. Copies of final subdivision map or condominium plan.
18. Copies of any contracts with independent contractors or professional managers.
19. Lists of names, addresses, and telephone numbers of unit/lot owners.
20. List of unsold lots/units held by the developer.
21. Copies of warranties on appliances, equipment or items of personal property, or warranties of contractors or sub-contractors.
22. Complete inventory of personal property belonging to the association, including fixtures, machinery and equipment.

23. Copies of insurance policies covering the project or personal property owned by the association.
24. Copies of leases entered into by the association.
25. Copies of any budgets, proposed assessments, financial statements, or similar documents prepared by the developer or by the board controlled by the developer.

9.17 Adjournment. A motion to adjourn can be made at any time, although it is normally made at the appropriate place on the approved agenda. A motion to adjourn is not debatable, cannot be amended, and must be seconded. It must be voted on immediately after a motion and second. If the motion fails to carry by a majority vote, the meeting continues. A motion to adjourn can be reconsidered at any time. *See Chapter 10.17.*

If a directors meeting is to be adjourned to another time and place, the concurrence of a majority of directors present is generally required. The project legal documents and state statutes may prescribe the requirements for adjournment of a general membership meeting to another time and place. If a meeting is adjourned to a time more than a certain number of hours later, notice may be required to be given to members or directors who were not present at that meeting. Some state laws require that notice of a meeting that has been adjourned to another date be posted in the common area within a certain period of time after the meeting. For a simple adjournment of a meeting where it is not the intention that it be adjourned to another time, it is only necessary to move that the meeting be adjourned.

CHAPTER 10
Conducting a Meeting

Manager's Note: Just as in our local, state and federal governments, regular meetings of the "governing body" are held to conduct the business of the association. Homeowners and board members alike should consider this a "must read" chapter.

10.1 Robert's Rules of Order. In 1876, H.M. Robert published a book called ROBERT'S RULES OF ORDER. The book is a short treatise on parliamentary law, the purpose of which is to provide various organizations and societies with a set of rules for organizing and conducting the business of meetings.

It is important that a meeting be run with certain rules of procedure. Those conducting the meeting should know the rules and see that they are followed. This chapter will summarize some of the highlights of ROBERT'S RULES OF ORDER. It is recommended that large associations, particularly those that hold frequent meetings, appoint a parliamentarian, and provide him or her with a copy of ROBERT'S RULES OF ORDER.

The entire book of ROBERT'S RULES OF ORDER is too long and too complex to be properly included in this book. What is presented here are some of the more basic rules of procedure, which should be sufficient to handle most of the business that will come before the association.

10.2 Motions. A motion is a proposal by an individual that the assembly take a certain action or make a specific statement. A motion is made by a member, who has obtained the "floor" (or permission to speak by being recognized by the chair) stating, "I move that...," followed by a statement of the action that (s)he proposes to have taken or the stand (s)he proposes that the assembly take.

There are many rules pertaining to motions contained in ROBERT'S RULES OF ORDER. Some motions are debatable and others are not. Some motions require a second and others do not. Some motions take precedence over other motions. Some motions can be amended and some cannot.

For a summary of these rules, see the table included below in Chapter 10.22.

There are cases in the ordinary course of business where the chairperson may put a "question" (or a call for a vote on an issue) to the membership without waiting for a motion. However, in most cases, a motion should first be made.

10.3 Resolutions. There is a subtle difference between a motion and a resolution. A motion is a proposal that the assembly take a certain action or express a certain viewpoint. For example, a member may move to adjourn, to amend a motion, to bring the matter to vote without further debate, or may move that it be adopted.

Where motions are very long, or where they are to contain some important business that needs to be preserved in the form of a written instrument, they are usually stated as resolutions, beginning with the words "Resolved..." The reasons for a resolution are usually stated in a preamble, with each reason preceded by the word "Whereas." Each "Whereas" clause should be separated by a semicolon, except for the last one, which should begin with "Now, therefore, be it resolved that..." *See Form 11 for a sample resolution.*

10.4 Seconding Motions. Most of the time, a motion must be seconded in order to be properly debated and voted upon by the assembly; however, there are exceptions to the rules. (*See the table below in Section 10.22 for some examples of motions that do not require a second.*) If a motion is made but not immediately seconded, it is customary for the chair to ask: "Is there a second to the motion?" If the motion is not seconded, it is not proper to proceed to debate or discuss the motion, or even to vote on it. Any member may raise a "point of order" (*see Chapter 10.5*) by calling the chairperson's attention to the lack of a proper second, and thus stopping any further consideration of the motion unless and until there is a second. A second is made by a member saying "I second the motion," or "I second it," and can be made without first obtaining the floor.

A motion is not before the assembly for consideration until it has been made and seconded, and the chair has put it before the assembly by restating the motion. Until the chair either states a motion or rules it out of order, members may suggest modifications of the motion. The person who made the motion can, without the consent of the person who seconded it, make modifications or even withdraw the motion entirely, provided the chair has not yet stated the motion to the assembly. After the chair has stated the motion, however, the motion cannot be withdrawn without the consent of the assembly.

10.5 Point of Order. A "point of order," sometimes also called a "question of order," refers to a member of the assembly raising a procedural question by addressing the chair and stating: "Question of order" or "point of order." The chair is required to recognize that member, even if (s)he is interrupting someone who has the floor at the time. A point of order does not require a second, and is decided by the chair without any debate, unless it is a doubtful case, in which event the chair may submit it to the assembly for a decision.

Any member who notices a breach of the rules of procedure has the right to call it to the attention of the chair and to insist upon the rules being followed. If the chair rules that the point of order is well taken, then the assembly must abide by the ruling unless there is an appeal. For example, if someone makes a motion, but there is no second and debate begins, it is appropriate for a member to raise a point of order, and call the attention of the chair to the fact that the motion has not been seconded. The chair would then rule the point well taken and call for a second. If no second is obtained, then the debate on the motion ceases. The decision of the chair to uphold or deny a point of order may be appealed, provided it is appealed at the time the ruling is made. *See Chapter 10.8.*

10.6 Obtaining the Floor. To ensure an orderly discussion of issues or items before the assembly, an individual who wishes to speak to the assembly must first obtain the "floor." (S)he does that by addressing the chair and requesting or indicating that (s)he wishes to speak. In a large group, the individual wishing to speak should rise and address the chair. The chair will then recognize that person by addressing him or her by name or in some other way indicating that (s)he has the floor. The person who rises and addresses the chair first is normally entitled to the floor. If two people ask for recognition at the same time, the chair will decide who gets the floor. There are certain instances where a member is entitled to be given the floor even though another has risen and addressed the chair. Consult ROBERT'S RULES OF ORDER for a more detailed discussion on this subject. If a particular measure is being hotly debated, it is a good policy for the chair to alternate between opponents and proponents of a measure by giving preference to a member opposed to the last speaker.

10.7 Calling for the Question. If at any time a member feels that a motion has been debated for a sufficient length of time, (s)he may move to limit the debate and to bring it to a vote. The motion can either be to bring the matter to an immediate vote, to limit debate to a certain number of speakers, to limit the time available to each speaker, or to close debate at a certain hour. For example, if a member wanted to limit debate to a particular time, (s)he could say: "I move that debate on this motion be limited to 10 minutes."

A motion to limit or close debate must be seconded, and is not debatable. ROBERT'S RULES OF ORDER requires a two-thirds vote of the assembly to adopt a motion to limit debate. It is not appropriate for a member merely to shout from the floor: "I call for the question." It is necessary that (s)he be recognized, make the motion, and let the motion be seconded.

10.8 Appeals. A member may appeal a decision, but (s)he must make it at the time that the action to be appealed is taken, not at some later date after other debate or business has intervened. An appeal is made by asking for recognition, and stating the request to appeal the decision of the chair. If the appeal is seconded, then the chair states the question, states his/her reasons for the decision, and asks for a vote to either uphold the decision of the chair or not. A majority vote to sustain the ruling of the chair means the appeal is denied. A majority vote against the ruling of the chair means the appeal is allowed and the decision of the chair is reversed.

10.9 Motions Relating to Nominations. Unless there are specific rules in the project legal documents concerning nominations, any member may nominate a candidate for election to the board of directors at a meeting called for that purpose. A nomination does not require a second, and it is not debatable.

Before proceeding to an election, if nominations have been made, the chair should inquire if there are any further nominations. If there are no responses, (s)he may declare the nominations closed. In large assemblies, it is customary to make a motion to close the nominations. A member can move to close nominations to fill the vacancies on the board. A motion to close nominations cannot be debated, and according to ROBERT'S RULES OF ORDER requires a two-thirds vote. A motion to reopen nominations can be made, and can be adopted by a majority vote. A motion to reopen nominations is not debatable, and it does require a second.

10.10 Amendments. Whenever a motion or resolution is under consideration, a member may propose an amendment to that motion or resolution by obtaining the floor, moving the amendment, and having the motion seconded.

Manager's Note: For example, if the board of directors is discussing a motion to approve the purchase of two new pool filters, but Ms. Smith feels only one pool filter should be purchased, she may amend the motion. She would amend the first motion (to purchase two filters) by obtaining the floor, and then making a motion to amend ("I move that the first motion be amended from the purchase of two filters to one filter"). The motion to amend would require a second from another member of the board of directors.

Once a motion to amend has been made and seconded, the assembly then proceeds to debate and vote on the amendment. If the amendment passes, it then proceeds to complete the debate and vote on the main motion, as amended. If the amendment is defeated, the assembly proceeds to conclude its debate and vote on the main motion. An amendment requires only a majority vote.

Under ROBERT'S RULES OF ORDER only two amendments may be considered at one time. That is, when a motion is before the assembly, an amendment to the motion may be offered for consideration, and before a vote is taken on that first amendment, a second amendment may be offered. However, a third amendment would be out of order. The way to handle such a situation is to dispose of either the first or second amendment by vote, thus leaving room for another amendment to be made.

10.11 Substitute Motions. In the process of amending a motion, the sense of the original motion may at times be so changed that the amendment becomes more than an amendment, and really becomes a substitute motion. A substitute motion may be in the form of substituting an entire paragraph, or it may be in the form of an entirely reworded motion. In such case, the substitute motion is voted upon. If it fails to pass, then the assembly continues to debate and vote upon the original motion. If the substitute motion passes, all that has happened is that there has been a vote to substitute one motion for another, but the assembly still has to vote to adopt the substitute motion after it has been substituted for the original motion.

The motion to substitute can either be to substitute a paragraph or to substitute an entire new motion. If something less than a paragraph is being substituted, then it is more properly termed an amendment.

10.12 Privileged Motions. Under ROBERT'S RULES OF ORDER, certain motions are privileged, which means that they take precedence over other business. That means that if another motion or question is pending and a privileged motion is made, the assembly has to give priority consideration to the privileged motion. Under ROBERT'S RULES OF ORDER, privileged motions are ranked in the following order of priority:

1. To fix the time for adjournment;
2. To adjourn;
3. To take a recess;
4. To raise a question of privilege;
5. To call for orders of the day.

When a privileged motion is made, the chair will decide to make a parliamentary ruling and to have the motion considered, if it is appropriate. For example, if the assembly is in the middle of a debate on a motion, or has finished its debate on a motion, and is about to go on to some other business, a motion to adjourn is privileged and takes precedence over the conduct of other business at the meeting. Privileged motions are generally not debatable, and must be seconded, except for a motion to call for orders of the day.

10.13 Orders of the Day. A call for orders of the day is a demand that the assembly conform to its agenda. It can be made at any time when no other privileged motion is pending and there is a variance from the order of business. It requires no second, and it can be made even when another person has the floor. It cannot be debated or amended. The chair either has to announce that the assembly has to return to the agenda, or (s)he will put the question to vote, in which case a two-thirds vote will prevent the assembly from following the agenda and disrupting its current proceedings.

10.14 Suspension of the Rules. At some time, the assembly may wish to take action that cannot be done without violating its own rules, or violating the principles of parliamentary law. In such a case, it is possible to suspend the rules. A motion may be made to suspend the rules. The motion must be seconded, is not debatable, and cannot be amended or reconsidered. A motion to suspend the rules for the same purpose cannot be renewed at the same meeting except by unanimous consent. The motion must be passed by at least a majority vote, and sometimes a vote greater than a majority is required. *Consult ROBERT'S RULES OF ORDER, Chapter 10.22 below, for more detail.*

10.15 Request for Information. A member may ask for information by rising or obtaining the attention of the chair and saying "point of information" or "request for information." The chair directs him or her to state the point upon which (s)he desires information. If (s)he is asking for information from the individual holding the floor at the moment, (s)he may request the chair's permission to ask that person a question. The chair will ask the person who holds the floor if (s)he is willing to be interrupted, and, if consent is given, the chair will direct the inquirer to proceed with the question. The chair has to be careful to avoid the point of information privilege being misused as a method of interrupting debate or getting the proceedings off track.

10.16 To Lay on the Table. A motion to lay on the table is made in order to enable the assembly to attend to more urgent business, or to lay aside a pending question so that it can be reconsidered later. It must be seconded, it is not debatable, and is passed by a majority vote. To reconsider a motion after it has been laid on the table, the motion must be made to take a question from the table. The motion requires a second and is not debatable. It cannot be made unless some business has been transacted since the question was laid on the table.

Manager's Note: *A motion to lay on the table or to "table" an item most commonly occurs when the board of directors feels it did not have enough information or was not given enough time to review important documents in order to make a decision. If, in order to make an informed decision, the board requires more research, or additional time (or an expert opinion) is needed to review lengthy documents, the board may "table" the action until a later date, rather than prolong the meeting.*

10.17 Reconsider. The motion to reconsider is required by ROBERT'S RULES to be made by one who voted with the prevailing side when the matter was previously voted upon. It must be seconded, by any member. It is not debatable only when the motion to be reconsidered is not debatable, otherwise it is debatable.

10.18 Decorum. Members should confine themselves to the question before the group, and attempt to avoid personal attacks and criticism. It is perfectly proper to condemn, in strong terms, the nature or consequences of an action or proposed action, but it is not considered proper to attack the speaker or the maker of a motion or to criticize his/her motivation or personality.

Members should not interrupt or attempt to obtain the floor without being recognized by the chair. Members should not disturb the proceedings by talking among themselves while debate or discussion is going on. Politeness should be the rule at all times.

Manager's Note: *The maintenance of a businesslike decorum is vital at association board or membership meetings. Unfortunately, there may come a time when an emotionally charged member may make repeated attempts to disrupt the speakers and meeting. In this case it is advisable to adjourn the meeting and reschedule it for a later date to transact the remainder of the association's business.*

10.19 Voting. When it is time for a vote, the chair should ask if the assembly is "ready for the question?" After a moment's pause, if no one objects, (s)he should put the question to a vote. Votes are usually by voice. It can also be by show of hands or by standing, by roll-call vote, or by ballot. If the bylaws permit, it may also be by mail.

It is the responsibility of the chair to decide how the vote has come out. If (s)he is in doubt, (s)he should count the hands or count the people standing. It may be necessary in some cases to have a roll-call vote to make sure that only eligible voters are voting, and that only one vote per member has been exercised.

The chair should avoid any confusion by informing the assembly of the effect of the vote after the motion is either carried or lost. (S)he should then move on to the next business. If there is a tie vote, the motion is lost. The chair may vote to make a tie. (S)he may also vote to break a tie, provided (s)he has not voted to make the tie. No one can vote on a question in which they have a direct personal or pecuniary interest. However, a member may vote for himself or herself for any office or committee. The chair has the prerogative to expedite business by avoiding the formality of motions, seconds, and votes when it comes to disposing of routine business on questions of little importance. For example, the chair can ask, in the case of approving the minutes, if there are any questions, and if there are none, or if there are none after some have been offered or suggested, and there are no further corrections, the chair can say: "there being no corrections or no further corrections, the minutes stand approved." If anyone objects to that, (s)he then calls for a motion, a second, and a vote.

10.20 Recess. A motion to take a recess is made when someone wants to take a break from the proceedings. It can be amended as to the length of the recess. It takes effect immediately. If there is no other motion pending when the motion to take a recess is made, then it is treated like any other motion, meaning it is debatable. If it is made when other business is before the assembly, it is not debatable.

10.21 Adjournment. A motion to adjourn may be made at any time. It takes precedence over other motions except a motion to fix the time to adjourn to, and it yields to that motion. It is not debatable and cannot be amended. A vote on a motion to adjourn cannot be reconsidered, but may be repeated if there has been intervening business. It may only be made by a member who has the floor. It cannot be made when the assembly is engaged in voting or verifying a vote, but is in order after the vote has been taken. No appeal or question of order or inquiry should be entertained after the motion to adjourn has been made unless it is of such a nature that its decision is necessary before an adjournment. Where the business is not finished and a motion to adjourn passes, the business that was unfinished is the first business to be taken up after the reading of the minutes at the next meeting.

10.22 Table of Parliamentary Rules. The following table explains some of the basic rules of parliamentary procedure. In some cases, the application of the rules is more complicated than indicated here, and the reader should consult ROBERT'S RULES OF ORDER or any text on parliamentary procedure to get complete rules. An asterisk indicates there is an exception to the rules stated under certain conditions, and ROBERT'S RULES OF ORDER should be consulted.

Motion	Is Second Motion Needed?	Can Speaker Be Interrupted?	Debatable?	Can It Be Amended?	Votes Needed To Pass
Adjourn	Yes	No	No*	No	Majority
Amendment	Yes	No	Yes	Yes	Majority
Amend an Amendment	Yes	No	Yes	No	Majority
Appeal from Decision of Chair	Yes	Yes	No (1)	No	Majority
Debate, to Limit	Yes	No	No	Yes	2/3
Motion	Yes	No	Yes	Yes	Majority
Nominations:		No			
To Make	No	No	No	No	No (2)
To Close	Yes	No	No	Yes (3)	2/3
Order, Questions of	No	Yes	No	No	N/A
Parliamentary Inquiry	No	Yes	No	No	N/A
Privilege, Question of	No	Yes	No	No	N/A
Recess, To Take	Yes	No	Yes (4)	Yes	Majority
Reconsider	Yes	Yes	Yes (5)	No	Majority
Substitute Motion	Yes	No	Yes	Yes	Majority
Suspend Rules	Yes	No	No	No	2/3
To Lay on Table	Yes	No	No	No	Majority
To Take From Table	Yes	No	No	No	Majority

Notes to Table:
(1) If relating to indecorum; yes in other cases
(2) No vote on nominations; just on election
(3) Yes, under certain circumstances
(4) Yes, if another question is before the assembly
(5) Yes, unless motion to be reconsidered is not debatable

* (With certain exceptions)

Chapter 11
VOTING/ELECTION

Manager's Note: One of the most important duties of each owner/member is selection of the members who will become the board of directors. Unlike other nonprofit organizations whose board members make no operating decisions, the decisions of the board of directors for an association affect each owner/member. This chapter is a definite "must-read" for both owners and (potential or current) directors of the board.

11.1 One Vote Per Owner/Member. In residential associations, the general rule is one vote per residential dwelling. There are some exceptions to this in states that permit "weighted" voting. In these cases, the votes normally are assigned to a unit based on square footage of interior living space.

Where there is more than one owner, the owners must decide how to cast the vote. Splitting of votes is generally not allowed. If co-owners show up at a meeting and cannot agree on how to vote or who gets to vote, their vote is not counted.

11.2 Weighted Voting. In commercial projects, it is customary to weight voting in accordance with relative square footage of usable floor space. Occasionally, you find a project where the voting among commercial units is based upon fair market value as determined by initial sales price. Weighted voting should be provided for in the legal documents, and generally an exhibit is attached which indicates the number of votes assigned to each unit. In an election where there is weighted voting, it is necessary to have written ballots rather than vote by voice, show of hands, or standing (although a roll-call vote may also be practical).

11.3 Two-Class Voting. In some states, consumer protection regulations permit developers' projects to create two classes of voting membership. The developer constitutes one class, and everyone else (meaning the buyers of units or lots) constitute the other class. Usually the developer has special privileges attached to its memberships that may take the form of treble (or triple) voting. This means the developer is entitled to three votes for every membership that it holds, giving the developer enough votes to elect a majority of the board of directors until it has sold 75 percent or more of the units or lots in the subdivision. At that point, its 3-to-1 advantage in voting no longer gives it enough votes to control the board.

Where such arrangements are permitted, they are perfectly valid, and are based on sound reasoning. The developer, after all, has the biggest stake in the project, and it is important for the future success of the project that it be given sufficient authority over the management and operation of the project to ensure its success. It should not have to deal with a hostile board of directors that is in control of the owners association during the time that it still owns a substantial number of the units or lots in the project. Generally, when the developer's remaining interest in the project dwindles to below 25 percent, it is deemed appropriate, at that time, to allow control of the board of directors to pass to the buyers of units or lots. Consumer protection regulations typically terminate treble voting rights when the ownership percentage of the developer dwindles to below 25 percent.

Some legal documents will protect the minority rights of the non-developer owners during the time that there are two classes of membership, or during the time that any other device exists which gives the developer a voting advantage. The protective device generally utilized is a provision that the members, other than the developer, are entitled to elect at least one director to serve on the board even if the developer has enough votes to elect the entire board. Other protective provisions would require the vote of a majority of both classes of membership in order to take certain actions such as amending the project legal documents.

11.4 Voting Register. The secretary of the association should keep an updated register or list of all members. The register should indicate the name of the current record holder of title to each unit or lot, and his/her address and telephone number. It should also indicate whether the owner's voting rights are suspended for delinquency in payment of assessments, or for some violation of the project legal documents. It is important that the voting register be kept current. This may be difficult if the association is not advised of all transfers of title to units or lots in the project.

In large associations it may be necessary for the secretary to establish a cut-off date, so that the voting roll can be established as of a specific date, similar to what a large publicly held corporation would do. It is a bit more difficult to adopt and enforce a record cut-off date, since strict adherence to the cut-off date will mean that any new owners who have closed escrow after the cut-off date and shortly before a meeting at which an election is to be held will be unable to participate. A practical solution to this would be for the new owner of a unit or lot who has acquired title after the record date to obtain a proxy from the prior owner from whom (s)he acquired the property. In that case, the new member can attend and vote by using the proxy from the former owner, whose name appears on the voting register as being entitled to vote at the meeting.

Manager's Note: New owners should be encouraged and invited to attend the annual or general membership meetings. If a proxy from the former owner authorizing the new owner to vote at the meeting was not delivered prior to the meeting, another proof of membership, such a copy of the deed, should be allowed as verification of ownership.

11.5 Transfer of Membership. The membership in an owners association is appurtenant to the ownership interest in a lot or unit, and transfers automatically with title to the lot or unit. Common interest subdivision state statutes provide for mandatory and automatically transferable membership. In addition, membership provisions are usually found in the recorded declaration and in the bylaws of a common interest subdivision project.

The legal documents may define an owner to be either the buyer or the seller when a unit or lot has been sold under a contract of sale where the contract provides that the seller shall deliver possession to the buyer, but the seller shall retain record title until the buyer has completed a series of installment payments over a number of years. In such a case, the membership and the vote appurtenant to the membership may reside either with the seller until title is ultimately transferred, or with the buyer at the time the buyer takes occupancy, depending upon the provisions in the legal documents.

The death of a member does not terminate membership rights, because those rights are appurtenant to the subdivision interest. Upon the death of a member, however, the membership automatically passes with title to the subdivision interest.

11.6 Proxies. A proxy is a written authorization signed by a member giving another person the power to vote on behalf of that member. The signature on a proxy may consist of a manual signature, a typewritten signature, telegraphic or faxed transmission, or other appropriate manifestation of intent to authorize the proxy.

A proxy continues in effect until it is revoked, unless a statute limits the term of a proxy to some maximum term of months, or unless the legal documents for the project limit the term of a proxy. A proxy may be revoked by:

- Delivering a written revocation to the association;
- A later proxy executed by the same person;
- Attendance at a meeting by the member, and voting in person.

A proxy revoked by attendance and voting is not revived if the member leaves before the meeting is adjourned. In such case, the member should re-execute and redeliver the proxy, or execute a new proxy before leaving if (s)he wants to revive it. Some statutes provide that the death or incapacity of a member or termination of the membership as a result of death or incapacity does not revoke a proxy unless written notice of such death or incapacity is received by the association before the vote is counted.

Some state statutes provide that certain proxies are not valid with respect to a vote on certain proposals unless the general nature of the matter to be voted on was described in the proxy. This usually includes such matters as:

- Removing a director without cause;
- Filling vacancies on the board of directors;
- Amending the articles of incorporation;
- Selling, leasing, conveying or otherwise disposing of substantially all of the association's assets;
- Approving a contract between the association and one or more directors or between the association and an entity in which a director has material financial interest;
- Electing to wind-up and dissolve the association; or
- Approving a plan of distribution of assets.

Some statutes require that in large associations a written proxy must provide on its face an opportunity for the holder of the proxy to specify a choice between approval and disapproval of certain matters to be voted upon. The secretary of the association should be familiar with any such rules that may apply to the association.

If the association is unincorporated, the legal documents creating the association should make provisions for proxy rights and the use of proxies, if the intention is to make use of proxies. Without such provisions in the legal documents there is some uncertainty about whether members of an unincorporated association have proxy rights.

Where proxies are used, the association should obtain a complete description of all applicable laws concerning proxies from counsel for the association.

All notices of meetings requiring proxy voting should be announced at least 30 days in advance, so there is ample time to allow for mailing and receipt of proxies. A proxy form may include the name of an officer or member of the board of directors when it is mailed out, or it may be left blank, so that the member can fill in the name of any unit or lot owner. The proxy may include instruction on how to vote in the case of specific proposals that will be brought before the membership for a vote at the noticed meeting. *See Form 4 for a sample proxy.*

11.7 Cumulative Voting. Some state statutes require cumulative voting for all elections in which more than two positions on the board of directors are to be filled. In other cases, cumulative voting is optional. Cumulative voting may or may not be provided for in the project legal documents. Cumulative voting requirements are intended to protect minority interests by ensuring that a minority will be able to have representation on the board even though a majority block of votes may control the board.

A provision authorizing cumulative voting may be inserted into the legal documents by a vote of the required majority of the membership. The legal documents may also be amended to terminate cumulative voting, as long as state law does not require cumulative voting.

Cumulative voting works in the following manner. Each owner is allowed to cast as many votes as there are directors up for election. The owner of one lot or unit will have three votes to cast in an election where there are three vacancies on the board of directors. The owner may cast three votes for one nominee, or two votes for one nominee and one vote for another, or one vote for each of three nominees.

An example of how cumulative voting can be used by a minority block of votes to gain representation on the board is as follows. Assume an association with 100 members and three directors to be elected. If cumulative voting is used, there will be a total of 300 votes, three for each membership. It will take 100 votes to ensure the election of one director or, if a minority block of 34 out of 100 members cumulates their votes and votes them all for one director, that director would be elected with a total of 102 votes. *See Chapter 12.6.*

11.8 Majority. Sometimes legal documents will provide for a majority vote, and it will not be clear whether that means a majority of the total voting power of an association or the majority of those present and voting in person and by proxy. Ambiguities that exist in the legal documents should be amended.

Some statutes define the term "majority" either to mean a majority of all members or a majority of the votes represented and voting at a duly held meeting at which a quorum is present.

11.9 Extra Majority. There are generally a number of situations in which the legal documents and/or state laws will require more than a 51 percent vote to take a certain action or adopt certain resolutions. For example, many recorded declarations require a vote of two-thirds or three-fourths of the members in order to adopt amendments. In projects which have legal documents drafted to qualify for federal loan guarantees, such as FHLMC or FNMA (*see Chapter 1.4*), two-thirds or more of the total membership may be required to take certain action, such as selling or encumbering a portion of the common area.

11.10 Secret Ballot. Some state laws and some legal documents require secret written ballots to be used in electing directors. The election of directors does not have to be by written ballots unless required by state law or by the project legal documents. Some laws provide that written ballots will be used only when a member demands election by written ballot at the beginning of the meeting, before the voting commences. However, if cumulative voting is used, it will be necessary to use written ballots in order to be able to correctly tabulate the votes.

11.11 Vote by Mail. Where the legal documents permit (and state law does not prohibit), members may vote by mail. The secretary can mail out ballots and tabulate the results when the ballots are returned.

If the project legal documents provide for the adoption of an amendment by "vote or written consent of a majority of the members," the directors can either call a special meeting to take a vote on the proposed amendment, or they may send the proposed amendment out to the members and ask for the written consent of each member. The forms sent out by the board should provide a space for the member to sign and signify consent to the amendment. When the forms have been returned and the tabulation indicates that a majority of the members gave their written consent, the amendment can be signed by the secretary to certify the approval of a majority of members.

11.12 Developer Votes. Some state statutes permit and some legal documents provide for multiple votes for the developer. The privilege is designed to extend the control of the developer over the board of directors of the association past the time when the developer has sold a majority of the subdivision interests. Where the developer chooses to exercise its multiple voting privileges, the members other than the developer can still obtain representation on the board of directors. The members may obtain board representation by cumulating their votes or relying on state law, consumer protection provisions, or the provisions in the legal documents that guarantee minimum representation of the non-developer members on the board of directors.

See Chapters 11.3, 11.7 and 12.1 regarding developer votes.

11.13 Nominating Committee. A nominating committee may be provided for in the project legal documents. Even if not required, one should be appointed in all but the smallest associations. The committee should study the membership, determine the best potential candidates, and contact each of those candidates to determine whether or not they are willing to serve. The committee should put together a slate of candidates to be presented to the general membership at its annual meeting for consideration of the members in electing a new board.

Manager's Note: *The nominating committee should be very conscientious about selecting candidates for the board who have both the ability and the willingness to serve effectively as directors and officers of the association. It is unfortunately true that many times the members of the association who are most qualified to serve on the board are often reluctant to do so. The nominating committee should attempt to identify those members who have the most potential to be directors and officers, and should attempt to persuade those individuals to allow themselves to be nominated. It is also true that there are members who are not particularly well qualified to serve on the board but who are eager to serve. In some cases, such persons may already have served on the board and would like to continue to serve.*

It is the job of the nominating committee to come up with the best slate possible, having in mind the interests of the association and its members, without at the same time creating animosity or ill will. Some associations follow a procedure of asking a nominee to sign a written acceptance agreeing to the submission of his or her name as a nominee and agreeing to serve if elected.

When the nominations are made, it is a good idea to read or publish with the meeting notice and proxy material a short biography of each nominee. It is also a good idea to have each nominee make a brief statement indicating his/her willingness to serve, and expressing any particular thoughts that (s)he may have concerning the role of a director and what (s)he hopes to achieve, if elected.

The nominating committee, or whoever is in charge of procedures for the election, should prepare in advance for the election. The nominating committee or the person in charge of election procedure should decide and announce in advance whether candidates' speeches will be permitted; if so, rules should be established which would include such matters as numbers of speeches for each candidate, length of time and other appropriate matters.

11.14 Elections. Elections of directors are held at the annual meeting or at a special meeting called for the purpose of electing or removing directors. *See Chapter 11.18.* The project legal documents will spell out the basic requirements for the annual election, including date, time, place, and notice requirements. If a nominating committee has been appointed, it should be prepared to present a slate of candidate names to the membership for nomination to the board. The developer may submit a slate of proposed nominees at the first annual meeting.

The initial board of directors of the newly formed association has a very difficult task to perform. For many of the new board members, operating an owners association will be a new experience, and they will learn as they go along. Usually, the initial board of directors will set or shape the standards that will be followed by future boards. It is therefore especially important to elect the most highly qualified people to the first board of a newly formed association.

The presiding officer for the election can either be the association's president, or the chairman of the nominations committee, or a person appointed to handle the election. The presiding officer discusses the election procedure, tells the members the number of directors to be elected, and explains cumulative voting and proxy voting. The nominating committee members are introduced, and the candidates selected by the nominating committee, or any slate that is presented, are introduced. The members are told that nominations may be made from the floor, and the presiding officer then calls for nominations. The candidates selected by the nominating committee are nominated. If there are any slates to be presented, they are presented by nomination. Members who wish to nominate or be nominated from the floor may do so. When all nominations have been made, a motion should be made to close the nominations. *See Chapters 6.5 and 6.6.*

The presiding officer then explains the voting procedures if cumulative voting is to be used, or if there are more nominations than there are vacancies on the board. Written ballots are then distributed to the members. It is important that the instructions be given clearly, and that they be understood.

The board may appoint inspectors for the election in advance of the meeting, or the chair may appoint inspectors at the meeting. The inspectors determine the number of memberships outstanding, the voting power of each class of members in the event there is more than one class, the number represented at the meeting, the existence of a quorum, and the authenticity of proxies. The inspectors also resolve any challenges or questions concerning rights to vote.

The first election of directors is required either by statute or by the provisions in the legal documents. The association may be required to hold the first election within a certain number of days after the association has been formed, or after the closing of escrow on the sale of the first lot or unit to be sold in the project, or a certain period of time after 51 percent of all the total interests authorized for sale have been sold and closed escrow.

Where written ballots will be used, they should be prepared in advance. *See Chapter 11.16.* If a ballot box is to be used, it should be obtained or prepared in advance. The ballot can be as simple as a box with a slot or a cardboard box.

Tally sheets should be prepared in advance. For larger associations having many members, a summary sheet should be prepared upon which the totals of the tally sheets can be recorded. A supply of paper, pens and pencils should be on hand. A place should be set aside for the inspectors to work in counting the ballots. Members have to be appointed to collect the ballots, to put them in the ballot box, and to deliver them to those who will count the ballots. If there are many ballots to be counted, then "readers" and "tally clerks" should be appointed. The readers read the ballots, and the tally clerks keep track of the votes.

An inspector or a judge should be available to answer questions concerning the ballots. For example, suppose that ballots were passed out with preprinted names on them, and the instructions were to mark an "X" after the name of each nominee that is being voted for. If a ballot has names circled but does not have any "Xs" there may be a question whether it should be counted. The inspector or designated judge appointed in advance should have authority to make the decision as to whether or not to count the ballot.

What should be done if there is a tie between two nominees? For example, suppose that three directors are to be elected, and five have been nominated. If one received 50 votes, the second 45 votes, and then two directors each got 35 votes, what should be done? The best answer is probably to have a run-off election between just the two directors getting 35 votes each, to determine which will fill the third slot on the board.

At the beginning of the election meeting, the secretary or a clerk or a committee appointed for that purpose will check in each owner and make sure that a complete record is obtained of the number of owners present who are eligible to vote, and of the number of proxies held by those in attendance. If ballots are passed out, a record should be kept of the name and unit or lot number of each owner to whom a ballot has been distributed. There should also be a list of those owners who are ineligible to vote because their voting privileges have been suspended. The notice of the meeting should include a reminder to members that delinquent assessments must be paid prior to the meeting or the delinquent member will be ineligible to vote. Ballots should be given to those members who hold valid proxies.

If during the meeting someone "spoils" a ballot and asks for another one, the "spoiled" ballot should be exchanged for the new one.

Once the members have all checked in, the checklist or tally sheet can be used to determine that a quorum is present and that the meeting is official. *See Chapter 9.10.*

A reasonable period of time should be allowed for people to mark their ballots, and then the ballots should be deposited in the ballot box or collected and delivered to the readers and tally clerks.

The final summary showing the candidates and the number of votes for each should then be given to the presiding person, who announces the names of those elected and the number of votes for each candidate. In the case of a tie, a run-off should be conducted. Some associations use different-colored ballots so that it is easy to distinguish between the ballots for the run-off election.

11.15 Checklist for Elections. The following is a general checklist to be used by the association in preparing for and holding an election.

1. Review project legal document provisions pertaining to election procedure.
2. Appoint nominating committee and election committee.
3. List notice requirements and review and summarize requirements and procedures for voting, proxies and ballots.
4. Interview prospective candidates.
5. Obtain signed acceptances from nominees.
6. Obtain biographies from nominees.
7. Notify owners concerning election date, nomination procedures, and other necessary information.
8. Prepare proxy forms and instructions.
9. Prepare ballots and instructions on voting and cumulative voting.
10. Select meeting place and make list of supplies and equipment needed such as tables, chairs, sound system, ballot box, ballots, different-colored ballots (if necessary), tally sheets, summary sheets, pens, pencils, owner roster and sign-in sheet.
11. Appoint presiding person to handle election procedures.
12. Appoint readers, tally clerks and judges.
13. Prepare and mail or distribute notices to owners including proxy forms, names of nominees and biographies, instructions on voter eligibility and on making nominations from the floor.
14. At the meeting describe the procedure, including cumulative voting, and introduce the nominating and the election committee.
15. Call for nominations.
16. Introduce all candidates and, if appropriate, allow statements by the candidates.
17. Instruct members how to mark ballots, how to vote cumulatively (if applicable), and what to do with spoiled ballots.
18. Explain the procedures for counting and tallying, and introduce ballot readers, tally clerks, judges and others involved in the election.
19. Actual voting.
20. Counting of votes.

In counting the votes, if a box is used, have the box opened by the designated group in charge of counting. Readers should read ballots while tally clerks tally the votes. Questionable ballots should be referred to the designated judge for ruling. The tally clerks will record the votes, prepare a summary that is reviewed by the judge, and then given to the presiding officer who will announce the results. In the event of a tie vote, a run-off will be held between the tied candidates. Finally, the presiding officer will announce the names of those elected, and will close the election proceedings.

11.16 Ballot. Ballots for elections of directors should be prepared in advance of the meeting and should have the names of directors who are nominated by the nominating committee preprinted. Blanks should be left on the ballot for names of directors nominated from the floor at the meeting. The ballot should also contain blanks to be filled in with the name of the owner and his/her unit or lot number or address. Each name or blank to be filled in with the name of the person nominated should be followed by a check "box" or space to indicate the vote or number of votes (in the event of cumulative voting) being cast.

Where the declaration permits, voting on such matters as approval of resolutions and amendments to the legal documents may be done by written consent rather than actually holding a meeting. The election of directors, however, must be done at a meeting. The ballot requesting written consent should contain the actual wording of the resolution or the amendment to the legal document to be voted upon. It should contain a place for the owner to indicate that a vote is cast for or against, or that the member abstains from voting. The ballot should also contain a place to fill in the date and to print or type the name and address of the owner and the lot or unit number. The ballot should indicate that if the lot or unit is jointly owned, all owners must date and sign the ballot. It should also indicate a closing date in the event that the project legal documents establish a closing date for voting. *See Chapter 11.4. See Form 6 for a sample ballot.*

In some states, laws require the rotation of names on ballots, so that every candidate's name appears at the top, bottom and middle an equal number of times. Some laws require incumbents to be listed at the top and challengers below. Unless state law or the legal documents themselves require something different, listing the candidates alphabetically by last name is the most simple.

Absentee ballots are generally not used in owners associations. There is no need for absentee ballots, since most associations permit the use of proxies and a proxy can serve the same purpose as an absentee ballot.

11.17 Changing the Number of Directors and/or Terms of Office.

The developer of a project makes the initial decision on the number of directors and the length of their terms. Once the buyers of the units or lots have taken over the association, they may wish to change the number of directors to make it either larger or smaller. Most states require that a board of directors consist of at least three (3) members. There should always be an odd number to avoid tie votes, and although there is seldom any legal limit on the total number of directors, there are practical limitations. The number of directors generally bears some relationship to the number of members. The larger the membership, the larger the board of directors (up to certain limits), and for every association there is certainly an optimum size.

Once a decision is made to change the number of directors, the officers or directors who are attempting to do so should first check with the association's attorney to make sure there are no statutory limitations or requirements of which they are unaware. Next the legal documents should be reviewed. In some cases, the articles of incorporation may prescribe a certain number of directors, so to change the number of directors it may be necessary to amend the articles. In states where articles have to be filed with the secretary of state, amending the articles can be somewhat complicated and may require the assistance of an attorney. The articles may specify the number of directors, but may also provide that amending the bylaws can change the number.

The bylaws are generally fairly easy to amend. Usually a simple majority vote of the members is all that is required to amend the bylaws. Except in those states where recording is required, the bylaws may be amended without recording and filing of record with the county. Some associations may have duplicate provisions in the recorded declaration and the bylaws that specify the number of directors. If that is the case, both documents should be amended unless the declaration provides that the number of directors may be changed simply by amending the bylaws.

The amendment procedure in the legal documents should be reviewed carefully. An amendment to change the number of directors may require a majority vote, more than a majority, or only a majority of a quorum. Amending the bylaws may be accomplished at a special meeting or at the annual meeting, or, in some cases, it may be done without having an actual meeting by sending out written ballots.

Once the number of directors has been changed, action must be taken to implement the change. If the board is to be increased in size, additional directors can be elected at the annual election, or a special election can be called for that purpose. If the board is to be reduced in size, the amendment reducing the number of directors should not take effect until existing directors have served out their terms. If board members are presently serving staggered terms, the reduction can be done a step at a time as terms expire, or one or more directors may be elected for a shorter term in order to be able to reduce the board to the new lower number at the expiration of the longest existing term of office.

11.18 Removal of Directors. The association documents should (and normally will) contain provisions concerning the circumstances under and method by which directors may be removed. State law may also impose certain requirements upon the process of removing directors. The power to remove a director should be reserved to the members, and not be given to the board. Although the board has power to appoint directors under certain circumstances, the board should not have the authority to appoint a director who has been removed by a vote of the membership. *See Chapters 6.8 and 6.9.*

11.19 Vesting of Voting Rights. The project legal documents may provide that voting rights do not vest until assessments have been levied against an owner's unit or lot. There may also be certain exceptions to that rule.

11.20 Protecting Minority Interests. Cumulative voting requirements are designed and intended to protect the interests of a minority of the membership. State laws or association documents may impose other restrictions to protect minority rights such as requiring a minimum representation on the board by owners other than the developer, where the developer has a controlling interest in the association. Restrictions on the removal of directors, which provide that a board member who has been elected solely by votes of members other than the subdivider may be removed from office only by a vote of at least a majority of the voting power of the members other than the subdivider, are also to protect minority interests. *See Chapter 6.8.*

11.21 Notice of Election Meeting. State law and association documents generally provide for a minimum period of notice before the date of a meeting. Notice must be given to each member who is entitled to vote at the meeting. The content of the notice is also generally prescribed and, as a minimum, includes the date, time, and place of the meeting. Usually, the notice will also include the names of all persons who have been nominated as of that date.

State law and association documents usually prescribe how notices are to be given, either personally or by mail—first-class, registered or certified. Generally, notices are required to be addressed to a member at the address of such member appearing on the books of the association or given by the member to the association. *See Form 2 for a sample form of Notice of Meeting.*

11.22 Nominations. Nominations should be formally made at the meeting by following established procedures. A nomination can be by slate or can be done by individual nominations, one at a time. Nominations need not be seconded. *See Chapters 6.5 and 6.6.* A good shortcut to save time at an election where the nominations are closed and only the number of directors necessary to fill the existing vacancies has been nominated, is to move that a unanimous "white ballot" be cast to elect the nominees. A voice vote can then be taken.

11.23 Suspension of Voting Rights. Association legal documents normally provide or should provide for the suspension of voting rights for failure to pay assessments or, in certain cases, for violation of rules and regulations of the association. Due process must be followed in suspending voting rights. *See Chapter 29.1.*

11.24 Contesting Elections. An action to contest the validity of an election must generally be commenced within a certain period of time after the election. That period of time would certainly be prior to the next election, and it may be shorter than that if prescribed either by statute or by the association's documents. State laws generally provide that if an action to contest the validity of an election is not commenced on a timely basis, in the absence of fraud the election of a director is conclusively presumed valid after a specified period of time has elapsed. Some state laws require that an action to challenge the validity of an election must be accompanied by notice to the state Attorney General's office, which has the authority to intervene in the process.

11.25 Record-Keeping. All the records pertaining to an election, including the notices and announcements, certificates of mailing, acceptance of the candidates, biographies, sign-in sheets, proxies, ballots, tallies, summary sheets, and spoiled ballots, should be kept at least until the following year's election. The shortest period of time that such material should be kept is until the time has expired for filing an action to contest the election.

CHAPTER 12
Voting Privileges of the Developer

Manager's Note: If your association is new, or the developer is still involved in the project, pay special attention to these privileges of the developer!

12.1 Multiple Voting Privileges. Developers of new projects like to retain control during the period of construction and sales. Control is retained principally through the developer's right to elect a majority of members of both the board of directors and the architectural review committee.

Voting control is retained through various means, the most common of which is for the developer to have a special class of membership that permits it to have more than one vote per lot or unit. By "weighting" the developer's votes, it can out-vote the rest of the owner/members who belong to a second class of membership. *See Chapter 11.3.*

12.2 Creation of Special Voting Privileges. The association documents are the source of the developer's special voting privileges. The documents will specify how many votes per membership the developer will get, and how long those special voting privileges may be retained and exercised. Consumer protection laws may put limits on the length of time the developer may retain its special voting privileges.

12.3 Elimination of Special Voting Privileges. The developer's special voting privileges may be automatically eliminated by the passage of time, according to the provisions in the association documents.

State law or consumer protection regulations may also provide for elimination of special voting privileges upon the elapse of a certain amount of time, or after the occurrence of a certain event, such as the closing of escrow on the sale of some percentage of the total lots or units in the project.

The developer may waive the special voting privileges. In a phased project, the voting privileges can be kept in force by annexing the next phase prior to the time when the developer's share of the votes in the existing phase of the project drops below the number which would cause it to automatically lose special voting privileges. For example, if more than 75 percent of the homes have closed in the first phase of a project, the developer's treble voting privileges will no longer afford it control of the total voting power. By annexing another phase to the project, the number of lots or units owned by the developer will increase, thus increasing the number of votes available to the developer. Where such circumstances exist, the developer may inadvertently lose its special voting privileges by failing to annex the next phase on a timely basis.

12.4 Extension or Revival of Special Voting Privileges. In some phased projects, state law and association documents permit the special voting privileges of the developer to be extended, or, if lost due to sale of a certain percentage of lots or units in prior phases, to be revived upon annexation of a subsequent phase.

12.5 Exercise of Special Voting Privileges. The developer has the option to use or not use its special voting privileges. The two situations in which the developer is most likely to use its special voting privileges are at the annual election of the board of directors, and when an amendment to the legal documents is proposed. If the developer feels it necessary to retain control of the board by electing members of its organization, or wishes to see that the directors elected to the board are friendly to the developer (or at least not unfriendly), the developer may exercise its special voting privileges. Similarly, a developer is likely to exercise special voting privileges to ensure passage of an amendment to the association documents sponsored by the developer, or to defeat an amendment sponsored by the other members if the developer is opposed to the amendment.

Some developers are reluctant to exercise their special voting rights because they believe (sometimes with good cause) that it appears heavy-handed or undemocratic, and can antagonize the members.

12.6 Cumulative Voting by Developer. Where cumulative voting is used *(see Chapter 11.7)*, the developer can cumulate its votes in the same way that other members can. For example, if a developer is entitled to three votes for every membership held, and there are three vacancies on the board of directors, the developer has nine votes for each membership held, which it can vote cumulatively.

12.7 Minimum Representation on Board. Even though the developer has special voting privileges and is able to out-vote the general membership, most state laws and association documents will provide for minimum representation on the board by members other than the developer or its employees, even if it means the general membership can elect only one member to the board.

12.8 Annexation of Phases. The legal documents for a phased project will normally create and preserve the right of the developer to annex subsequent phases. Under such provisions, automatic annexation at the option of the developer without consent of the owners can be accomplished at any time within the limits prescribed by the legal documents or by the state consumer protection laws. The developer can also automatically increase its voting strength by annexing the next phase. *See Chapter 12.4 and Chapter 58.*

CHAPTER 13
Minutes

Manager's Note: The minutes of the association become the official written record of the business that was transacted by the association board of directors or the membership. The minutes may be taken by the association's secretary, the association manager, a transcriptionist, or a member who is assigned the job of note taking at meetings.

13.1 Minutes of First Board Meeting. Since developers form most associations, the developer or the developer's attorney will generally prepare the minutes of the first board of directors' meeting. These minutes will deal with such things as the adoption of the bylaws, the appointment of first officers, adoption of a corporate seal (which will be done for most incorporated associations), the opening of a bank account, and the adoption of a fiscal year.

See Chapter 6.27 for more information about the developer's first meeting of the association.

The minutes of the first meeting of the general membership, where the association's board is elected, are usually prepared by the newly elected secretary, although sometimes the developer or the professional manager (if one has been retained) will assist in the preparation of the minutes. *See Form 8 for a sample of Minutes of the First Board Meeting.*

13.2 General Membership Meeting. The minutes of the general membership meeting should be complete and accurate. While the minutes are not intended to be detailed transcripts of a meeting, it is a good idea to summarize the remarks made by each speaker which are relevant to the proceedings and contain material that should be preserved as part of the records of the meeting. Motions, however, should appear in the minutes exactly as they were made in the meeting. A tape recorder can assist the secretary in ensuring that the motions are properly transcribed in the minutes.

When the minutes are read at the next meeting, it is important that any corrections to the minutes be made at that time. It is helpful to have the minutes circulated to the members prior to the meeting, so that there will be enough time to read them and make any corrections. It is difficult for the board members to make corrections to the minutes if they have not had an opportunity to review them before the meeting. The recorded tapes (if any) of the meeting should be preserved until the minutes have been approved at the next meeting. In the event of any possible controversy or litigation over a particular event occurring at a meeting, the tape of that meeting (if one exists) should be preserved along with the minutes of the meeting until the controversy has been resolved.

Manager's Note: Association boards faced with controversial subject matter or possible litigation in their meetings may consider videotaping the board meetings, and retaining copies of those videotapes until the issue has been resolved or passed.

Video cameras can provide an excellent record of the proceedings of a meeting, and, unlike audiotapes, speakers can be visually identified.

Styles vary greatly in taking minutes of a meeting. An association should try to develop a uniform style or format, adopted as a standard so that the minutes from one meeting or from one administration to the next do not vary greatly in form or content. The minutes should always be signed by the person who prepared them.

It is helpful to have a detailed, typewritten or printed agenda prior to each meeting. The agenda is helpful in keeping the business of the meeting organized and flowing efficiently. The agenda is also helpful in preparing the minutes of the meeting. A copy of the agenda should be filed with the approved and corrected minutes in the association's corporate minutes book.

13.3 Minutes of Directors' Meetings. Minutes of directors meetings should contain more detail than for a general membership meeting, because the board is involved in considerably greater detail than are the members at a general membership meeting. In addition, the board is action-oriented, and will generally pass a number of resolutions or motions during the course of the meeting. Actions taken in the form of motions should be set forth in separate paragraphs.

Some secretaries like to use the abbreviation "MSP" or "M/S/P," which stands for "Motion, Seconded and Passed." It is not necessary to include the name of the person making a motion, or the name of the person seconding the motion, although some secretaries prefer to do so, and some associations adopt that as a standard format for their minutes. *See Chapter 9.14*. Minutes of executive session meetings (*see Chapter 6.31*) are not normally kept, due to the often sensitive nature of the meeting; however, if written records of an executive session are made, these are not distributed to the membership. Actions taken as a result of the executive session will be generally noted in the minutes of the open session.

13.4 Action Without A Meeting. The association documents may permit the board of directors to take an action without holding a formal meeting. *See Chapter 6.29*. In such cases, minutes of the last meeting should be prepared, and they should indicate that an actual meeting was not held, but that the action taken was approved by unanimous written consent of the directors.

13.5 Telephone and Electronic Meetings. Some association documents permit the board of directors to hold a meeting by telephone or video conferencing equipment. *See Chapter 6.30*. As is the case of action without a meeting, detailed minutes should be kept, and they should indicate that the meeting was held by conference telephone or videoconferencing equipment.

13.6 Resolutions. A resolution is a motion that takes on a certain form. The standard form is to include some "whereas" clauses, which give background or reasons for the action, followed by a "Now, therefore, be it resolved" clause, which leads into the actual wording of the resolution.

A resolution is a formalized motion that is used for approving some official action to be taken by the association, such as opening a bank account, approving a contract, or amending the legal documents. *See Chapter 9.15.*

13.7 Minutes Book. Some state statutes require an association to keep a minutes book. Most legal documents also require that a minutes book be kept. In any event, <u>a minutes book should be kept by every association</u>. It can be a simple three-ringed binder with the name of the association on a label affixed to the binder or it can be an official minutes book, which can be purchased from an office supply store.

A well-organized and properly maintained minutes book is essential. It is part of good record keeping, and can be invaluable in the event of litigation or a dispute of any kind concerning action taken by the association or by the board of directors. The minutes book should be maintained by the secretary and should be kept with the permanent records of the association.

In addition to the minutes of meetings, the minutes book should also contain original association documents such as certified articles of incorporation, a file-endorsed copy of the original recorded declaration of covenants, conditions and restrictions pertaining to the project, and the original executed copy of the bylaws. The original executed copies of all amendments to the legal documents should also be kept in the minutes book. *See Chapter 14.2.*

CHAPTER 14
Association Records

14.1 Records to Keep. There are statutory requirements applicable to owners associations that require associations to keep certain records and to preserve them for specified periods of time. These legal requirements may be incorporated into the association's legal documents; however, the legal documents may not be up-to-date with respect to recent amendments or additions to the law, so the record-keeping requirements imposed by law may actually be different from the records referred to in the legal documents. It is important that the association keeps current with respect to record-keeping requirements. The following checklist contains important items that an association should consider keeping on a routine basis:

1. Books and records of accounts.
2. Minutes of general membership meetings.
3. Minutes of board meetings.
4. Minutes of committee meetings.
5. Record of names and addresses of all members (the membership roster).
6. Annual reports to members.
7. Where required, a copy of the annual corporation statement that must be filed with the state or county.
8. Annual budget.
9. Annual balance sheet.
10. Annual financial report.
11. Statement of association's policies and practices in enforcing remedies for defaults in payment of assessments or violation of rules and regulations.
12. Annual federal and state tax returns or informational returns.
13. Copies of association insurance policies.
14. Copy of an inventory of any personal property owned by the association.
15. Copies of contracts entered into by the association.
16. Contracts of employment and payroll records.
17. Copies of leases entered into by the association.
18. Official permits relating to boilers, pools, kitchens, garages, and other association facilities and improvements.
19. List of unsold units or lots held by developer.
20. Warranties covering association property, equipment, appliances, and improvements.
21. Original recorded legal documents and any amendments.

Manager's Note: Many of the items listed above, which will become the permanent records of the association, are unique, and copies are not normally distributed to owners/members (Items 7, 12 through 18, 19 through 21). Owners/members will receive and should retain annual reports distributed by the association as part of their ownership records (Items 2, 6, 8, 9 and 10).

14.2 Association Minutes.
Minutes of annual meetings may or may not be distributed to all members following the meeting. The minutes, of course, should be kept with the permanent records of the association and a copy should

always be available at the association's administrative office for review or copying at the request of any member. Minutes of directors' meetings should be distributed to all directors as soon as it is practical after each meeting. Minutes of each meeting should always be approved, either as prepared or with corrections, at the following meeting.

For more information regarding the form and content of association minutes, see Chapters 9.14 and 13.3.

14.3 Plans and Specifications. The developer may or may not have provided the association with a complete set of plans and specifications of the project. Providing plans is optional, so deciding to provide plans is left to the discretion of the developer. If the association requests a copy of the plans and the developer does not supply them, it is possible that a set of plans and specifications may be obtained from the local governmental authority, such as the city or county planning department which issued the building permit for the project.

If the developer refuses to provide a set of plans to the association because the plans belong to its architect, the association might ask the architect to furnish a set of plans. The architect is entitled to request that the association agree not to use the plans to build any other improvements, and agree not to make the plans available to any other builder. The architect may also charge a fee to have the plans duplicated and delivered to the association. A copy of the plans and specifications should be kept on file with the permanent records of the association.

14.4 Subdivision Maps. If the project has been subdivided, a civil engineer will prepare and have recorded a subdivision map. The association should obtain a good, readable copy of this map, and keep it in the permanent files. A map can be obtained from the title company or from the county recorder's office. The association may also be able to obtain a full-sized copy of the map either from the developer or from the civil engineer.

14.5 Condominium Plans. The association should also have as part of its permanent records a good, readable copy of the recorded condominium airspace plan. Sources for this document are the developer, the county recorder's office, the title company, or the civil engineer.

14.6 Parking Assignments. In some projects, assignments are made to unit or lot owners for the exclusive use of certain common area parking spaces. Records of those parking space assignments should be maintained as part of the official records of the association. It is important to have those records available in the event any questions are raised concerning rights to the use of such parking spaces.

14.7 Exclusive Common Area Assignments. In condominiums or planned developments where portions of the common area are assigned to the exclusive use of a particular unit or lot owner, a record of such assignment should be kept by the association as part of its permanent records.

14.8 Membership Roster. The records of the association should include an up-to-date membership roster and voters' register. The name, address and unit or lot number of each owner should be kept on that list. In addition, the voting register should indicate whether or not a member's voting rights have been suspended for failure to pay assessments or as a result of discipline for a violation of association rules or regulations. *See Chapter 4.2.*

CHAPTER 15
Corporate Seal

15.1 Corporate Seal. The question often arises as to whether or not an association should have a corporate seal. Some state statutes specifically require a corporate seal. Others specifically provide that a corporate seal is not required. Others are silent on the matter.

Legal documents for projects may or may not contain a provision requiring a corporate seal. Generally speaking, a corporate seal is not of much use to a nonprofit corporation unless it is required by law or unless it is customary to provide a corporate seal on documents required by banks or financial institutions with whom the association does business. A substitute for a corporate seal can be a resolution certified by the secretary and signed by two or more corporate officers.

It is easy to obtain a corporate seal. All states have privately owned corporate supply outfits that will provide a corporate seal, minute book, membership certificates, and anything else that an association needs for a nominal fee.

CHAPTER 16
Association Administration and Operation

16.1 Association Rules and Regulations. The first set of association rules and regulations may be initially prepared and adopted by the developer. The buyers of lots or units in the project will later generate their own rules and regulations based upon their experience in living in the project.

Rules should be consistent with the association's legal documents. To some extent, the rules may be repetitious of some of the basic provisions of the declaration and/or bylaws, but generally the rules will go into more detail with respect to conduct prohibited or required within the project and its recreational facilities. The legal documents should contain provisions authorizing the adoption of association rules and regulations by the board of directors. If they do not, they should be amended to provide and include the authority to enforce such regulations. Association rules and regulations may extend beyond ordinary regulation of conduct, and may include such things as detailed provisions for architectural review of proposed alterations, modifications or additions to dwellings, and procedures for discipline of members for violation of the rules by a disciplinary committee or the board of directors. *See Chapter 47. See Form 16 for a sample of association rules and regulations for a residential project. See Form 17 for a sample of procedures for enforcement of association rules.*

The association's rules should be a "living document," which means they are frequently reviewed and subject to periodic revisions. The rules and regulations should not be allowed to get out of date. Only essential revisions should be included, and those that are included should be rigorously enforced. Failure to enforce rules can lead to a condition where the rules are actually waived, and it becomes impossible to enforce them. *See Chapter 28.7.*

16.2 Review of Legal Documents and Procedures. The board of directors should review annually the basic association legal documents, including the declaration, articles, bylaws, and rules and regulations, as well as any management agreement and major service contracts. Needs and circumstances change, so an annual review of these documents is necessary to accommodate changes. Laws also change, sometimes more than once a year, and it is important that the legal documents properly reflect and are current with respect to those changes. It may be necessary to consult an attorney for advice and a periodic review of the legal documents.

16.3 Adoption of Budget. The board of directors, as one of its first official acts, should consider the budget. It begins by referring to the original, officially approved budget that was prepared by the developer and presented to the association at the beginning of the project. This budget may have been reviewed by a state regulatory agency, and was probably created using estimates and generally recognized guidelines.

Once control of the project has been handed over to the association, the new board of directors should immediately begin evaluating the accuracy of the initial budget, and should be prepared to make any changes necessary to reflect the actual financial needs of the association. If the initial budget is totally inaccurate to the point of fraud or misrepresentation, there are legal remedies available to the association that the board should vigorously pursue. *See Chapters 37.1 and 37.5.*

Specialized help is usually available to assist the board in preparing or revising a budget. Organizations exist that will prepare a budget for an owners association for a fee. In some states, the Department of Real Estate or other regulatory agency may publish a book of guidelines that contains operating cost estimates that can be used to forecast expenses, such as landscaping, exterior painting, pool maintenance, repair of streets and parking areas, and other usual costs and expenses.

Perhaps the most important part of the budget is the reserve account. Some states require that adequate reserves be funded on an annual basis, and that the amounts set aside each year be reasonably accurate with respect to the items that must be repaired or replaced. Sometimes after the buyers take control of the board, the new board decides to reduce assessments by cutting the contribution to the reserves. This is not sound financial planning. In the shortsighted effort to minimize and lower the current assessments, the owners will subject themselves and future owners to rather large and/or unexpected special assessments when it comes time to replace equipment or undertake much-needed major repairs and renovations.

At a minimum, a budget should consist of the following information:

1. Estimated revenue and expenses, on an accrual basis.
2. The amount of the total cash reserves of the association currently available for replacement or major repair of common facilities and for contingencies.
3. An itemized estimate of the remaining life of, and the methods of funding to defray the costs of repair, replacement or additions to major components of the common area and facilities for which the association is responsible.
4. A general statement setting forth the procedures used by the association for the calculation and establishment of reserves.

The board of directors, in carrying out its obligation to maintain adequate reserves, should begin by referring to the original or initial budget that was approved by the state regulatory agency, if the project is one which went through the process of review by a state agency. There may also be published guidelines and operating cost manuals available from the state's Department of Real Estate. Estimates can also be obtained from contractors who specialize in areas such as roof repairs, plumbing, solar heating, swimming pool equipment, landscape maintenance, driveway resurfacing, and other reserve components. The contractors or other experts can be asked for estimates of the remaining life of the components and the probable cost of replacement. The information that is used as a basis for setting the reserves should be kept on file as evidence to support the reasonableness of the board's decision to establish reserves at the chosen level.

The association's reserve account must be allocated among the components to be replaced. The board then calculates the replacement cost, and the amount that will need to be set aside to pay for replacement. An allowance for increases in costs due to inflation and for interest income on reserves should be included in the computation to determine the amount of the monthly assessments. Once a reserve-funding program has been established, it should be reviewed and updated annually.

16.4 Bank Account. Newly elected directors need to change the signature cards for the bank accounts of the association. This means obtaining a copy of the bank signature card, and executing the standard form of bank resolution authorizing certain persons to sign checks. The bank resolution should be incorporated into the minutes of the meeting of the board of directors. The directors should obtain from the developer the checkbook, check register and old bank statements, as well as a current bank statement and a current audit of the association accounts, at the meeting at which control is passed from the developer to the newly elected board.

It is best to require two signatures on all association checks, and, indeed, some state laws require two signatures on the account, particularly on the reserve account. Sometimes the association will retain a professional management firm to collect the assessments and pay the bills. In such case, it is preferable to have one member of the board of directors and one officer of the management company sign checks and manage the association's financial affairs.

Generally, it is best to have at least two accounts, one general account and one for reserve. This way the reserves can be kept separate, and there is less chance of the reserve fund being allocated to current expenditures. In some states the law requires, and in some associations the legal documents require, one or more trust accounts to be set up for insurance, utilities and reserves.

16.5 Use of Computers. For a large association, a computer is an excellent tool to process the information that the association board or the manager of the association is required to maintain. While the association must perform a variety of functions, there are many commercially available software packages that can be easily modified to suit the needs of property owners associations. Consultants are available to help in the selection and modification of hardware and software.

A committee should be appointed to thoroughly investigate the potential computer systems and software available to serve the association. The committee should get expert advice whenever it can. Service is an important element in picking the company to supply the hardware and to provide continuing maintenance and repair service.

Manager's Note: There are many fine commercially available software programs that can assist the association in managing its files and performing vital functions. At a minimum, the association's software library should include an accounting program, a spreadsheet program, a word-processing program and, for larger associations with many members and components, a database program. Choose software produced by well-known, reliable companies that will provide technical support for their products.

16.6 Security. Security systems can consist of the minimum alarm system that can be connected to a central station, or can include entry gates with or without a guard, guards who patrol on foot, and roving patrols who patrol by automobile with police radio connected to the police station. Many associations will appoint a committee in charge of security. The committee can look into such things as neighborhood watch systems, establishing anti-solicitation rules to prevent people posing as solicitors from casing homes for later burglaries, checking perimeter security, common area lighting, and cooperation with neighborhood police departments. The security committee can prepare suggestions to be distributed to members on how to handle situations where strangers appear at the doorway, ask for directions, ask to use the telephone, purport to be involved in some sort of contest, or claim to be soliciting donations for charitable organizations. *See Chapter 54 regarding security.*

16.7 Start-Up and Initial Organization. In the first days of organization of an association when control is transferred from the developer to the new board, there are certain initial organizational steps to be taken by the board and the officers. The following is a suggested checklist for some of the basic steps:

1. Obtain original executed copies of all association documents, including the declaration, articles and bylaws.
2. Obtain all financial records, including bank account records, checkbook, check register and deposit slips.
3. Obtain copies of architectural plans and drawings, subdivision maps and condominium plans.
4. Obtain copies of all contracts entered into, including the landscape contract, maintenance contract, swimming pool contract and security contract.
5. Obtain copies of the developer's budget or any existing budget for the association.
6. Obtain the original copy of all insurance policies held by the association.
7. Set dates for board meetings and for the annual membership meeting.
8. Order supplies to be used by the secretary and the treasurer.
9. Obtain copies of warranties on all appliances or equipment owned by the association. Obtain a bill of sale or inventory for all association equipment.
10. Set up an association "library" to include copies of relevant state rules and regulations, budget, homeowners association manual, insurance guide, association legal documents, and reference guides to assist officers and directors in conducting association business.
11. Select a CPA for the association.
12. Check on tax status (has exemption been claimed and obtained?). *See Chapter 42.6.*
13. Select the association's attorney.
14. Negotiate and enter into contracts for all services required. *See Chapter 19.1.*
15. Review all existing contracts and determine whether or not to terminate, modify or renew.

In general, the board of directors will need to establish a firm basis for future operations for the association.

16.8 Attorney for the Association.

The association should have a lawyer that it can contact for legal advice. Only a very large association can afford to have a lawyer on a retainer. Small- to medium-sized associations will have to be content with establishing a relationship with a lawyer or a law firm that can handle legal problems as they arise. For the most efficiency and least expense, it is advisable for the association to use an attorney or a firm that has a high degree of expertise representing owners associations. The association's attorney should be able to draft amendments to the association documents, advise the association regarding changes in laws applicable to owners associations, and provide advice regarding their relationship with the project developer and state regulatory agencies. Other areas where the association will rely on the expertise of an attorney will include the enforcement of the legal documents, collecting assessments, imposing discipline in the form of fines or suspension of voting rights, breach of contract and developer defect litigation.

The services of a CPA experienced in handling owners associations will usually be adequate for tax assistance, but occasionally the need for a tax attorney may arise. The association should make an effort to determine what areas of expertise are required, and should then attempt to find the attorney or other professional who can best supply the needed skills.

There are various ways to find an attorney. The best method is to seek referrals from other attorneys (who perhaps do not specialize in that particular area), or title company officers, professional association managers, state regulatory agencies (such as the Department of Real Estate), bar association directories, and banks or lending institutions that do business with or make loans to owners associations.

The committee or person in charge of selecting an attorney to represent the association or to handle a certain matter for the association should feel free to conduct personal interviews with several attorneys before making the final selection. Some of the things to keep in mind prior to selecting an attorney include:

- Does the attorney represent any other owners associations?
- Does the attorney represent developers?
- Has (s)he formed a number of associations and been responsible for the preparation of association documents?
- Does the attorney have the time to handle the association's affairs?
- Does the attorney appear to have sufficient experience in the area?
- Is the attorney's practice primarily in other areas so that the owners associations constitute only a minor part of his/her practice?
- Is the attorney willing to provide a fee schedule?
- What are the hourly rates charged by the attorney and, more importantly, what is the attorney's estimate of the fee required for the particular matter?

It is not wise to select an attorney simply based upon a comparison of hourly rates. A higher hourly rate may, and in most cases does, indicate a greater degree of expertise, a higher degree of efficiency, and therefore a better overall job, and perhaps a lower overall bill. Sometimes it is necessary to experiment and try out two or three different attorneys on small matters in order to select one. An association should not feel any compulsion to continue using an attorney (or any other professional) with whom it is not totally satisfied. *See Chapter 18.1.*

16.9 Loans. Occasionally an association may need to borrow money. This would be true in the case of emergency repairs or in the case of repairs to or replacement of a major component, such as the roof or the swimming pool filter and pump. Where the reserves are found to be inadequate and there is not sufficient time to establish and collect a special assessment, the legal documents should be reviewed along with state law provisions to determine whether or not the association has the authority to borrow money and, if necessary, pledge the assets of the association as security. Lenders will ask for assurance that the board has the authority and the power to borrow money and pledge assets. Officers and directors should never be required to nor should they consent to sign for the loans personally or give personal guarantees for loans to the association. *See Chapter 56.*

16.10 Central Filing System. Particularly for a large association, a comprehensive filing system should be established. The files should include minutes of all meetings of the board and of the general membership. Minutes of key committee meetings should also be included. The filing system should be available for use by the board, officers, and all committee members. Unit or lot owners should also have the right to access any non-confidential files during normal business hours.

The following is a list of suggested items to be kept on file:

1. Project legal documents.
2. Architectural plans and specifications.
3. Condominium plans.
4. Sales literature used in marketing the project.
5. Public reports obtained from the state used in marketing the project.
6. Inventory of personal property, equipment, fixtures and machinery owned by the association.
7. Copies of purchase agreements entered into with the developer.
8. Warranty agreements entered into with the developer and warranties on personal property, appliances and equipment owned by the association.
9. Contracts, including the management agreement and contracts with maintenance, service and security companies.
10. Employment contracts with employees of the association.
11. Insurance policies, including the master policy and any other policies.
12. Official permits for pools, boilers, garages, elevators, etc.
13. Membership directory, including the name, address, telephone number and lot or unit number of each owner.
14. Directory of service, repair, and maintenance personnel.
15. Directory of consultants, including accountants, attorneys and other professionals with whom the association has done business.
16. Complete financial and accounting records of the association.

Manager's Note: *For protection of the association and its membership, some files, such as employment and payroll information, personnel files, owners' telephone numbers, executive meeting minutes, etc., should be treated as confidential information, which is only available for review by the board of directors and management.*

16.11 Checklist of Items to be Addressed by Association After First Organizational Meeting. The board of directors and any appointed committees should, as soon as possible after control of the association is transferred from the developer, address the following items.

Financial. Set up a bank account or transfer over existing bank account assets to a new account; or obtain, complete and return to the bank new signature cards. Obtain all corporate financial records, including ledgers, bank deposit slips, bank accounts, checkbook, check register, savings accounts and certificates of deposit.

Contracts. Check all management and service contracts. Decide whether to terminate and, if so, review termination provisions. Check expiration dates and decide whether to renew. For contracts that will be terminated or not renewed, prepare to enter into new contract with another supplier of services.

Notices. File corporate notices indicating the change of officers and directors with appropriate state agencies.

Corporate Records. Obtain official records of the association from the developer, including the minute book, corporate seal (if applicable) and original, executed legal documents, including all amendments. Review all records and prepare summaries of important points, such as dates of annual and monthly meetings, requirements for notices of meetings, financial reporting requirements, and dates for billing and collecting assessments.

Change of Address. File or mail forms to appropriate places indicating the change in name and address of the secretary, treasurer, and the association office.

Tax Returns. Establish due dates and a system for getting federal and state tax returns filed. Find out if a tax exemption has been claimed and/or obtained, and if not, see that it is done.

Meetings. Review the date, time and place set for board meetings and membership meetings. Decide whether to change, and take appropriate steps.

Committees. Appoint committee chairs and members.

Budget. Review the budget. Appoint members to the budget committee, and prepare new budget. If necessary, hold budget hearings prior to adopting and presenting the budget to membership for approval.

Assessments. Review assessments in connection with the current budget. Decide whether to increase or decrease assessments. Check provisions of the declaration to see whether the board has the authority to increase or decrease assessments. Notify members.

Insurance. Obtain copies of policies and certificates of insurance; set up a file to monitor termination and renewal dates. Be sure sufficient funds will be available to pay renewal premiums.

Maintenance and Operation Items. Obtain keys to all common area locks. Obtain list of location of meters and valves for all utilities.

Instructions for Equipment. Obtain instructions on operation of recreational facilities, including pool, spa and gym equipment.

Sprinkler System Diagram. Obtain a diagram of the sprinkling system and, if computerized, obtain instructions for operation of computer.

Lighting. Obtain a diagram of the outdoor lighting system and, if computerized, obtain instructions for operation of the computer.

Fire and Security Systems. Obtain diagrams of the location and installation of fire and security systems and instructions for use, maintenance and operation. Recharge fire extinguishers.

Landscaping. Obtain records regarding the frequency and type of fertilizing, aerating, pruning, trimming and spraying.

Pest Control. Obtain records of control measures and inspections to date. Review the contract with the pest control service company. Consider retaining the pest control service company to monitor such things as termites, dry rot and insects.

Pool Maintenance. Review the pool maintenance contract. Establish procedures for regular inspection and maintenance to ensure a healthy environment.

Annual Meeting. Set the date, time and place; take care of physical arrangements. Prepare a notice to members, including agenda, proxies, financial reports, proposed resolutions, proposed nominations, and nominees' biographies. Establish election procedures, including appointment of election clerks and judges; prepare ballots, a check-in list, voting tally sheets and election rules; check on the eligibility of voters; prepare an explanation of cumulative voting, voting instructions, and quorum requirements; appoint a presiding officer for the election. *See Chapter 11.14.*

Notice to Contractors. Notify companies such as public utility companies and various contractors and subcontractors of the name and address of the person to send bills to or to contact regarding problems or communications.

Continuing Education. There are a number of organizations that serve homeowners associations, such as the national organization called the Community Associations Institute (CAI). Another organization, based in California, is the Executive Council of Homeowners (ECHO). There are many other similar organizations, some national in scope, some statewide, and some covering local metropolitan areas.

Many of these organizations publish monthly newsletters or magazines that contain valuable information. They also sponsor educational seminars to train association officers, directors and committee members. Organizations of any size will soon find membership in these organizations to be a wise investment.

Many organizations like CAI and ECHO sponsor periodic seminars and conferences, which non-members may attend. The attendance fees paid for these conferences are usually rather minimal, so that all interested board members may attend. However, if the association chooses a delegate to attend these seminars, it should be someone who is conscientious and well equipped to brief the association on the information provided at the conference or seminar.

CHAPTER 17
Management

17.1 General Discussion of Management. In the early stages, the project developer will usually control the management functions for the owners association. As soon as possible, however, members will be involved in the management of the association. Usually this begins with one or more members being elected to a board while it is still controlled by the developer. During this time, it is important that those members cooperate with the developer, learn about the administration and operation of the project, and educate themselves so they will be ready when the developer relinquishes its seats on the board.

The developer may manage the association, or it may have retained a professional manager to handle the business affairs of the association. One of the earliest and most important decisions to be made by the new board is whether or not to retain a professional manager or management company, or to have the board and the officers handle the management functions.

17.2 Management by the Board of Directors or "Self-Management." Depending upon the amount of common area items to be maintained, the age of the complex, and the legal requirements imposed on the association, some small associations (under 10 units or lots) may find it more practical for the board to manage the administration and maintenance of the project. This type of arrangement is often called "self-management."

In self-managing, the board will appoint committees to supervise and perform the jobs that would normally be done by a professional manager, such as periodic inspection of the complex with contractors, or contacting maintenance contractors to obtain bids for needed repairs. The board can hire landscapers and other contractors to work for the association. The treasurer and secretary, working together, can send out the monthly or periodic assessment statements, collect the funds, pay the bills for the association, and handle the finances.

Manager's Note: The volunteer secretary and treasurer/CFO can easily handle the chores of sending out monthly assessment statements and paying operating expenses. Unless one of these individuals has the expertise and training to complete monthly or quarterly financial statements, the association would be well advised to hire a qualified CPA or accounting professional to provide assistance in compiling financial statements and fulfilling year-end tax requirements.

Self-management, however, requires members serving in key positions to perform considerable amounts of work and to be willing to volunteer significant amounts of their own time to complete these monthly tasks. If the association's membership does not include people with both the ability and the time to serve, then even the smallest association may have to hire a professional management company.

Frequently in a small organization the same individuals continue to take on more than their share of responsibility. As long as they are willing to do so, the other members can take advantage of the situation and the association can keep its assessments down by not having to hire outside management.

Manager's Note: *In some cases, professional management companies will offer limited services to small associations at a reasonable fee. Another alternative to hiring a professional management firm is to hire an association management consultant, who can negotiate to handle only those services required by the board of directors. See Chapter 17.5 below for more information about the management consultant.*

17.3 In-House or On-Site Management. An association may employ either a part-time or full-time resident manager. The manager employee can be trained to complete ordinary management duties such as responding to service requests and complaints, supervising contractors and repairmen, and performing limited bookkeeping duties.

There are advantages and disadvantages for the association if the paid in-house manager is also a member of the association. The advantage of a member manager is knowledge of the organization, its needs and its members. Because the member is essentially working for and with neighbors, (s)he may also have a strong motivation to do a superior job. There are also potential problems because of the built-in conflict of interest, and fixing the compensation at a reasonable level is always a problem. In most cases, such managers tend to serve for fees that are lower by comparison to what outside professional management companies would charge. Use of an in-house resident manager may be a good compro-mise for a small- to medium-sized association that does not want to take on the financial burden of hiring an outside professional management company.

Manager's Note: *In some instances, smaller associations will hire a member to serve as the association manager. In return for providing management services, the association may "waive" the monthly assessments of the member manager. If both the association and member manager agree to this arrangement, it is a perfectly acceptable method for payment of the manager. The association should remember, however, to provide the member manager with the appropriate tax disclosure (usually a 1099-MISC form), as the "waived" assessments would be considered income to the manager.*

17.4 Professional Management. There are many professional management companies that offer a full range of services. The professional manager can perform all of the operational functions, such as selection and supervision of contract services, collection of assessments, payment of bills, bookkeeping and preparation of financial statements, newsletters, notice of meetings, minutes of meetings, and tax returns. The cost of such services is related to the range and frequency of services requested and the size of the project. A minimum level of professional management may be adequate for a small- to medium-sized association in which the governing body has the time, inclination, and experience to assist in the duties of management. For the larger association, however, comprehensive management and financial services are available. Not all management companies provide the same level of service, and not all associations require the same level of management services.

Some lending agencies, such as FNMA and FHLMC, require that professional management be retained by an association, and that once professional management has been retained, a decision by the association to establish self-management be approved by a certain percentage of votes of the owners (FNMA currently requires 67%), and a certain percentage of the votes of units or lots subject to mortgages or deeds of trust held by lenders holding first deeds of trust. FHLMC requires that any management agreement entered into by an association be for a term not to exceed two years, and contain provisions for termination without cause and without payment of termination fee upon 90 days' or less written notice. FNMA requires that contracts for professional management include a right of termination upon 90 days' or less notice without cause or payment of any penalty. Some state regulations prohibit the board of directors from entering into a management contract for a term longer than one year, except a contract approved by FHA or VA or a contract approved by the vote of a majority of the voting power of the association residing in members other than the developer.

17.5 Management Consultant. A relatively new entry into the field of association management is the professional management consultant. Similar to management companies, the management consultant can provide comprehensive management and financial services to associations of any size. However, unlike the management company, the consultant will often provide services on an "as-needed" basis to the association clients. As such, the consultant is often called upon to provide management services to smaller associations that are too small for conventional management contracts, and to very large associations as a supervisor or expert that oversees the work of on-site personnel.

17.6 Selection of Manager.
Whether the association is considering selecting professional management or a management consultant, the prospective candidates should answer a number of questions before the board makes its final decision.

The following checklist contains examples of questions that can be asked of the management firm or consultant:

1. Does the manager have a regular place of business, such as an office? This may be important if the association does not have an on-site management office. The board may want to be able to come to the management office to discuss problems and transact association business, so proximity to the project may be an important factor.
2. How many units or lots does the company currently manage? How many of those projects are of a nature or type similar to your association?
3. What is the reputation of the company in the community? How long has it been in business? Is its business growing or declining?

4. What do other projects that the company manages look like? The board should visit those properties, and check on the quality of maintenance and talk to some of the members to find out their degree of satisfaction with the management company.
5. Who will be assigned to handle the management problems? How experienced is the manager, and does (s)he have a personality that relates well to the board members with whom (s)he will be working closely?
6. Does the association need the manager to provide comprehensive management services or just limited aspects, such as financial management? Can the association compartmentalize its services, and pay a fee in accordance with the number of different types of services?
7. How strong is the management company's experience in financial matters such as assessments, budgeting, and cost accounting, and in negotiating and obtaining favorable insurance rates?
8. How does the company rate in the industry? Does it belong to any organizations such as the AMO (Accredited Management Organization), or do any of its individual officers have credentials such as CPM (Certified Property Manager), PCAM (Professional Community Association Manager), or CCAM (Certified Community Association Manager)?
9. Do the references of the management company, such as banks, professional relationships and personal references, respond favorably to your inquiries about its service?
10. Does the management company or consultant have bonds for its employees who handle the association funds? Does the management company or consultant carry E&O (Errors & Omissions) insurance?

Manager's Note: Depending on the state requirements governing certification and/or licensing of professional managers, E & O insurance coverage may not be available to individuals in the association management industry.

11. Does the management company have enough trained personnel and backup staff to satisfy the needs of your association?
12. Does the company or consultant offer a cash or accrual method of accounting? Does the company or consultant know how to convert your books from cash to accrual and/or vice-versa?
13. Does the management company or consultant compile the financials in-house, or does another company perform the financial functions? Computerized accounting will enable the association to have faster, more accurate and complete reports, and if the management association has its own computer, it has greater control over the system, can provide greater flexibility, and can operate on a more timely basis.
14. Review the systems used by the management company or consultant. For example, does it send out monthly assessment notices, or does it rely on owners to send in their payments on their own? What is the method used for late-pay-

ment notices and collection of delinquent assessments? Ask to see the forms, procedures, and (if available) the administrative manual the association follows in collecting assessments and following up on delinquencies. If the association is well-organized and experienced in collecting assessments, it will have its own system and its own forms, including delinquency notices, collection letters, notices of default, and assessment lien forms.

15. What is the management company or consultant's fee structure? Are the fees based on the number of units or lots in the project or an hourly rate? Precisely what services are included in the management fees?

Manager's Note: *An often overlooked advantage of hiring an association manager or consultant is the continuity that a manager brings to the association. Volunteers seldom make long-term commitments to serve on the board of directors; however, the association manager often remains with a management assignment for several years or more, and can be a source of valuable "historical" information.*

17.7 Management Contract. The board of directors has in most cases the authority to enter into a contract for management. Any contract entered into by the developer prior to the election of a board consisting of the new members should either be terminated or ratified by the new board with appropriate resolutions and notations in the minutes of the first meeting.

If any director or officer of the association has a material financial interest in the management firm, there must be full disclosure of that interest to the members prior to approval of the contract. *See Form 30 for an example of a resolution approving a management contract where one director has a financial interest in the management entity.*

Similarly, if a member of the board or an officer of the association intends to enter into a management agreement with the association, or has a material financial interest in the entity with whom the association plans to contract, the facts of the transaction and the director's interest must be fully disclosed to the board, the disclosure should be recorded in the minutes, and the agreement should be approved in good faith by a vote of disinterested directors. Even so, the agreement will have to be "fair, just and reasonable" as to the association at the time it is entered into.

A management contract should state the duties and responsibilities of the association and of the manager, the amount of compensation, the term of the agreement, and manner in which the contract may be terminated. In the interest of efficiency, it is best to have a limited number of people from the association authorized to communicate directly with the manager or managing agent. The contract should provide the managing agent with the authority needed to carry out his/her responsibilities under the contract. It is important that the portions of the agreement detailing the manager's duties and responsibilities be sufficiently precise and detailed to avoid any disagreement between the parties.

The actual form of the contract can be a form presented by the manager or prepared by the association's attorney. If the association's attorney does not prepare the management contract, it should certainly be reviewed and approved by counsel prior to retaining the manager. *See Form 28 for a sample of a management contract.*

It is important to distinguish between individuals who are actually employees of the association from those who are independent contractors. There are some rather complex rules for determining whether an individual is an employee or an independent contractor. A number of "tests" are also applied to determine whether or not an individual is an independent contractor. Some of the questions to be asked include:

- Is the person performing services engaged in a distinct trade, occupation or business?
- Is this kind of occupation usually done under the direction of the "employer" or by a specialist without supervision?
- What amount of skill is required in the particular occupation?
- Does the "employer" or the person performing the services supply the tools and the place of work?
- What is the length of time for which the services are to be performed? What is the method of payment—is it based on time or by the job?
- Is the work a part of the regular business of the association?

If there is any doubt about whether an individual hired by the association is hired as an independent contractor or an employee, the association should consult its attorney for an opinion. If an in-house manager is hired, (s)he could be either an independent contractor or an employee, depending upon the circumstances. If the individual is an employee, the association should have workers' compensation insurance, an employer identification number, and unemployment insurance coverage, and should withhold income tax and social security from the employee's paycheck.

17.8 Termination of Management Contract. Where the developer has entered into a management contract with a professional management firm, and the new homeowner board takes over during the term of the contract, the board may be able to terminate that contract. There is likely to be either a federal or state statute or a provision in the legal documents that gives the board the authority to terminate the management contract, without cause, on fairly short notice (generally, 30 to 90 days).

The board should certainly consider the contract and decide whether to terminate it, ratify it or extend it, and the minutes should reflect the discussion and the decision of the board in that regard. If the board wishes to terminate a contract that it has entered into, ratified or extended, it will have to check the provisions of the contract regarding termination. If the board wishes to terminate the contract "for cause," it should consult with its attorney before notifying the other party to the contract of its intention to terminate. The attorney may be able to advise the association on how to proceed in terminating the contract under circumstances that will not leave the association liable for any damages.

17.9 Handling Member Complaints. The board should establish a procedure for logging and handling complaints. Records should be kept of every complaint, whether verbal or written. The name, date and nature of the complaint should be noted in a daily complaint "log" or register, as well as the disposition and resolution of the complaint subject matter. The complaint log or register is useful for observing trends and for review of contractors' and vendors' performance to the association.

17.10 Site Inspections. The board should establish regular site inspection routines, so that rather than rely solely upon third-party reports, the members of the board are personally aware of the condition of the project, by inspecting landscaping, exterior maintenance, recreational facilities, streets, landscaping, and other components of the project. Written standards should be adopted and passed on from one board to the next.

17.11 Delegation. Officers and directors may delegate some, but not all, of their duties. The project documents should permit the delegation of a major portion of powers, duties, and responsibilities to a management representative. However, the board bears ultimate responsibility for the operation of the association, even though the day-to-day operations have been placed in the hands of the manager. Delegation has the advantage of spreading out the burden of administration, but there are certain risks involved in delegating, because officers or directors do not escape responsibility for failure to perform their duties or for negligent performance on the part of the manager just because they have delegated those duties.

Project legal documents will typically include some limitations on the delegation of its duties by the board. State law or governmental regulations such as those prescribed by FNMA, FHLMC or FHA may also prohibit the board from delegating certain matters or from taking certain actions without the approval of the association members.

In performing their duties, directors are entitled to rely upon information, opinions, reports, and statements prepared or presented by officers or employees of the association whom the directors believe to be reliable and competent, or information, opinions or reports prepared by counsel or by independent professional consultants.

There are certain responsibilities or duties that the board should not delegate, which generally include:

- Final control over the budget and the amount of assessments;
- Establishment of association rules and regulations, and the administration of those rules and regulations, including the imposition of fines and penalties;
- Opening of bank accounts;
- Purchase, sale or leasing of assets or property of the association;
- Borrowing or lending funds;
- Entering into contracts involving more than a certain amount of money (generally prescribed by the declaration or the bylaws); and
- Making a decision to initiate litigation or to settle or dismiss litigation.

CHAPTER 18
Consultants

18.1 Attorney. As the property owners association industry ages, the legal questions become increasingly more complex. Coupled with the trend among lawyers to become more and more specialized, the association would be well served to find an attorney who is a specialist in community association law. There are several good places to look for an attorney. The developer's attorney may be a specialist in community association law; however, if (s)he represents the developer, and the developer still has an interest in the project, there is a built-in conflict of interest which prevents the attorney from representing both the association and the developer.

There are many ways to locate a qualified attorney who specializes in the field of common-interest development or property owners association law:

Local Bar Association. The local bar association may have a list of lawyers who specialize in community association law.

Referrals from Trade Organizations. The association can check with members of other associations for referrals. They can also check with the Executive Council of Homeowners (ECHO) or the Community Associations Institute (CAI).

Other Real Estate or Owners Association Attorneys. Lawyers who practice in the field of real estate or real property will probably know of firms or attorneys that specialize in community association law.

Management Companies. If the association has engaged the services of a professional association manager, the manager will usually have a list of attorneys whom he or she recommends to clients.

Once a list of potential attorney candidates has been assembled, the board should delegate members to a committee to contact and interview each attorney. The attorney should be given the specifics about the association including the type of project, age, amenities, number of board members, and the number of total members. In general, it is best to avoid lawyers whose practice is very broadly based, even though they may claim to have experience in handling association legal affairs. One very important function of the lawyer representing the association is to prevent legal problems from arising, and to keep the association out of trouble. An attorney who is not experienced in handling association matters will not be as skilled in this kind of preventive legal work as one who is experienced.

In interviewing attorney candidates, the same approach should be taken in each interview. The same amount of time should be allocated, and the same questions should be asked. When all the interviews have been completed, the committee should then make its recommendation to the board of directors. The candidates should be rated, and the pros and cons should be given to the board along with the committee's recommendation. One of the key questions will be what the attorney would charge the association for services. The attorney may offer to charge a monthly retainer, or (s)he may prefer to charge everything on a time basis. If a retainer is to be paid, both parties should be clear on exactly what services are included in the retainer. It is difficult for the association to evaluate what level of service it is getting if it pays a monthly retainer to an attorney and the services vary greatly in scope from time to time. Retainers tend to be unfair to one party or the other over a period of time, and it is generally better to pay the attorney on a job or hourly basis. Hourly rates are important, but should not be the sole determining factor. Sometimes the attorney who charges a lower hourly rate will take longer to do the work, will have less expertise, and may be less efficient.

One possible method of evaluating the attorney candidates would be to ask each of the final candidates to undertake a fairly simple task that can be done for a nominal fee, such as providing a sample violation notice to be used when homeowners disobey the association's rules. Without informing the attorneys that they are being tested, ask each to perform the same service, and then compare the results, taking into consideration the time that it took for the attorney to complete the service, the quality of the result, and the amount of the total fee.

Once an attorney has been selected, it is important that his/her services be used as often as needed. To ensure that the attorney's time is used efficiently, it is best to discourage or prohibit individual members from contacting the attorney with legal questions on behalf of themselves or the association. In fact, it is best that as few members of the board or as few officers of the association as possible are authorized to contact the attorney. Any contact with the attorney should normally be authorized in advance by the board after discussion. Most attorneys bill for telephone calls in the same manner as for office visits—on a time basis, unless they are on a monthly retainer that includes routine telephone calls. Whoever is authorized to consult with the attorney should always prepare himself or herself in advance so that (s)he will use as little of the attorney's time as possible.

Generally, it is not necessary or advised to have an attorney attend board meetings or general membership meetings. Exceptions to this would be where there are difficult legal points involved, or where, for example, a proposed amendment is to be presented to the general membership, the amendment has been drafted by the attorney, and the board feels that there will be some questions about the form, content or purpose of the amendment, the answers to which may involve technical legal matters which are best explained by the attorney. If it is decided to have the attorney present at a meeting, the business of the meeting should be scheduled so that the appearance of the attorney will take as little of his/her time as possible.

Some developers will authorize their attorneys to assist the association and the board of directors at the first general membership meeting of the association and at the first directors' meeting. The attorney may be made available for consultation with the officers and directors of the association for a limited period of time after control of the association has passed from the developer to the members. However, as long as the attorney is still representing the developer, even though (s)he may be very helpful to the association and the new board, the board should keep in mind that the attorney's loyalty is to his/her developer/client, and the board should establish a relationship with its own counsel who is independent of the developer as soon as possible. *See Chapter 16.8.*

18.2 Certified Public Accountant, Enrolled Agent or Certified Financial Planner. Every association needs the services of a financial expert at some point. Depending upon the length of time the developer controls the association, there may be an accounting system in place when the homeowner board takes control, or there may not be any formalized sets of books. Unless the association has engaged the services of a professional association manager, a CPA or accounting professional should be consulted to assist in properly setting up a bookkeeping system and training the board members on how to enter specific information.

Every association must qualify under either federal and state tax law as a tax-exempt owners association. Usually, the association must file annual federal and state tax returns and pay taxes. In such cases, the association needs to continue to operate as, and must comply with federal and state tax return requirements for, a nonprofit owners association. If the developer has not obtained tax-exempt status by filing an exemption claim form, then the association should retain a CPA or tax professional to do so.

For larger associations, an annual audit or review by a CPA may be required by the legal documents or by state law. If the association hires a CPA to perform the routine financial operations of the association and/or prepare the monthly financial statements, another CPA firm will need to be hired to complete the annual or periodic audit or review of the books.

The preparation of annual statements such as balance sheets and profit-and-loss statements as well as financial reports should be under the supervision of an accountant.

In selecting a CPA or any financial professional, many of the same considerations apply as in the case of selecting an attorney. *See Chapter 18.1 above.* The CPA should have experience in representing, auditing, reviewing, and working with homeowner associations or property owner associations. In selecting an auditor, it is important to know if the auditor has experience in auditing property owners associations, and should obtain references from other association clients. The association should also know, in advance, the fee it will be charged for an annual audit and whether the cost of the audit or review will include the preparation of state and federal income taxes.

Manager's Note: *There are also many fine enrolled agents who have begun working exclusively for homeowners associations. An enrolled agent is an individual who is authorized to "practice before the IRS." Enrolled agents are required to pass a rigorous test that is administered* *by the IRS, and many enrolled agents are former IRS or state tax department employees. While an enrolled agent cannot provide audit or review services—only a CPA may perform these duties—enrolled agents can prepare annual federal and state tax filings.*

Depending upon the size of the homeowners association and its age, there will come a time when the association may have a fairly sizeable reserve fund for the eventual repair and maintenance of building and common area components at the project. Investing these funds in a suitably secure, high-yield investment is important to ensuring that the funds grow at a rate commensurate with the economy. While bank CDs are relatively safe, if the association's reserve exceeds the $100,000 limit insured by FDIC, it's time to look at the services of a qualified investment broker or certified financial planner. Financial planners and investment brokers, who operate either individually or as a part of a larger corporation such as a stock brokerage, can provide extremely valuable information regarding investments in T-bills and large or jumbo Certificates of Deposit. There may be provisions in the association's legal documents or some state laws that prohibit funds being placed in speculative or "risky" investments. When in doubt as to what is an acceptable form of investment, contact your association's attorney for more information.

18.3 Insurance Broker. The insurance industry has developed a number of highly specialized insurance policies to meet the needs of condominiums and planned developments. It is important that the board of directors have access to a knowledgeable insurance broker who is experienced in dealing with property owners associations' insurance policies, and who is familiar with the laws governing adequate insurance for owners associations. Too many insurance brokers or agents are not familiar with the types of policies and coverages available, and many such brokers and agents have not obtained proper coverage for owners associations.

One of the first tasks of the newly elected board will be to obtain and review the insurance policies currently in effect that were purchased by the developer or by the initial board appointed by the developer, and which may or may not be adequate. An early determination should be made as to whether the coverage is sufficient and whether the rates are reasonable. A survey of other alternative policies that are available should be made as soon as possible so that the board can make adequate plans to provide for its insurance needs. Among other things, the board should consider the extent of the coverage, the adequacy of the policy limits, and the financial stability and reputation of the insurance company issuing the policy.

Manager's Note: *Among the types of insurance the board should consider are the following:*

- *Liability insurance for common area*
- *Fire insurance for the buildings (normally required for condominium complexes)*
- *Directors' and Officers' liability insurance*
- *Fidelity bonding for those who handle the association's funds*
- *Earthquake or flood insurance*

The insurance broker should be able to explain each type of coverage thoroughly to the board of directors, and should be able to recommend both types of coverage and amounts.

The premium structure also should be evaluated, and the board should consider whether changing the type or amount of the coverage would save money on premiums. The cost of insurance has gone up to the point where insurance coverage is now one of the major expenditures of an association. It is more important than ever that a knowledgeable and experienced insurance broker be available to the association to help it in obtaining good quality insurance at a reasonable cost.

18.4 Manager. *See Chapter 17 for a discussion of the role and duties of the association manager.*

CHAPTER 19
Contracts

19.1 General. The association will enter into a number of contracts. Some of these will involve large amounts of money, so it is important that care be taken to ensure that the association enters into a contract only after all the essential steps leading up to the signing have been completed. One of the most important first steps is to outline, in detail, the scope of the work or the specifications for the contract. Before even talking to potential parties to the contract, the board of directors should discuss in detail exactly what is to be accomplished by entering into a contract.

19.2 Authority To Enter Into Contracts. The clauses in the legal documents describing the purposes, powers, and duties of the association and the board of directors should provide sufficient authority to enter into the proposed contract. If the specific authority is not apparent, the documents should be amended to clearly authorize the association to be able to enter into a contract. Occasionally, uncertainty about the authority of an officer or officers to bind an association may make third parties reluctant to enter into contracts without some written consent from the general membership. In the case of an incorporated association, the consent of the governing body, or even of the officers, should be sufficient. Sometimes a corporate seal may be required (*see Chapter 15.1*).

Where the officers of a corporation have entered into a contract without the advance consent of the board, the contract can be ratified later by the board, and a certified copy of the resolution can be given to the other contracting party. Without this resolution, the other party to an unauthorized contract may not be able to enforce the contract against the association, and the members of the association may not be obligated to pay assessments for costs incurred in connection with this unauthorized contract. In the event the owners cannot be assessed to meet the contractual obligations, the officers who executed the unauthorized contract may become personally liable.

For unincorporated associations, the rules are not quite as clear. There is no legal presumption that a contract signed by a representative of an unincorporated association is in fact authorized. This makes it somewhat more difficult for unincorporated associations to enter into contracts with third parties, unless the signatures of all members are obtained, or unless all members sign a document authorizing the contract to be signed by their representatives.

19.3 Types of Contracts and Contract Templates. Contracts come in many different forms and styles. The association can approach the subject in two ways:

1) It can rely upon the contracting party to prepare the basic contract form, and then modify that form to fit the situation, or
2) The association can establish its own basic form of contract, and then adapt that for use in different

situations. The association will be in a better position in the long run (and perhaps also the short run) if it develops its own basic forms to use over and over.

This basic template is especially useful when the party with whom it contracts remains the same, but the subject matter changes. When changing landscapers, for example, the association does not have to review or approve an entirely new form of contract, but can use the template, modified to fit the new circumstances. The same basic form of contract can also be used for different services. Since most of the wording and many of the provisions in contracts are legal "boilerplate" which change very little from one contract to another, having a standardized form or template that can be used again in many different situations will save the association and its attorney time (and money) in reviewing contracts. There are also certain disadvantages to using the same form repeatedly, particularly if it becomes outdated or otherwise needs improvement.

The association should never allow itself to become so wedded to a particular form that it tries to force it into situations where it does not fit. Never overlook opportunities to include new clauses or to modify the template in ways that are beneficial. The various forms of contracts that appear in the forms supplement to this book should be used as guides only; there is no one form of contract comprehensive enough to suit every situation or jurisdiction. Each state has its own particular set of laws. Only a qualified attorney practicing in that state can determine whether or not a particular form of contract meets all of the legal requirements of that state.

19.4 Management Contract. The association should try to develop its own form of management contract to ensure consistency of service between different management companies. *See Chapter 17.7 for a discussion of management contracts. See Form 28 in the Forms Supplement for a sample Management Contract.*

Before entering into a management contract, the board of directors should decide the exact level of management it wants and how much it is willing to pay. If it is not able or willing to obligate the membership to pay for the cost of a full-service management contract, it should identify those areas in which it desires professional management services and limit the contract to such matters.

Manager's Note: In the event that the association cannot afford full-service management (which, in most cases, includes site management, administration and financial services), the other more reasonably priced option is to hire a management consultant who works only when needed to handle specific tasks for the board of directors. Consultants are often paid on an hourly basis, and only bill when time is spent on a designated project.

19.5 Maintenance Contracts. The number and variety of maintenance services that work for the association vary with the size of the project and the amenities involved. The following is a brief description of some of the most common maintenance contracts that the board may review.

Landscaping. The contract for landscaping will be one of the association's largest expenditures. Before considering proposals from landscape contractors, the board of directors or the landscape committee should carefully consider their expectations. Does the association want minimum maintenance of existing landscaping? Does the association want major changes in the landscape plan, or an extremely high level of maintenance? Should the maintenance include simply cutting the grass and raking up the leaves ("mow, blow and go"), or should it include pruning, weeding, fertilizing, planting of annuals, replacing diseased or dying plants, and watering? If the board is uncertain of its needs, and does not have anyone within the association who can determine these specifications, it would be a good idea to have an outside consultant assist in preparing specifications to be given to potential landscape contractors. *See Chapter 20.6 for more information regarding landscaping specifications.*

Washer, Dryer and Laundry Operaions. Some associations with central laundry facilities contract the operaion, maintenance and supply of laundry equipment and related supplies to a laundry service or concessionaire. This laundry equipment and service contract should detail the terms and conditions of the concession and the duties and obligations of the concessionaire. The contract should also specify the type and number of pieces of equipment, the cost to operate the coin-operated machines, hours of operation, and the maintenance and repair obligations of the concessionaire. The association should have the authority to cancel the contract at any time for cause, which should be defined to the extent possible. For example, the frequent breakdown of equipment should be cause for termination of the contract. Also, failure by the contractor to replace old or inefficient equipment should be cause for termination. The contract should provide who will pay for the costs of installation and removal of the laundry equipment. At termination, the concessionaire should be obligated to restore the premises to the conditions existing at the beginning of the contract (reasonable wear and tear excepted), including repair of damages caused by leaks and overflows. If the equipment is located near dwellings, the contract should include specifications about shock mounting, noise abatement and vibration.

Pest Control. Some association legal documents specify whether the association or the individual owners have responsibility for pest control. When something must be done and it is unclear who has the duty for pest control, the board should consider proposing an amendment to the declaration to give the association the authority and the responsibility for pest control in the project.

Once the authority is established, the association must then determine what type of pest control or what type of preventative measures should be undertaken, and what sort of company should be contracted. For garden pests, the landscaper's contract may already address the removal or eradication of some pests. A termite inspection company is probably the preferable alternative for termites, dry rot and fungus. A licensed pest control operator can control rodents and most crawling and/or flying insects.

If the project has an ongoing or persistent pest problem, it is best to hire an experienced and capable pest control firm. Periodic inspections and periodic preventative measures, rather than waiting until the problem becomes acute, will reduce the need to take more drastic, costly measures to reduce the pest population. As in the case of landscape contracts, it is important to know what chemicals are being used and whether they are potentially harmful to pets, plants or humans. The contract should specify that only "safe" chemicals can be used and that they can only be used at levels that are within the prescribed safety limits.

Cable Television. New projects are now constructed with cable television access already installed. In such cases, the project legal documents may provide that either the association or the individual owner is responsible for contracting with the cable franchise company. If access to cable television is not built into the project and the decision is made to obtain the service, the association will need to enter into the contract with the cable franchisee.

Security. *See Chapter 54 for a general discussion of security.* The security contract should include provisions that cover the term of the agreement, compensation, duties to be performed, number and frequency of patrols, number of security personnel on duty, days and hours of operation, and specifications on the authority of the guards or security patrol. For example, should the security force observe and report parking violations and enforce parking and vehicle regulations? What about animal control or excess noise provisions? Should the security force be limited to protecting the project against intruders from outside the project? Will the guards use dogs or carry weapons? Should the security force be bonded or carry insurance?

Garage Maintenance. Where the association owns an underground garage, it may be best to contract for the operation and maintenance of the garage to a company offering such services. The contracting party can be responsible for controlling ingress and egress, parking of members and guests, and deliveries. The garage floors should be cleaned frequently to remove deposits of oil and grease that could cause accidents or fire if allowed to remain.

Janitorial/Window Cleaning Service. In most one- and two-story projects, window cleaning can be left to the individual owners. For safety reasons, it is best to have windows in high-rise projects cleaned by professionals.

A janitorial firm should perform basic upkeep on the corridors, hallways, elevators, lobbies, and other interior common areas in large condominium projects. The janitorial contract should clearly define the responsibilities of the contracting company. If windows are included in the janitor's duties, the contract should specify how often the windows are to be cleaned and whether they are to be cleaned both inside and out or just outside. Owners should clean the interior portions of their own windows. The janitorial service will maintain the cleanliness of the windows in the common areas.

Painting. Painting is one of the largest expenditures the association will make. Adequate reserves should be set aside to provide for periodic painting. Before deciding to paint, a thorough inspection of the project should be made. Each building and unit should be inspected, and a written report and recommendation should be made to the board regarding what needs to be painted. The association should maintain permanent records regarding when a building was painted, the color(s), paint manufacturer, painting contractor, and any other pertinent information about the job. During the inspection, careful note should be made of any defects such as cracks in stucco, delaminated plywood, or other areas that need special attention before paint can be applied.

The association should not rely solely on the painting contractor to decide how to do the job, but should make its own inspection. The work should also be inspected by the representative of the association while in progress as well as after completion. It is particularly important that the preparatory work, such as sanding and caulking, be inspected before the paint is applied.

Experts recommend that at least two or three bids be obtained from different painting contractors. As in the case of other contractors, references should be checked, a list of other jobs should be obtained, and the contractor should be required to carry adequate insurance. Unless the painting contractor has a preference, the association should choose the brand of paint and specify the color and type (flat, gloss, semi-gloss, etc.). As a precaution to prevent dilution of the paint by the contractor, the association could require the paint to be delivered in sealed cans to the job site, and to keep this paint on the site until the work is completed. The contract should specify when the painting will start, when it will be completed, and what penalties will be imposed if the time limits are not met. Reasonable time allowances should be granted for inclement weather for exterior painting work. *For more information about painting, please see Chapter 20.13.*

Street Repairs. If the association is responsible for street repair, there should be a system of accumulating reserves or funds to pay for periodic street maintenance. *See Chapter 22.6.* Before any maintenance or repair is performed, it is important to survey the condition of all paved surfaces in the project. *See Chapter 20.10 for specific information regarding maintenance of the streets.*

Snow Removal. Projects located in areas where snow falls annually should either have their own equipment and operators for snow removal or should contract with a service company for regular snow removal to supplement the snow removal service provided by local governmental agencies.

Garbage and Trash Disposal. Where there is a central deposit area for trash pickup, the association should have a contract with the local trash collection or scavenger company.

Other associations do not provide a centralized place for trash pickup, and each owner will make arrangements and pay for individual trash pickup. If the city trash service does not regulate the type, style and placement of the trash can, the association should create rules concerning the placement and maintenance of garbage cans. Generally, the city grants a franchise to one scavenger company, and the association should attempt to negotiate the best deal that it can within the existing limits. Often, as with local utilities and telephone services, there will not be a formal contract entered into with the local trash collection company. Nevertheless, there should be some exchange of correspondence indicating the type and frequency of service to be provided.

19.6 Contracts With Consultants. The business relationship between the association and its consultants, such as attorneys and CPAs, should be clearly stated. Even if services are performed upon request or at an hourly rate, there should be some letter or memorandum in writing that delineates the terms of employment and compensation. *See Chapter 18.1.*

19.7 Capital Improvements. Before undertaking any capital improvements, the association legal documents should be checked to determine the authority of the board to make capital improvements and the vote of the membership required in order to approve special assessments for capital improvements. If, for example, the board decides to build a tennis court or add another tennis court, swimming pool, or recreation room, the procedural steps specified in the project legal documents to obtain the necessary authority to enter into a contract and assess the members for the cost of the improvements must all be carefully observed.

It may be necessary to enter into a series of contracts in order to construct capital improvements. Services of an architect, a landscape architect and a general building contractor may all be required. The association's insurance policy will have to be modified to include coverage for the new capital improvements.

19.8 Remodeling. If the association decides to remodel or refurbish the common areas or the common area facilities, it will have to deal with a general contractor or, if it intends to act as its own contractor, will have to deal with a number of subcontractors and suppliers. If bids are to be obtained, the services of an expert should be sought to advise the association on how to draw up the specifications for the contract. The specifications should be prepared in writing, so that the job can be standardized and all bids can be compared. It is wise to consult with the contractors who are expected to bid on the job in order to get their input about what should be in the specifications. *See Chapter 20 for helpful hints about choosing and working with contractors.*

CHAPTER 20
Maintenance

Manager's Note: One of the most important reasons for the existence of a homeowners association is to maintain the property. This chapter provides useful information to familiarize the owner and board member with terminology of specific maintenance items, and a basic understanding of the different types of maintenance required.

20.1 Maintenance Responsibility.

Occasionally questions arise about the maintenance responsibility of the association in a planned development or a condominium project. The legal documents may define the different areas of responsibility. Typically, in a condominium project the association maintains all project exteriors. In a planned development project, however, sometimes the association maintains the exteriors of the dwellings, and sometimes the individual homeowners are responsible for exterior maintenance.

In some cases, the legal documents are not entirely clear about where the "dividing line" is between the maintenance responsibility of the association and that of the individual owner. In such cases, if the legal documents are unclear, the board may have to consult with its attorney for an interpretation. In a situation where there is no way to tell from a review of the legal documents where maintenance responsibility lies, the board will have to make a decision one way or the other, or will have to amend the documents to clarify the situation. Project legal documents tend to be drafted in broad terms, as it is generally not possible to predict all possible situations that may arise. Rather than over-draft the documents with endless detail in an attempt to anticipate all situations that may arise, it is more important that the responsibilities of the association and of the board be well defined. For example, if it is the board's responsibility to maintain the fire and smoke detection or alarm system and they fail to do so, and a fire occurs with some damage or injury resulting, the association (and possibly the board members, if they were personally negligent) could be held responsible for the damages or injuries. Similarly, the owner who is responsible for maintaining the fire or smoke alarm in his or her unit and who removes the battery could be held liable for the resulting damage and/or personal injury if a fire starts in his/her unit.

It is often recommended that condominium projects and planned development projects with common walls or "party walls" have broad powers to maintain fire detection and prevention equipment. If the association has the responsibility to maintain equipment that is located within dwellings, it also has to have the authority to enter the dwelling units in order to inspect and maintain that equipment.

Manager's Note: In soliciting bids or proposals from contractors, at a minimum the association should require the following:

1. *Contractor's license number.*
2. *Number of years in business.*
3. *A bank reference.*

4. The name of their insurance carrier or carriers and the amounts of coverage.
5. A list of suppliers and subcontractors.
6. A list of comparable jobs completed.

References should, of course, be checked. Avoid the temptation to accept the lowest bid simply because the price is the most appealing. The best practice is to accept the lowest responsible bid.

It is important that the insurance references are checked to make sure that the contractor is fully covered by workers' compensation and liability insurance. It is a good practice to have the contractor's insurance company provide a certificate of insurance to the association, certifying that the contractor does carry adequate workers' compensation and liability insurance.

It is also a good idea to check the contractor's credit references and find out if (s)he pays his/her bills, and if (s)he has a good reputation. For large construction or remodeling jobs, the association may want to ask the contractor to post performance and labor and materials bonds to ensure that the job is completed, that all the bills are paid, and that there will not be any liens against the project.

20.2 Common Area Maintenance. The association is responsible for maintenance of the project's common areas. The level of maintenance depends upon the size of the budget and the amount of assessments allocated for maintenance. The level of maintenance should be sufficient to protect and preserve property values by preventing deterioration that can be avoided by proper maintenance. A high level of maintenance will help maintain property values and will certainly facilitate home sales. Inadequate maintenance can cause a project to slowly deteriorate, diminishing property values and affecting the overall morale of residents of the project.

Officers and directors who are charged with the responsibility for maintaining the common area can be subject to personal liability if they are provided adequate funds to maintain the common areas but fail to do so.

20.3 Maintenance of Restricted Common Areas. The association's legal documents may provide for certain exclusive-use areas, such as assigned or deeded parking spaces, balconies, decks, storage areas, and patios that are reserved for certain owners, and may also prescribe maintenance responsibilities for these areas. If the legal documents are silent on the subject of maintenance responsibility and the association is required to maintain common areas, that obligation will extend to include the restricted or exclusive-use common areas. If there is uncertainty about maintenance responsibilities, the legal documents should be amended to clearly specify who has the responsibility for maintenance of restricted common areas.

20.4 Private Area Maintenance. The project legal documents usually will require each owner to maintain his or her private premises up to certain minimum standards, or the standard prevalent throughout the project. The association needs the authority to take care of maintenance problems that develop on private property because an owner fails to comply with his/her obligations. In such cases, the association should have the authority under the legal documents to collect the cost of such maintenance from the owner of the unit or lot in question. *See Chapter 28.2 for a discussion of enforcement procedures.*

20.5 Swimming Pools. Swimming pool maintenance can be complicated. Because of health hazards that can develop if the chlorine content of the water is improperly regulated, the association should always have professional pool maintenance personnel in charge of the pool. Expensive repairs to the pool equipment can also be avoided or made much less frequent if professional personnel are involved in periodic inspecting, servicing and cleaning of the pool equipment.

20.6 Landscaping. Landscaping maintenance is a critical part of any project. The overall level of maintenance of a project will first be evident by the appearance of the landscaping. In a new project, the landscaping will usually be covered by a warranty from the landscape contractor or the developer for a period of several months and perhaps as long as a year after installation. During that time, the original landscape contractor or the developer may replace any damaged or dead plants and repair any problems with the irrigation system and controller. The developer also may elect to care for the landscaping during the period of the sales program.

Whenever the developer or the landscape contractor stops maintaining the landscaping, the association should be prepared to have a landscape maintenance contractor under contract to assume that responsibility. *See Form 30 for an example of a landscape contract.*

In some cases, the legal documents may require individual owners to maintain the landscaping within their own lots or the exclusive-use areas for the units. In other cases, the legal documents will require the association to maintain landscaping within the unfenced portions of private lots or units. These are matters of discretion, and the association documents can, of course, be amended at any time to shift the responsibility for landscaping either to the association or to the individual owners.

The association should always maintain common area landscaping. The board should be specific about what standard of maintenance it requires for the landscaping in the project. The following is a checklist of items to be considered when entering into a landscape contract:

1. Equipment, tools and supplies; who will furnish and pay for these?
2. Lawn care; how often should the lawn be cut? To what height should the grass be cut? Is edging around buildings and sidewalks and planting borders to be included?
3. Ground cover maintenance; how often should ground cover be trimmed or pruned?
4. Weed control; how frequently should weeds be removed? Who will pay for the chemicals?
5. Irrigation and sprinkler repair; is sprinkler repair included as part of the maintenance fee paid to the landscaper? Of course, the landscaper should repair any sprinklers that are broken by his/her men or equipment, without charge. As to other routine breakdowns in the sprinkler system, should that be included in the basic contract or is it an

extra? Should a separate contract be entered into with an outfit specializing in irrigation systems?
6. Vandalism; suppose someone drives over the lawn, leaving tire marks, and the lawn has to be repaired. Is that included in the contract or is that an extra?
7. Replacement of damaged, dead and dying plants, and planting of new plants from time to time; how will this service be billed—as an extra or included in the monthly maintenance fee?
8. Debris removal; is the contractor responsible for removal of cuttings, trimmings and leaves?
9. Trimming of big trees; should this be a part of the landscape contractor's duties or should a tree surgeon be called in for such work?

Manager's Note: *Unless the landscaper has an arborist on staff, and even if the landscaper can trim trees, it is often safer (and certainly more beneficial to the trees) to have a professional tree surgeon or arborist trim common area trees.*

10. Control of pests; should the landscape contractor be responsible for control of pests such as snails, slugs, ants, rodents, or flying insects, or should a pest control firm be hired?
11. Sweeping of streets and carports; is that part of the landscape contractor's job?
12. Hours of maintenance; should the contract specify that mowers and blowers will not be used on weekends, particularly early on Saturday and Sunday morning?
13. Use of chemicals or pesticides; should the contract provide that no chemicals or pesticides should be used on the premises without having them specifically approved, in advance, by the board or by someone retained by the board to advise on the relative safety of the chemicals being used on the premises?
14. Noise level of equipment; should gasoline-powered mowers or blowers be used, or should electrical equipment be required? Should there be a limit on the number of decibels of noise output permitted? *See Forms 30 and 31.*
15. Emergency service; will the landscape contractor provide emergency, 24-hour service in the event of a water line break or irrigation system problem?

20.7 Equipment. If the association owns equipment such as computers and printers, calculators, electric typewriters or photocopy equipment, the maintenance of the equipment may or may not be covered by a service or maintenance contract. If the equipment does not have a maintenance contract, some consideration should be given to establishing a reserve fund for the periodic maintenance, repair or replacement of such equipment.

20.8 Elevators. Elevators are required to be periodically inspected and licensed. They should also be covered by a long-term maintenance contract with an experienced and reputable elevator maintenance contractor.

One question that sometimes arises is whether the cost of maintenance and insurance of elevators should be spread equally among all lot or unit owners in a project, or whether it should be pro-rated, so those who use the elevator more than others will pay a larger share of the costs. The answer depends partly on the design of the project. If a project consists of one high-rise building and a number of low-rise buildings, with the only elevators being in the high-rise building, a case can be made that only the unit owners in the high-rise building should pay the costs of elevator maintenance, insurance and repair. However, the counter argument in this example would be that the cost of maintaining roofs in the low-rise buildings is greater than the cost of maintaining a single roof on the high-rise building. Thus, when all pay equally into a roofing reserve, the payment of elevator maintenance costs balances out the discrepancy, so there is no reason to prorate either expense. The developer, in most cases, will have considered this issue in the beginning and will have tried to make the assessments reasonably fair to all parties. The assessment ratios can always be changed if sufficient votes for an amendment to the documents can be obtained.

20.9 Chimneys. In projects having fireplaces, some thought needs to be given as to whether the individual owners or the association will assume the responsibility of paying for chimney sweeping. In projects with attached housing, the rationale for having the association assume chimney-sweeping responsibility is that a creosote fire in one chimney can quickly spread to the other units in the project. In these cases, it is better to avoid this risk by having the association handle chimney sweeping, even if it costs a little more to do so. In associations where a portion of the units does not have chimneys, the cost of chimney sweeping is assessed only to units or lots with chimneys and fireplaces.

20.10 Streets and Driveways. Maintenance of streets and driveways is required periodically, which can be a major expense. It is important that adequate reserve funds be set aside each year to pay for the expense of resurfacing, repaving, or repairing the streets and driveways.

The following information would be helpful in determining whether the street or driveway requires maintenance:

Raveling. This is the progressive separation of aggregate particles in a pavement from the surface below. The fine aggregate usually comes off first and leaves small "pock marks" on the pavement surface. Eventually larger particles are broken free and the pavement has a rough and jagged appearance. Raveling is caused by lack of compaction during construction or construction during wet or cold weather. It can also be caused by dirty or disintegrating aggregate, too little asphalt in the mix, or overheating of the asphalt mix.

Alligator Cracks. Alligator cracks are interconnected cracks forming a pattern resembling alligator skin. In most cases, alligator cracking is caused by excessive deflection of the surface over unstable subgrade. Unstable subgrade is usually the result of improper compaction, or uneven or water-saturated subgrade. Alligator cracking can also be caused by repeated loads that exceed the load-carrying capacity of the pavement.

Shrinkage Cracks. Shrinkage cracks are interconnected cracks forming a series of large blocks. They may be caused by changes in the asphalt mix or in the base or subgrade.

Grade Depressions. Grade depressions are low areas of limited size that are sometimes accompanied by alligator-like cracking. They may dip an inch or more below grade, and tend to collect water. The depressions may be caused by traffic loads that exceed the load capacity of the pavement, by settlement of the sub-grade, or by poor construction or poor grading.

Potholes. Potholes are bowl-shaped holes in the pavement resulting from localized disintegration. They are usually caused by weakness in the pavement that can result from too little asphalt, asphalt that is too thin, or improper mixture of asphalt.

Lane Joint Cracking. Lane joint cracks are long, straight separations which follow the joint between two passes of the paver. The crack is usually caused by a weakness in the joint between adjoining paving lanes.

Upheaval. Upheaval is the localized upward displacement of pavement due to swelling of the subgrade. It is most often caused by expansion of ice in the subgrade or by swelling of expansive soils subjected to moisture.

Evaluating the Condition of the Pavement and Recommended Maintenance Procedures. Following are examples of pavement conditions and the recommended remedial measures:

- Pavement surface is in good condition—two to four years old—with no cracks, but the fine aggregate is on the verge of raveling. Remedy is to apply an asphalt emulsion slurry seal coat.

- Pavement is in good condition, but exhibits fine cracking and/or some raveling. Pre-fill any cracks larger than 1/8 inch wide, and apply an asphalt emulsion slurry.

- Pavement is in good condition, with random cracks up to ½ inch in width, and/or fine aggregate has raveled. Remedy is to pre-fill cracks and seal entire surface with asphalt emulsion slurry.

- Pavement in fair condition; local alligator-cracked areas, upheaval or potholes, and/or aggregate has raveled. Patch failed areas using full-depth techniques; seal entire area with asphalt emulsion slurry or apply an asphalt overlay over a petroleum mat ("petromat") to increase strength.

- Pavement in fair condition, local alligator cracks, upheaval or potholes, random cracks up to ½ inch wide, and/or aggregate has raveled. Patch failed areas using full-depth technique, pre-fill cracks, and seal entire area with asphalt emulsion slurry or apply an asphalt overlay over a petromat product.

- Pavement is in fair to poor condition; local alligator-cracked areas, upheaval or potholes, random cracks to ½ inch wide, depressions, aggregate raveled. Patch failed areas using full-depth techniques; pre-fill cracks with asphalt emulsion slurry; apply leveling course; seal entire area with asphalt emulsion slurry or apply an overlay over a petromat product to increase strength.

- Pavement is in poor condition, extensive failed and cracking areas, depressions, potholes, difficult to salvage. Remedy is to reconstruct the street using standard techniques recommended by the Asphalt Institute.

Repair Techniques:

- Crack filling; cracks must be cleaned by use of a broom and compressed air. Vegetation must be removed using either a torch or a chemical weed killer. Soil sterilants should be used to prevent future weed growth. Fine cracks up to ½ inch wide should be routed to a minimum of 3/8 inch with depth equal to width before filling. Filling should be accomplished with an emulsion slurry or a fine sand/asphalt hot mix. Cracks measuring below 3/8 inch in width may be filled, but these require application of an undiluted asphalt material.

- Full-depth asphalt patching; in instances where pavements require patching, this should be accomplished by the full-depth technique as follows:

    (i) Remove the surface and base as deep as necessary (minimum four inches to reach firm support, extending at least 12 inches into good pavement outside the cracked area). Make the cut square or rectangular with faces straight and vertical.

    (ii) If water is a cause of the failure, install drainage. Compact subgrade until it is firm, hard, and unyielding.

    (iii) Apply tack coat to the vertical faces.

    (iv) Backfill the hole with a dense grade hot asphalt mix.

    (v) Compact in layers if the hole is more than six inches deep. Compact each layer thoroughly. Compaction should be done with equipment suited for the size of the job. A vibrating plate compactor is good for small patches. A roller should be used for large areas.

    (vi) Use a straight edge to check the alignment of the patch.

    (vii) Fog seal; this is a slow-setting asphalt emulsion generally diluted with water and sprayed on.

    (viii) Emulsion slurry seals are a mixture of asphalt emulsions, fine aggregate, mineral filler and water. They may be mixed in a mixer or in a special machine, or in a wheel-barrow in small quantities. A mixture is prepared in the form of a slurry and is applied to an average of 1/8 inch. The new emulsion sealant, which no longer has oil in it, is currently being used in most states for environmental reasons.

    (ix) Avoid applying an asphalt overlay over cracked surfaces, as the cracks will simply migrate through the new three- or six-inch asphalt overlay without a proper petromat product being embedded into the old asphalt with slurry.

For further information and specifications, contact an industry association such as the Asphalt Institute in Sacramento, California.

20.11 Reciprocal Maintenance of Streets and Parking. Sometimes a project will share streets and parking with an adjoining project. In such event, there should be a written reciprocal maintenance agreement. This agreement should define the responsibilities for maintenance and the formula by which the cost of maintenance will be shared. In the absence of such an agreement, some statutes provide that the cost of maintaining a shared easement area will be borne by each party using the easement in proportion to the percentage of that party's estimated use of the easement.

20.12 Roofs. In some planned development projects with attached housing and in most condominium projects, roofs are maintained by the association. The amount of maintenance depends, of course, upon the type of roof. Tile roofs are said to have an unlimited life; however, even they will require periodic maintenance to replace broken tiles and flashing. Flat roofs generally require the most frequent maintenance. Wood shakes will also require replacement; the heavier the shake, the longer the interval before replacement is required.

There are certain economies of scale in roofing. The association could benefit from a lower per-unit cost to re-roof if the entire project is completed by one contractor, rather than a series of small contracts for re-roofing individual dwellings. As with other contracts, it is important that a number of bids be obtained from responsible roofers before entering into a contract. *See Chapter 19.1.*

Occasionally, the cause of chronic leaks is not a problem with the roof, but is a problem with the flashing or the caulking. Leaks can result from negligent or inadequate construction techniques that have little to do with the roof itself. If wind-driven water gets into cracks in the roof and siding of a building without paper or a moisture barrier, water can intrude into the interiors of the dwellings. In this case, the solution is not replacement of the roof, but removal of the siding, so that building paper and flashing can be properly installed. A maintenance program that includes annually caulking areas where water can invade can save significant amounts of money over time by prolonging the life of roofs and siding. Occasionally, roofs fail not because of the fault of the roofer, but because of the design of the building itself.

20.13 Painting. Painting can be a significant expense for the association, so a reserve fund should be set up to cover the painting expense. In addition to choosing paint colors, paint types and a painting contractor, the association should insist upon a guarantee of workmanship and materials for at least two years from the date of completion. The guarantee should include peeling, flaking and fading beyond normal limits, with the provision that work to be redone under the guarantee shall be done corner-to-corner to the nearest natural break, and with the redone work to be guaranteed from the date that it is redone.

The specifications on preparation of surfaces to be painted should be rather specific. The contractor should be required to clean, scrape, sandpaper and caulk all surfaces, and perform whatever other duties are necessary to ensure proper adhesion of the paint. The contract should require that experienced, skilled painters apply all materials in a thorough, workmanlike manner, with no sags, drips, thin spots or laps. If the association specifies a particular type or brand of paint, and the contractor wants to use an equivalent alternative, (s)he should be required to submit some panels of each color for approval. Brands should not be mixed without prior color approval. The contract should also specify that all surfaces that are not to be painted should be kept free of paint.

It is a good idea for the association to require lien releases to be submitted with invoices for payment. The association should consult its attorney about the procedures for use of lien releases.

How long should a good paint job last? One expert says five to seven years on the unweathered side of wood siding, and a minimum of four years on a weathered side. Stucco paint should last from seven to ten years. Depending upon exposure to the sun and water, varnish on doors should be reapplied every year-and-a-half to two years.

20.14 Maintenance Standards. The standards of maintenance for any project may be prescribed in a number of different ways. First, the legal documents for the project will spell out the areas of responsibility for maintenance and may say that maintenance shall be conducted in a "first-class manner" or similar language.

The local governmental entity may also have imposed certain standards of maintenance. These standards may appear in local ordinances, or they may appear in the use permit, planned development permit, or tentative map conditions. Sometimes a city will have reserved the power to intercede to maintain a project, and will charge the expense to the association if the association has failed to meet its obligations. Insurance companies may also impose a certain level of maintenance as a condition of issuance and renewal of the policy.

A certain minimum level of maintenance may also be important in preserving warranty rights. One area of dispute between owners associations and developers or contractors is in the area of exterior maintenance. For example, the association may claim the contractor or the developer is at fault for a leaking roof. The contractor and the developer, in turn, may claim that the owners association is at least partially at fault because it failed to keep the gutters, catch basins and drains free from accumulation of leaves and other debris. If the association is careful to set and follow certain standards of maintenance, it can avoid arguments of that kind and can clearly establish responsibility where it belongs.

20.15 Decks, Balconies, and Patios. The association legal documents may place the burden of maintaining decks, balconies and patios on either the association or the individual owners. Maintenance obligations may also be split so that the association, for example, is responsible for painting, and the individual owners are responsible for landscaping or resurfacing the deck, balcony, or patio surfaces. It depends upon the design of the project as to which makes more sense.

20.16 Fences. The association generally maintains exterior perimeter fences. The owners usually maintain fences that enclose yards of individual planned development lots. Occasionally the documents will require the association to paint the exterior of those fences in order to maintain uniformity of appearance. Where owners maintain their individual fences, the association should have the authority to perform the maintenance if the owner fails to do so, and bill that owner for the cost of the maintenance.

20.17 Carports and Garages.
Normally, the association will maintain carports and underground and non-enclosed garages, unless the garage is included within the unit. Maintenance obligations can be split, so that the owner having the exclusive right to the use of a restricted common area garage or carport is responsible for interior maintenance, and the association being responsible for exterior maintenance.

20.18 Storm and Sanitary Sewers.
The local municipality, a special sewer district, or the association may maintain storm and sanitary sewer mains. Maintenance of laterals can be the responsibility of either the association or the individual owners. Jurisdictional problems can arise where the association is responsible for maintaining sewer laterals, but blockage occurs within the private area of a lot. The legal documents may be unclear as to whether the owner or the association has the responsibility for the cost of such repairs. The first time such a problem arises, the board should review the legal documents to determine whether or not an amendment is necessary, or at least to be sure that a clear policy is established and is made a part of the records of the association.

20.19 Windows and Janitorial.
Usually, individual owners perform window cleaning, except in multi-story buildings where professional window cleaners under contract with the association should perform exterior window cleaning. *See Chapter 19.11.* Breakage of windows is generally the responsibility of the unit owners. Some legal documents provide that to the extent there is insurance coverage under the master policy, the association will take care of glass repairs. Certainly wherever glass breakage is the fault of an owner, that owner should be required to pay for the cost of the repairs, even if they are made by the association or covered under the association's insurance policy.

Janitorial service varies greatly, depending upon the type of structure and the quality of service desired. The following checklist should be helpful in choosing the level of service desired:

1. Windows; washing inside and out.
2. Wood and vinyl floors; sweeping, waxing, wax stripping.
3. Carpeting; vacuuming and shampooing.
4. Bathrooms, shower rooms and toilets; cleaning, supplying toilet tissue and paper towels.
5. Kitchen; cleaning general kitchen area and appliances, including oven, refrigerator, and range.
6. Dusting, emptying ashtrays, wastebaskets and trash cans.
7. Walkway sweeping.
8. Vacuuming of furniture; spot-leaning of upholstery, carpets, and drapes.

20.20 Common Foundations, Walls, and Roofs. In a planned unit development project where there are common foundations, walls, or roofs, the legal documents may put the burden of maintenance on either the association or individual owners. If the documents are silent, the owners of adjoining units are jointly responsible for maintenance costs of their common walls, roofs, and foundations. The owners usually must cooperate in sharing costs and agreeing on when maintenance is required. If the legal documents require a certain standard of maintenance of the owners, the board of directors may, from time to time, direct owners to undertake and to pay for maintenance of their walls, roofs, and other shared components.

20.21 Shingles. Cedar shingles, either on the roofs or as exterior siding, can be treated annually with a clear wood sealer to preserve the original appearance and to prolong shingle life. Acrylic paints and solid color stains will last longer and require less maintenance than the wood sealant.

20.22 Stucco. Stucco may be either pigmented (pre-colored) or painted. Stucco should be painted every seven to ten years. To increase the life of stucco, cracks should be immediately patched to prevent moisture invasion.

CHAPTER 21
Insurance

21.1 Master Policy. State laws pertaining to condominiums and most project legal documents creating condominiums require the association to carry a master insurance policy covering the entire project including the individual units. This is the only approach to insurance that makes any sense in a high-rise project, and in most lateral projects it also makes sense because of the interrelationship of individual condominium units and the project's common areas.

In planned unit developments, the advisability of having a master policy depends to some extent on the type of construction. With attached townhouses or rowhouses it is possible that a master policy is preferable to individual policies covering each dwelling. A master policy may cost less money than a collection of individual policies; it is also easier to ensure adequate coverage for the entire project with a master policy than it is with individual insurance policies issued by different companies. Usually the developer of a project will have purchased an insurance policy that will be in effect at the time the board of directors is taken over by the new owners. The project legal documents will generally specify whether the insurance policy should be a master policy covering all of the improvements in the project, or whether it covers only the common area improvements or improvements owned by the association, and leaves it to individual owners to insure their own property.

Certainly the most efficient way to handle insurance in either a condominium or a planned unit development project is to have a single master policy covering all of the units or lots. Each separate unit or lot owner would then carry only liability insurance and personal property insurance covering the contents of his or her dwelling or office. This will eliminate conflicts among carriers because of overlapping coverage, will save overall premiums, and should eliminate gaps in coverage as well as duplication in coverage.

21.2 Individual Policies. Individual condominium unit owners can obtain a special condominium policy covering the contents of the unit and personal liability. This is usually called or referred to as an "HO-6" policy. Such a policy will cover loss or injury within the unit, but will not include liability for actions occurring in the common area, and will not include damage to the common area. The unit owner can obtain additional endorsements to the HO-6 policy, including:

- An "all-risk" endorsement;
- A living expense endorsement;
- A rental coverage endorsement (to cover loss of rent as a result of fire or other damage); and
- Loss assessment coverage (to cover special assessments levied by the association to cover uninsured losses).

The owner can also obtain a special endorsement for rain damage, which may be important because the master policy will generally exclude rain damage and the HO-6 policy may not cover it.

Manager's Note: *For the protection of both the homeowner and association, reminders should be published annually in newsletters or with other important documents (such as the rules or budget) of the need for a homeowner to purchase an HO-6 policy. Often there is a prevailing misconception among condominium owners that the master policy will cover all losses both outside in the common area and <u>within</u> the home. Check with the association's insurance agent to determine what types of losses would NOT be covered under the master insurance policy, and make a point of reminding homeowners of these areas that they must cover with their own insurance or personal funds.*

Where individual policies are required instead of a master policy, the association legal documents should set minimum insurance standards to be met by each owner, and copies of policies should be required to be filed with the association.

Procedures should exist for applying insurance proceeds to repair of the property, even if that requires proceeds to be made payable to a trustee who will contract for all repairs using the proceeds of all the individual policies. Some master policies exclude rain damage to the interior of the building unless the rain entered through a hole made by the wind. Other policies allow for depreciation to be deducted on any loss to carpets and built-in appliances, and limit coverage on glass breakage to a specific amount per pane with a maximum per occurrence, unless the loss is caused by fire, wind or hail. Therefore, the individual owner must purchase his or her own insurance coverage with riders to cover personal property, including furniture and clothing; fixtures (depending upon whether the master policy covers fixtures); glass breakage (depending upon master policy coverage); additional living expenses; loss of rental income; personal liability; and loss assessment.

21.3 Casualty Insurance. "Casualty" insurance is a broad term that is used to describe property insurance. It is sometimes called "all-risk" or "comprehensive" insurance.

21.4 Liability Insurance. Liability insurance protects the association from damages due to bodily injury or property damage caused by an occurrence covered by the insurance policy. Although liability (or "public liability," as it is sometimes called) covers many areas, there are also certain matters that are generally excluded from liability coverage. Some of these include injuries from automobiles, boats or aircraft; injury to employees arising out of employment; injuries arising from discharge of smoke, fumes, or chemicals; damages for false arrest, malicious prosecution, wrongful entry, eviction, libel or slander; contractual liability; host liquor liability; and non-owned automobiles. Most if not all of these exceptions can be covered under separate policies or additional riders. The best method of protecting individual members of an association, whether incorporated or unincorporated, from unlimited tort liability is through a comprehensive insurance program including adequate public liability insurance. In addition to public liability coverage included in the master policy, each individual homeowner should carry his or her own public liability policy to cover injuries or damage that occur on the premises rather than the common area.

21.5 Comprehensive or All-Risk Coverage. Comprehensive or all-risk coverage is also referred to as "extended coverage" or "special form coverage." "All-risk" usually means that you are insured for "all forms of physical loss" except for specific exclusions that are mentioned in the policy. Fire, theft and vandalism are normally included in an all-risk or comprehensive policy.

21.6 Earthquake Insurance. Although available, earthquake insurance costs may be prohibitive; but in earthquake-prone areas, this coverage may be a worthwhile investment despite the high premiums. The project legal documents may require earthquake insurance. If the board elects not to carry earthquake insurance, the membership should be so informed.

Manager's Note: Board members of associations located in earthquake-prone areas should annually update and review their earthquake policies and coverages, as these change quite frequently. Also, boards would be well advised not to make the decision of whether to purchase earthquake insurance without consulting the membership. An annual poll or vote of the membership will determine if the earthquake insurance costs are higher than the membership is willing to bear, or if the membership wishes to continue or expand that particular coverage.

In a planned development project, if the association carries a master policy but does not include earthquake coverage, the individual homeowners may obtain earthquake insurance as additional coverage under their individual policies. If the association carries a master policy, it is probably not practical for the individual owners to try to carry earthquake coverage only on their dwellings without any other casualty coverage. However, it is possible that by judiciously shopping around, an owner can find limited earthquake coverage for the contents of the home even though the exterior elements and structure itself are covered under the master policy for earthquake coverage.

If earthquake insurance is desired for a condominium project, it must be included in the master policy. Individual condominium unit owners cannot obtain earthquake insurance on their own units. However, some insurance companies offer individual condominium owners coverage for assessments that are levied by the association following earthquake damage. Insurance companies may also offer earthquake insurance on buildings if all the owners in the building purchase the insurance. Condominiums with fire insurance are covered if a fire caused by an earthquake destroys the project. However, each policy should be examined for escape clauses.

21.7 Flood Insurance. Flood insurance may or may not be desirable, depending upon the project's location. In designated flood hazard areas, flood insurance may be required by lenders or by secondary lending agencies such as FNMA and FHLMC. If the project is located in a designated flood hazard area, the master policy should include flood damage, and the individual policies that the owners carry on their contents should also include flood damage.

21.8 Workers' Compensation. If the association has any employees, it is generally required to carry workers' compensation insurance. Independent contractors, who are not paid a salary and are not on the association payroll, are not employees and do not need to be covered. The total employee payroll generally determines the amount of the premium. Uncompensated volunteers of non-profit organizations are not usually considered employees for purposes of workers' compensation, unless the board of directors has specifically declared, prior to any injury occurring, that the people performing such voluntary services are deemed to be employees while performing such services. An association might wish to so declare, in order to provide some insurance coverage for injuries of members serving voluntarily without pay. Examples of employees that should be covered by workers' compensation insurance if they are on the association payroll would be maintenance personnel, on-site or resident managers, guards, and gardeners. In some states, laws require that workers' compensation be carried for workers or contractors who work on the premises even though they are not employees of the association. In case of any doubt, consult your insurance broker and your association attorney.

21.9 Automobile Insurance. In the event the association owns any vehicles, each vehicle should have adequate automobile insurance, including personal injury, liability and property damage, medical and comprehensive, including fire, theft, and vandalism.

21.10 Non-Owned Automobiles. If the association does not own an automobile and does not have automobile coverage but has a basic public liability policy, that policy may exclude from coverage the damages or liability arising out of the use of non-owned automobiles. The association should obtain an endorsement to its liability policy that will include non-owned automobile insurance coverage. This will cover the association if an officer, director, or employee of the association should be using his or her own automobile on association business when a loss occurs.

21.11 Directors' and Officers' Insurance. Officers and directors of an association may be subject to personal liability for suits brought by owners and third parties. The association should obtain adequate insurance protection to cover its officers and employees. The association's documents should contain specific authorization for the purchase of this type of coverage. The insurance will not cover liability for intentional acts, liability arising from civil rights violations, or liability resulting from failure to purchase adequate insurance for the project. Although sometimes difficult to obtain and expensive, directors' and officers' liability policies are necessary if the association expects to have its members serve in positions that subject them to potential personal liability.

Some officers' and directors' liability policies are issued on a "claims made" basis, which means that they offer protection only for claims made during the policy period based upon acts occurring while the policy was in effect. Other policies may protect against claims arising during the policy period regardless of when the act occurred. Some policies will not cover officers and directors for liability from claims arising from actions taken while they were on the board, when the claims are made after they are no longer on the board. The association should shop around and try to get the broadest coverage possible, and should inform officers and directors of the exact coverage. Of course, the association should indemnify its officers and directors against personal liability that is not covered under the association's policy.

21.12 Rain Damage. Most blanket insurance policies exclude rain damage to the interior of units unless rain enters through a hole made by the wind. Even if the rain is forced in by the wind, there may not be coverage unless the building sustained actual damage first. A homeowner can obtain rain damage coverage by asking that the standard unit owners policy (HO-6) be broadened to include rain damage. Rain damage coverage is normally included in the standard HO-32 rider. The coverage under policies varies greatly, of course, and it is important that the unit owner determine exactly what coverage there is under the master policy and what coverage can be obtained under his/her unit policy by adding riders. This is to eliminate the gaps in coverage so that no matter how or where the loss or damage occurs it is covered by some policy.

21.13 Auxiliary Structures. Auxiliary structures such as fences, signs, pools, carports, etc. may not be covered under a standard comprehensive or all-risk casualty policy unless they are specified. The board should be sure that auxiliary structures are covered, and that if necessary, their values are included in computing the total amount of insurance to be carried.

21.14 Glass Coverage. It may be necessary to add glass coverage or "plate glass coverage" as an additional rider to an insurance policy in order to get full coverage.

21.15 Dram Shop Coverage. If the association operates a bar or at any time dispenses alcoholic beverages, it is essential that the association get a dram shop coverage rider added to its liability policy.

21.16 Personal Property. If the association owns personal property such as recreation room furniture, pool furniture, or pool-cleaning equipment, that personal property should be insured to full actual cash or replacement value under the association's master policy. Standard "all-risk" insurance policies may exclude theft of property that is not part of the building, and therefore exclude theft of personal property. Care should be taken to be sure that such personal property is covered on a replacement cost rather than a depreciated value basis.

21.17 Boiler and Machinery. In a project that has a steam boiler, there should be a "boiler and machinery" policy to cover damage to the boiler and to the structures caused by an explosion of the boiler. Generally, "all-risk" protection on the building will not include or will specifically exclude boiler coverage. Boiler and machinery coverage can also cover sudden and accidental breakdown of pumps, compressors, boilers and motors.

21.18 Umbrella Coverage. An association should probably have liability coverage of at least $1 million, and for a large association, insurance substantially higher than that should be considered. One way to obtain higher coverage limits is to purchase an umbrella policy that covers liability to limits in excess of what is covered by the basic policy, and offers coverage that is somewhat broader than the basic liability package policy. Umbrella coverage premiums tend to be considerably less, because it depends upon there being some underlying coverage to handle the liability up to a specified level.

21.19 Title Insurance. When the new board of directors takes over the operation of the association, it should check to see whether or not the developer of the project purchased title insurance on property deeded over to the association. If so, that insurance can be relied upon in the event there is any problem with title to the association's property in the future. In a phased project, the board of directors might consider requiring a title insurance policy on any common area property that is annexed to the association as part of an additional phase.

21.20 Property Damage Insurance. This coverage is intended to protect the association's property, including buildings and all commonly owned property such as recreation room furniture or pool furniture, from loss or damage from hazards such as fire, windstorm, collapse of the building, and other hazards. Property damage is generally included in an "all-risk" coverage policy; however, it is important to note what exceptions are listed even in an "all-risk" policy. *See Chapter 21.5.*

21.21 Product Liability Insurance. If the association operates dining or food service facilities or has vending machines that dispense food under its operation and control, it should include product liability coverage.

21.22 "Claims-Made" or "Occurrence" Coverage. In purchasing liability insurance, particularly in the case of officers' and directors' liability insurance (*see Chapter 21.11*), it is important to distinguish between a policy offering "occurrence" coverage or "claims-made" coverage. Claims-made policies provide coverage only if loss or damage occurred <u>and</u> is claimed during the policy period. If the event causing the claim occurred during the effective period of the claims-made policy, but the claim is not made until after the expiration of the policy, there will not be coverage. Alternatively, if a claim is made during the period the policy is in effect, but the event occurred before the policy period, there might be coverage, depending upon whether or not the policy specifically excludes claims for events occurring prior to the period of coverage. If the coverage is "occurrence" coverage, then a claim arising out of an event that occurred during the period the policy was in effect will be covered, even if the claim is made after expiration of the policy.

21.23 Replacement Cost Endorsement. Unless there is a special endorsement, a standard policy will depreciate a structure in the event of loss so that the depreciated value is the extent of the coverage. A special endorsement should be added that would provide for coverage based on replacement value rather than depreciated value.

21.24 Inflation Guard Endorsement. It is possible to obtain an endorsement that provides that the amount of insurance will automatically increase by a specified percentage every few months or by the amount of the increase in the cost of living index or some other construction cost guide. This is particularly important coverage to have during periods of rapid inflation.

21.25 Nonconforming Building Endorsement. If the project does not conform to present building or zoning codes, which may be the case for a rental apartment building that was converted to a condominium, and more than 50 percent of the building is damaged, it normally cannot be repaired without bringing the building into conformity with current building codes and zoning ordinances. Normally, insurance would not cover the extra costs to bring the building up to code or to add additional parking spaces, if that is what is required. These extra costs can be covered with the purchase of a special endorsement for nonconforming buildings.

Policy Exclusions. It is important to be aware of what exclusions exist in policies that are supposedly "comprehensive," "special form," or "all-risk." Generally, the following are excluded unless covered by specific endorsements or riders:

- Damage from termites, dry rot or fungus;
- Damage from underground water;
- Damage from rust;
- Damage from settling of the building;
- Damage from animals or birds;
- Damage from electrical shortages (unless fire should occur);
- Glass damage;
- Damage to signs;
- Damage from explosion of steam boilers (*see Chapter 21.17*);
- Damages from "acts of God," such as earthquake, flood, war, or landslides;
- Rain damage to the interior of the building (except when created by a hole caused by wind-driven rain);
- Water damage that occurs over an extended period of time.

21.26 Waiver of Subrogation.
Under a standard insurance policy, after the insurance company has paid for physical damage to the property, the company has a legal right to recover its loss from the parties who were negligent and caused the loss. The association's policy should contain a waiver of this right of subrogation (transfer recovery rights) against the individual owners, so that the insurance company will not attempt to collect the amounts paid by the insurance company from the individual owners. A typical waiver of subrogation clause would read as follows:

"The insurance company for and in consideration of $_____ and other good and valuable consideration covenants and agrees that, in the event any sums are paid to the insured under the insurance conditions of this policy, it will not exercise any legal or equitable right it may have as a result of the payment of such sums, as against any unit or lot owner, officer, the board of directors or the manager. The insurance company further covenants and agrees that, in the event this endorsement or the policy to which it is attached is cancelled, reduced in amount or its conditions altered, it will give 10 days' written notice of such changes to each of the above persons."

21.27 Co-Insurance. Most insurance policies require that a building be insured to at least a substantial percentage of its full value or the full value, because the higher the value insured, the higher the premium. The insurance company does not want to be in the position of having to pay more for a building than the insured value, so they often require an association or policy holder to carry 80 percent (80%) or more of the value of the building in casualty insurance. In the event of inadequate coverage, the coinsurance clause will penalize the policyholder by making them a co-insurer (or a participant in the cost of the claim). As a general rule, it is best for the association to carry insurance in the amount of 100 percent of the replacement value of the improvements.

21.28 How to Purchase Insurance.

The board of directors should appoint an insurance committee or should delegate one of its members to be responsible for investigating and recommending what insurance to purchase. As is the case with lawyers and accountants, insurance brokers tend to specialize, and homeowners association insurance is an area of specialization. The association should only deal with a broker who is experienced in handling owners association insurance and should ask for information about the broker's level of experience and how many owners associations are currently insured through the broker.

It is customary to get two or three bids or proposals from different insurance brokers or agencies prior to acquiring the insurance policies. The same specifications should be given to each insurance agent who will be providing a proposal, as there is a great difference in the coverage and language of insurance policies offered by different companies. Since most insurance policies are so complicated that they are not easily read and understood by laymen, the association has to rely upon the expertise of its broker in interpreting and comparing the policies to find out which policy offers the best coverage at the best rate.

If there is some doubt about the liquidity or stability of the insurance company, the broker can consult the latest "Best Report." The Best Report rates insurance companies based on their financial strength and overall conduct of business.

21.29 Cross-Liability Endorsement.

A cross-liability endorsement provides coverage when one unit or lot owner sues another owner or the association for injuries resulting from an accident in the common area. If there is no specific cross-liability endorsement, it is possible that the definition of "insured" appearing in the master policy will solve the problem. There may be coverage if "insured" means any person or organization qualifying as an "insured" in the "person insured" provision of the applicable insurance coverage, and the insurance applies separately to each insured against whom a claim is made or a suit is brought. Check with your broker to make sure that the language of the policy either automatically includes the cross-liability endorsement or that the endorsement is added to the policy.

21.30 Checklist of Specifications for Insurance Coverage.

1. Blanket, comprehensive, all-risk protection on improvements, including buildings, pools, fences and auxiliary structures, and "all-risk" contents coverage including theft. Coverage to include:

- All improvements and betterments (including those added by owners).
- Stipulated amount clause.
- Inflation guard endorsement.
- Waiver of subrogation clause.
- Low deductible ($100, for example).
- All losses payable to association as trustee for owners.
- Replacement cost endorsement.

- Additional owner coverage will not reduce master policy coverage.

2. $_____ in liability protection, including:

- Personal injury with no exclusion relating to employees.
- Non-owned automobiles.
- Comprehensive general liability endorsement.
- Severability of interest clause.
- Products and host liquor liability.
- Owners as additional insureds (for common area).
- Contractual liability.
- Minimum amount per-person guest medical payments (for example, $1,000).
- Cross-liability endorsement.
- Personal injury rider to cover slander, libel and related claims.
- Automobile insurance for employees.

3. $_____ in directors' and officers' liability insurance; specify deductible and participation. Policy must be on a "claims made" basis, and should include protection for prior acts.
4. $_____ blanket bond to cover directors, officers and employees.
5. $_____ umbrella coverage.
6. Workers' compensation.
7. Title insurance on association real property.
8. Common charges insurance, where one owner defaults and the others have to pay their share to make up the default.
9. Clause prohibiting cancellation without 30 days' notice from the insurance company.
10. Flood insurance.
11. Earthquake insurance.
12. Water damage coverage.
13. Watercraft liability (where applicable).
14. Garage keepers' liability (where applicable).
15. Golf cart coverage (where applicable).
16. Machinery and equipment (owned or leased) located in the common area.
17. Loss of rental insurance (commercial condominium or planned unit development project).
18. Emergency shelter rider.
19. Rental loss insurance.

21.31 General Insurance Discussion. Each unit or lot owner should know precisely what is and what is not covered by the insurance policies carried by the association. Since each owner is required to pay assessments even if the dwelling is uninhabitable due to fire or other damage, his or her policy should include an emergency shelter rider to cover additional living expenses and obligations to pay assessments. Owners who rent their units or lots should also carry rental loss insurance. Owners should be required to notify the association of any alteration in the improvements to their unit or lot that would add to their replacement cost, so that appropriate adjustments in the master policy can be made.

Care should be taken to ensure that the master insurance policy covers all common areas, and that there are no gaps between the master policy and the individual policies that can result in a lack of coverage on a portion of the project. The board of directors has the responsibility to see that adequate insurance covers the perils against which good business judgment indicates the project should be insured, for the preservation of the property of the owners and the payment of claims against them. Failure to make prudent provision may result in personal liability. The directors must review the insurance policies that are in existence when they take over the association to make sure that the insurance is adequate. Although the directors may and should obtain assistance from specialized insurance brokers, finding and filling gaps in coverage and ensuring that insurance provides adequate coverage for all potential areas of loss is the ultimate responsibility of the board.

Most policies contain some deductible clause. An important question is how much of the initial loss is the association prepared to assume in order to reduce its premiums? In a project having a large number of separate buildings, a clause setting a deductible per building may be undesirable. Similarly, in a large high-rise, a single large deductible clause may be undesirable in a situation in which the damage is confined to a few units, unless the owners of the damaged units carry their own insurance.

When several different insurance companies are involved, a loss that affects the common area and some of the units or lots requires adjustment between the carrier for the association and the carriers for the owners. Prorations and decisions have to be made as to who receives the proceeds of the policies. A question of what control is exerted by the association over insurance proceeds payable to individual unit or lot owners must also be answered. This problem could, of course, be reduced or eliminated by having a single company cover the common area and all property not owned separately by unit/lot owners.

Where the master policy fully insures the buildings and individual unit owners have their own policies, there may be over-insurance. This may lead to total recoveries that exceed the actual loss, unless the insurance company can apply co-insurance clauses. It may also result in proration or division of the liability of the different carriers. Total recovery exceeding the loss will probably be resisted by the insurance companies, but there is precedent for such recovery.

Estoppel may prevent pro-ration where the same insurance company issued the master policy and one or more unit policies and had accepted duplicate premiums on a single risk. Under a "valued" policy, where the carrier agrees to pay the face value of the policy regardless of the actual value of the insured's interest, recovery would also be possible. However, in most cases where there is multiple coverage, the loss will be prorated among the different carriers so that the total insurance proceeds do not exceed the total loss. Where there is pro-ration, the association should receive a sufficient amount of the proceeds to reconstruct the project, including all the common areas that have been damaged. The unit owners should receive only enough of the proceeds to repair what was damaged or destroyed within the units after the association had received sufficient funds to rebuild the common area.

To avoid conflicts and complications arising from the existence of several different insurance policies, the declaration can prohibit owners from carrying individual policies that duplicate the master policy. This might eliminate some of the problems, but it might also prevent the owner from being able to insure permanent improvements and fixtures in the unit or lot, and could create problems in obtaining a loan. An alternative is to coordinate all of the unit or lot owners' policies. However, this does not necessarily eliminate all of the loss adjustment and subrogation problems. Another alternative would be to require unit owners to place their policies with the carrier issuing the master policy for the association; however, some state laws would prohibit that as an "unfair insurance practice."

In condominium projects, the association should have a general policy known as a "special multi-peril" or "SMP" policy. A general form for condominiums is MLB-29. The MLB-29A is a special, all-risk type of insurance covering buildings, additions and extensions, fixtures, personal property of the association, and everything else not excepted from coverage. Exceptions include property within any of the units except for common building elements such as pipes and wires. Under the MLB-29A policy, there is no coverage for doors, carpets, interior partitions, appliances, etc. MLB-29B provides coverage for fixtures, interior partitions and installations within the unit. Landscaping, signs, pools and retaining walls are not covered under an ordinary condominium policy, and the association needs a special endorsement for such coverage.

The master policy should cover the liability of unit or lot owners in the common area, since their individual policies will not extend coverage into the common area. The master policy should also include the owners as named insureds (by referring to them as a class, not necessarily individually by name).

If the association carries only an MLB-29A policy, then the unit owners will have to add to their HO-6 policies additional coverage for all improvements and betterments to their units beyond the bare floors, wall and ceilings, and this can create a problem. Under the MLB-29A policy, the lender on a condominium unit will need to be named as an additional insured on both policies, because the master policy will cover a portion of the property that secures the lender's loan and the HO-6 policy will cover the balance. Under an MLB-29B policy, however, all lenders can be included in one policy. When condominium unit sales are closed, the name of the lender on each unit is forwarded to the company and an additional certificate of insurance is issued to that lender.

The following is a checklist of specific recommendations concerning the casualty insurance program that should be considered for a common interest project:

1. The declaration and the master policy should preclude contribution between the master policy and policies purchased by unit owners.
2. Conduct of a unit owner should not constitute grounds for avoiding liability under the master policy.
3. Authority to adjust losses should be vested in the association, not the insurance companies.
4. The association or a trustee should control expenditure of insurance proceeds to rebuild a damaged project.
5. Coverage sufficient to pay assessments while a unit is uninhabitable following a casualty loss should be included.
6. A waiver of subrogation rights with respect to the association and unit owners and a cross-liability endorsement should be included.

7. Each unit owner should have an individual liability policy covering personal exposure for torts, whether occurring in his/her unit or elsewhere.
8. If the master policy contains a coinsurance clause, unit owners should be required to notify the association of all improvements to their units, or the master policy should state that the value of the project for coinsurance purposes includes only improvements installed by the association. This is to prevent the inadvertent failure to insure to the coinsurance percentage required, and as a result not recover the total proceeds necessary to compensate for a loss.
9. Individual policies should be filed with the association so they can all be reviewed to eliminate potential conflicts with the master policy.
10. The question of whether insurance proceeds should be used to restore a destroyed project, or be paid to the association for distribution to the members or to mortgagees, should be resolved with the company issuing the master policy at the time the policy is purchased.
11. In the case of commercial condominiums or mixed residential and commercial condominiums, proper allocation of premiums must be made to the units generating excess insurance costs.

CHAPTER 22
Financial Management

22.1 Budget. The annual budget or pro forma operating budget is an estimate of the association's income and expenses for the coming fiscal year. Usually, the upcoming year's budget is based on estimates in the previous year's budget, updated with information from actual income and expenses for the year. In the initial year of operation of an association, however, there is no "performance data" upon which to base a budget. In most cases, the developer will provide the initial budget. *See Chapter 16.3.* It is important that the budget be as complete and as carefully tailored as possible to the project. The following items should be considered basic for most association budgets:

1. Management fee.
2. Association office expenses including telephone, stationery, supplies and office equipment.
3. Legal and accounting fees.
4. Maintenance of common areas.
5. Maintenance of units or lots (exteriors).
6. Utilities, including gas, electricity and water, furnished to common areas or to units on a master meter.
7. Insurance.
8. Recreational facility maintenance and operation.
9. Security (if provided).
10. Refuse collection.
11. Pest control.
12. Specialized services such as snow removal, tree trimming, garden spraying, fire and safety equipment inspection and chimney sweeping.
13. Reserves for repair and replacement.

Time-share projects will require additional budget items to cover:

1. Reservation service.
2. Unit care services (maid service, linens, towels, etc.).
3. Reception desk.

See Form 21 for a sample form of budget.

22.2 Start-Up Funds. In some projects, the developer will have collected, in advance, one or two months' assessment deposits from each purchaser, so that the association will begin with a cash "cushion." In some states, it may be required that two months' assessments be paid in advance at the close of escrow of each home in a new condominium or planned development project.

22.3 Original Budget. The newly created project will have an original budget prepared by the developer. The budget will be based upon general estimates for similar projects or guidelines developed by a regional or state source. The budget may also have been approved by a state regulatory agency.

Efforts are made to keep the initial budget accurate, but occasionally one will be either too high or too low. If the budget is too high, the simplest remedy is to adjust the expenses and reduce the assessments. If the budget is too low, increased assessments or perhaps a special assessment will be required. Under certain circumstances, if the budget is unreasonably low, there could be some liability on the part of the developer or the budget preparer for grossly underestimating the budget.

22.4 First Budget by New Board.
Prior to preparation of the first budget by a newly elected board, the directors, committees and manager or management company should be asked for recommendations and input that will be used in creating the budget. It is important to obtain as much input as possible before finalizing the first budget to be adopted by a newly elected board. The board will rely upon the budget furnished by the developer at the beginning of the project, but undoubtedly some changes will be made based on the maintenance and operation experience of the project.

22.5 Increases or Decreases in Assessments.
Some project documents and state laws limit the amount by which assessments may be increased or decreased without the consent of a majority of the members. The board should determine whether any such restrictions are applicable before adopting either large increases or decreases in the budget and/or assessments.

22.6 Reserves.
The budget consists of two parts—current operating expenses and reserves. It is advisable and almost always required by the legal documents and state laws to set aside funds in a reserve. Where it is *not* a legal requirement, some owners would prefer *not* to set aside reserves, especially those who are planning to sell their home in the near future. The problem with not setting aside reserves is that one never knows when major expenditures will be required, and if there are no reserves to pay for these expenditures, a large special assessment will be required to pay for the expense. One way to consider these reserves is as payment for "usage." For example, as a new roof with a life of 15 years ages, the members of an owners association will contribute approximately 1/15th of the cost annually to the reserve account. At the end of the roof's useful life, there will be an adequate amount on hand to pay for the cost of re-roofing.

Estimated life expectancies are available for certain assets such as swimming pools, wood siding, tennis courts, asphalt paving, built-up roofs, shingle and tile roofs. There are various sources from which these estimates can be obtained, but these estimates are only *guidelines*. The actual life expectancy of the various components can vary greatly, depending upon such considerations as climate, materials used, type of use, design of the project, and the amount of periodic maintenance that is performed. Obviously, asphalt paving in a mild dry climate will last much longer than asphalt paving in a climate that experiences severe winters and stormy summers.

22.7 Financial Procedures and Management.
Depending upon the size of the project and common area elements, preparation and distribution of a budget may take between three and six months. Owners should have the new budget between 45 and 60 days prior to the beginning of the new fiscal year. In addition to these commonsense requirements, there may be legal requirements imposed either by the project's legal documents or by state law.

The budget should include both the annual operating budget and detailed information regarding how the contributions to the reserves were calculated. Backup material to support the calculations for the reserves should be assembled and retained in the permanent files.

Life expectancies or anticipated maintenance of major components such as roof replacement, painting of exterior siding, and resurfacing driveways should be estimated and re-evaluated annually based on the best information available at the time of preparation. Provisions should be made for investment of reserve accounts in a manner consistent with maximum safety and greatest return on the invested funds. Past budgets and backup calculations should be retained in the permanent records of the association.

Manager's Note: One of the points of particular interest to members is the annual budget. If the association is large enough, a finance or budget committee can be formed to analyze operating expenses, and to work with the professionals who will provide the information to be used in calculating the contributions to the reserve funds. Committees are excellent ways to "grow" future board members, and the budget or finance committee allows homeowners an opportunity to experience first-hand what it takes to operate the association each month or each year.

If a committee is employed in the budget process, however, the association should allow several months to prepare the budget.

22.8 Investing Association Funds.

Owners associations, particularly larger ones, can build substantial funds in the reserve accounts over a relatively short period of time. These amounts should be invested to maximize the return on income without sacrificing safety or security.

The operating income account of the association should also be deposited into an interest-bearing checking account. The balance maintained in the checking account should be just enough to cover payment of monthly bills, plus, if necessary, any minimum-balance requirement. All excess funds should be transferred from the checking account to an interest-bearing savings account. Reserves can be invested in higher-yielding accounts, such as treasury bills, federally insured bank accounts or certificates of deposit, and instruments that are backed by the full faith and credit of the United States government.

Whoever is in charge of recommending investment options for the association, which is usually either the association treasurer or the professional manager, should get the best rates available, consistent with safety. The association board should not speculate with the association's funds, as it is acting in a fiduciary capacity with respect to the assets.

The total amount of funds in all accounts should not be allowed to increase over the maximum insured amount. An association that has one or more "jumbo" accounts or certificates should spread the business around to other banks so that the accounts are not at a single institution. An active chief financial officer who constantly monitors market rates can get a better return when investing the association's funds than can one who does not track the market and simply invests all the money until maturity in an account currently returning the best rate at the time. Some larger associations may actually retain an investment counselor to advise them on how to get the best return on their accounts.

If the association has treasury bills, notes, bonds or any negotiable instruments, it should rent a safe deposit box where these items can be stored.

The interest earned on the association's investments is taxable, even though the association is qualified as a tax-exempt owners association. The effect of the exemption is to avoid income tax on assessments. However, income that is unrelated to the assessments, or "non-function income" such as interest income on investments, is subject to tax. In the case of an association with very large reserve accounts, the income tax on the reserve account interest income can be substantial. In setting up the budget for the coming year, the treasurer, chief financial officer or budget committee should consider the amount of interest or investment income that will be earned by the association.

22.9 Estimating Expenses. Assistance in estimating expenses can be obtained from various sources. A state regulatory agency such as the Department of Real Estate may publish and make available an operating cost manual to assist homeowners associations, developers and newly organized associations in preparing accurate budgets. The association can also talk with the board members from other associations to determine what others are experiencing in their geographical region. In most cases, the board will have the benefit of some prior operating experience during the first few months of operation of the association.

After an association has operated for several years, it becomes much easier to accurately forecast a budget for each coming year. During the first year or two it may be necessary to make adjustments during the fiscal year, and perhaps even to levy a special assessment to bring the budget into line with the actual expenses.

22.10 Allocating Income and Expense Items. While establishing the budget, the board needs to carefully consider the various needs of the association. In order to avoid drawing on the reserve funds to meet operating expenses, the amount budgeted for reserves should be set aside in a separate reserve account. In addition to the reserves for repair and replacement of major components such as roofs, there should be adequate funds in the budget to handle such periodic expenses as insurance, replacement of common furniture and equipment, and a reserve to handle unexpected contingencies.

CHAPTER 23
Financial Reports and Accounting

Manager's Note: *All Board members should read this chapter; however, it is especially critical that the chief financial officer (CFO) or treasurer of the association be well versed on the information in this chapter.*

23.1 Financial Reports That Are Legally Required. Owners associations are required to provide certain financial reports. The requirements may be contained in the project legal documents and/or in the state statutes and regulations. The board of directors, and particularly the treasurer or chief financial officer of the association, are responsible for knowing what reports are required and for seeing that those reports are properly prepared and distributed on time to the membership.

23.2 General Financial Reporting Requirements. Owners associations are required to mail or distribute financial reports to all members and to inform the members of their right to obtain reports upon request. In most states, owners associations are required to prepare and distribute an annual budget prior to the beginning of each fiscal year.

23.3 Profit and Loss Statement. The "profit and loss" or income statement, which is sometimes referred to as an operating statement, should be prepared as soon as possible after the close of each fiscal year. The report will contain the total income and expenses for the year and indicate whether operations resulted in a surplus or deficit. It is helpful to have a form that combines the budget together with the operating statement. The first column of the report will contain the budget figures and the second column will be the actual expenditures and income. Having two columns in a single report allows budget and performance to be compared.

23.4 Statement of Assets and Liabilities. The statement of assets, liabilities and equity is also referred to as a "balance sheet." A balance sheet can be prepared as of any accounting date, but normally is prepared the last day of the month. It should include the schedule of assets, liabilities and equity. Some project legal documents and state laws require that a balance sheet and an operating statement be distributed to all members within a certain number of days after the close of the fiscal year.

23.5 Statement of Reserves. Reserves should be accounted for at least annually. Some associations keep track of their reserves on a monthly basis, indicating the amounts broken down into major categories that are on hand, that have been expended, and the total amount of reserves set aside for each major category.

Manager's Note: *What is the difference between an income statement and balance sheet? For accountants, we say that a balance sheet is a "snapshot" in time, showing exactly what the association has, owes and is worth on a specific date. The balance* sheet for the very next day would contain different figures due to changes in the assets, liabilities and equity. On the other hand, an income statement provides "performance" information that spans a specific period of time. For example, an income statement prepared for the first quarter of the year would show only the income and expenses collected over three months. Together, the income statement tells the reader the association's financial performance over a period of time, and the balance sheet gives the reader information regarding what that performance "yielded" in assets, liabilities and equity at end of that time.

23.6 Annual Statement of Policies.
Some state laws require that an association annually distribute, within a certain time prior to the beginning of the fiscal year, a statement of the association's policies and practices in enforcing its remedies against members for defaults in the payment of assessments, including the provisions for recording and foreclosing liens against members' subdivision interests. It is the responsibility of the board and particularly the chief financial officer to be aware of and to comply with such requirements.

23.7 Distribution of Annual Report.
Most legal documents and a number of state statutes require that an annual report, consisting of the balance sheet, an income statement, and statement of changes in financial position for the fiscal year, be distributed within a specified number of days after the close of the fiscal year. In some cases, such statements are required to be audited or prepared by an independent accountant. A report stating that the financials were prepared from the books and records of the association without independent audit or review should accompany the report if a CPA did not perform an audit or review. Refer to the project legal documents and your attorney to determine the requirements.

23.8 Accrual vs. Cash Basis Accounting.
There are two basic methods of accounting, "cash basis" and "accrual basis." Although cash basis accounting is easier to understand, as it relies only on recording income received and checks sent during the month, accrual basis accounting is more accurate and more useful, as it recognizes the expense or income in the month incurred.

Under the cash basis method, all revenue is recorded when received rather than when it is earned, and expenses are recorded when they are paid rather than when the obligation is incurred. This method of reporting can be misleading, because while it tracks income accurately, cash basis tends to understate the actual expenses.

Accrual basis accounting, on the other hand, allows the association to accurately compare the financial status of the current year with that of the previous year, and to create a picture of any financial trends. Accrual basis accounting is often required, and the association does not have an option to select cash basis accounting.

Manager's Note: *A third possible method of tracking income and expenses in the association's financials is to use a "hybrid" method of accounting, which combines the best elements of cash basis with accrual accounting. In a hybrid method, income is posted when received, but expenses are posted when incurred.*

Thus, the financial picture, while not as accurate as an accrual method, will not understate the monthly or quarterly expenses.

A CPA or qualified financial professional should be consulted to create the proper format and train personnel in using the hybrid method of financial reporting.

23.9 Audits. In some states, associations, particularly very large ones, are required to have an annual audit or review by an independent certified public accountant. Even if not required by law, some associations prefer to have the financial records audited or reviewed each year. The board should select an auditor who is experienced in auditing owner associations.

An internal audit can also be conducted by the chief financial officer or the finance committee. The typical internal audit would consist of the following actions:

1. Assemble all financial records, including the journal, ledgers, checkbook, assessment records, canceled checks, invoices and bank statements.
2. Select, at random, one or two months' records to spot-check.
3. Check all invoices for markings indicating that they were approved for payment.
4. Check invoices against the checkbook and the canceled checks. Check endorsements on checks. See that the expense was allocated to the proper account.
5. Check journal and ledgers for entries to match the invoices and the canceled checks.
6. Check the monthly financial statement against the ledger accounts.
7. Check the accounts of the members, and if any questions arise, test a few by making inquiries as to whether the account shown on the books is consistent with the owner's records.
8. Check bank balances. The report from the bank should, of course, coincide with the association's records.
9. Check the fidelity bonds for the officers to make sure they are adequate in amount.
10. Check on the secretary's record-keeping. Check the minutes book and book of resolutions, contracts and correspondence. Make sure these are all in order and up-to-date.

If the association decides to have an audit performed by an outside CPA, two or three firms should be contacted to provide bids or proposals. After one firm has been selected, partly on the basis of fee and partly on the basis of reputation, the treasurer or chief financial officer should assemble the financial records for the audit, which will include:

- All general, cash and sales journals;
- Subsidiary ledgers;
- Records of individual accounts;
- Chart of Accounts;
- Bank statements, passbooks, certificates of deposit, bank reconciliations, canceled checks and check stubs;
- Invoices, paid and unpaid bills;
- Budget for the current year;
- Balance sheets and income statements prepared during the year;
- Minutes book;

- A statement or description of any litigation in which the association is currently involved; and
- A copy of the association's current insurance policy.

CHAPTER 24
Corporate Reports

24.1 Statutory Reports. Each state has a number of statutes requiring corporations to file periodic reports. These reports include income or franchise tax forms or informational reports for tax-exempt owners associations, and domestic corporation statements stating the names and addresses of the current officers and the agent for service of process. The officers should have a list of the statutorily-required reports, and should ensure that the corporation complies with the statutory deadlines. In many cases, there are monetary penalties for failure to file the reports on time.

24.2 Association Document Requirements. The association's legal documents may contain a number of requirements for filing of periodic corporate reports and for distribution of documents to the members. The responsible officers (secretary and chief financial officer) should be familiar with the requirements, and should see that corporate reports are prepared and distributed on a timely basis as required by the project legal documents.

24.3 Disclosure Requirements. Some states have adopted consumer protection laws that require an owners association to furnish certain reports to prospective purchasers and new owners. The board should familiarize itself with those legal requirements to ensure that they are followed. The failure to make a required disclosure to a purchaser who becomes an owner may result in an inability of the association to collect delinquent assessments or impose a special assessment upon the new buyer under certain circumstances.

24.4 Inspection and Copying of Reports. Members of an association have a right to inspect and copy the official records and reports of the association, which is usually delineated in the legal documents or state statutes. Typically, members may inspect association records and obtain copies at a nominal charge, and within a reasonable time upon a certain number of days' prior written request.

The accounting books and records and the minutes of the board and committee meetings are always open to inspection upon request of any member at any reasonable time for a purpose reasonably related to his/her interest as a member. Any officer or director has an absolute right at any reasonable time to inspect and copy all books, records, and documents of the association. In most cases, the board is authorized or has the authority to establish reasonable rules with respect to the notice to be given to the custodian of records, the hours and days of the week when inspections may be made, and the payment of the cost of reproducing copies.

Manager's Note: What are reasonable hours, and what is a reasonable request? To avoid confusion and to provide the best response to interested members, the board needs to create rules that specifically answer these two questions. Typically, if the association is professionally managed, "reasonable hours" are the normal business office hours of the management company (9 a.m. to 5 p.m., Monday through Friday, for example). However, if the association does not use professional management, "reasonable hours" might be the hours that the president or secretary of the board can be present to open the records (for example, 5 p.m. to 7 p.m., or on a Saturday morning). The board should also establish a policy to determine how many days in advance the member should submit a written request to see the documents. For example, it is probably not reasonable that a member ask to see all the records with a notice delivered only two hours before the member wishes to arrive.

What documents should be available for review, or what constitutes a reasonable request? While members have a right to inspect most documents, there are some records restricted for review only by members of the board of directors or officers of the association. These restricted records may include minutes of executive sessions of the board of directors, payroll records for association employees, medical records or personnel information of employees, bids and quotations from vendors, contracts, unit files containing correspondence from other owners, confidential litigation information, and certain letters from the association's attorney.

To prevent potentially confidential information from being distributed, copied or viewed by members, the board should consult with the association's attorney regarding what documents may not be viewed by the members. Also, to make it easier on the individual who will be preparing the documents for review, the member should be asked to include a list of the documents (s)he would like to review with their written request to view records.

24.5 Minutes Book. Associations are required to keep a minutes book, which should contain copies of all the basic legal documents of the association together with all meeting minutes and resolutions. The minutes book can be a simple three-ring binder, or a more elaborate minutes book can be purchased from corporate suppliers. See Chapter 13.7.

CHAPTER 25
Assessments

Manager's Note: Board members (especially the chief financial officer or treasurer) and homeowner members should be familiar with the following information.

25.1 Original Assessments. The original assessments for any project are computed by the developer of the project based on estimates of expected income and expenses. The assessments may be assessed to each unit equally, or may be pro-rated among units or lots on the basis of square footage or on the value of the home as a percentage of the total value of the entire project.

In projects regulated by the state's Department of Real Estate or other consumer protection agency, the amount of the assessment will have been reviewed and approved by that state agency based on its review of the project. Under most project legal documents, the assessment charged to a unit or lot is a debt of the owner at the time the assessment is levied. If unpaid, the delinquency becomes a lien upon his or her interest in the project upon recordation of a notice of assessment together with a description of the unit or lot.

Assessments are authorized both by the legal documents and by state laws pertaining to planned developments, condominiums and other common interest subdivisions.

Manager's Note: How soon after the association is "turned over" to the homeowners should the assessments and budget be adjusted? The original assessments are based solely on estimates of usage and expenses to be incurred by the association. As soon as the board of directors has taken over the association, a thorough review of all the actual expenses and income should be done to determine if the assessments will be sufficient to cover the actual expenses. Adjustments to assessment amounts should be made as soon as the board is aware of any shortfall in income.

25.2 Determining the Assessment and Pro-ration. The assessment amount must be set at a level to ensure availability of funds necessary to manage, operate, insure and maintain the project. The project legal documents are required to set forth the procedure for calculating and collecting regular and special assessments.

In most cases, the amount of ownership in the "common area" or the "undivided interest" in the project is the same for each unit. However, this is not always the case. Sometimes, the undivided interests in the project are based on square footage of the unit, while assessments are equal.

It is not advisable to allocate assessments based on the appraisals made by the county assessor's office, as this may result in inequitable assessments. The formula and method used by the county assessor in determining the value of a property may not be uniform and/or may be subject to limited adjustments that benefit owners who own their homes longer, while drastically increasing the assessed value of the home for a new owner.

Occasionally, the formula originally used to determine the amount of the assessment results in inequities. In such cases, it is possible for the association or one or more of the members to bring an action to amend the legal documents to create a more equitable distribution of assessments among all the owners.

The relative size of the dwelling units is not in itself the sole determining factor in setting assessments, although it is the most popular basis for pro-ration. The owner of the smallest unit in the project can make the same or greater use of the recreational facilities and open spaces of the project as the owner of the largest unit. Probably the most accurate and equitable method to pro-rate assessments is to allocate most expenses equally, except for certain items that are more directly related to square footage, such as exterior building maintenance, insurance, and reserves for roofing and painting.

Another method occasionally used to pro-rate assessments is the fair market value of the units, generally based on sales prices. This is not as reasonable a method as the square footage method, because value may have nothing to do with the cost of maintenance or upkeep. In a high-rise building, the unit on the top floor may have a higher value than one on the ground floor, but the cost of maintenance and upkeep may be identical. Quite often hybrid formulas are used. For example, assessments can be equal except for certain items that are based on square footage.

In the event of alterations in units as, for example, where one owner decides to add on a couple of bedrooms and receives permission from the architectural committee to do so, if the assessments in that project are based on square footage, there should be an adjustment in the allocations to take into consideration the increased size of the unit.

In commercial condominiums, the uses of the units may be taken into consideration. For example, a restaurant or a laundry would use much greater amounts of hot and cold water and gas or electricity than would an office in the same condominium project. If the utilities were not separately metered to the units, then the units having the greater usage of utilities should pay proportionately more.

25.3 Regular Assessments. The project declaration should provide the authority for the association to levy regular assessments on an annual basis that can paid in monthly installments. The regular assessments should be sufficient to pay for all of the expected expenses in the current budget of the association.

25.4 Special Assessments. Special assessments may be necessary from time to time to construct capital improvements, to pay for extraordinary expenses, or to pay for a shortfall in reserves. Special assessments are normally allocated in the same manner as are the general assessments. However, in some cases, state laws require that special assessments to raise funds for rebuilding or for major repair of the common area of the project be levied on the basis of the ratio of the square footage of the floor area of each unit. The board should consult the project legal documents and applicable state statutes to be sure that special assessments are not improperly allocated.

Boards may be required by the project legal documents or by state law to obtain the consent of a majority of owners before levying a special assessment that exceeds a certain percent of the budgeted gross expenses of the association for that fiscal year.

25.5 Increases in Annual Assessments. Some project documents and state laws limit the authority of the board to increase assessments by more than a certain percentage above the preceding year's assessment unless approved by a majority of the owners. There may be certain exceptions, such as assessments for maintenance or repair of the common areas or payment of emergency expenses. The board should always consult its legal documents and be familiar with state laws that apply to assessments before making a substantial increase. *See Form 20 for an example of a Notice of Increase in Assessments.*

25.6 Decreases in Assessments. Some legal documents and some state laws limit the authority of the board to decrease the assessments beyond a certain percentage below the assessments of the prior year. This is intended to protect and preserve the property rights of the members by ensuring that the funds available for the maintenance and upkeep of the project are not jeopardized by the actions of the board of directors. In such a situation, the approval of a majority of the owners will be required to decrease the assessments by more than the stated allowable percentage.

25.7 Notice of Assessments. In most states, associations are required to give written notice to the members of the amount and due dates of annual and special assessments. Normally, assessments become a lien only when a notice of assessment is recorded. The notice must take a certain form; usually the description of the subdivision interest against which the assessments has been made and the name of the record owner must be included in the recorded document. In some states, the notice must also state the name and address of a trustee authorized by the association to enforce the lien by sale if the lien is to be enforced by power of sale. The officer or committee in charge of notices of assessments should be familiar with the legal requirements to ensure that there is full compliance.

25.8 Commencement. Assessments normally begin on the first day of the month following the close of escrow on the sale of the first subdivision interest in the project. In phased projects, the assessments within a particular phase generally begin on the date of the first closing or on the first day of the month following the closing of the first conveyance in that phase. Sometimes assessments may be partially delayed on improvements still under construction under certain conditions as provided in the legal documents and/or by state law.

One of the responsibilities of a newly elected board is to check the records to see if assessments were started when required, and if the records indicate that these have been paid up-to-date. If not, the board has a responsibility to collect the assessments.

25.9 Phased Assessments. In some projects the developer is required to pay assessments on all of the units or lots that it owns, starting from the time of sale of the first unit or lot in the project. In a large project, this can become very financially burdensome. In order to reduce assessments during the initial period of sales, the developer may decide to divide the project into several phases. Assessments in phased projects are levied only against the units or lots in a phase in which units or lots are currently being sold, and no assessments are levied against homes in subsequent phases until the sale of the first such home in that phase. This way, the developer can avoid paying assessments on homes that have not yet begun or are still under construction. This method also avoids building up a large surplus of association funds at the expense of the developer. It is the responsibility of the board in a phased project to see that assessments commence on time and that collections start when required as new phases are annexed to the project.

25.10 Exemption from Assessments. Some project documents and state laws permit the developer to exempt certain subdivision interests from a portion of assessments that would otherwise be attributable to those separate interests while the buildings or amenities are under construction. The exemption is generally limited to certain specified items, which include such things as reserves for roof replacement and exterior maintenance, walkway and carport lighting, refuse disposal, cable television, domestic water supplied to living units, and insurance attributable to completed dwelling units. Generally, where such exemptions are allowed, they are limited in time. For example, they may terminate automatically when a notice of completion has been recorded, or a certain number of days after issuance of a building permit for a dwelling. Partial exemptions of this type will have an effect on the association's budget.

25.11 Payment of Assessments. Due dates are usually established by the project legal documents. Assessments not paid when due will generally accrue interest, and sometimes a late penalty if the legal documents allow. Some states have laws that limit the amount of interest and penalties that can be charged. These same laws may also prescribe a certain grace period during which no interest or penalties can be charged. The board should be familiar with these laws to ensure compliance. Generally, the project's legal documents provide that annual assessments may be collected in monthly installments.

Periodically, homeowners or the developer of the project may become delinquent in payment of their monthly or annual assessments. In these instances, the board will need to collect the amounts due in a timely manner. *See Chapter 26 for information about collections.*

25.12 Challenging Assessments. An owner may challenge an assessment that (s)he believes is beyond the authority of the association to levy by bringing an action for declaratory and injunctive relief in the state court system. An owner may defend against the enforcement of an assessment by alleging waiver (the association has not enforced the provision before) and estoppel (similar to waiver, except there must be some inducement on the part of the association). Both owners desiring to contest enforcement actions and the association should seek legal counsel in such cases where technical defenses are used to challenge assessments.

25.13 Accelerating Assessments. Regular assessments are usually made for a one-year period and collected in monthly installments. If the declaration does not provide for monthly installments, there is a potential risk that an assessment is not technically in default until the end of the fiscal year. If the declaration provides for acceleration in the event of default in the payment of a monthly installment, the association can then exercise the acceleration clause and collect the entire assessment when the installment becomes delinquent. However, some state regulatory agencies disapprove of acceleration clauses.

If acceleration is provided for and an assessment has been accelerated based on default, the foreclosure of a first lien prior to the association's lien may extinguish not only the delinquent assessments up to that point in time, but also the assessments for the remainder of the fiscal year, unless the declaration specifically provides that in the event of foreclosure of a lien subordinate to a senior deed of trust, the transferee will take title subject to any installments that have not yet become due and payable as of the date the transferee takes title by foreclosure.

25.14 Billing for Assessments. The bill for an annual or monthly assessment should be in a standard form and sent to all members.

CHAPTER 26
Collection of Assessments

26.1 Successful Collections. Collection techniques include telephone calls, demand letters, imposition of monetary penalties, late charges, interest, suspension of membership in the association and privileges for use of common area facilities, and suspension of voting privileges. If none of these techniques are successful, the association may either sue the owner directly or establish a statutory assessment lien and begin foreclosure proceedings (*see Chapter 27.3*).

Some banks or savings and loans offer collection services for a small charge, and most management associations include collection of assessments as part of their service. The service may include filing liens and small claims court actions, although those would, of course, have to be authorized in advance by the board.

Manager's Note: The best and most successful collection methods are those in which action is taken early and consistently to collect outstanding assessments. As for all businesses, the longer that an amount remains delinquent, the less likely are the chances of collecting it.

26.2 Collection Methods. The treasurer or chief financial officer, or whoever is in charge of collections, should have available a series of standard methods to collect assessments. First should be a form letter that goes to members who have not paid by the due date, which may be 15 days after the assessment was due. *See Form 23 for a sample reminder notice.*

If the form letter fails to cause the delinquent owner to pay, a Notice of Delinquent Assessment can be recorded, stating the description of the delinquent owner's separate interest in the subdivision, the name of the owner, the amount of the delinquent assessment, and the amount of any interest or penalty that has been added to the assessment. *See Forms 24 and 25 for sample forms of the Notice of Delinquent Assessment.*

26.3 Collection of Assessments from Developers. Developers of a project are required to pay assessments on all units or lots that they own, just like all the other owners. Most state regulatory agencies require developers to post a bond, cash, letter of credit or other form of security to ensure payment of the assessments on the developer's units or lots for a certain period of time. A typical state statute would require the developer to post a bond equal to six months' worth of assessments on all the homes that are for sale in the project, and would require that the bond be kept posted until 80 percent of the units or lots have been sold. The bond would then be released only if the developer was current in the payment of all of its assessments. The project legal documents and the state laws in such cases should provide the remedies for enforcing the bonded obligation of the developer who is delinquent in the payment of its assessments. The association has the same remedies against the developer that it has against its own members; that is, to file suit for delinquencies or to file a notice of delinquency, and to file a notice of foreclosure and actually foreclose against the developer's units or lots.

Under certain circumstances, the developer or its officers, agents or employees may become personally liable for assessments. An example would be where the developer and its staff functioned as the board of directors of the association for several months, during which time the association failed to collect assessments from the developer. In such circumstances, the developer and its employees who were serving as members of the board of directors could be liable in their fiduciary capacity to the association. They may be required by the courts to personally pay the amount of the assessments still owed by the developer, in the event that the amounts of the assessments cannot be collected from the developer.

Frequently, developers will fail to pay assessments to the association and will instead pay all of the expenses of the association. When the books and records of the association are turned over to the newly elected board, the developer may represent that all expenses and bills have been paid and that the developer has taken care of all those matters, and the associaion can now commence with assessents. In such case, the association may have the legal right to hold the developer responsible for all of the uncollected or unpaid assessments on the units or lots that the developer has owned and still owns up to that point. Even where the developer has paid all of the expenses of the association over a period of time, it may be still liable for the assessments that it should have paid to the association during that period of time, although it may be entitled to an offset for the expenses that it has paid.

26.4 Delinquent Assessments.
The association may or may not be required by state law or by project legal documents to notify an owner prior to recording a notice of delinquent assessment. Once an assessment is delinquent, the association has several remedies besides filing a notice of delinquency. It may be empowered to declare monetary penalties, temporary suspension of voting rights, or temporary suspension of rights to use the recreational facilities. Certainly a notice of delinquent assessment should be filed promptly in every case where an assessment is delinquent. Among other things, that will protect the association against the possibility that the unit could be sold before an assessment lien could be established of record and the association would then be unable to collect the past-due assessment, unless it sued the selling owner personally. The association always has a choice between litigation, through a suit in small claims court, municipal court or some trial court of lower jurisdiction, or pursuing foreclosure either by using the power of sale or by judicial foreclosure.

26.5 Assessment Liens. An assessment, including charges such as interest, costs, late charges, penalties and attorneys' fees, becomes a lien on a separate subdivision interest when a notice of delinquent assessment is recorded properly. *See Forms 24 and 25.* In some states, monetary penalties cannot be included in liens that are enforceable by foreclosure using power of sale.

26.6 Costs Incurred in Collecting Assessments. In collecting assessments, the association may sue the owner or member directly on the obligation, or follow the lien and foreclosure procedures authorized by the declaration and by state statutes (*see Chapter 27.1*). Costs incurred by the association in bringing an owner into compliance with the project restrictions or to repair damage to the project common areas can be collected by lawsuit or can be included in a special assessment against the owner, which assessment can then be enforced by lien and foreclosure in the same manner as a regular assessment. In some states, special assessments imposed as penalties for failure to comply with the restrictions or to reimburse the association for costs incurred or to repair damage to common area facilities may not be enforced by lien and foreclosure proceedings.

26.7 One Form of Action Rule. Some state statutes provide what is known as the "one form of action" only rule. It provides that if the association wishes to enforce an assessment lien, it has to take its choice between foreclosure of a lien and a suit for collection. Where the one form of action rule applies, the association must make an election either to file suit in court or, in the alternative, elect a foreclosure remedy by filing and foreclosing a lien under the foreclosure statutes, either by power of sale or by judicial foreclosure. *See Chapter 26.10.*

26.8 Subordination and Priorities. Most condominium and planned development declarations contain a mortgagee protection clause that provides for subordination of any lien for assessments to the lien of a first mortgage or deed of trust against a subdivision interest. This means that any lender who records a mortgage or deed of trust prior to the recordation of a notice of delinquent assessments will have priority over the assessment lien. This is generally true even if a deed of trust was subordinated to the recorded declaration, either by reason of the developer having signed the declaration or because it signed a separate subordination agreement. The reason for giving the first lender priority over assessment liens is because if it could not be assured of such priority, it probably would not make loans to purchasers of lots or units.

Mortgages or deeds of trust that are filed of record after an assessment lien is filed will be subordinate to that lien. Most lenders will not make a loan on property secured by a mortgage or deed of trust unless they can be assured that there are no assessment liens of record against the property on the date that their mortgage or deed of trust goes of record. Some declarations distinguish between first and second liens with respect to the priority of assessments. First lenders may be given the protection of priority, but second and third lenders are not. Some state regulatory agencies prohibit giving priorities to second and third lenders. This may have the disadvantage of discouraging institutional lenders form making loans secured by second deeds of trust under conditions where there is still a substantial owner's equity in the property, above and beyond the combined total of the first and second trust deeds. However, it also protects the association against an owner who might otherwise put a large second deed of trust on his/her property and then vacate the unit, leaving the association with its delinquent assessments subject to first and second liens which together equal the total value of the unit. That would preclude the association from collecting the delinquent assessment by foreclosing its lien, because it would have to take the unit subject to the first and second deeds of trust and there would be no equity in the unit.

26.9 Foreclosure. Once a lien has been established (*see Chapter 27.2*), the association may foreclose the lien by power of sale. This is sometimes referred to as a trustee's sale, or non-judicial foreclosure. *See Chapter 27.3.*

26.10 Judicial Foreclosure. As an alternative to non-judicial or power of sale foreclosure, the association may file a civil action to foreclose the lien. *See Chapter 26.11.*

26.11 Collection By Suit. In lieu of establishing an assessment lien and foreclosing on that lien, the association may elect to sue the owner directly on the debt. An assessment is the debt of the owner at the time it is made, which is normally at the beginning of each month.

In determining whether to file foreclosure of a lien or to sue, the association should consider such factors as:

- The amount of the obligation;
- The potential defenses;
- Other assets of the owner that may satisfy a money judgment;
- Time considerations;
- Prior actions of the association against similar obligations;
- The extent to which such an action would set a precedent; and
- The probable costs, including attorneys' fees.

If the association elects to sue, it will have a choice between small claims court, where there is a jurisdictional limit and where no attorneys are allowed to participate, or a municipal court or other lower civil court, where attorneys can participate and the limits of jurisdiction are much larger than in small claims court. One advantage of suing in municipal court and not in small claims court is that attorneys' fees may be recovered, provided the project legal documents allow recovery.

Suing in small claims court is less expensive than suing in a higher court, but the association cannot be represented by counsel. Also, in some jurisdictions there is no appeal from a small claims court decision if the association loses, and the unit or lot owner may be entitled to appeal and have a new trial.

26.12 Personal Liability for Assessments. The project's declaration may provide that the owner of a subdivision interest is personally liable for payment of assessments, so that if the owner should sell the unit, the association can still file a lawsuit and collect a personal judgment for the delinquent assessments.

26.11 Late Charges and Interest. Late charges may be imposed against an owner for delinquent assessments. In some states and under some legal documents, the maximum amount of the late charges is limited. Interest may also be charged on delinquent assessments. Assessments generally become delinquent after 15 or 30 days; interest normally begins to accrue on a certain date, which may be specified in legal documents or may be prescribed by state laws. Some legal documents and some state laws put limits on the amount of interest that can be charged. The chief financial officer of the association should keep current on what the maximum late fees and interest charges are, and ensure that the association follows these rules. The legal documents should be amended from time to time, if necessary, in order to bring them into compliance with changes in the law.

26.13 Attorneys' Fees. The project legal documents may provide for the recovery of attorneys' fees when collecting delinquent assessments or for enforcing provisions of the project legal documents. In some cases, even if the project legal documents do not so provide, state statutes may permit the recovery of attorneys' fees by an association that is successful in a collection or enforcement action. The board of directors should review its legal documents to determine whether or not the attorneys' fees clause is included, and if not, the board should amend the documents to include a provision for collection of attorneys' fees.

26.14 Homestead Exemption. Some states have homestead exemption laws that permit an owner to file a declaration of homestead against the property and protect it from any liens or foreclosures. Usually, enabling statutes create an exception in the case of a homeowners association lien, so that a homestead exemption does not protect the owner against foreclosure of an assessment lien. It is possible that a valid homestead exemption could protect an owner against a judgment obtained by the association, as distinguished from the foreclosure of an assessment lien. State statutes should be reviewed in any case where this question could arise.

26.15 Estoppel Certificates. The owner of a property in a common-interest subdivision is required by many state laws and by some legal documents to provide a prospective purchaser with a written statement from an authorized representative of the association. This statement will include the amount of any unpaid assessments, including late charges, interest, and cost of collection, which are due as of the date the statement is given. Some state laws require an association to deliver such a statement in writing within a certain period of time. The association may be permitted to make a nominal charge for this service. Once such a statement is given, the purchaser is entitled to rely upon it, and the association is said to be "estopped" from thereafter claiming that assessments were delinquent or from attempting to collect delinquent assessments that are not included in the statement provided by the association.

CHAPTER 27
Liens

27.1 Authority for Liens. The project legal documents should provide for the creation of a lien by filing a Notice of Assessment.

In some projects, a blanket assessment is filed against all units or lots in the project at the beginning of each year. That establishes the lien for that year's annual assessment as a matter of record, so that a priority over subsequently recorded liens and encumbrances is established. However, there are some drawbacks to blanket liens. A release of lien must be recorded when the assessment charges are paid. Assessments generally are not satisfied all at the same time, so the recording of multiple releases may be required. It is also possible that the association may have to file monthly releases as monthly installments are paid.

Where blanket liens are not allowed or are not made use of, an individual lien must be filed against a unit or lot when the owner becomes delinquent in payment of the assessment. To establish a lien, a notice of the delinquent assessment must be recorded with the county recorder of the county in which the unit or lot is located. *See Forms 24 and 25 for samples of a Notice of Delinquent Assessment.*

Some association documents do not provide the association with the authority to record a lien against the project. In such cases, the association's remedy is to file a suit to collect delinquent assessments. It may be possible in such a case for the association to amend its documents to permit the filing of liens, but it will probably require the unanimous vote of all owners. If the lien is to include charges in addition to the assessment, such as interest, penalties, costs and attorneys' fees, the notice must specify the charges, and the declaration must authorize such charges to be included in the lien. A notice of lien must be signed by an authorized representative of the association, usually either an officer or member of the board of directors.

In some states, a lien will expire automatically one year after the date of recordation, if the lien is not satisfied or released or enforcement proceedings initiated within that time. It is also possible in some states to extend the lien for an additional period of time by recording a written Notice of Extension.

27.2 Notices. A number of different notices must be filed in connection with the enforcement of assessment liens. A notice of assessment can either be filed as a "blanket lien" against all units or lots, or individual notices of assessment can be filed against each unit or lot. Some legal documents and some state statutes provide for filing Notices of Assessments, while others provide for filing Notices of Delinquent Assessments. Generally, the form is substantially the same. It requires the legal description of the unit or lot, the name of the owner, the amount of the assessment lien including assessments, penalties, interest and other charges, and the notice must be signed by an authorized representative of the management body of the association, which means an officer, director, or duly authorized and designated representative.

If the assessment is delinquent and the association wishes to follow lien foreclosure procedures, under most state statutes a Notice of Default must be filed. *See Form 26 for a Notice of Default.* If the lien is not paid after filing a Notice of Delinquency, the association may proceed to file a Notice of Default, which sets in motion a statutory time period (usually three months), during which time the owner of the unit or lot may pay the assessment, plus interest and fees. The final notice is a Notice of Sale that is recorded several times in a newspaper published in the county in which the property is located. The Notice of Sale indicates the date, time and place at which the property will be sold to satisfy the lien.

27.3 Enforcement by Foreclosure of Lien. An assessment lien may be foreclosed either by power of sale or by judicial foreclosure. Foreclosure by power of sale is sometimes referred to as "non-judicial foreclosure." Under some state statutes, the validity of a foreclosure by power of sale conducted by an association is questionable, so it may be advisable for the board to file a judicial foreclosure action or to file suit instead of pursuing the foreclosure by power of sale remedy. To enable the association to pursue a foreclosure by power of sale, the legal documents should authorize the naming of a trustee to enforce the assessment lien by sale, and the Notice of Assessment should state the name and address of the trustee authorized to enforce the lien. When no trustee is named, it may be difficult to get someone to act as trustee and to obtain title insurance from a title company, insuring a trustee's deed from the foreclosure sale. As a practical matter, the action to foreclose by power of sale seldom ever gets to the point where the home is actually offered for sale at the title company or on the courthouse steps. Generally, enough pressure is brought to bear on the owner by the foreclosure action itself that the owner will pay the delinquency rather than permit the property to be sold.

If the association elects to file a judicial foreclosure action, it will have to retain an attorney to pursue the action in court.

27.4 Satisfaction, Release and Removal of Liens. Upon payment of the assessment and any interest or other charges specified on the Notice of Delinquent Assessment, the association is required to record a Notice of Satisfaction and Release of Lien. There may not be any time specified in either the legal documents or under laws within which the release of lien must be recorded, but the association should proceed to do so within a reasonable time in order to avoid any potential liability to the owner for clouding the title. *See Form 27 for a Notice of Satisfaction and Release of Lien.*

27.5 Use of Liens to Collect Fines. Some statutes prohibit associations from using their assessment and lien powers to collect penalties or fines imposed as a disciplinary measure against a member, or to collect reimbursement of costs incurred to repair common area damage caused by a member. Statutes may also prohibit the association from using lien powers to bring the member and the unit or lot into compliance with the governing instruments of the project. In some cases, the statutes and regulations that prohibit using assessment powers to collect liens or fines only apply while the project is being offered for sale under a public report issued by the state Department of Real Estate or consumer protection agency. After the project has been fully sold, the new owners are free to amend their legal documents to give the association the power to use its lien and assessment powers to collect fines or penalties.

If the association does go through with a foreclosure sale to the actual bidding process, the association will bid in the amount of its assessment lien, including all interest, penalties, attorneys' fees and costs or expenses incurred with respect to the publication of the Notice of Default, Notice of Sale, and the holding of the sale. If there is a higher bid, it must be for cash. The cash from the successful bidder in the amount of the association's lien will be paid to the association. If there is a first deed of trust of record against the property, the successful bidder will take the property subject to that first deed of trust. If no one overbids the association's opening bid, the association will have bought the property for the amount of its lien. It will then own the property, subject to the deeds of trust that are of record at that time. Depending upon whether second trust deeds are given any sort of priority over assessment liens, if there is more than one deed of trust, it is possible that the assessment lien may wipe out the junior encumbrances. If the association acquires title to a unit or lot, it will be able to rent the property or offer it for sale. Meanwhile, if the unit or lot is subject to a deed of trust, the association will have to keep the payments current to prevent a foreclosure sale brought by the lender.

27.6 Mechanics' Liens. Mechanics' liens are liens filed by persons or companies furnishing labor, materials or equipment used in connection with the construction of a project. The purpose of mechanics' lien laws are to protect contractors, laborers and suppliers of material, by giving them an opportunity to collect money from the owner of property who has benefited from their work or by the supply of their material, where the owner or contractor who was supposed to pay them has defaulted. State statutes specify who is entitled to file liens, and what the procedures are for filing and perfecting liens.

In a condominium project, it is possible for a mechanics' lien claim to be filed against the entire project, even though work was only done in one area of the project and the claim was filed prior to the completion of the project and for conveyance of title to the first unit. Even after completion of the project and conveyance of title to one unit, if all owners own an interest in the common area, a mechanics' lien claim can be filed against the entire project if work was done in the common area. It is also possible for unit owners to give either express or implied consent in the case of emergency repairs, and this consent would entitle the person performing those repairs to file a lien. In a condominium project, the owner of a unit may, if permitted by statute, remove a lien from the unit by paying the fraction of the total lien attributable to the unit under the recorded declaration.

Where a condominium is divided into several separate buildings and/or separate lots, and the common area property owned by the association is also on a separate lot, it is possible to insulate units from mechanics' lien claims filed on other units where the work was actually done. In planned development projects where each owner owns fee title to the lot, the work done on one particular lot may entitle the person doing that work to file a mechanics' lien claim against that lot. It does not entitle him or her to file a mechanics' lien claim against other lots in a project.

There are often technical and complicated rules for filing, perfecting, and removing mechanics' lien claims. Any time a mechanics' lien claim appears and alleges to affect a condominium or planned development project or any of the homes therein, the association's attorney should be contacted.

CHAPTER 28
Enforcement of Restrictions

28.1 Enforcement of Non-Monetary Obligations. The best way to enforce the restrictions, and particularly use restrictions, is by preventing violations from occurring, by making certain that each owner is aware of the restrictions and association rules and regulations that are adopted and changed from time to time. The association should make sure that every owner is fully informed at all times, by being given copies of the current provisions of the legal documents for the project.

Manager's Note: A monthly newsletter, which is carefully laid out and written, is an excellent means of "reminding" homeowners and residents about the association rules and any changes to the rules. In addition to a newsletter, the association should generate a homeowner's handbook that provides a succinct, easy-to-read explanation of the general rules and restrictions.

28.2 Authority to Enforce Restrictions. Associations derive their authority both from state law and from the project's legal documents. The authority to enforce a restriction rests with the board of directors, and can be delegated by the board to officers and, to a limited extent, to the professional manager hired by the association.

28.3 Obligation to Enforce. The association has a duty to administer and enforce the covenants, conditions, and restrictions, and cannot legally refuse to administer or enforce such provisions. The association acts as a quasi-government in exercising its functions, maintaining the project, enforcing the restrictions and collecting assessments. The directors of the association are held to a high standard of responsibility with respect to members, and have a fiduciary duty to act in the best interests of the membership. An association could not, for example, arbitrarily refuse to enforce architectural or use restrictions. In addition to having the authority to enforce by virtue of state laws and the legal documents themselves, there are many judicial decisions that give associations the authority and the duty to enforce the legal documents for the project.

28.4 Prerequisites to Enforcement. There are certain prerequisites to the proper enforcement of an association's restrictions. First, the association must follow its own rules and procedures, which are set forth in its legal documents and meeting minutes, and are contained in other customary procedures that it has previously followed. Second, the association must enforce rules that are fair and reasonable. If the association adopts unfair and unreasonable rules and attempts to enforce them, the members against whom such rules are being enforced may have legal defenses or other remedies available to them. Third, the board of directors or the officers who are involved in enforcement are required to make a good-faith determination that there has indeed been a violation, and that enforcement actions should take place. Fourth, before an enforcement action can take place, the matter should be brought to the attention of the board, and the board should meet to consider the matter. The decision to proceed with an enforcement action should be made part of the minutes of the board meeting.

28.5 Enforcement by Developer. During the time that the project is still under the control of the developer, the developer has the authority (by virtue of its control over the board of directors and its position as declarant) to enforce the restrictions. It also has the duty to enforce the restrictions and can be held accountable by individual owners who are concerned that violations are neither being corrected nor rules being enforced.

28.6 Responsibility of Officers and Directors for Enforcement of Restrictions. The board of directors and the officers of an association have a fiduciary responsibility as well as a legal duty to enforce the restrictions. Non-enforcement of the restrictions can constitute a breach of the director's fiduciary obligation, for which the director can be held personally liable.

28.7 Waiver. If the association fails to enforce a certain restriction over a period of time, this may result in the permanent waiver of the restriction and make the association powerless to enforce it in the future. It is possible to authorize temporary suspension of the rules or of the rights of owners, provided notice and a hearing are given, without any waiver resulting.

28.8 Discipline of Members. The board may take disciplinary action against an owner for failure to pay assessments or for violation of the rules and regulations or use restrictions. The disciplinary action may take the form of a fine or suspension of certain rights, such as the right to use the recreational facilities, or the temporary suspension of voting rights. However, the board cannot cause a forfeiture of an owner's right to the enjoyment of the home due to a failure to comply with provisions of the governing instruments of the project. The exception would be a court judgment, a decision arising out of arbitration, or a foreclosure sale, either under power of sale or judicial foreclosure. The right to the full use and enjoyment of the owner's home is such a basic right that the association is not allowed to deprive him or her of that right through its own internal mechanisms, without the concurrence of an independent third party in the form of a court or arbitration hearing. The association can fine a member or impose certain limitations upon the rights to vote or to make use of common area facilities, but it cannot expel the owner from the subdivision.

28.9 Fines. Fines can be a very effective means to enforce association regulations. In order to levy fines, however, the association must be given the authority under either its legal documents or state law. In order to impose a fine, due process must be followed, which means, at a minimum, that the owner who is to be fined must be given reasonable notice of a hearing and the opportunity to be heard. *See Chapter 29 for a discussion of due process and the conduct of hearings.*

28.10 Enforcement by Owners. Violations of the declaration give rise to an individual cause of action for damages against the defendant violator and in favor of a plaintiff homeowner residing in the subdivision, and/or a member of the association. A member of an association can bring an action against another member who is in violation of the restrictions if the board fails to take action. A member may also bring suit to require the association to enforce the declaration.

28.11 Remedies and Defenses.
The remedies available for an action arising out of a breach of the restrictive covenants include:

- Injunction against future breaches, with or without damages for past breaches;
- Temporary injunctive relief pending the determination of the applicability and enforceability of a restrictive covenant;
- Injunctive relief to restrain a continuing violation, to prevent threatened violations, or to compel removal of prohibited structures; or
- Declaratory relief.

In some cases, the courts may grant a temporary restraining order to the association prior to the hearing on the question of a preliminary injunction. In such a case, the association might have to post a bond to obtain prompt relief as a safeguard against a later finding that the restraining order was erroneously granted.

Depending upon the provisions of the legal documents and the applicable local rules, attorneys' fees may be recoverable by the prevailing party in an action to enforce the declaration. If the action was resolved unfavorably to the association, it might not only fail to get the injunctive relief that it sought, but might also have to pay the defendant's attorneys' fees.

The following defenses might be raised to an action for enforcement of restrictions:

- The covenant was not properly adopted or amended;
- The defendant was released from his or her obligation under the covenant;
- The association acquiesced to the defendant's conduct or waived or abandoned the right to enforce the restrictions;
- The association delayed too long in attempting to enforce the covenants; or
- It is estopped from enforcing the restrictions because of its own conduct.

The doctrine of hardship or "changed circumstances" may be asserted to defeat the enforcement of a covenant. The changed circumstances defense alleges that the restriction has outlived its usefulness and should no longer be enforced. Where the doctrine of relative hardship comes into play, the court is asked to balance the equities, and to compare the harm resulting from enforcement against the benefits to be gained. For example, if the architectural restrictions required the use of pine siding, and an owner used fir siding, the court might say that requiring the owner to remove the fir siding and replace it with pine siding would be inequitable, particularly where the owner could show that pine siding was difficult to obtain in that location.

28.12 Arbitration. Arbitration is an alternative to litigation. The matter in dispute is heard by an arbitrator rather than a judge or jury. The arbitrator can be one person or a panel of two or more persons.

The American Arbitration Association and other similar organizations provide numerous experienced professionals from which to select arbitrators. Arbitration generally produces faster results at less expense than would litigation.

Arbitration can be binding or non-binding. If binding, there is no opportunity to appeal the decision from an unfavorable ruling.

Project legal documents and state statutes frequently provide for non-binding arbitration or mediation (*see Chapter 28.13*) to be attempted first, before the courts will allow a lawsuit to be filed. The term "alternative dispute resolution" or "ADR" refers to the use of arbitration or mediation as an alternative to litigation.

ADR has become increasingly popular as the most effective method to resolve disputes between members of an association, or between the association and its members. For a complete set of rules and forms, contact the local chapter of the American Arbitration Association.

28.13 Mediation. Mediation is a voluntary process whereby the parties to a dispute seek to resolve their differences with the aid of a neutral party who acts as a facilitator. Mediation is always non-binding. The mediator has no authority to make any ruling or to decide the matter in favor of any participant. The mediator can only reason with the parties and use persuasion and logic to bring the parties to an agreement.

In the hands of a skilled mediator, mediation is surprisingly successful in resolving disputes between homeowners and between the association and its members. Mediation is also quick and relatively inexpensive.

***Manager's Note:** Mediation, or arbitration, or litigation? Before choosing litigation, the association should work quickly to educate or understand the position of the homeowner or members. The more quickly the association reacts and remains open to possibilities for resolving disputes, the greater the likelihood that mediation or arbitration can bring a satisfactory resolution for all parties.*

There may be state statutes that require an association to attempt mediation or arbitration to resolve a problem prior to engaging in litigation. When in doubt about whether such requirements affect the association, the attorney should be consulted for more information and advice on the proper procedures to ensure the best results.

CHAPTER 29
Due Process

29.1 Due Process Considerations. All associations are subject in some way to the rule of due process. Due process under the United States Constitution has certain legal meanings. Generally, the clause is applied under the United States Constitution in cases where action taken by an entity which is part of the state government has allegedly deprived an individual of life, liberty or property without adequate and appropriate legal process and procedures. Obviously, a homeowners association is not an arm of the state government, so it is unlikely that action by a homeowners association would violate U.S. constitutional rights. However, homeowners associations are like quasi-governments, and courts have imposed rules of due process upon them.

Action by a homeowners association may also violate the due process protections of a state constitution. Courts have generally applied a minimum standard of due process of law to the activities of associations and their governing bodies. In some court decisions, the following test has been used in order to determine whether or not the action of the association meets the basic legal requirements of reasonable due process:

1. Is the action taken or proposed clearly within or reasonably related to the purposes of the association?
2. Is the action clearly within or reasonably related to the association's powers?
3. Is the action taken reasonable with respect to its application and the scope of its application?
4. Has the association acted with reasonable due process in carrying out the action?

Whether the action or proposed action is reasonably related to the purposes of the association and is within the power of the association can normally be decided from a review of the association's legal documents. Whether the action is reasonable in application and scope depends on the circumstances in each case. Whether the association has acted with reasonable due process depends upon whether the association has reasonable rules, and has followed those rules.

Minimum standards of reasonable due process in carrying out an action require, initially, notice to the owner of the rule which he/she is alleged to have violated. An association cannot pass a rule on Monday and then seek to immediately fine an owner for violating it on Tuesday, if the owner has not had reasonable notice of the rule. Notice also means that the owner is given notice of the claimed violation, an opportunity to be confronted with the charges brought against the owner, to see and hear the witnesses who have seen the violation, and to be allowed to present his or her own defense. Project legal documents and/or state statutes may contain notice provisions such as sending notices a certain number of days in advance, and sending notices by first-class or registered mail.

Due process also requires some form of hearing if requested by the accused member. In most associations that have established procedures in this regard, discipline is not imposed without noticing a hearing and giving the accused member reasonable opportunity to attend the hearing, listen to the evidence presented, and present evidence in his or her own defense. Due process implies that the member will have the right to cross-examine witnesses who testify against him/her, and will have the right to be confronted by those witnesses (e.g., no anonymous accusations).

Some statutes require a delay between the decision to impose a penalty and the enforcement thereof in order to give the owner time to take appropriate corrective action or to appeal, if an appeal is warranted. One exception to the hearing and notice procedures is the enforcement of delinquent assessments through the imposition of lien and foreclosure remedies or the imposition of penalties or late charges. However, if additional penalties such as suspension of membership rights or voting rights are planned, notice and hearing procedures should be followed. In some associations, a disciplinary committee handles disciplinary proceedings. In such cases the committee should follow all of the due process requirements. An additional requirement of due process would be that the owner would have the opportunity to appeal the decision of the committee to the board of directors.

29.2 Attorneys. An accused member should have the right to bring an attorney to represent him/her and to defend him or her at any hearing held by the association for the purpose of imposing discipline.

29.3 Evidence. Evidence at the hearing should be, as it is in any courtroom hearing, presented in the form of witness testimonies, exhibits or written documents. Witnesses should be subject to cross-examination, and should testify under oath. Documentary evidence should be authenticated. Exhibits such as photographs should be properly identified and preserved as part of the record.

29.4 Preservation of Record of Hearing. The record of the hearing should be preserved for a reasonable period of time, or at least until any appeal period has expired. The records should consist of any exhibits or documentary evidence presented, and should be either a taped transcript of the meeting or detailed written notes. If it is a meeting before the board and a resolution was adopted to impose the discipline, the resolution should be included in the official minutes of the meetings.

29.5 Appeals. There should be a provision for appeal from any committee or any hearing body that is subordinate to the board of directors. The association need not specifically provide for an appeal from a decision of the board of directors to the courts. That option is always available to any member who feels that (s)he has been treated unfairly or that due process has been violated. Some statutes put a limitation (such as one year) on the right to appeal from disciplinary action taken by an association against a member.

29.6 Delegation to Committees. Some associations delegate the entire process of hearings and imposing discipline to a committee charged with that responsibility. In a larger organization, this is probably a worthwhile idea. The committee can become quite efficient and judicious in conducting hearings and imposing appropriate discipline; however, this system may deteriorate if the wrong people are permitted to serve on the committee. The rules should permit any member who appears before the committee to appeal an unfavorable decision to the board of directors.

CHAPTER 30
Legal Actions and Lawsuits Against the Association

30.1 Actions Against the Association. Actions by third parties may be brought against an association, whether incorporated or unincorporated. A member may also bring actions against the association, despite the fact that, at least theoretically, (s)he is suing himself/herself. For example, if a member is injured when (s)he trips over a sprinkler head in the common area, (s)he may be able to bring an action against the association to recover for his/her injuries. As a member of that association, (s)he may have to contribute through his/her assessments to the association's expenses, including the purchase of an insurance policy to pay claims and payment of the deductible amount. An association is a separate legal entity and can be sued as such and served with process, and will have to defend itself and pay any judgments rendered against it.

30.2 Tort Liability of Associations. An owners association is potentially liable in tort for its negligence or the negligence of its employees, officers or agents. Some examples of acts or omissions that may cause an association to be liable include:

- Failure to maintain the common areas;
- Negligence of maintenance personnel who are employees of the association;
- Failure to adequately supervise pools, playgrounds or recreational facilities;
- Failure to properly inspect and maintain fire detection equipment;
- Wrongful entry of an owner's unit;
- Automobile accidents involving vehicles owned by the association or driven on association business;
- Product liability, where food, beverages or consumable products are served by the association or dispensed by vending machines owned or operated by the association.

A homeowners association has been held liable in tort based on negligence for failure to provide adequate lighting of the common area under circumstances where the lack of lighting was alleged to have been a contributing factor in the case of assault upon a homeowner. *See Chapter 33.2.*

An association can also be liable for breach of its fiduciary duty to the members of the association who are owners of units or lots in the project for failure to enforce the restrictive covenants contained in the declaration.

30.3 Contractual Liability of Associations. Owners associations have the authority to enter into contracts and can be sued for breach of contract. An association can also bring suit to enforce contracts on its own behalf. If an association enters into a contract for landscaping of the common area, and it breaches the contract by failing to pay the landscape contractor, that contractor may sue the association. If (s)he wins the case and obtains a judgment against the association, (s)he can also levy execution on the association's property. If the association owns real property, (s)he may be able to execute against its bank account, including its reserve account. If an unincorporated association had no assets whatsoever, (s)he could collect directly from the members, in most cases. An incorporated association may offer some greater protection for its members. *See Chapter 4.10.*

30.4 Defense by Insurance Company. Depending on the type of action filed against the association, the association's insurance company may provide defense. Most tort actions would involve maters that are covered by liability insurance, so the insurance company would be obligated to provide a defense and to pay any judgment against the association. In the event that an association is made a defendant in a lawsuit, if there is some possibility that insurance may cover the matter, the association should tender the matter to its insurance company. This is done in the form of a letter that should come from the association's attorney. The letter is sent to the insurance company and it "tenders the defense" of the action to the insurance company in accordance with the provisions of the policy. If it is not absolutely clear there is coverage, the insurance company may agree to defend the action, but it may do so "under a reservation of rights," which means it reserves the right not to pay any judgment although it will pay for the cost of the defense. In such case, whether the association is entitled to its own choice of counsel probably depends upon the terms of the policy. In some cases where the insurance company is defending under a reservation of rights, the association has a right to retain independent counsel to ensure that the attorney hired by the insurance company is adequately defending the case. In this way, if there is a judgment against the association, it will be one that the insurance company is obligated to pay. One of the issues that often arises in such cases is whether the insurance company has to pay for the independent counsel in addition to the attorney that it has retained to defend the action under a reservation of rights.

Occasionally an insurance company is guilty of what the courts refer to as "bad faith" in defending or settling or refusing to settle a case brought against an insured association. In such circumstances, the association may have a right of recovery directly against the insurance company. In matters involving issues such as these, the association should have the advice of its own attorney, plus the advice and counsel of its own insurance agent.

CHAPTER 31
Legal Action and Lawsuits by the Association

31.1 When Should an Association Bring Suit? Whenever possible, the board and the officers should take actions that will keep the association out of court. Litigation is expensive, and the outcome of any lawsuit is uncertain. Nevertheless, there are times when a suit must be filed, and in such instances the board should be certain that the general membership will support any action that is filed by the association. In case of doubt, a vote of the membership should be conducted.

31.2 Standing to Sue. In most states, either under statutes or court decisions, associations have the power and the standing to bring suits in the name of the association and on behalf of members of the association. The association may bring a suit against the developer of a condominium or planned development project that involves allegations of damage to or defective construction of commonly owned lots, parcels or areas, or individually owned lots, parcels or areas that the owners association is obligated to maintain or repair. In such case, the board of directors of the association may sue on behalf of the association and assess the members of the association for the costs associated with the suit.

31.3 Choice of Court. After deciding to file, the association needs to make a decision as to the court where the action will be filed. If an amount is small enough, the association may use the small claims court. The advantage of small claims court is that no attorneys are present and the expenses are kept to a minimum. The disadvantage is that the person who will be representing the association will have to do all of the research, appear before the judge, present arguments, etc. Under most small claims court procedures, if the association is the plaintiff and loses the suit, it will not be able to appeal. The defendant, on the other hand, may be able to appeal from the adverse small claims court decision and get a new trial in a higher court.

If the suit were not to be filed in small claims court, what other court would be the proper court? This will depend upon the type of action. If the suit involves collecting money, the amount of money will determine the proper court. If it involves equitable relief such as obtaining an injunction, it may go to a different court. These matters will need to be decided by the attorney retained by the association to file the action.

31.4 Attorneys' Fees. Whether or not attorneys' fees are recoverable in a suit generally depends upon the statutes in that jurisdiction. Normally, there is no recovery for attorneys' fees unless permitted by some statute or contractual agreement. In the case of suits brought by an association arising under the provisions of the project legal documents, there is a basis for attorneys' fees being awarded to the prevailing party if the legal documents provide that the prevailing party in any action brought under the documents is entitled to attorneys' fees.

31.5 Depositions and Discovery. Soon after a suit is filed, the attorneys may take depositions. This means that the officers and directors and possibly other members of the association may have to appear before a court reporter with attorneys for both sides present and submit to questioning under oath. The questions and answers are transcribed, and the resulting document is called a "transcript." Deposition transcripts may be used in court under certain circumstances in the absence of a witness. They may also be used to impeach the testimony of a witness whose testimony at trial varies from the deposition. "Discovery" is a general term used to describe depositions and other forms of discovering the strengths and weaknesses of an opponent's case prior to trial.

31.6 Interrogatories. Interrogatories are written questions directed by one party in a legal action to the other. The interrogatories are prepared by the counsel for the party asking the questions, and the answers are prepared by the attorney for the other party. Both sides are entitled to submit written interrogatories. The purpose of interrogatories is to discover as much information as possible about the other side's case before trial, and is designed to limit the length of the trial.

31.7 Subpoenas and Summons. When a lawsuit is filed, the complaint is served upon the party being sued, together with a document called a "summons," which is used to compel the defendant to respond. Subpoenas are documents issued by parties to a lawsuit that are served upon defendants in order to compel appearance of a witness at a deposition or trial. If an association or any of its officers or directors is served with a summons and complaint or subpoena, the documents should be turned over immediately to the association's attorney.

31.8 Alternative Dispute Resolution. When faced with the possibility of a lawsuit, the association should always consider the alternatives of mediation or arbitration. *See Chapters 28.12 and 28.13.*

CHAPTER 32
Condemnation

32.1 Partial Condemnation. Condemnation is the commonly used term to describe the process whereby a government, or an instrument of the government, uses the power of eminent domain to acquire private property for a public purpose. The United States Constitution and the constitutions of the individual states require that "just" compensation be paid when private property is condemned for public purposes.

When one or more lots or units in a common-interest subdivision are condemned but the balance of the project survives, the owners whose property was taken by eminent domain are entitled to adequate compensation. If one or two units in a condominium project are taken, should all of the proceeds of condemnation go to the owner or owners whose units were taken, or should some of the proceeds go to compensate the remaining owners who may have been damaged in some way by the eminent domain? For example, after an eminent domain action, suppose money has to be spent to reconstruct walls, streets, or certain portions of the common area, such as landscaping. Should the owner whose unit or lot was condemned be compensated just for the value of the property taken? Or should compensation include a portion of the value of the interest in the common area to the extent that the common interest was not included in the value of the property? The answers to these questions are not always entirely clear. The legal documents may or may not cover the question explicitly enough to be of assistance.

State laws tend to be rather general and broad in scope; however, there are certain principles that usually apply. Certainly, the owner of property that is taken is entitled to the fair market value of the property, including both the lot or unit that was actually taken plus the appurtenant interest in the common area, to the extent that interest was not included in the value of the property or to the extent that the common interest adds an increment of value to the unit or lot. In addition to compensation to the owner, if the taking results in some damage to the remaining property owned by the other owners, or diminution in the value of the interest of the other owners, they too should receive some compensation from the condemnor. In some cases, it may be necessary to have an appraisal of the lot or unit being taken, and another appraisal of the effect of that taking on the balance of the project. If more than a certain percentage of a common-interest subdivision is taken by eminent domain, leaving the remainder of the project unable to be economically viable, the entire project may have to be terminated and sold. The proceeds of sale and the proceeds of eminent domain would be distributed equitably among all owners.

32.2 Taking of an Entire Project. When an entire project is condemned, the proceeds of condemnation should be distributed among the owners and their mortgagees.

The distribution will be based on the relative values of the interests affected by the condemnation, as determined by independent appraisal and in accordance with the procedures set forth in the governing instruments and in applicable state laws.

When a standard condominium project is taken by eminent domain, all the owners must be joined as defendants, because the owners association (although it may be a corporation having a separate existence) does not own title to the property. In a standard condominium project, title is held individually and collectively by the owners of all the units, all of whom must be joined as defendants in such an action. In a planned unit development project, where the owners association holds title to some of the land and possibly improvements thereon (such as recreational facilities), the owners association must be joined as a defendant. In a project that combines aspects of a planned development and a condominium (sometimes referred to as a "plandominium"), both the association and the individuals would have to be named and joined as defendants in an eminent domain action affecting the entire project.

One of the questions regarding valuing a condominium or planned development project is whether each unit or lot should be valued separately, or whether the entire condominium or planned development should be valued as one parcel. There are two conflicting principles in the law here. One is that in eminent domain, the fair market value of the whole, not the cumulative value of the various parts, is the value for eminent domain purposes. The other competing principle is that the value of the separate units or lots cannot be adequately reflected by a lump-sum valuation. Where deeds have created a number of separately owned interests in a project, multiple valuations should be required where a combined appraisal would create manifest injustice. If the total amount of the appraisal under a lump-sum appraisal would be less than the aggregate total consisting of the sum of the separate valuations of all of the parts, then multiple valuations should be required.

32.3 Negotiation and Representation. In an eminent domain action involving more than a single lot or unit, the question arises about whether each owner should represent himself or herself, or whether the association should represent all owners in negotiating with the condemning authority. As usual, the legal documents for the project and state law should be reviewed for possible application. When the association owns common area, it has to represent the owners in the condemnation proceedings, because the association holds record title to such property. In a condominium project, if the units are not valued separately by the condemning authority or by the court, the association should participate in the negotiations and be involved in the process of selecting the method for dividing the proceeds of condemnation.

32.4 Settlement. The process of condemnation may result in a settlement prior to the case actually going to trial. In such case, the proceeds of condemnation will be paid in accordance with the provisions of the settlement agreement, which would be signed by the condemning authority and by the owner or owners whose property interests were being condemned, including the association, if the association's property (common area) is involved. The settlement agreement should include provisions for payment of the agreed-upon value of the property, and should also make provision for payment of costs and attorneys' fees and for the use of funds to make repairs or restoration in the case of a partial taking.

Once a final settlement is reached, a deed or deeds will have to be recorded transferring title to the condemning authority. Lenders will be paid off, deeds of trust released, and, if necessary, legal documents will have to be amended. In the case of a partial taking, the legal documents may have to be amended to state the new percentage interests in the remainder of the property and to reallocate the assessments. In the case of a taking of an entire project, the condominium or planned unit development declarations should be rescinded. Additionally, subdivisions may need to be reverted to acreage, depending upon local practice, and the owners association will be dissolved. Any proceeds received by the association will be distributed equitably among the members after payment of bills.

32.5 Distribution. Distribution of the proceeds of condemnation is apportioned among the owners, either by court judgment or by agreement between the condemning authority and each of the owners. Distribution of proceeds is according to relative values of the interests affected by the condemnation as determined by independent appraisal, and in accordance with the procedure set forth in the government documents and in applicable state laws.

Some project legal documents containing FHLMC provisions (*see Chapter 1.4*) may require that no provision of the legal documents gives any owner priority over the rights of any first mortgagees. Other lender protection provisions of the legal documents may contain similar requirements. Where such provisions apply, the obvious purpose is to protect lenders by ensuring that if and when condemnation proceeds are paid to the owners of lots or units encumbered by deeds of trust, the lenders who hold those deeds will receive sufficient funds from the condemnation proceeds to retire the loan. In the event that legal documents are silent about distribution of condemnation proceeds and percentage ownerships, there will be a presumption that ownership in the common area is equal, and the distribution will be made accordingly.

Project legal documents as well as state laws should provide that the assets be distributed to the members upon dissolution of an owners association. Some association legal documents, drafted before Internal Revenue Code § 528 was amended to recognize the existence of homeowners associations and grant tax-exempt status, may contain provisions that provide for distribution of the assets of the association upon liquidation or wind-up of the affairs of the association to another homeowners association or another association qualifying as a tax-exempt organization. Such provisions should be amended to provide for distribution of the proceeds in an equitable manner among the members of the association. It is no longer necessary to provide for distribution of the assets of a residential association to another tax-exempt organization upon dissolution in order to qualify for tax exemption. *See Chapter 42.14.*

32.6 Condemnation of Condominium. In the condemnation of a standard condominium project where each of the unit owners owns an undivided interest in the common area, the association should be a participant in the negotiations, representing the condominium owners. The proceeds of condemnation should be payable to the association or to any trustees appointed by the association for the use and benefit of the condominium owners and their mortgagees as their interests may appear. Upon making an award and payment of the proceeds for condemnation, the owner of each unit should receive his or her portion of the award. The owner's lender, who has a security interest in the unit, should receive its share of the proceeds, and both owner and lender would then be divested of all interest in the project.

The association should participate in the negotiations and propose the method of division of proceeds, where the condominiums are not valued separately by the condemning authority or by the court. The proceeds of condemnation should be distributed among the owners and their mortgagees according to the relative values of the units affected by the condemnation. If there is a substantial taking of the property (more than 50 percent), under most state statutes and project legal documents the owners may terminate the legal status of the project by bringing a partition action, if required by local statutes, and would then distribute the proceeds from the partition sale to the owners and their mortgagees.

32.7 Condemnation of Planned Development Project. In the event of condemnation of a planned development project, if all or any part of a lot (except the common area) is taken by eminent domain, the award is disbursed to the owner of the lot, subject to the rights of the mortgagee. If the taking renders the lot uninhabitable, the owner is divested of any further interest in the project, including membership in the association, and the interests of the remaining owners are adjusted accordingly. If all or any part of the common area is taken by eminent domain, the proceeds of condemnation are used to restore or replace that portion of the common area affected by the condemnation, if restoration or replacement is possible. Any remaining funds after payment of fees and expenses relating to the condemnation are distributed among the owners in proportion to their interests, subject to the rights of their mortgagees. If necessary, the remaining portion of the project should be resurveyed to reflect the taking.

Where common area is taken, the planned development owners association will participate and represent the lot owners in negotiations with the condemning authority, and will propose a method of division of the condemnation proceeds from acquisition of the common area.

32.8 Condemnation of Stock Cooperative Project. Normally, a stock cooperative's legal documents will specify the procedures to be followed in the event of a partial or total taking of the project. In the event of a total taking, the board of directors of the stock cooperative would normally represent all the owners in the action, subject to the rights of first mortgagees of record. In the event of a partial taking, the legal documents should provide for the handling of the distribution of proceeds and the payment of expenses. The proceeds are first applied to balances due on any mortgages of record and on any fees due to the stock cooperative. Some portion of the proceeds may also be applied to repair and restoration of the project.

CHAPTER 33
Liability Issues

33.1 General Discussion of Liability Issues. Among other things, the general trend today in common-interest subdivision living is toward a greater amount of litigation. Litigation is not confined to construction disputes between builder/developers and those who buy their products (*see Chapter 34*), but also involves disputes between owners of interests in common-interest subdivisions and between officers and directors of associations and association members. Owners associations are being sued with increasing frequency, and courts are in the process of increasing the extent to which individuals are at risk when they assume the role of an officer or director of an owners association. As an example of expanding liability, associations are now responsible for taking reasonable measures to protect their members from foreseeable risks of crime. In many jurisdictions, associations are now required to monitor criminal activity in the community, to establish crime prevention procedures that will protect members and their property, and to ensure that security techniques and procedures are followed and observed by all residents of the project.

Whenever condominium or planned development owners own common area in undivided interests as tenants-in-common, they are exposed to personal liability as co-owners. They may be viewed as employers responsible for the actions of maintenance personnel and subject to liability for their injuries. They may also be viewed as property owners, liable for injuries to guests, invitees, and occasionally trespassers. As landowners, members of an association have a duty to take adequate measures to protect individuals who are or will be present on the premises against dangerous conditions and foreseeable criminal acts of third parties.

33.2 Tort Liability. One of the most significant areas of liability for members, officers and directors of an owners association is tort liability. In the field of tort law, negligence is probably the most common claim. The negligence can either be active (creating slippery floors that cause people to fall and injure themselves) or passive (failure to note a dangerous or defective condition due to deterioration over time and to take corrective action). Owners are, of course, liable for their own torts and may also be liable for the torts of the association to which they belong. Members are generally not personally liable for the acts of other members of the association, if the acts were done without their participation, knowledge or approval.

Owners are liable for torts arising from injuries to third parties resulting from the owners' failure to exercise ordinary care to keep their property reasonably safe. Owners are also liable for torts committed by their employees in the scope of their employment. Owners of undivided interests, as tenants-in-common, are liable for failure to exercise ordinary care to protect persons entering the common areas.

If the association holds title to the common areas rather than by individual owners as tenants-in-common, the owners are somewhat protected from claims based on negligence or other torts. It is not certain whether ownership of common areas by an unincorporated association affords as much protection as ownership by an incorporated association. Certainly in some cases an unincorporated association does not afford protection. *See Chapter 4.10.* In some jurisdictions, courts have held that where a judgment was obtained against the association for injuries or damages occurring in the common area, each individual owner's liability in the judgment should be proportionate to the owner's share of assessments or interest in the project, which could be discharged by paying only his or her share of the judgment. However, in other jurisdictions the unit owners as tenants-in-common are "jointly and severally liable" for injuries occurring in the common areas. "Joint and several liability" means that all owners are jointly liable, but that they are also individually liable for the entire amount of the judgment.

The traditional answer to avoiding exposure from tort liability is to carry adequate insurance, which means that the association should carry public liability insurance and each owner will individually carry public liability insurance. *See Chapter 21.4.*

33.3 Contractual Liability. Members of an incorporated association are not liable for the association's contractual obligations. Members of an unincorporated association are liable in some jurisdictions for the contractual debts of the unincorporated association.

Assuming that the board of directors and the officers have authority to execute a contract on behalf of the association, individual members would not be exposed to contractual liability as a result of a contract entered into by the association. In order for a member to be personally liable, (s)he must have authorized or ratified the contract. For example, a member who accepts the benefits of a contract would be said to have "impliedly" ratified the contract, and in some jurisdictions that owner might be held personally liable in contract for the debts of the association. In a properly formed and validly existing stock cooperative association, individual members would not be personally liable for contracts entered into by the stock cooperative. However, if the stock cooperative breaches its contract, its creditors could appropriate the assets of the corporation and would effectively deprive a member of his or her property just as if a judgment had been levied against the owner personally.

33.4 Limited Liability. Perhaps the best way for members of a common-interest owners association to limit their personal liability is to carry adequate personal insurance for claims against the association, and to be sure that the association carries adequate liability insurance. Insurance can be expensive, and even the most comprehensive policies have their shortcomings. Incorporating the homeowners association provides some degree of additional protection for members from claims against the association. If the owners association owns the common areas rather than the individual owners having undivided interests in the common areas, this adds some additional degree of insulation from liability.

Manager's Note: *For those who own condominiums or live in attached housing, it is especially critical to remember to purchase adequate insurance coverage for your home and possessions. While the association's blanket liability policy will provide some protection for the structure and limited interior amenities, it will not cover theft, loss, "slip and fall" or other liabilities that may occur within the interior of the home. Perhaps the biggest mistake made by most common-interest development homeowners today is the reliance on the association's policy to cover all losses both within and outside of the home—nothing could be further from the truth. The best defense against finding oneself unprotected in the event of a loss is to purchase appropriate insurance for the home.*

Where insurance and the protection of the corporate veil prove to be inadequate, and one member of an association has been required to pay more than the pro rata share of a judgment against the association, that member may use the courts to enforce a contribution from the other members to equalize their respective contributions toward payment of the judgment. Where the claim is actually the common responsibility of all the members, the courts will enforce each member's obligation to contribute a proportionate share.

Incorporation of the association and ownership by the association of the common areas, plus adequate insurance coverage, offer the greatest protection for individual owners against liability from claims arising against the association. However, owners should be aware that if a claimant obtains a judgment against an association and the insurance coverage is inadequate, the owners may have to levy a special assessment against all members, should the association have insufficient assets to satisfy the judgment and the claimant has levied against the association's common property. A similar situation exists in the case of a stock cooperative. A judgment against the cooperative must be satisfied either out of the corporation's insurance proceeds or its assets, including the reserves. To the extent that insurance proceeds and the corporation's assets and reserves are inadequate, the judgment plaintiff will be in a position to have the co-op's property sold to satisfy the judgment. In that case, the owners will need to contribute via a special assessment in order to satisfy the judgment and preserve the ownership of the project by the corporation in which they are stockholders.

CHAPTER 34
Construction or Design Defects

34.1 Handling of Construction Defects and Owner Complaints.

Any large newly constructed project will eventually exhibit signs of design or construction defects. Some may be relatively minor, while others may be substantial. The defects may show up in individual units, in common area improvements, or both. With respect to common area problems, the owners association (acting through its board of directors), should serve as the vehicle for handling and resolving complaints. Individual owners should present their complaints to the board, and they should consolidate these complaints and present them to the builder/developer and to any other parties responsible for the alleged defects. In the case of complaints of defects within individual units, if the problem areas are under the control of the association, that is, if the association is obligated to maintain and/or insure those areas, then once again the association should handle the matter. If the complaints involve matters that are strictly within the interior of a unit and not within the common area, individual unit owners may attempt to resolve their complaints by:

- Contacting the builder or developer directly; or
- Joining together in a class action; or
- Asking the board of directors of the association to act on behalf of all owners having similar complaints.

There is an understandable tendency on the part of developer-controlled boards not to vigorously pursue the developer over alleged design or construction defects that arise during the early months of the project. However, the failure of board members appointed by the developer to actively seek remedies for design and construction defects from the developer may result in personal liability on the part of the board. *See Chapter 34.4.* Once a board of new owners has been elected, that board should move quickly to survey the situation and determine the nature and extent of construction or design defects. To ensure that a thorough and complete investigation is made, each owner should be required to complete a form listing any defects that have come to his or her attention, whether the defects are within a unit or in the common area.

34.2 Plans and Specifications.

The board of directors should try to obtain from the developer a copy of the plans and specifications for the project. Sometimes developers are reluctant to provide such plans and specifications because of a concern that the association will check whether the project, as built, conforms to the plans and specifications. If there is any material degree of nonconformity, it could be the basis of a lawsuit. Sometimes builders are unable to provide copies of plans because the plans belong to the architect, who will not agree to release them. In such case, it may be possible to get a duplicate set of plans from the city or local governmental agency that issued the building permit. If there is some reason to believe that there have been material deviations from the plans and specifications, a thorough review should be made by an independent expert retained by the board.

Litigation over construction or design defects may well center on an interpretation of plans and specifications. The architect or engineer who prepared the plans and specifications may contend that the contractor failed to properly follow the plans, while the contractor may contend that the plans and specifications were in error and that (s)he should not be held responsible for having followed them. Unfortunately, that kind of infighting can lead to prolonged disputes and result in expensive litigation of matters that should be settled out of court. *See Chapter 34.6.*

34.3 Responsibility of Developer.
Subdividers, developers and contractors are liable for damages for defects in the products they build and sell. Liability runs not only to initial purchasers, but also to subsequent purchasers. In some states, developers and contractors who build residential projects have been held strictly liable in tort to the owners association, as well as to individual owners, for defective design and construction of projects. Home builders have a duty to use reasonable care in the construction of projects to all who may foreseeably be injured or damaged by defective construction.

The liability of builders, developers and contractors is based on theories of negligence or strict liability. If an action is based on negligence, the plaintiff has to prove that the contractor, architect, engineer, builder, developer, or other responsible party was negligent in some way, and that the negligence caused or contributed to the damage or injury. If the claim is based on a theory of strict liability in the case of residential construction, the owner has only to prove that a defect exists, and does not need to prove that its existence resulted from negligence. It is unclear whether the doctrine of strict liability applies to commercial as distinguished from residential property, although the courts appear to be moving in the direction of imposing strict liability on builders, developers and contractors regardless of whether the project is residential or commercial.

34.4 Responsibility of Directors.
The board of directors of the association has a fiduciary duty to investigate design or construction defects, to determine their nature and extent, and to decide whether the builder/developer and/or the agents should be held accountable for those defects. The failure to recognize and pursue a design/construction defect claim may be a breach of the board's fiduciary duty and, under some conditions, might result in personal liability for board members. *See Chapter 6.17.* Thus, if board members have a reasonable suspicion that a faulty condition exists resulting from defective construction or design, the board has a duty to investigate and, if necessary, to commence legal proceedings against those responsible. For example, if a member of the board received complaints from owners about leaky roofs and the board failed to investigate the complaint, or investigated and determined there were substantial problems with the roof but failed to pursue a claim against the developer, the board would clearly have violated its

fiduciary obligation to act responsibly to the association and its members. If the board completed an investigation of the leaks and obtained a repair estimate from a reliable roofing contractor for $6,000, the board could then present a claim against the developer or the roofer who did the job. If the claim is rejected, the board should then consult its attorney for advice on the prospects for litigation. If the attorney advises that the exposure of the developer is probably only 50 percent because at least half of the leaks are due to normal wear and tear, the board is then faced with a decision whether to sue for $6,000 with a chance of only collecting half the amount. If the attorney advises that it would cost $3,000 to prosecute the suit, then the board is looking at what may very well be just a break-even situation. In such an event, the board may decide not to file suit, but try to settle with the builder or roofer on a "cost of litigation" approach. That means the board would offer to settle for an amount of money which the defendants would be likely to expend to defend the case. To put it another way, the board does not have to pursue every remedy to its ultimate conclusion, regardless of costs, risks involved, and chances of recovery. It does have to act responsibly and in a reasonably prudent manner.

Any time the board gets involved in an investigation of design or construction defects in the project, it should consult its attorney, and should obtain the services of investigative firms who have expertise in areas where defects are suspected or alleged to exist. Written reports from independent investigators or inspectors should be obtained in all cases where material defects are suspected or alleged.

34.5 Typical Defects. Most disputes over design and construction defects involve water leakage. Leakage most often occurs due to defective design and construction of the roof; however, leakage can occur as a result of wind-driven rain penetrating through siding or improperly sealed windows and doors. Water intrusion can also be a problem in foundations, basements, and crawl spaces, where standard construction techniques have not been followed or improper materials have been used.

A second major source of claims for defective construction and design is soil problems, which can result from improper design of a foundation, or improper or inadequate soil studies, or inadequate preparation of the soils underneath the building pad.

The third major source of construction disputes is in the area of landscaping and irrigation. This can be a tricky area because of the conflicting claims of the owners that the landscaping materials were improperly selected or improperly planted, or improperly maintained during the initial construction period, and the counter-claim of the builder/developer or landscape contractor that the landscaping has been inadequately maintained after the owners association took over the landscape maintenance responsibility.

The fourth major area of design or construction defects includes a variety of claims such as defective tile or masonry work; windows or doors that do not operate properly; appliances, heating, ventilating, or air conditioning equipment that does not work properly; or paint or other materials that peel, flake, delaminate, or are otherwise defective.

In order to preserve and maximize the legal rights of the association and its owners to hold those responsible for defective design and construction liable for the cost of repairs, the board itself must act with diligence and prudence. It must investigate defects thoroughly and promptly, and be diligent in establishing and following its own maintenance and operational procedures. If the irrigation system is suspected of causing deterioration in the landscaping, the board should make every effort to see that it is made to perform properly by adjusting time clocks, altering spray patterns, and similar measures. The failure of the association to attempt improvements or corrections will give the developer or the irrigation system contractor a defense, or at least a partial defense, if a claim is brought for the cost to replace dead landscaping.

Similarly, if interior damage from leaks is suffered by a number of units in a condominium project, the ability of the association and its members to recover the repair costs from those responsible may depend in part upon the ability of the association to show that lack of basic maintenance (such as an annual inspection and caulking program) was not the cause of the leakage, but rather was caused by defects in design or construction.

Defects that ultimately cost the association and its members money, either in damages or costs of repair, can be the result of many different things. Poor design is one cause of defects. For example, a roof that is designed to shed water may sag and actually result in water ponding because the architect or structural engineer failed to properly calculate the strengths of the load-bearing beams or trusses. Damages from moisture accumulating beneath interior floors may be the result of the failure of the architect to specify a waterproof membrane, or it may be the result of the negligence of the contractor in failing to install the waterproof membrane that was included in the specifications. The delamination that occurs in plywood siding may be the result of the architect failing to specify exterior grade plywood, or it may be the result of the painting contractor failing to follow the specifications for the exterior finish. The cracking of driveways or patios may be the result of improper soil analysis by the soil engineer, improper foundation design by the structural engineer or architect, or it may be the fault of the concrete supplier who supplied faulty material to the job.

When a material defect surfaces in a project, the board has an obligation to hire experts who are specialists. These specialists can, on the basis of their experience, properly determine the cause of the defects or the cause of the damage, and can advise the board on who is most likely responsible for the defects and the likely remedial costs.

34.6 Avoidance of Litigation. A board of directors that does its work properly will conduct a thorough investigation and establish the causes of defects that have surfaced, while demonstrating that lack of maintenance was not a contributing factor. This information should be fully and fairly presented to the builder/developer/contractor or other party allegedly responsible for the problem. Then, the chances are very good that the matter can be settled to everyone's satisfaction without litigation. Boards of directors should learn to work with builder/developers and architects and other professionals responsible for the project. In some cases, the problem may be caused by the manufacturer or supplier, and then the association and the builder/developer and/or contractor should be allies against the manufacturer. This requires investigation in the beginning to determine the cause of the defect, and then cooperation between the association and the builder/developer/contractor to present a united front against the manufacturer. The manufacturer will then be much more likely to settle the claim by replacing the defective material. If the association comes in with a "shotgun" claim against everyone involved, it provides an opportunity for the manufacturer (who may be the real culprit) to place part of the cost against the architect or the contractor. In such cases, it is much more likely to wind up in litigation rather than being settled early.

34.7 Litigation. If the association is unable to settle its claim without litigation, it will have to resort to legal action. As soon as it becomes apparent or even reasonably probable that litigation will have to be initiated, the association should consult with an experienced and qualified litigation expert. Neither the association's regular attorney, nor an attorney retained by the association to provide advice and counsel about organizational and administrative matters, should be asked to represent the association in preparing for or filing a lawsuit. Litigation is a specialty, and an attorney specializing in real estate or association law is no more qualified to pursue a lawsuit on behalf of the association than a litigation attorney is qualified to draft amendments to the association's legal documents.

The association's regular attorney may be qualified to assist the association in negotiating settlements; sometimes attorneys who are not primarily litigation-oriented can do a better job of settling a case before positions harden and animosity begins to interfere in the process. Even if the association's regular attorney is involved in trying to negotiate a settlement, an experienced litigation attorney should be consulted early in the process to make sure that if the negotiations do break down, the association has not weakened its case in trying to work out a settlement. For example, the key to winning a case may be to select the best qualified and most experienced expert who will make the best investigation, write the best report, and who will make the best witness if the matter goes to court. The chances are that the litigation attorney will be better able to locate the most highly qualified investigator who will do the best job in these areas. In addition, the selection of the appropriate expert witness early in the litigation may well increase the chances of an early favorable settlement of the case. The importance of expert witnesses and their testimony in construction defect cases cannot be overemphasized, and one of the major benefits of having the best expert available early on is to maximize the chance of an early favorable settlement. Without an accurate report from a qualified expert, the association, in most cases, will not be in a good position to negotiate a fair settlement on behalf of its members.

When the association settles with the builder/developer/contractor, the association will sign a release of all claims which will be broad enough to waive any rights to assert future claims against the same parties. If additional defects surface later, and it turns out that those defects could have been discovered by a more adequate investigation or a better investigative report, the association and its members may well be unable to recover more damages for such additional defects.

In settling claims, the builder, developer or contractor may ask that 100 percent of the owners agree to the terms of the settlement. It is rarely possible to obtain the written consent of 100 percent of the members of an association to anything. The demand for unanimous agreement among all the members may be impossible to meet, and may result in a case having to be tried that could have been settled. One way to avoid such a result is to have the settlement agreement approved by a majority of all the owners, and then find a way to protect the developer, builder or contractor from additional claims brought by individual members who disapproved of the settlement. The builder, developer or contractor can be protected against claims by individuals dissatisfied with the settlement approved by a majority of the members by providing in the settlement agreement that the association will indemnify the builder, developer or contractor against any future claims. Such an indemnity provision would simply provide that if any owner who has refused to sign the settlement agreement and release files his or her own lawsuit against the defendants, the association will step in and defend the case. The association can then use its influence to prevent such a lawsuit from being filed by one of its members. If it cannot prevent the suit from being filed, the association can pay the cost of defense and collect those costs in the form of special assessments against all members, including the one who filed the suit.

34.8 Statutes of Limitation.

Statutes of limitation are laws that set time limits on the enforcement of certain rights. If claims are not brought within the applicable statutory period, a lawsuit is barred. If the board of directors is ignorant about the statute of limitations and/or fails to file a suit within the statutory limits, it can be in breach of its fiduciary duty, and the members of a board could, under certain circumstances, be held personally liable for the breach.

There are various statutes that apply, and the time limits vary within jurisdictions. Generally, there are fairly short statutes (one to three years) for personal injuries suffered as a result of defects. There are slightly longer statutes (two to four years) for actions based on a breach of contract. Some states have even longer statutes (up to ten years or more) for "latent defects." A latent defect is a defect which is not apparent from a visual inspection of the property, and was not discovered or could not have been discovered with reasonable diligence until the time when the defect surfaces for the first time. Once a latent defect becomes known, the shorter statutes apply and action must be taken promptly thereafter.

There are varying circumstances that start the running of a statute of limitation. In some cases, it is the close of escrow and transfer of title. In other cases, it is the completion or substantial completion of the improvement, or the date of final inspection or the date of recordation of a notice of completion. It may also be the date that use or occupancy commenced, or the passage of a certain amount of time after completion of the work on the project.

It is important that the board consult with its attorney as soon as any defect is known or suspected, so that the statute of limitations can be determined and a course of action adopted to ensure that a claim is filed before the statute runs. In some cases, if the statute is about to run, it may be necessary to retain a litigation attorney to file a claim to prevent the statute from running, and permit the parties to continue with settlement negotiations.

34.9 Alternatives to Litigation.

Mediation or arbitration should always be considered an alternative to litigation. *See Chapters 28.12 and 28.13.* Project legal documents and/or state statutes may require the association and the builder or developer to participate in some process of alternative dispute resolution (ADR) prior to filing a lawsuit in a construction defect case.

CHAPTER 35
Obligations of Developer

35.1 Contractual Obligations. Developers of common-interest subdivision projects such as residential or commercial condominiums, planned unit developments and residential stock cooperatives have certain contractual obligations to the purchasers of interests in such projects. The primary obligations are based on written contracts. The contracts take the form of deposit receipt agreements or purchase and sale agreements. The terms of the contract may be found in certain reporting documents, such as sales brochures and escrow instructions. Such documents must be reviewed in their entirety in order to determine the contractual obligations between developer and buyer. Additional contractual obligations may be found in an express (written) warranty given by the builder/developer. (*See Chapter 36.1.*) In addition to express warranties, certain implied warranties may also be the basis for establishing liability or responsibility of the builder/developer to the buyer. *See Chapter 36.2.*

35.2 Statutory Obligations. In almost every state, there are certain statutes that regulate the construction and sale of housing to the public. Generally, there tend to be more numerous and stringent regulations in the case of residential housing than commercial development. These statutes impose certain obligations upon builder/developers or "merchant builders." Anyone who wants to understand all the obligations and responsibilities of merchant builders to their customers (buyers) must consult statutes and, in some cases, administrative regulations or guidelines.

36.3 Consumer Protection Laws. In most states, a state agency such as the Department of Real Estate or a similarly named agency has been empowered to adopt and administer consumer protection regulations to protect the buying public against some common abuses of the housing industry. The purpose of such consumer protection laws is to eliminate or minimize the extent to which less sophisticated members of the public can be victimized by dishonest or incompetent builders. These regulations impose certain obligations upon developers, which can be very extensive. The basic thrust of most of these regulations is to require the developer to:

- Make full disclosure about all material aspects of the project being offered for sale to the public;
- Ensure that the project is not misrepresented to the public; and
- Provide a means of forcing the builder/developer to fully perform all promises.

35.4 Common Law-Imposed Obligations. In addition to statutes, regulations, contracts, and express warranties, there are certain obligations imposed upon builder/developers by the courts. Not all of the laws that apply in this area are contained in statutes and regulations. There are many important appellate and Supreme Court decisions that have a significant impact on the building industry. One example is the doctrine of implied warranties, which is a principle based on a long line of legal decisions. Simply stated, an implied warranty is a legal obligation imposed upon a builder to deliver a product that is fit for the purpose for which it was intended; that is, a home or an office that is "habitable."

35.5 Bonded Obligations of Builder/Developer.

In most states, consumer protection laws and regulations impose certain requirements on merchant builders, primarily residential builders. Typically, such regulations impose a requirement that the builder posts a bond, cash or some other approved form of security to secure the builder's obligation to fulfill certain promises or representations. The bond or other security may be posted with a state agency or with a title or escrow company. A typical example would be a requirement that a builder post a bond in an amount sufficient to pay for the completion of the subdivision improvements, including common area facilities. Under such arrangements, the builder would have the option to either (1) complete the entire project, file a notice of completion, and then close escrow and sell lots or units to the public, or (2) post adequate security to ensure completion of the balance of the subdivision and common area improvements, so buyers would not be left exposed and unprotected if the builder failed to complete the project. Where such obligations to post security exist, there generally are provisions for enforcement. A typical example is a condominium project consisting of ten buildings, each containing ten units, plus a swimming pool and tennis court. If the builder wants to be able to close escrow and complete the sale of twenty units in the first two buildings before completing construction of the swimming pool and tennis court, landscaping, streets, utilities, etc. in the rest of the project, the builder would be required to post a bond in the amount necessary to complete those other facilities. If the builder sold and closed escrow on the twenty units and then stopped building and did not complete the swimming pool, tennis court and other facilities, the buyers of the first twenty units would be entitled to take the security posted by the developer and to use those funds to complete such improvements.

Another common regulation would be applicable where a developer has completed construction of a fifty-unit planned development project and has closed escrow on the sale of the first lot. The legal documents and state laws would usually provide that the sale of that first lot would obligate the developer to begin paying assessments to the owners association. At that point, the first buyer would own one lot and the developer would own the remaining forty-nine lots. A typical regulation would have required the builder to post a bond, cash, or other security sufficient in size to ensure that the builder's assessments on all the remaining unsold lots will be paid until enough lots closed escrow. This is done so that the association can operate successfully on the assessments paid only by the members. The regulation might provide that the developer put up a bond or cash in an amount equal to six months' worth of assessments on all fifty lots, and that the security remain in place until 80 percent of the lots (or, for our example, forty total) in the entire subdivision have been sold. If at any time the developer defaulted on the payment of the assessments, the association could proceed against the security. Once the point has been passed at which the developer is no longer required to retain the security, the bond would be cancelled and returned to it, or the cash or other deposit would be refunded to the builder. Boards of directors of owners associations need to be aware of the existence of such secured obligations on the part of the developer, so that the board can proceed against the security if the developer runs into trouble in meeting its obligations.

Some governmental or quasi-governmental agencies such as FNMA may in certain areas require that a residential project be funded with money from the builder/developer and the buyers during the initial sales period. A typical FNMA regulation might require that each time a unit or lot is sold, two months' worth of assessments be paid into the association's treasury. Where such requirements are imposed, the board of directors needs to be aware of these requirements. For example, does the condition require that two months' worth of assessments be paid by every purchaser of a lot or unit in the project until completion of the entire sales program? Once sales have been completed and the association has a full two months' worth of assessments in its account, how long must the extra funds remain there? Does there come a time when the association could either reduce the monthly assessments until the surplus was used up, or apply the entire surplus to one month's assessment, so that every owner would have a one-time, one-month assessment "holiday"? Similar questions can be asked about other arrangements that are made that are based on some sort of governmental regulation. The answers in each case will depend upon the facts and circumstances. Members of the board of directors need to be aware of the facts and circumstances, and it is their obligation to ask the right people enough questions to find out the answers and then to act accordingly.

Another form of bond is a completion bond, which is typically required by the city or local governmental agency that approves the construction of the project. Usually the builder or developer is required to post a bond with the local governmental agency in an amount estimated to be the cost of completing the "off-site" improvements, such as streets, curbs, gutters, sidewalks, sanitary and storm sewers, and utilities to the site. Those bonds are not necessarily intended to protect the ultimate purchasers of the project, but are for the protection of the general public. This bond ensures that when the "privilege" of subdividing a parcel is granted to a developer, the city and its citizens will not be inconvenienced or offended by the presence of a half-completed subdivision should the builder fail to complete the project once it has been started.

Another form of bond is a subsidy bond, which is sometimes required of developers of large residential projects. For example, in a 200-unit residential project containing an Olympic-sized swimming pool, clubhouse, and several tennis courts, the cost of operating and maintaining the recreational facilities would be very high. If the cost were spread among all 200 owners, the monthly charges for those facilities might be $200 per month. If the cost were spread among 50 owners, the cost might be $800 per month per owner, and would be more than those 50 owners would be willing to pay. Therefore, it is necessary for the developer to subsidize the association by paying the extra amounts required to operate and maintain the recreational facilities while still keeping the assessments down to $200 per month for the units that have been sold.

Another area in which developers are typically obligated on an ongoing basis and may be required to provide some security is for the maintenance of streets and landscaping in the project. Some cities may require the developer to post security for a period of a year or so after the streets in a project have been completed and dedicated to the city. The same may be true of landscaping in a project. The developer may be required to post security to maintain the landscaping for an initial period of time so that if plants die, they can be replaced.

35.6 Disclosure. One of the long-held traditions of the English and American common law systems has been "caveat emptor," or "let the buyer beware." The trend today is more and more in the direction of protecting the buyer, by requiring that the seller make full and complete disclosure of all material facts concerning the real property and improvements that would reasonably be expected to have a material effect on the value. Some recently adopted disclosure legislation requires very detailed reporting on the part of the seller and occasionally on the part of the real estate brokers and salesmen participating in the sale. Buyers and members of the association's board of directors need to be aware of these disclosure laws. The purpose of the laws is, of course, to protect the buying public and to eliminate or minimize chances of fraud or deception in connection with the sale of real property. Typically, the remedies for nondisclosure or for violation of the disclosure requirements are rescission or damages. "Rescission" means the buyer of a property who has been the victim of nondisclosure has the right to void the contract, give back the property, and get all of his or her money back. "Damages" means the buyer may be entitled to keep the property, but have the price reduced or be awarded an amount of money. Often the reward is calculated to compensate the buyer for the reduced value of the property resulting from the facts that the seller failed to disclose prior to the completion of the sale.

35.7 Obligations of Developer as Board Member. Owners associations are usually created by the developer of the project and initially staffed by the developer and his or her employees or agents. When the developer and the employees or agents serve on the board of directors of the owners association, they have a built-in conflict of interest. The failure of the developer's directors to fully perform their obligation to the association has been a frequent source of litigation. Where such cases have come to court, the courts have been very strict about holding the directors responsible for performing their fiduciary obligations to the association and its members. *See Chapter 6.11.*

CHAPTER 36
Warranties

36.1 Builder Express Warranties. Most home builders offer the buyer some type of written warranty agreement that guarantees new construction for a certain period of time. A typical warranty will define areas that are covered and excluded by the warranty. Many buyers believe there is a universal one-year warranty on all new construction, but unless the state has adopted a specific statute to that effect (which is unlikely), there is no one-year required warranty period.

Most warranty agreements do not specifically address any of the common areas of a common-interest project. Unless there is some specific reference to such areas, they would not be covered by an express written warranty, but would instead be covered by the implied or common law warranties. *See Chapter 36.2.*

Express warranties can either be contractual (in the form of a written agreement provided by the builder) or statutory. For example, the Uniform Condominium Act contains detailed warranty provisions that would apply in those states where a form of the Uniform Condominium Act has been adopted.

One of the problems with an express written warranty is that its scope tends to be somewhat vague and general. This occurs because not enough effort is put into tailoring the warranty agreement to a particular project. There is a tendency on the part of the developer to use the same form over and over again without modifying it to fit the unique aspects of the project. A considerable degree of doubt exists about the enforceability of express written warranties in connection with the sale of residential real estate. The courts in most states have yet to determine whether or not an express written warranty prevails over the doctrine of strict liability (*see Chapter 34.3*). Until various forms of express warranty agreements are tested by litigation, it will not be known whether a written warranty agreement limits the liability of a merchant home builder to the warranty agreement terms when claims are made for defects appearing after the expiration of the warranty term.

36.2 Builder-Implied Warranties. Where no statutory or express written warranties exist, there are implied warranties. Over the years, the courts have imposed an implied warranty on builders that dwellings be fit for habitation and be constructed in a reasonably workmanlike manner. The courts have also imposed implied warranties that dwelling units be constructed in accordance with the specifications contained in the building plans approved by the local governmental authority. One court has said that an implied warranty arises by operation of law and exists regardless of any intention by the builder to create it. Such warranty is said to arise from the builder's breach of a duty to the purchaser, which, by reason of the builder's superior knowledge or the reliance by the purchaser on the builder's representations or judgment, means the builder has taken advantage of the purchaser. The courts have in some cases imposed implied warranties on the builder that condominium units have been constructed in accordance with plans and specifications approved by the local governmental authority. Thus, the builder has an obligation to file modified specifications with the government for approval and to make these new specifications a matter of public record. In one case, the court found the developer in breach of the purchase and sale contract and the implied warranty of fitness when inferior features were substituted for those described in the attachment to the purchase agreement.

The implied warranty extends to the common elements as well as to the units in the condominium project. Some courts have distinguished between sales of new housing and resales of "used" housing, and, in some cases, the doctrine of implied warranty has not been extended to a resale. However, if the resale involves a condominium conversion project where certain building modifications have occurred, there is little difference between the application of an implied warranty to a new project or to a converted project.

36.3 Condominium Conversions.
In the case of a condominium conversion (conversion of a rental apartment project into for-sale condominiums), the developer of the condominium conversion is held to substantially the same standards as that of a merchant builder of new housing. This means that the doctrine of implied warranties applies both to the units and to the common areas. *See Chapter 36.2.*

Many states have imposed additional burdens upon condominium converters, with respect to construction and, particularly, disclosure and representations. Consumer protection laws in some states require developers to disclose to buyers certain information concerning the renovation or replacement of important major components of a converted building. In some states, condominium converters are required to post security for renovation or replacement work that has not been completed at the time units are sold. In some cases, condominium converters are required to furnish prospective purchasers with a written statement disclosing all substantial defects and malfunctions in major systems of the unit or the common area, or disclaiming any knowledge of such defects or malfunctions. If the builder fails to make full and proper disclosure, the buyer could rescind the agreement and have the purchase money refunded or could sue for damages.

36.4 Pick-Up or Warranty Work.
Where the builder uses an express warranty, it may contain certain provisions describing what warranty or "pick-up work" the builder intends to perform. The term "pick-up work" or "warranty work" refers to the maintenance, repair and replacement customarily provided by the developers for a certain period of time after the sale and close of escrow. Written purchase agreements or express written warranty agreements may spell out the intentions and duties of the developer. Where there are no express warranties and the purchase agreement is silent on the point, many builders have a policy of doing pick-up or warranty work for a period of one year after the close of escrow. Most builders, if approached reasonably and rationally, will do pick-up

work for at least one year, if not longer.

It is important for a new home buyer to make an early and thorough inspection of the home, preferably just prior to the close of escrow, to create a list of all observable defects. The owner should keep a copy of the list and should deliver a copy to the builder. It is the builder's responsibility to take care of the defects listed within a reasonable period of time. The homeowner should check with the developer and see that this work is completed. A problem can arise when additional defects are noted at a later date and are then brought to the attention of the builder, which can lead to arguments regarding the cause of the defect. For example, if a purchaser complains two months after close of escrow about chipped tiles, gouged cabinets or counters, the owner is at an obvious disadvantage if such defects were not included on the inspection list prior to the close of escrow.

There are other kinds of defects, however, which appear several months or perhaps even years after the close of escrow. Such defects are known as "latent defects." Some states have long statutes of limitations (as much as ten years or longer) which apply to latent defects. *See Chapter 34.8.* There are certain defects that in the natural course of events will show up in any new building project, without negligence by anyone involved. Examples of this are hairline cracks in stucco, slight separations in corner moldings above doors, and minor stress cracks in concrete. Buyers who make an issue of claimed defects that are only natural results of new construction are not helping themselves, and are likely to put the correction of real defects in jeopardy.

Most builders want to be responsible and ethical, and if approached in a reasonable manner, will make an effort to stand behind their product. Of course, there are always exceptions. When a builder arbitrarily and unjustifiably refuses to complete the pick-up work in a common-interest subdivision, the association's board of directors should take a part in representing the owners and the association in negotiating with the builder. The owners and the association have a number of options available:

1. Bring in the association's attorney to put pressure on the builder to fulfill its obligations.
2. If the project is under the jurisdiction of a state agency such as the state Department of Real Estate, file a complaint with the regulatory branch of that department.
3. File a claim with the state contractor's licensing board.
4. File a complaint with the Better Business Bureau.
5. File a lawsuit against the builder. *See Chapter 37.7.*
6. Check to see whether the builder has posted any security, such as a bond or cash deposit, that can be called upon to satisfy the builder's obligations.
7. If the builder is still involved in building and/or selling units in the project, the owners can organize a picket line. This is particularly effective on weekends and during prime sales time. It is always best to try the friendly, cooperative approach first to give the builder an opportunity to demonstrate its integrity before making accusations

attacking the builder's motives and reputation.

36.5 Appliances. New appliances that are included in completed dwellings should carry their own individual warranties. These warranties should be passed on to the buyers, so they may enforce these warranties directly against the manufacturers. Certain fixtures will carry their own warranties, including items such as hot water heaters, forced-air furnaces, solar heating systems, ovens, ranges, dishwashers, trash compactors, garbage disposals, built-in vacuum cleaner systems, and built-in security systems. The owner should obtain the original warranties on all fixtures from the developer. Some builders' express written warranties will exclude coverage of "consumer products," leaving the purchaser to pursue the manufacturer under the manufacturer's warranty.

Some federal legislation exists that applies to consumer products installed in new homes. This legislation imposes certain minimum warranty requirements upon the manufacturers and distributors of appliances customarily installed in homes.

36.6 Materials and Equipment Warranties. Certain warranties, either express or implied, may attach to nursery materials (plants, trees, and shrubs), irrigation systems, and recreational facilities and equipment. Where defects in such items occur, the association can pursue either the developer or the manufacturer's supplier or installer, or both simultaneously. It is usually best to first ask the developer to resolve the problem. If that fails to produce immediate results, the association should feel free to approach the manufacturers or suppliers directly.

CHAPTER 37
Actions Against the Developer

37.1 General Liability of Developers. Suits against developers have serious effects on an association. Suits can often be accompanied by increases in dissension among the membership, and increased harassment of the board by members who are upset by the special assessments needed to pay legal fees connected with a lawsuit. The delays and expense of the legal process can create serious problems for associations. One very adverse side effect of a suit against the developer is the depressing effect such a suit has upon resale of units.

Builders and developers of common-interest subdivisions are potentially liable based on a number of different legal theories:

1. Contractual liability to purchasers of subdivision interests for defective construction.
2. Tort liability to purchasers for misrepresentation or fraud.
3. Tort liability for defective construction.
4. Liability for breach of fiduciary obligations as directors or officers of the owners association.
5. Liability for violation of local ordinances.
6. Liability for violation of state laws or regulations.
7. Liability for failure or refusal to enforce restrictive covenants.

37.2 Liability of Developer for Failure to Complete Construction or Deliver Promised Facilities. Occasionally a developer will fail to deliver certain promised recreational amenities. In those jurisdictions where the development is regulated by a consumer protection agency such as a branch of the Department of Real Estate, any promised facilities that are not completed at the date of close of escrow will be bonded for completion. The security may be in the form of a corporate surety bond, cash, or letter of credit. *See Chapter 35.5.* In any event, there will be mechanisms in place for proceeding against that security if it becomes necessary to enforce the obligation of the developer to complete certain facilities. In such event, the board should review the legal documents and the public report from the state Department of Real Estate or similar governmental agency, to familiarize itself with the available mechanics to enforce the developer's obligation and pursue the security. In cases where no security exists and the developer has simply breached its promise to deliver facilities, the association may have to file a lawsuit against the developer. *See Chapter 37.7.*

37.3 Design and Construction Defects. Subdividers, developers, and contractors are liable for damages or defects in the products they build and sell. Liability is based on traditional notions of contract law, and extends from initial purchasers to subsequent buyers. Liability is based on a variety of different legal theories. *See Chapter 37.1.*

Developers who build residential projects and sell them to the public have been held strictly liable to buyers and, in a common-interest subdivision, to the owners association for defective design and construction. To date, it is not clear whether the strict liability rule extends to commercial property or is limited to residential property. *See Chapter 35.2.*

37.4 Changes by Developer in Design or Unit Mix. In a large or multi-phased project, suppose the developer starts out with a particular design and proposes a certain mix of units to include specified numbers of one-, two- and three-bedroom dwellings, and then halfway through the project, the remaining units are redesigned and the unit mix changed dramatically. Do the buyers of homes in the early phases have any right to object? If the developer has reserved the right to change its design and unit mix by appropriate provisions in the project legal documents, the buyers clearly have no right to object. However, even if the right to change the design and unit mix in subsequent phases has been reserved, if the project is still under the regulation of a state agency such as the Department of Real Estate, the developer will have the burden of establishing that the change will not have a materially adverse effect on the purchasers in the initial phases of the project.

If the developer has not reserved the right to change the design or unit mix, can changes be made if it can be demonstrated that there will not be any adverse consequences to the initial buyers? For example, what if the design of units in later phases is architecturally quite different from the design in earlier phases? Can the owners of dwellings in the earlier phases object on the grounds of aesthetics alone? The answer might depend upon what provisions there are in the declaration concerning architectural control. Did the developer reserve the absolute right to change its design without having to go through architectural review? Was an architectural review process even set up in the original declaration? If an architectural review is required, and the developer dominates the committee but did not reserve the absolute right to change its design, is it appropriate for the developer's representatives to approve a radical new design opposed by the minority on the committee who represent the existing buyers? The answers to these and similar questions will depend upon the circumstances, and each case would have to be evaluated on its own merits. When such issues arise, the association should have advice from independent legal counsel.

37.5 Promises and Representations by Developer. Where a developer makes promises about the building of facilities in future phases that are contained in recorded documents, they will be binding upon the developer and any successor developer. If the agreements or promises are not contained in recorded documents, they may only bind the developer and would not necessarily be binding on subsequent developers who acquired the balance of the project without knowledge of the promises. Promises concerning future developments that are contained in something other than contracts or recorded covenants, such as, for example, in sales brochures, may not be as enforceable as if they were contractual in nature, but may serve as a basis for a claim of misrepresentation or fraud. For example, if a sales brochure showed that part of the project was going to be left as an open-space park, and later the developer sought to build an apartment house on that parcel, the purchasers of lots or units in the project who had been induced to buy their homes based partly in reliance upon the promised open space rather than an apartment house at that location should be able to get the court to intervene and prevent the developer from building the apartment house. If the promises to deliver future facilities were made as part of the application for a public report or permission to sell to the public, the state regulatory agency may have the authority to force the developer to keep those promises. The leverage may be in the form of a bond, letter of credit or other security posted to ensure completion of the other facilities (*see Chapter 37.2*), or it may be in the form of power to restrain the developer from making any further sales.

37.6 Warranties. Warranties of builders or developers come in two types—express warranties and implied warranties. Express warranties may be contained in a written warranty agreement provided by the builder or may be provided by statutory provisions that contain certain legally required warranties. Implied warranties may be the result of verbal statements made by the builder or agents of the builder. An example of an implied warranty would be a statement by a sales representative of the builder that "this entire project and all the materials in it are of the finest quality." The implication here is that construction materials are of such a nature that they will outlast and out-perform all but the most expensive and highest-quality products. Courts have found implied warranties of fitness for an intended purpose applicable to the products of merchant builders. A common implied warranty is that a dwelling is constructed in a reasonably workmanlike manner and is fit for habitation. The courts have also imposed implied warranties that new condominiums or townhouses be constructed in accordance with the specifications contained in the building plans approved by the local governmental authority. *See Chapter 36.2.*

37.7 Suits for Defective Construction. An individual homeowner may bring a suit for defective design and/or construction against the builder or developer. If the suit involves allegations of damage to common property or individually owned lots or areas that the association is obligated to maintain or repair, a lawsuit may be brought against the homeowners association. In some cases, one or more owners on behalf of all owners may bring a class-action lawsuit. The association's board of directors may also bring an action on behalf of the association and its members, and can assess the members of the association for the costs of prosecuting the action. *For a discussion of the various causes of action that may be alleged against a developer, see Chapter 37.1. For a discussion of statutes of limitation, see Chapter 34.8.*

37.8 Purchaser's Right to Rescind. The buyer of a unit or lot may rescind the contract, if the facts can be established to substantiate a cause of action for fraud against the developer. The right to rescind exists independently of any damages that may or may not have been incurred. For example, if a builder fraudulently concealed material defects in construction, the owner who learned of the fraudulently concealed defects after (s)he acquired the property would have the right to tender the property back to the developer and receive a refund of the money (s)he had paid. In some jurisdictions, (s)he would also be entitled to recover for damages suffered as a result of the fraud. Of course, (s)he could always elect to keep the property and sue for damages. The most common measure of damages in such a case would be the amount of the diminution in the value of the property resulting from the concealed defects. Under certain circumstances, a purchaser might be entitled to punitive damages in a particularly aggravated case of fraud or concealment.

Where the builder or developer has violated regulations promulgated by the state in connection with a consumer protection program, such regulations generally provide for an absolute right on the part of the buyer to rescind the contract wherever there is a violation of the consumer protection regulations, even though the violation may only be a technical one. *See Chapter 35.3.*

37.9 Product Liability Insurance. All developers would be well advised to carry product liability insurance as coverage against suits for defective construction. While most builders choose to carry such insurance, some cannot because of the expense, others because of their poor track record, and still others are unable to obtain this insurance simply because it is not available in the geographic area where they build or does not cover the product built. With the trend toward more and more litigation involving merchant builders, builders should carry at least enough product liability insurance to take care of the defense costs in any construction-related lawsuit. *See Chapter 37.7.*

37.10 Failure to Enforce Restrictive Covenants. During the initial stages of the project, developers regulated by restrictive covenants have a special obligation to administer the project in accordance with the project's legal documents. In most common-interest subdivisions, the developer will have created an owners association (either incorporated or unincorporated), and the board of directors will be composed of persons appointed by the developer. If the developer and/or the board of directors do not enforce the restrictive covenants of the project, and, as a result of this failure damage is done to the project forcing subsequent buyers to take corrective action, the courts may hold the developer responsible for failing to enforce the restrictive covenants. In some cases, members of the board of directors who failed to enforce the covenants have been held personally responsible and liable for damages. *See Chapter 6.17.*

The developer of a new common-interest subdivision generally has special powers and privileges under the legal documents prepared by the attorney for the developer. A developer has a fiduciary obligation to fulfill the responsibilities it has assumed by virtue of those documents. The failure to discharge such responsibilities can result in the developer being liable for damages to the association and its members. For example, suppose the recorded covenants called for the creation of an architectural review committee to review any changes in architectural design of any of the homes in the project. One homeowner adds more rooms or a garage or a carport to his home in direct violation of the restrictions, but the builder/developer fails to prevent him from making this addition or fails to appoint an architectural review committee. If the association must go to court to get an order requiring the homeowner to remove the unauthorized improvements, the developer who failed to enforce the covenants could be held liable for the attorneys' fees and court costs incurred by the association.

CHAPTER 38
Custodian Unit

38.1 Authority to Acquire Custodian Unit. Some project legal documents will contain provisions authorizing the association to acquire a dwelling unit within the project for use as a residence for a custodian or office for the resident manager. Without such a provision in the documents it is doubtful that the association would have this authority. In a large project, it may be desirable to have a resident manager. If the economic level of the typical owner is fairly high, it may not be possible for a resident manager to afford to live in the project. The association's legal documents can be amended to accommodate a resident manager or custodian by authorizing the purchase of one of the units as a custodian unit, or to authorize the board to subsidize a resident manager or custodian by guaranteeing a loan and paying a salary sufficient to pay the loan and monthly assessments.

Manager's Note: There are many developers who design large projects with a custodian's unit or manager's office on the premises. Often a management office is simply a small unit on the project. A custodian or "groundskeeper's" unit may be a small home located on the perimeter of the complex. In such cases, the units are deeded to the association soon after the close of the first escrow in the project.

38.2 Assessments Against Custodian Unit. The custodian unit may be subject to the same assessments as any other unit in the project, or it may be exempt from assessments during the time that it is occupied by a custodian or resident manager.

38.3 Voting Privileges of a Custodian Unit. The custodian unit may or may not a have voting membership. If the unit is exempt from assessments, it should not carry voting privileges.

38.4 Insurance on Custodian Unit. If the custodian unit is part of a condominium project, the master policy will cover everything except the unit's contents. *See Chapter 21.1.* A custodian who lives in the unit should have some kind of insurance for the contents of the unit and to cover personal liability. *See Chapter 21.2.* The association can subsidize the cost of such insurance as part of the compensation package, if the legal documents so permit.

Manager's Note: In the case of an on-site management office which is not the home or residence of the manager, it is customary for all costs associated with the office to be paid by the association. Such costs would include all utilities, insurance and property taxes on the manager's unit. As with a custodian's unit, if the management office is also a residence, all or a portion of these costs can be paid by the association or can become part of the compensation package given to the resident manager.

38.5 Use of Custodian Unit. Where the legal documents permit the use and occupation of a unit by a custodian or resident manager, they should also provide that the occupant of the unit is subject to all of the restrictive covenants, including the association's rules.

38.6 Sale or Rental of Custodian Unit. Where the legal documents authorize the existence of a custodian unit, the terms of occupancy should be specified in the employment agreement. Normally, the association will hold title to the unit and a custodian will not be permitted to sublease the unit.

CHAPTER 39
Rental of Common Area Office to Developer

39.1 Rental to Developer. In most cases, the developer of a new common-interest subdivision will make provision for the location of its construction and sales activities. Usually a developer will use certain units for model homes and for a sales office. Construction activities are generally handled from construction trailers brought to the site.

In a large project where the developr must maintain a sales office on the site for a number of years, it is sometimes necessary to locate the sales office somewhere other than in the models or in one or more of the units. In such cases, the developer may wish to occupy a room or rooms in the common area facilities, such as the recreation building or common meeting room. Where this occurs, there may be certain regulations adopted by the state consumer protection agency that put limitations on the terms under which the developer may use common area facilities as a sales or rental office. For example, if the developer entered into a long-term lease of a portion of the project's recreation building for use as an office, and the board of directors signed the lease at a time when a majority of the board were officers or employees of the developer, state laws or regulations may exist that would make this long-term lease voidable at the option of the members of the association or the newly elected board of directors.

39.2 Rental to Real Estate Broker. In very large projects, particularly condominium projects, there will generally be a fairly heavy level of rental activity within the project. If the project's declaration does not permit a business to be operated on site, it would be a violation of the use restrictions to permit a real estate broker to occupy space within the project unless the legal documents are amended to permit such activity. In addition to amending the use restrictions to permit the continuing presence of a real estate office, the provisions granting powers to the board of directors may also require amendments to permit the board to rent space in one of the common area buildings to a real estate brokerage office. Certainly, no board should undertake to permit such use without being granted clear authority in the legal documents or without having the matter put to a vote of the general membership.

39.3 Legal Authority. In order to determine whether or not an association or board has the legal authority to rent either a unit or a part of the common area to a broker for use as an on-site sales or rental office, the board should consult the project legal documents to determine if such arrangements are authorized. The association should also review local zoning ordinances to see whether the operation of a business or commercial activity is permitted within the residential area of the project. In addition, if the project was developed under PD zoning and a use permit was granted, it is possible that the establishment of a real estate sales or rental office on the project site may violate the use permit or the PD permit, and permission of the city would have to be sought.

39.4 Rental Agreement Form. *See Form 32 for an example of a rental agreement to be entered into between an association and a developer.*

39.5 Reconversion of Rental Office or Custodian Unit. In the event the project legal documents permit a custodian unit or an on-site sales or rental office, and such a facility, after a period of legally authorized use, is no longer necessary, the association may desire to terminate the arrangement and convert the space back into recreational use if it is part of common area, or it may wish to dispose of the unit occupied by the custodian. At this point it is necessary to consult the legal documents to determine what restrictions have been placed upon the unit. If the unit has no vote and is not subject to assessments, the legal documents may have to be amended. If the association owns the unit, the association will have to decide whether it wants to rent or sell the unit.

Long-term rental of the unit would have to be authorized by the legal documents. The legal documents may have been created to provide for the eventual termination of the use of the unit as a custodian unit or termination of the occupancy of a part of the recreational facilities by the developer.

CHAPTER 40
Destruction or Obsolescence of Project

40.1 Obsolescence. Common-interest owners associations will find that over time their legal documents become outdated. This poses no problem if the owners are able to agree on suitable amendments. Updating obsolete documents can become a problem when an extraordinary majority is required in order to adopt any amendments. *See Chapter 3.12.*

Obsolescence due to changed circumstances such as a decline in the neighborhood, construction of new highways or nearby public buildings, drastic changes in zoning, or obsolescence caused by rapid technological advances or changes in concepts of building design and materials are more serious problems. If an entire project becomes functionally obsolete over a period of time, it may be necessary to terminate the project. *See Chapter 41.*

40.2 Destruction. Where destruction of a common-interest subdivision occurs, a number of choices exist. If the destruction is partial, the destroyed area should be rebuilt. If the association has insurance to cover the loss, the insurance proceeds may be used to rebuild. If the insurance proceeds are insufficient, there may be a special assessment to cover the shortfall. *See Chapter 25.4.* Although it seldom occurs, if the project is totally destroyed, the decision whether to rebuild using insurance proceeds or a combination of insurance proceeds and special assessments may not be quite so obvious. In most cases, the project legal documents will contain provisions covering total or partial destruction. There may be a formula that defines major and minor destruction and requires different solutions in each case. An extraordinary majority vote may be required in order to rebuild a project that has been substantially destroyed. For slight damage, repair or rebuilding may be automatic unless an extraordinary majority votes not to repair.

Federal and state legislation must also be considered. In some states, laws address how insurance proceeds are to be distributed to the membership when more than half the project has been destroyed. In these states, insurance proceeds must be distributed to the members and the damaged project must be sold by partition action, with the proceeds distributed to owners and their secured lenders, unless a vote by an extraordinary majority demands reconstruction. The rules vary from state to state and from project to project. In most cases, where state provisions address the question of partial or total destruction, the rules or statutes provide that the owners of the project are free to make other provisions, and the statutory rules only operate in the absence of any provisions in the legal documents.

There are many competing considerations that affect the decision of whether the emphasis should be on rebuilding a damaged project, or on selling it and distributing the funds together with the insurance proceeds. The approach that is adopted is an arbitrary decision made by the original developer at the time the project legal documents are created. The owners should carefully consider the provisions of the legal documents and the applicable state and federal laws to decide what provisions should apply in the event of destruction of all or a portion of their project. Some draftsmen of project legal documents prefer to leave the documents vague as to what happens in the event of partial or total destruction, leaving it to the owners to decide the most equitable solution at that time.

In mixed-use projects, where commercial property occupies the lower levels and residential property occupies the upper levels, there may be two different associations, and the ownership of the residential and commercial areas may be separate. In such a case, the residential area above the commercial area will have easements for ingress, egress and support. If the entire project is destroyed and the residential area owners wish to rebuild but the commercial area owners do not, how can the residential area owners proceed to rebuild? Using easement rights provided for in the project legal documents, the residential owners could construct the necessary foundations to support their residential building. However, if the commercial owners decided not to rebuild and had the power to make such a unilateral decision, the added costs of building up to the level where the residential property begins might make the total cost of rebuilding the residential area too great. In this case, the residential owners might consider purchasing the residual value of the commercial real estate and developing it itself, or selling it off to another party interested in developing the commercial area.

The legal documents may provide for a vote of both the residential and the commercial owners on the question of reconstruction. A common provision in mixed-use documents is that insurance proceeds must be used to rebuild the project unless an extraordinary majority of the residential owners and the commercial owners vote against reconstruction. If partial destruction occurs and insurance proceeds are not sufficient to rebuild, should all of the owners be required to contribute to the costs of rebuilding, or only the owners whose units were destroyed? On the one hand, it does not seem reasonable to require owners of undamaged units to pay special assessments to rebuild other units that were damaged. However, a condominium, stock cooperative or planned development project can be considered a joint endeavor where all owners have cast their lots together, sharing project benefits and catastrophes, and thus have either expressly or impliedly agreed to share the risks.

It is not clear whether the various mathematical formulas pertaining to percentage of destruction, or requiring certain extraordinary majorities to vote on whether to rebuild or to distribute insurance proceeds and sell the project, really work. A formula that works for a single high-rise condominium building may not work at all for a low-rise garden apartment project with a number of detached and independently operating buildings. Compulsory repair of partial damage may at times run counter to sound business judgment and the desires of most owners. Automatic dissolution and distribution of insurance and sale proceeds may not be preferable in every case where there is substantial or total destruction. Some legal analysts caution against substituting arbitrary legal judgments in place of a post-casualty determination by a majority of the owners, made in light of the facts and circumstances such as the amount of destruction, the cost of repairs, the age and location of the project, and other relevant data.

40.3 Insurance Proceeds. The project documents should specify the rights of the association and its members with respect to the use of insurance proceeds. If the documents and/or applicable statutes require insurance proceeds to be used to rebuild the project, that will control; however, if the owners have the option to vote, then the matter must be put to a vote. If the documents provide that under the circumstances insurance proceeds must be distributed, then consideration must be given to how to distribute the proceeds. Lender protection provisions, either in the legal documents or lender's deeds of trust, will require that lenders receive that portion of the proceeds necessary to pay off their loans. The distribution of the remaining proceeds should be made by a formula established by the legal documents or pursuant to the statutory requirements. Where there are neither statutory requirements nor provisions in the legal documents, distribution will have to be based on common sense, good judgment, and the will of the majority.

In the event of a partial or total destruction of a common-interest subdivision, coupled with the members' election not to rebuild, some state regulations require that insurance proceeds be distributed among the owners and their mortgagees according to:

1) The fair market values;
2) A formula set forth in the governing instruments; or
3) Some other method approved by the state regulatory agency.

Standard provisions require insurance proceeds to be used to rebuild, but with an escape clause in the form of an option to distribute the proceeds to owners and lenders on vote of an extraordinary majority of members.

If a project was substantially destroyed and has not been rebuilt or repaired within a certain period, some statutes provide that the project may be terminated and partitioned by sale. The proceeds of the sale, plus the proceeds of insurance, would be distributed to owners and their lenders on the vote of a majority of the owners.

The owners of one building in a single development of free-standing buildings should not be able to elect among themselves to take their insurance proceeds, pay off their lenders, retain the balance of the proceeds, and leave their destroyed building as a problem for the remaining owners. A project potentially vulnerable to such a situation should have its legal documents amended to prevent such an occurrence. The FHLMC Sellers and Servicers Guide provides that insurance proceeds payable for loss due to destruction of a condominium project must be used for repair or reconstruction unless two-thirds of the first mortgagees or two-thirds of the owners agree otherwise.

The FNMA Lending Guide requires that damage due to destruction must be repaired unless other action is approved by the first mortgagees of units having 51 percent (51%) of the votes of units subject to first mortgages where the lenders have met certain FNMA requirements.

Some lenders have included language in their deeds of trust that gives the lender the right to have insurance proceeds applied against the unpaid balance of the loan rather than be used to repair the property. A court has held that a lender is under a duty to apply the insurance proceeds to rebuild the improvements unless the lender can show special circumstances under which its security would be jeopardized unless the proceeds were used to apply to the loan. The decision prevents the lender from applying the insurance proceeds to the loan, and leaving the property owner with insufficient money to rebuild and pay any remaining loan balance to the lender.

If insurance proceeds are insufficient to rebuild and a special assessment is necessary to raise funds to rebuild or repair, on what basis should it be levied? The legal documents will generally provide the answer. There may be some question about whether the assessment should be pro-rated on the basis of square footage, or market value, or if it should be equal. In a planned development project where the destruction is to common area improvements, the assessments should be equal, because theoretically every owner has an equal right to use the common facilities. Where damage is to individual townhouses insured under a master policy, a special assessment should probably be on the basis of square footage or some assessment formula that takes into the consideration the size and the difference in value of the units. It would not be reasonable to require the owner of a single unit that was damaged to make up the difference between the amount of insurance proceeds available from the master policy and the cost of rebuilding his/her dwelling. That is because where legal documents provide for a master insurance policy, the members of the association have elected to spread the risk of loss so that they all share in it regardless of where it falls within the project. Furthermore, in many cases the master policy provisions of the declaration will prohibit each owner from carrying his/her own hazard insurance in order to avoid having an insurance company invoke the co-insurance clause and reduce the proceeds payable under the master policy. *See Chapters 21.1 and 21.27.*

Legal documents should provide the procedure by which insurance proceeds are collected and used to restore or reconstruct the project. The association should be given authority to handle the insurance proceeds and to supervise the reconstruction activities wherever the construction involves common area property or property insured under the master policy.

In a partially destroyed condominium project where the owners elect not to rebuild the project and, at the same time, do not vote to acquire the interests of the owners whose units were destroyed, the insurance proceeds would be distributed equitably to all owners. The owners of the destroyed units would receive some proceeds and would still own an undivided interest in the project as well as continuing to own the airspace where their unit had been located. In such a case, the owners of the destroyed units would have several possible remedies. The legal documents or state statutes may provide that if the project is not rebuilt within a certain period of time, the owners can bring an action for partition and force a sale of the entire project and a distribution of the proceeds. Each owner, of course, would be able to sell his or her unit to someone who would rebuild it in accordance with the original plans and specifications.

40.4 Distribution of Assets. Prior to the adoption of amendments to the Internal Revenue Code which granted tax exemptions to residential owners associations, such associations were subject to income tax on their assessments to the extent that assessments for the year exceeded expenditures for the year. In order to avoid having to pay tax, some associations were set up as if they were public benefit corporations. In such cases, the articles of incorporation provided that in the event of termination of the project and dissolution of the association, the assets would be contributed to another non-profit corporation. At that time it was believed by some tax advisors that such provisions were necessary in order to establish tax-exempt status. Such provisions are no longer necessary to achieve that end, and wherever such provisions appear they should be deleted by amendment and replaced by wording which indicates that in the event of dissolution of the association, the proceeds shall be distributed equitably among the members. *See Chapter 42.14.*

CHAPTER 41
Extension of Projects; Termination of Projects

41.1 Extension of Projects. Most common-interest subdivision project legal documents provide that the project and the recorded covenants, conditions and restrictions will continue for a number of years, after which they may be extended or may terminate. Some documents provide for automatic extension unless a certain number (more than 50 percent) of the members vote not to extend or to terminate. Some state statutes as well as some legal documents provide that no single extension may exceed the initial term of the declaration, or some fixed number of years, whichever is less. Generally, there is no limit on the number of extensions allowed.

In some states there are technical rules of law derived from English common law that put limits on the maximum term that covenants, conditions and restrictions may apply to real property. Usually the drafters of the documents will have taken those rules into consideration and will have made provision for the maximum term. Such rules are subject to change by state legislatures. Legal counsel should be consulted in any event when questions of extension or the maximum term of existence of project legal documents is under discussion.

If a project comes to the end of its initial term, it will be terminated in accordance with its legal documents unless there is a vote to extend. If the required majority of the owners does not vote in favor of extension, or votes against extension, the project will have to be terminated. If the legal documents do not provide for what happens in that event, it is possible that state statutes may be helpful. If help cannot be found in either the legal documents or state statutes, the members will have to decide among themselves how to terminate the project and distribute the assets. There are, of course, a number of alternatives. The entire project could be sold to a developer who may start a whole new project or may operate it as a rental project. Individuals could sell their lots or units to other individuals who collectively could elect to continue or to reconstitute the project. The entire project could be sold to a buyer who would convert it to an entirely different use. The proceeds of sale would be distributed equitably among the selling owners and their lenders.

41.2 Termination of Projects. A project may be terminated for a number of reasons. The project may have been taken by eminent domain (*see Chapter 32*) or may have become obsolete. *See Chapter 40.1.* The project may have been totally or substantially destroyed and the members may have decided not to rebuild. *See Chapter 40.2.* The project may be terminated because under the project legal documents or state statutes one or more owners have brought a partition action to have the entire project sold. One hundred percent (100%) of the owners of a common-interest development may have agreed to terminate it at any time, subject to rights of third parties such as lenders, and subject to local governmental restrictions that may have been placed on the project at the time of its creation.

In the case of a leasehold condominium, the expiration of the underlying ground lease may require the termination of the project unless the owner of the land elects to continue the condominium form of ownership. When a project is terminated, certain legal actions may be necessary. If the owners association was incorporated, the statutory steps for dissolution of an incorporated association must be followed. It may be necessary to record a rescission of the recorded declaration of covenants, conditions and restrictions in order to remove those restrictions and prevent them from being a cloud on the title to the property in the future.

CHAPTER 42
Taxes

42.1 Federal Income Taxes.
Owners associations, whether or not incorporated, are treated by the Internal Revenue Service as if they were corporations for tax purposes, and their "income" is subject to tax. Owners associations may qualify for exemption from tax. *See Chapter 42.7.*

Unless an association has achieved tax-exempt status, it is subject to tax on its income, which includes its assessments, interest received on its savings accounts, and rental income or concessionaire income paid to the association. The association is entitled to deduct its expenditures for ordinary and necessary expenses of operating, managing and maintaining the property. If expenses equal income for the association's fiscal year, it would not owe any income tax. However, reserves must be set aside, which will cause income to exceed expenses. The Internal Revenue Service has permitted associations to avoid paying income tax on the amount by which assessments exceeded expenditures, provided the excess receipts were specifically designated for reserves and were segregated into a separate account for that purpose. In other cases, if the excess receipts were applied on the following year's assessments or were returned to the owners, the association was allowed to escape income tax. While it is possible by means of careful handling of the association's receipts and expenditures to avoid income tax on assessment receipts, it is not possible to avoid paying income tax on interest or rental income. It is also possible to avoid income tax on assessments without having to engage in fancy financial footwork, merely by qualifying for tax-exempt status. *See Chapter 42.7.*

Any association planning to avoid income tax by proper handling of its receipts and expenditures, but without obtaining a tax exemption, should have the assistance of a CPA experienced in handling owners association tax problems. In addition to rental income and interest, the association must pay tax on amounts received from persons who are not members of the association for use of the association recreational facilities, or for special use of the association facilities. For example, if the association admitted members from an adjoining project to the association's recreational facilities and charged a monthly fee, those fees would be taxable income to the association. The association would be able to deduct expenses attributable to the rented areas so that only the net income would be subject to tax. Also, where common areas owned by the association are rented to third parties, the association should be entitled to deduct some depreciation.

Stock cooperatives are subject to slightly different rules. They are not specifically eligible for exemption under the Internal Revenue Code. Under certain state laws, they are exempt from state income tax. They may reduce or eliminate taxes on the excess of assessments over expenditures by refunding excess collections to the members before the end of the taxable year.

Commercial common-interest owners associations are not eligible for tax exemption. *See Chapter 42.7.*

42.2 State Income Taxes. The treatment of owners' associations under state income tax law varies from state to state. Some states have adopted their own version of the Internal Revenue Code that may or may not permit owners' associations to be exempt from state income taxes. Where exemptions are provided, the state rules may differ from the federal rules. *See Chapter 42.7.*

42.3 Local Taxes. In some cases, associations may be subject to some form of local taxation. For example, some communities levy a tax on fees received by residential time-share associations.

42.4 Real Property Taxes. In a condominium project where the common area is owned in undivided interests by the owners, the association will not own any property and is therefore not subject to any separate assessment, nor liable for the payment of any real property taxes. In cases where the association owns real property, whether or not it is subject to tax depends upon state statutes. In some states there is no separate tax imposed on common area property owned by a residential owners association. The value of the association-owned property is included in the tax assessor's appraisal of the individual units or lots, and each unit or lot owner is assessed his or her proportional share of that value along with the value of the unit or lot. In those states where a separate real property tax is assessed against association-owned property, the association must pay the taxes and should set aside reserves to make the annual or semi-annual tax payments.

42.5 Personal Property Taxes. In some jurisdictions, if the association owns personal property such as furniture, furnishings and office equipment, it may have to file an annual personal property tax return and pay some personal property taxes. There may or may not be an exemption from such tax available under state law in that jurisdiction.

42.6 Tax Exemptions. Homeowners associations can qualify as tax-exempt organizations under Internal Revenue Code § 528. Cooperative housing corporations and commercial common-interest owners associations are not eligible under that section.

Homeowners associations can elect to be treated as tax-exempt organizations by using the proper application form. *See Chapter 42.7.* If an association makes the election and is qualified as a tax-exempt organization, it is not taxed on receipt of its assessments. To qualify for election, an association must meet the test prescribed by Internal Revenue Code § 528. In order to qualify, the association must be organized and operate to provide for the maintenance and care of association property. Auxiliary uses, such as recreational facilities, laundry areas, storage or maintenance areas, are considered residential uses. Most of the income of the association must be derived from membership assessments received from owners of residential units. Most of the expenditures for the year must be made for management, construction, maintenance and care of association property. No part of the net earnings of the association can inure to the benefit of any individual except through such things as rebate of excess assessments. The association must elect to be treated as a tax-exempt organization for the tax year in question. These rules are technical, and can change from time to time with the adoption of new regulations. The association should have the advice of an experienced CPA or tax attorney in achieving tax-exempt status. In some cases, the original developer of the project may have obtained a tax exemption for the association, and, in other cases, the developer may not have done so, which will require the new board to apply for the exemption. *See Form 22 for an example of a resolution authorizing application for tax-exempt status.*

The association may elect tax-exempt status by filing Internal Revenue Form 1120H within the time prescribed for filing federal income tax returns for the year for which the election is made, including any extensions. Once the election is made, the association is not taxed on exempt income for that year, which means dues, fees, or assessments received from the owners of residential lots or units in the project. However, the association will continue to be taxed on income that is not exempt. Such income would include:

- Interest earned on reserves;
- Amounts paid by persons who are not members of the association for use of association facilities;
- Amounts paid by persons who are members of the association for special use of the association's facilities (an example would be rental of the recreation room for a private party); and
- Late charge penalties and fines.

Many states have also adopted tax-exemption statutes and have established forms for claiming tax exemptions. The association's CPA or tax attorney should be consulted about how to file for exemption from state income tax.

42.7 Application for Exemption. Homeowners associations may qualify as tax-exempt organizations under Internal Revenue Code § 528. They may also obtain tax exemptions from state income taxes under applicable state statutes. A developer may apply for a tax exemption at the time the association is formed, or any time thereafter. To qualify for exemption under the Internal Revenue Code, the association makes an annual election at the time it files its federal income tax return, using Form 1120H. Once the election is made, it is binding for that tax year and may not be revoked without the consent of the Commissioner of Internal Revenue.

If the developer has not obtained a tax exemption for the association under state law, and/or has not filed an election to be treated as a tax-exempt organization under the Internal Revenue Code, the board should follow through, with the help, if needed, of the association's CPA or attorney.

42.8 Denial of Exemption. An association that cannot meet the test of Internal Revenue Code § 528 and the regulations adopted thereunder will be denied an exemption. A stock cooperative corporation or a commercial condominium association will not meet the test. If a residential association is denied an exemption, it can appeal from the denial to the tax court or the federal district court, or in the case of a denial of an application by a state franchise tax board, an appeal could be filed in the state court system.

42.9 Mixed-Use Associations.

With the trend in favor of mixed-use projects with ground floor commercial and residential development above, the number of mixed-use owners associations is increasing. If an owners association consists of owners of commercial units in addition to residential unit owners, does that prevent the association from qualifying as a tax-exempt homeowners association under Internal Revenue Code § 528? It depends upon the facts. Presently, the code requires the association to be organized and operated to provide for the management, maintenance and care of association property, 85 percent of which is used by individuals for residential purposes. Although auxiliary uses such as recreational facilities, laundry areas, and storage and maintenance areas are considered residential uses, commercial property normally does not qualify. Does this mean that a project can be 15 percent commercial and still qualify because it is 85 percent residential? Any mixed-use association should consult its CPA and tax attorney on this question. Some developers that have created mixed-use projects have purposely set up separate associations for the commercial and residential owners partly to avoid jeopardizing the right of the residential owners to achieve tax-exempt status.

42.10 Adjusting Income and Expenses to Minimize Tax.

When an association cannot meet the qualifications for exemption from income tax, or elects not to file Form 1120H, that does not necessarily mean that it has to pay income tax on its assessments, or indeed any income tax at all. It is possible to adjust receipts and disbursements so that as of the end of the fiscal year the expenses equal the income and there is therefore no net income to be subject to tax. Also, assessments for capital improvements are not classified as income, if they are specifically earmarked as reserves for capital improvements and are not commingle with general funds.

42.11 Switching from Tax-Exempt to Non-Tax-Exempt Status.

There are some conditions under which it is advisable for an association not to make an election to be treated as a tax-exempt association in a particular year. If the association's reserves have increased to the point where the interest earned and the corresponding taxes are substantial, the association may save taxes by filing a standard corporate return and paying tax on its interest income at a lower rate. The association should consult its CPA each year to determine whether or not it is preferable to claim the exemption for that year. There is, however, some question about whether an association may file a Form 1120H in alternate years. Some Internal Revenue Service agents have apparently advised that once an 1120H election has been made, an association cannot abandon that election without Internal Revenue Service consent. That may or may not be true, and the association should seek tax advice on this issue.

If the association elects not to file an 1120H form for a particular year, in order to avoid being taxed on its assessments, its expenditures must equal its assessments or excess assessments may be refunded, providing that the decision to refund is made before the end of the taxable year. It can also pass a resolution prior to the close of the fiscal year to have the excess receipts applied against the following year's assessments, and this may serve to avoid tax. The association should also consult its accountant about whether or not it is entitled to depreciate its assets and to offset its assessment income with depreciation where the association is not qualified for exemption from tax.

Manager's Note: *To avoid taxes against assessments, homeowners associations are advised to adopt annually (usually at the annual meeting of the general membership) the provisions of IRS Revenue Ruling 70-604. Check with your CPA to obtain the correct wording for this resolution.*

42.12 Tax Returns. An incorporated association should have its accountant obtain a corporate identification number for federal income tax purposes. The association should file either a corporate return or Internal Revenue Code Form 1120H.

In the event an association expects to pay income taxes, it may be required under state law to make quarterly payments of estimated tax. Also, an association must file forms 1096 and 1099 MISC with the Internal Revenue Service in the event it has paid more than $600 per year to any person providing services to the association during that year. The tax laws of a particular state may treat corporate income tax differently than federal laws, and it may be possible to elect tax-exempt status under federal laws and at the same time elect not to be treated as a tax-exempt homeowners association under state law. The association's accountant should be consulted with any questions.

42.13 Audits. Certain state statutes require annual audits for associations having more than a certain number of members, or collecting more than a certain minimum amount in assessments or other charges during a single fiscal year. Statutes may specify the requirements for the audit.

The project legal documents may contain certain provisions requiring an audit under certain circumstances, such as where the association receives more than a certain amount in income during any one year. The association's legal documents may also provide that a member or certain number of members has/have the right to call for an audit at any time. Any time an audit is involved, whether voluntary or involuntary, the association should have the advice of an experienced CPA.

42.14 Distribution of Assets on Dissolution. Prior to the passage of the Tax Reform Act of 1976, many legal documents creating nonprofit homeowners association were drafted with provisions that provided for distribution of the assets of the corporation to a tax-exempt organization upon dissolution of the owners association. It was believed necessary to do that in order to qualify for tax-exempt status prior to the 1976 act. It is no longer necessary to have such provisions in order to qualify for tax-exempt status. Any owners association still having such provisions in its articles of incorporation or elsewhere in its legal documents should amend them to provide that upon dissolution of the association, the assets will be distributed on an equitable basis to all of the members. *See Chapter 40.4.*

42.15 Incorporated Compared with Unincorporated Associations. Unincorporated owners associations are in most cases treated as if they were corporations for tax purposes, and are subject to regular corporate tax rates. The Internal Revenue Code definition of a corporation extends to an association that has certain corporate characteristics, such as centralized management, continuity of life, free transferability of interests, and limited liability. Most owners associations have centralized management (officers and a board of directors) and continuity of life (unlike a partnership, the association continues on after the death of one or more of its members). Membership is transferable freely with transfer of a unit or lot. An unincorporated association that wishes to qualify for tax-exempt status should consult its CPA.

42.16 Tax Identification Number. The board of directors of the association should obtain a tax identification number, or ask its accountant to do so. Once obtained from the Internal Revenue Service, that number should be used on all correspondence with the Internal Revenue Service, as well as on all tax return forms.

CHAPTER 43
Utilities

43.1 Master Meter. A common-interest subdivision may be designed so that one or more master meters serves the entire project. In such cases the association will be billed according to the meter(s) for the utilities used. The utility bill will be included in the expenses of the association, and a portion of the utility bill will be included in the assessment paid by each member.

The association legal documents should specify whether utilities are to be pro-rated equally among all members, or are to be assessed on a formula basis. In some cases where formulas are used, they are based on square footage of interior usable space. That is not necessarily the fairest way to pro-rate utilities, however. It is fair and more accurate to pro-rate on the basis of usage, even if the usage is only estimated. Estimating usage has some difficulties, however, as it is not possible to forecast water usage, for example, simply based on the number of bathrooms in each dwelling serviced by a master meter. At the same time, it would be logical to assume that in a commercial condominium project a restaurant would use more water than an office occupied by a temporary secretarial service.

Developers who create such projects try to pro-rate the utilities on an equitable basis where master meters are used. If any members believe that the method of pro-rating utility charges among the members is unfair, the matter can always be brought to the attention of the board, and, if necessary, a special membership meeting can be called to consider the matter. It is always possible to amend the project legal documents to change the formula or the method of allocation, although it may require an extraordinary majority, or in some cases even a unanimous vote, to do so.

43.2 Individual Meters. Where individual meters are used for each unit or lot, pro-ration of charges for utilities takes care of itself. However, there may be some cases where the project has both master meters and individual meters, and some controls are necessary. For example, in a condominium or planned development project where garages or carports are part of the common area, but garages or carports (which are in the common area) are serviced by a master electrical meter, some control needs to be placed on the use of electrical power by the individual owners. One way of handling the situation is to have the legal documents provide that the association board of directors has the authority to assess a member for utility charges in the event that that member is found to be using more than his or her fair share of utilities supplied through a master meter.

43.3 Mixed-Use Projects. Mixed-use projects that combine residential and commercial units served by a master meter are rare, but do exist. In such circumstances, the association should attempt to have a separate meter installed for the residential units and one for the commercial units. If possible, it is also best to have individual meters on all commercial units, since the use of electricity, gas, water and other utilities can vary greatly among different commercial users.

43.4 Utility Assessment Adjustments. What if the members of an association believe that the formula for pro-ration of assessments or assessments based on utilities is unfair or inaccurate? How can the formula be changed? That depends on the circumstances. If the project is under the jurisdiction of a state regulatory agency, there may be restrictions on how the formula can be changed. The project legal documents will probably have to be amended, and there may be provisions that require more than a majority vote to change the formula. In some cases certain lenders may have the right to approve changes in the formula. *See Chapter 25.5.* It may be possible for one or more of the members to have a court intervene and actually reform the legal documents to make the formula for pro-ration of assessments more equitable.

CHAPTER 44
Public Relations and Communication

44.1 The Importance of Public Relations. Instituting good systems of communication and public relations is extremely important for any owners association. Few things are more destabilizing to a neighborhood than feuds between neighbors. Tension among owners living and working in close proximity in a residential or commercial common interest subdivision tends to degrade the quality of life. Good living and working relationships may be due to a fortuitous mix of owners, or, more often, is a combination of planning, foresight, and attention to establishing and maintaining a good community spirit or *esprit de corps* within a common-interest subdivision. *See Form 19 for an example of a letter to new owners.*

44.2 Use of Committees. One very effective way to establish and nurture an *esprit de corps* is to involve members in committee service. Committees, which can be helpful in terms of improving community spirit, can include a social committee, a security or anti-crime committee, an architectural control committee, and a new membership committee. In addition to getting members involved in the activities that are part of the solution rather than part of the problem, committees serve as a training ground for future directors and as a means of communication between the board and the owners. Committees should have as much authority and responsibility within their area as the board is authorized to delegate. (*See Chapter 6.15 regarding limits on the board's authority to delegate.*)

Certainly, the new member committee or social committee can do a great deal to integrate new members into the association by explaining the rules, acquainting them with the project, making them feel at home, and generating community spirit for the project.

44.3 Handling of Grievances. Every association should institute a method of handling complaints and grievances. Complaints are commonly funneled through the professional manager under contract to the association. In a large association, a grievance committee may be established to handle complaints.

Whether it is the manager or grievance committee, or a member of the board of directors, the job will involve logging the nature of the complaint, the date and time of receipt, the corrective action, and the completion or action date. Finally, the complaint log should contain an acknowledgement by the complaining owner that the matter has been resolved.

Manager's Note: Complaint logs do not need to be complicated in order to be efficient. For smaller associations, a log can be a simple spiral-bound journal noting the date, name of homeowner, and nature of the complaint. When the situation is resolved, a check mark and a date can be placed next to the entry. For larger associations, complaints may be logged in a large spreadsheet, which references a work order or job-tracking form. Databases are also excellent methods to track service requests and repairs, and to determine if any maintenance "trends" seem to be occurring.

44.4 Newsletters. Many associations that have established and continue to maintain a good community spirit are helped considerably by having a quality newsletter that is distributed monthly or quarterly to all members. Associations interested in having a newsletter should seek help from other associations by obtaining a copy of their newsletter. They can also contact organizations such as the Community Associations Institute (CAI) or the Executive Council of Homeowners (ECHO) to obtain sample copies of association newsletters.

***Manager's Note:** Many of today's most popular software programs allow even the smallest association to produce professional-looking newsletters.*

The best newsletters are the ones that are READ by the membership. To ensure that the newsletter is not "circular-filed," newsletters should include not only reminders of the association's rules, but events in the complex such as a community party or board meetings. Periodic stories about "doers" in the community or "good news" items acknowledging someone's hard work around the complex or their home encourages readership and fosters community awareness.

CHAPTER 45
Exclusive-Use Common Area Rights

45.1 Authority to Establish Exclusive Common Area Rights. All common-interest subdivision projects have certain areas within the project designated as a "common area." The common area may be owned in undivided interests by the owners of units or lots within the project, or it may be owned by the owners association, the members of which are the owners of the units or lots in the project. Designated portions of the common area may be set aside for or restricted to the exclusive use of certain members. The terminology used to describe such areas is usually "exclusive-use common area," "restricted common area," or "limited common elements." Examples of exclusive-use common areas are patios, balconies, decks, storage areas, carports, garages, parking places, yards, stairs, elevators, bay windows, greenhouse windows, and fireplace chimneys and flues.

The legal documents by which the project was created may describe restricted common areas and reserve the exclusive use of portions of the common area for certain units or lots. Such areas may be designated in the body of the declaration or in an exhibit attached to the declaration. They may be, in the case of a condominium, shown on the condominium plan. In some projects, the project legal documents will define certain exclusive common areas, but not specifically identify them. For example, a planned development declaration might provide that one common area parking place will be assigned to each lot, and that the assignment shall be made by the declarant and shall be included in the grant deed by which title to a lot is transferred to the initial purchaser. The declaration may also vest the board of directors of the association with the authority to make assignments of common area parking spaces or other common area exclusive-use rights.

Where the declaration or the declaration and the condominium plan or subdivision map create the exclusive common area rights, each exclusive-use common area can be located by consulting those documents. Where the exclusive rights have been created by a series of resolutions of the board of directors, those deeds and those resolutions will have to be consulted to identify and locate the exclusive-use common areas.

The nature of the right to the exclusive use of a portion of the common area is an easement or a right of use or occupancy. Having an exclusive right to use a particular parking space or a particular garage is not the same as having legal title to that parking place or garage.

45.2 Transfer of Exclusive-Use Common Area Rights. Most common-interest subdivision project documents provide that exclusive-use common areas are appurtenant to the unit or lot to which they are assigned initially, and may not be transferred separately and apart from the transfer of title to that home. The usual legal terminology is that the rights are "appurtenant" to the subdivision interest, which means that once established, the exclusive-use common area rights attach to title to the unit or lot to which they are initially assigned, and are conveyed with the transfer of title to that unit or lot. This is normally true even if the exclusive-use common area rights are inadvertently omitted from a deed in the change of title. For example, if the developer of a project deeds out a condominium unit, and the deed includes the exclusive easement to use a particular garage and a particular patio, the garage and the patio are appurtenant to that unit. If the purchaser of that unit fails to mention the garage and patio in the deed when (s)he subsequently transfers title to his/her unit to another buyer, the exclusive rights to the use of the garage and patio will remain appurtenant to that unit. These rights will pass to the new owner (unless state statutes provide otherwise).

Sometimes problems are created where the wrong exclusive-use common area is described on a condominium plan or in a deed. Recording a "Certificate of Correction" or a "Correcting Deed" will correct the description.

Occasionally owners of different units or lots will informally exchange parking places, carports etc. This may be done by informal agreement or unrecorded written agreement between the owners. Normally this does not cause a problem, unless the project legal documents or association rules prohibit such transfers. There may, however, be a problem when one of them sells his/her lot or unit. Since the informal arrangements would not affect title to the exclusive-use common areas, the new owner of the unit or lot would have to make the same agreement for exchanging the use of restricted common areas as his or her predecessor. Where owners try to record their agreement to exchange restricted common areas such as by exchanging deeds, there will be problems. The owners probably lack the authority to do so, because provisions in the project legal documents will restrict the ability of owners to make transfers of record of their exclusive-use common area rights. Therefore, any attempt to record an assignment of the right to use a parking place, garage, or other exclusive-use common area may be void, as it is in conflict with the provisions of the recorded project documents.

45.3 Use Rights. Where exclusive-use rights are assigned, the legal document creating the exclusive use will generally define the rights of use. The term "exclusive" means that no other owners are entitled to use or even to enter the area without permission of the exclusive user. The type of use that can be made is usually implied from the nature of the area. For example, a carport is obviously to be used for parking of vehicles, and not for use as a hobby shop. The project legal documents may contain certain rules and regulations for use of restricted common areas. The association rules and regulations *(see Chapter 47)* may also contain certain rules regarding uses of restricted common areas.

45.4 Maintenance. The project legal documents generally indicate who has responsibility for maintenance of exclusive-use common areas. In some cases, it may be the association, and in others it may be the owner who has been assigned

229

the exclusive-use rights. Occasionally the maintenance authority may be divided. For example, the association may have the responsibility to maintain the fencing around an exclusive-use patio area, but the owner of the unit to which the exclusive-use right has been assigned may have the obligation to maintain the landscaping within the patio.

45.5 Insurance and Liability.
Since exclusive-use common areas are by definition common area, such areas will be included in the master policy for casualty insurance. *See Chapter 21.3*. The unit or lot owner to whom exclusive use has been assigned should carry his or her own public liability insurance *(see Chapter 21.4)*, and the insurance should include liability for injuries occurring in the exclusive-use common area in addition to those occurring within the unit or lot. The association and the exclusive-use common area owner share the burden of potential liability for injuries occurring to persons entering the exclusive-use common area.

CHAPTER 46
Party Walls and Zero-Lot Lines

46.1 Party Walls. Unlike in a condominium, where the space within the walls between two adjoining units is common area, the boundary line between two adjoining lots in a planned development is an imaginary line. In the same way, the boundary between two subdivision lots is an imaginary line that is located and described by survey. Where two adjoining planned development townhouse units are located next to each other and share a common boundary line, the common wall between the two units may be a "party wall."

The type of construction used in party walls, of course, varies. Some party walls may consist of two entirely separate wall structures, with an airspace in between and a common roof overhead. In another case, a party wall may consist of a double wall with plywood or sheetrock and studs set back-to-back. In such projects, the legal documents normally spell out the maintenance requirements for party walls. Usually the cost of maintaining, repairing or replacing party walls falls equally upon the adjoining lot owners. Occasionally the legal documents may provide for repair and reconstruction of such walls by the association.

Where there is destruction by an insured casualty (such as fire), and the association carries a master insurance policy that includes casualty insurance on all dwellings in the project, the master policy proceeds would be used to rebuild the dwellings and the party walls. Where individual owners carry their own casualty insurance, the master policy will usually insure only the common area. In such cases, in the event of destruction of a party wall there may be two insurance companies involved—one for each adjoining owner, or perhaps only one insurance company if the same insurance company covered the adjoining dwellings, or if only one owner was insured. In either event, the adjoining owners are jointly responsible for the costs of maintenance and repair of party walls, unless the association is required by the legal documents to bear that responsibility.

Most states have statutory provisions that establish rights and duties with respect to party walls. Where party walls exist, there are also reciprocal easements between lots upon which party walls are located. Easements for the continued location of the wall and for access to maintain, support and replace the wall are standard. These easements are usually described in the project legal documents, and may also be mentioned in the deeds transferring title to the lots.

46.2 Zero-Lot Lines. The term "zero-lot line" is used to describe a planned development subdivision where some of the homes within the project are built on the boundary line between two lots, rather than being built on the side yard setback line, which is usually five or more feet. This type of construction is permitted by special zoning ordinances. The purpose is to create more useable yard space on one side of the house, while creating more of a feeling of open space within the subdivision. For example, standard side yard setbacks within a residential zone may be between 10 to 20 feet. If the lots are small, and the setback requirements are 10 feet, each house would have two 10-foot side yards. By moving each house so that one exterior wall is placed on the boundary line, a 20-foot side yard can be created on the other side of the house. In this case, the owner of the dwelling built on the boundary line between two lots will need an easement over the adjoining lot for access to maintain and repair the house that is built upon the boundary line. Such easements are normally created by the project legal documents.

Manager's Note: In order to allow adjoining neighbors to maintain the exterior of their homes, many maintenance agreements will prohibit the construction or installation of structures and "hardscape" elements such as raised decks, bushes, concrete pads or irrigation in the maintenance area. If such limitations appear in the legal documents, it is necessary for these restrictions to be enforced when reviewing and approving proposed architectural changes to side or rear yards.

46.3 Common Foundations. In a typical planned development project, homes on adjoining lots will share common foundations. Where such is the case, reciprocal easements for maintenance, repair and replacement of the common foundations exist between the adjoining lots that share the common foundation. Such easements should be provided for in the legal documents creating the project. In the event of a catastrophe such as an earthquake, the adjoining lot owners would share the costs of rebuilding the foundations. If the master insurance policy carried by the association included earthquake insurance, the proceeds of the policy would be used to rebuild the foundations on the adjoining lots (to the extent there was coverage).

46.4 Common Roofs. In planned development projects, the design of the project frequently requires construction of common roof structures, and there should be reciprocal easements among the owners of dwellings sharing a common roof. The project legal documents should provide for such easements and for the sharing of expenses of repair and maintenance of the common roofs. The project legal documents may provide for maintenance by the association of common roofs, or may require lot owners having common roofs to share their maintenance responsibilities. The master insurance policy for the association may or may not include insurance on common roofs. If it does insure roofs, then the association would repair any damage to the roof, using the proceeds of insurance to the extent they are sufficient.

CHAPTER 47
Association Rules and Regulations

47.1 Authority to Adopt Rules and Regulations. The legal documents should provide the board of directors with the power to adopt rules for operation of the common areas and facilities owned or controlled by the association. The board should also have the authority to adopt rules of conduct for the association members, their tenants and guests. The rules adopted by the board should not be inconsistent with the declaration, articles and bylaws of the association. The rules may to some extent be repetitious of the basic provisions of the project legal documents, but generally will go into considerably more detail with respect to conduct that is prohibited or permitted within the project.

47.2 Need for Rules and Regulations. Every common-interest project needs to have certain rules and regulations to control the conduct of its members in order to make project living as comfortable as possible for everyone. Most developers will leave the drafting of rules and regulations to the ultimate buyers of lots or units in the project. Rules tend to be very subjective, and most developers prefer to allow the owners and occupants of the project to develop their own rules and regulations based upon their experience in living in the project.

47.3 Adoption of Rules. Association rules and regulations are usually adopted by the board and then ratified by the membership in a subsequent meeting. The board should have authority to make changes in the rules from time to time. If the legal documents do not specifically give the board that power, the documents should be amended.

47.4 Subjects to be Addressed by Association Rules. Rules should govern the conduct of the members of the association, their tenants and guests. Guests may not be subject to all the rules that apply to members; however, guests and tenants should always be under the control of the owner whose unit they occupy. Rules should be enforced by the board against owners for the actions taken by their tenants or guests that may be in violation of the rules.

Examples of subjects that association rules and regulations normally address include:

- Use of recreational facilities;
- Conduct of pets and children;
- Storage in common areas;
- Obstruction of walkways or common areas;
- Obstruction of views;
- Types of vehicles that may be parked and driven on the property;
- Noise levels and hours of playing stereos, television or radio;
- Unit upkeep;
- Standards for garbage and refuse;
- Use of utilities;
- Storage of flammable materials or toxic materials;
- Use of identification cards, membership certificates or electronic card keys for entrance to the

project or entrance to recreational facilities;
- Replacement of lost keys or certificates; and
- Use of restricted common areas.

See Form 16 for a sample set of association rules and regulations.

CHAPTER 48
Use Restrictions

48.1 Use Restrictions in General. The declaration and other project legal documents will normally contain a set of use restrictions that control or restrict uses to which the property may be put. Usually, the developer will create a set of use restrictions that cover the areas that have in the past been customarily covered by project legal documents. The restrictions may not be particularly well tailored to the project, and the board of directors and members may wish to refine these once they have had experience in living with the use restrictions.

48.2 Population Density Restrictions. Many project legal documents prohibit more than two persons per bedroom from residing as permanent residents within a project. Reasonable population density restrictions have been upheld where they do not have the effect of discriminating against persons because of age, sex, sexual preference, marital status, race, religion, or other suspect criteria. The courts have held that it is a legitimate purpose to limit the total number of inhabitants of a project on a fair and equitable basis. Therefore, reasonable restrictions that are aimed at the total number of persons living in a particular dwelling unit may be enforceable, while at the same time restrictions on the relationships (for example, no more than one family in a dwelling), may not be enforceable.

48.3 Age Restrictions. With respect to age restrictions, some states have held that any restrictions that discriminate against families with children are unenforceable and constitute a violation of civil rights. In such states, enabling legislation has been adopted that does permit the establishment of some adults-only communities. However, there are usually strict rules for establishing adults-only communities, and there are limitations on the ages. For example, it may be necessary that the minimum age be sixty years or more in order to qualify as an adults-only community.

Many projects have been created with restrictions against children under a certain age, and the project documents have not been amended even though such restrictions may no longer be enforceable in the state where the project is located. In such case, the unenforceable provisions that prohibit children in the project can simply be ignored. However, it would be preferable for the association to amend its documents to remove the illegal and unenforceable restriction against children where such restrictions are no longer enforceable.

The federal civil rights statutes may be used to attack restrictions based strictly upon age, depending on the circumstances. Federal statutes do permit the establishment of adults-only communities under strictly enforced conditions. Families with children may find it increasingly difficult to purchase housing where restrictions apply which make some of the housing unavailable to them. In larger projects, it may be possible to reconcile these differences by providing one area for families with children and another area for adults only. However, in medium-sized and small projects, it may not be practical to segregate the project into family areas and adults-only areas. Not everyone wishes to live in a large project, and it would seem reasonable to expect that where age restrictions are illegal or unenforceable, state legislatures would make provision for the establishment of adults-only communities.

48.4 Signs. Most project legal documents will have provisions that restrict the number of signs, types of signs, and size and location of signs. Some state statutes specifically provide that the owner of a dwelling has a right to erect at least one (1) sign of a certain size and dimension, advertising the property for rent or for sale. The particular restrictions on signs may be found in the declaration, or there may be local ordinances or state statutes that regulate signs within the subdivision.

48.5 Window Coverings. Typically, developers will insert provisions in project legal documents that control what owners use as window coverings. A typical provision will provide that drapes or window coverings must be of certain colors, textures and materials that are approved by the developer, by the board of directors, or by an architectural control committee. The basic objective is to have an attractive project; without such regulations there is nothing to prevent owners from installing unattractive or unsightly material in their windows.

48.6 Clotheslines. In many projects, there will be restrictions against the use of clotheslines for drying laundry outside where it can be seen from other dwellings or from the common area. In some municipalities, however, it is not permissible to prohibit the use of outside clotheslines. Local ordinances must be consulted.

48.7 Antennas. Television, radio and satellite antennas are typically regulated by use restrictions included in the project declaration. The Federal Telecommunications Act of 1995 gave the Federal Communications Commission the authority to preempt local ordinances and recorded restrictions. Antennas or satellite dishes of one meter or less in diameter cannot be restricted, except to the extent provided in the FCC rules. Some restrictions are permissible, provided they do not unreasonably increase installation costs and do not preclude an acceptable quality of reception and depending upon the proposed location of the equipment.

48.8 Alterations or Additions. Project legal documents will normally require any owner who wishes to make alterations or additions to his or her home to submit plans and specifications to the board or to an architectural control committee for approval prior to the commencement of construction. In cases where a use permit or PD permit has been issued by the local governmental agency, it may also be necessary for the homeowner to apply to some local governmental body in order to obtain approval of any alterations or additions to dwellings in the project.

48.9 Architectural Committee. The project legal documents will normally provide for an architectural committee, charged with the responsibility of reviewing plans and specifications for construction of new buildings or alteration of existing buildings. The members of the committee may originally be appointed by the developer, and in some cases the developer retains the right to control the membership of the committee until (s)he has completed building and selling the dwellings in the subdivision. The board usually has power to appoint the members of the committee after the developer has relinquished the right to appoint. The project legal documents should define the duties of the architectural committee, and the committee itself should create and follow specific rules. Provisions should be made for review of plans and specifications and specifications. It is customary to provide that if the committee does not take action either approving or disapproving the plans within a certain period of time after they have been submitted (usually thirty to sixty days), the plans will be deemed approved and the owner submitting the plans will be permitted to proceed.

Sometimes a detailed set of guidelines will be prepared and will be available for review by all members seeking to obtain consent by the architectural committee for alterations or for new construction. The guidelines are generally a flexible document that may be changed periodically by the board.

Manager's Note: *In some areas, a detailed set of guidelines will be prepared by the city or county's planning and building departments or may be filed by the developer with the city or county. Members seeking to obtain consent of the architectural committee would be well advised to carefully review the guidelines on file with the city or county.*

If an owner fails to comply with the rules and regulations of the architectural committee, either by building without submitting his/her plans or by building despite rejection or disapproval of the plans, or making changes in plans that have been approved without submitting the changes for approval, the committee and the board should take action against the owner for the breach of the rules in order to prevent a waiver. It is possible for the architectural control provisions to be waived over a period of time if they are ignored and a certain number of owners are permitted to build unchallenged, without having their plans approved by the committee.

48.10 Vehicles and Parking. The regulation of motor vehicles is always one of the major problem areas for any common-interest subdivision. The declaration will normally include provisions regulating parking and controlling the types and use of vehicles within the project. These provisions must relate to and not be incompatible with local ordinances. Generally, there will be limitations on the size or type of vehicle that may be parked in the project as well as on the number of vehicles. Storage of inoperative or dismantled vehicles is generally prohibited, as is the conducting of major and lengthy vehicle repair or re-building operations, which should be done in a garage or more suitable location.

Vehicle restrictions will also cover parking, and in some cases may include rather specific provisions about illegal parking and enforcement of parking restrictions, including towing. In many jurisdictions, there are local ordinances or state laws that apply to the parking and the towing of illegally parked vehicles.

Where such statutory provisions exist they must be followed. They may, for example, require that an association post a sign of a certain size with a certain message on it before it is legal for the association to call a towing agency to have an illegally parked car towed from the premises. It is also possible that a project may submit its private streets and parking areas to the jurisdiction and control of the local law enforcement agency for purposes of patrolling and enforcing traffic and parking regulations.

The assignment and use of parking spaces is frequently a controversial area. Parking spaces in the common area may be assigned to the owners of units/lots in the declaration or in exhibits attached thereto. They may also be assigned in the condominium plan or in the deeds by which title to lots or units are conveyed to purchasers. The project legal documents may vest authority in the board of directors of the association to regulate and control parking, to make assignments of common area parking spaces, and to adopt rules and regulations pertaining to the use of common area parking spaces.

If permitted by provisions in the declaration, the board may charge a rental fee to a member of the association for use of common area parking spaces under the control of the association. In the absence of specific authority in the project legal documents, the board cannot assign exclusive rights to the use of the common area parking spaces or charge a fee for their use. The board does have authority to adopt reasonable rules and regulations for the use of common area parking spaces, including the right to prohibit parking in certain portions of the common area. The board also has authority to enforce the parking restrictions by such methods as towing of offending vehicles and disciplining or fining the owners of offending vehicles. There may be certain statutory requirements that must be complied with before vehicles can be towed. In order to avoid getting either the association or the members of the board of directors into trouble for illegally towing vehicles, the local statutes should be reviewed carefully to make sure that appropriate signs are posted and that legally required procedures are followed before vehicles are towed.

There are other less drastic methods of regulating and enforcing parking restrictions than having illegally parked vehicles towed. Putting notices on windshields or using the project newsletter for publicity concerning parking and parking violations can sometimes be effective in controlling violations of the parking rules and regulations. If parking violations occur in public street areas of the project, the local law enforcement agencies, rather than the board, will control. If the parking violations occur on private streets within the project, the board should have the authority to adopt and enforce rules and regulations to control parking. It is also possible that the project may, by appropriate documentation, submit itself to the jurisdiction of the local law enforcement agencies so that the local police department will enforce parking and traffic rules within the project.

48.11 Handicapped Regulations. Handicapped regulations now exist in the form of federal, state, and, sometimes local legislation. Although the requirements do not usually apply retroactively to existing buildings, they do apply to new construction, and under certain circumstances may apply to renovations, remodels, additions, or conversions from rental apartments to condominiums. Extensive modifications to uniform building codes have been made in order to assist handicapped persons by requiring newly constructed multi-family residential projects, such as apartments, stock cooperatives, and condominiums, to be built to accommodate wheelchairs. These requirements mandate construction of ramps to provide access, wide doors, special bathroom facilities, and special parking, including the designation of handicapped parking spaces.

When a newly elected board takes over a project from the prior developer, it should familiarize itself with the handicapped requirements. A certain number of the parking places may have been designated initially for handicapped persons. The board needs to find out the exact limitations on the use of those spaces. Where parking is tight in the project's garage and there are no handicapped residents living in the project, is it possible for the space that is designated "handicapped" to be assigned to a particular unit owner, or to be used by all unit owners or their guests for parking? These and similar questions must be answered after review of the applicable local and state regulations.

48.12 Hobbies. Typically, the use restrictions will limit or restrict hobbies requiring noisy or potentially hazardous equipment, such as car maintenance or carpentry. If the declaration of restrictions governing a project does not cover such subjects, it is possible for a board to adopt rules and regulations limiting the use of power tools and equipment. However, in order to be enforceable against good-faith purchasers of units or lots who may not be informed about the association's rules and regulations, it is best to have any permanent restrictions against such things as car maintenance included in the recorded declaration, by way of amendment. Any recorded document puts a prospective purchaser on notice of its contents whether or not (s)he reads it. On the other hand, restrictions contained only in a set of association rules and regulations that a buyer does not receive until after (s)he has closed escrow may present problems when the buyer claims the right to do a prohibited act of the rules because (s)he had no prior knowledge. *See Chapter 48.19.*

48.13 Noise Levels. Typically, the provisions of a declaration will not make any specific reference to noise levels. However, there will generally be a nuisance provision that prohibits any activities that may constitute an annoyance to other owners. Association rules and regulations usually provide specific restrictions on noise levels, including provisions regulating hours of play and volume of stereos, televisions, machinery, equipment, or other noise-producing activities. In some developments, there may be prohibitions against hardwood floors in upstairs units where the noise of people walking would be transmitted to the downstairs units. There may also be certain requirements with regard to soundproofing that have to be maintained. Local ordinances and building codes may apply and require a certain amount of soundproofing in areas between units and floors. Where there are disputes about noise or noise levels, it may be necessary to hire an expert equipped to conduct the tests, or to rent a decibel meter and conduct noise level tests. The results of the tests may be used as evidence at a hearing before the board to determine whether a violation of the association's rules and regulations or of the use provisions of the declaration has occurred.

48.14 Pets.

Control of Pets. The regulation and control of pets is always one of the two or three most controversial issues in any common-interest subdivision. The project legal documents created by the developer will usually contain some provisions that may limit the number and type of pets, the size or weight, and establish certain basic controls. The regulations will also cover such matters as the conduct of pets, where pets may be permitted within the project, leash laws, and mandatory cleanup requirements. The decision to impose such use restrictions is always arbitrary, and is not based upon any particular consideration as to the nature of the project or desires of the people who ultimately will inhabit the project. In some cases, pet restrictions or limitations are placed on a project by a developer as a market-enhancing device. The intent is to appeal to a more limited class of buyers, and to establish the project as somewhat more exclusive and therefore more expensive. Such an approach, however, limits the marketability of the project if persons with pets are unable to bring their pets with them to the project. The enforcement of the use restrictions regarding pets and the modification of those restrictions to fit the lifestyles of the inhabitants of the project inevitably falls upon the members of the association and the board of directors.

Typical Pet Regulations. Typical pet regulations will include the prohibition against the raising, breeding or commercial use of pets. Generally, the number of pets is restricted to no more than two (2) usual and ordinary household pets. In some cases, there may be a weight limit, usually stated as a maximum number of pounds allowed. Weight limits are always difficult to enforce, because it is impractical to have pets weighed. However, if the pet provision provides for a 25-pound weight limit, certain animals will obviously violate the rules. Pets may be prohibited in certain areas of the project; for example, dogs not being allowed in the swimming pool area. Owners may also be required to clean up after their pets, which is another difficult provision to enforce. Loud or obnoxious behavior on the part of the pets is more easily enforced. Courts have supported boards of directors when the boards have required a homeowner to remove an obnoxious or aggressive pet from a project.

Change in Rules; Amortization. What happens when pets have previously been allowed, but the rules have changed to prohibit them? The usual procedure is to adopt a pet amortization rule. Such a rule permits those who have pets with them to keep their pets as long as the pets live and the owner continues to live in the project. However, an owner is not allowed to replace a pet if it dies. Such pet provisions have been upheld by courts.

48.15 Parties.
The association rules and regulations may specifically regulate parties. The rules may require that parties, particularly those

with live or loud music, are terminated after a certain hour. Where the recreational room or other common area facilities are used, specific rules and regulations should be adopted and enforced.

48.16 Violations of Use Restrictions. Where someone has violated the restrictions, another owner will generally make a complaint. The owner who is complaining should be asked to come forward with evidence of the claimed violation. The evidence can be oral, initially, but if the board feels that written statements and/or photographic or other evidence are required, this should be obtained. In certain instances, such as those involving parties or noise complaints, noise tests may be required or photographs may be needed. Where the board is involved in making the decision as to whether or not to act on a complaint or to enforce the use restrictions, it may be necessary to hold a hearing, have witnesses testify, and present results of decibel meter tests and perhaps a recording or video tape. *See Chapter 48.19.*

49.17 Unreasonable Restrictions. It is possible that restrictions are so unreasonable or arbitrary as to be legally unenforceable. Courts have held that, for example, a restriction against the use of any pickup trucks by owners of units in a condominium project is so arbitrary as to be unenforceable.

48.18 Restrictions Which Are Discriminatory. Those restrictions that tend to discriminate on the ground of race, religion, sex, age or sexual preference may be ruled unconstitutional, or otherwise illegal and unenforceable. Such restrictions may be in violation of constitutional civil rights, federal statutes, state statutes, local ordinances, or the provisions of the legal documents themselves. If there is a serious question about an alleged discrimination, the board should refer the matter to its attorney.

48.19 Enforcement. The board is charged with the responsibility of enforcing the use restrictions for a project. Failure to enforce the restrictions or permitting a violation to continue can constitute a breach of the fiduciary obligation board members owe to the association, and could lead to personal liability on the part of board members. There are certain minimum requirements for enforcement. These include notice, hearing, and a reasonable opportunity to present a defense. "Due process" is required prior to any disciplinary action being taken by the board that would adversely affect the rights or the status of the homeowner. This means that every member is entitled to know what the rules are, to be given a fair hearing with adequate notice, and an opportunity to defend himself or herself prior to any disciplinary action. *See Chapter 29.1.*

CHAPTER 49
Tenants and Rentals

49.1 Restrictions on Lease and Occupancy. Sometimes a significant issue in a project is the percentage of absentee owners versus that of residents. In many condominium projects, particularly those in an urban area, investors who lease their units may purchase their units. There can be strong feelings where the interests of the resident owners clash with the interests of the absentee owners who lease their units. Naturally, the resident owners assume that other resident owners will be more conscientious about following the rules and taking care of the property than will a tenant who may be a short-term or transient occupant. In some cases, members have attempted to adopt amendments to the project restrictions that prohibit more than a certain percentage of the units being occupied by tenants. Such provisions may state that in the event more than 30 percent of the units are occupied by renters, no further rentals will be permitted, and any owner who wishes to rent his or her unit will have to wait until an existing unit reverts to occupancy by the owner. Thus, the percentage of absentee owner units will not exceed a 30 percent level. There is no reason why such restrictions, if appropriately worded and adopted by the required majority of the members, should not be enforceable.

In some high-rise condominium projects, associations have established a special fee for tenants who move in or out. The theory is that charging a special fee is justifiable, since moving furniture in and out causes some wear and tear on the elevators and on the interior hallways and lobbies.

The secondary mortgage market requirements imposed by such organizations as the FHLMC and the FNMA have an impact on common-interest developments. Such requirements are that the project be substantially owner-occupied in order to qualify for various sale and resale programs. A project dominated by investor-owned units occupied by tenants may lose its ability to qualify for the secondary mortgage market, which will greatly reduce the availability of loans to anyone seeking to buy units in the project.

There is also a commonly held perception that owners tend to take better care of the property than do tenants, and are more likely to participate in the affairs of the homeowners association. The quality of life in a project that is dominated by tenants is significantly different from that in a project that is dominated by resident owners. Restrictions on leasing are therefore quite legitimate and are enforceable in the courts. Regulations or requirements adopted by the FNMA or the FHLMC may limit the terms under which owners are permitted to lease their units. For example, a unit may not be leased for transient purposes (generally defined as a term of less than 30 days), and maid service or other customary hotel/motel amenities may not be supplied to tenants renting units in a common-interest subdivision if the subdivision is to qualify for access to the secondary mortgage market.

49.2 Tenant Relationships. In most cases, the board of directors has the authority to enforce the rules and regulations against tenants to the same extent as they would against owners. The most effective power that the board possesses is the ability to discipline a member and then lien his or her unit in the event that the fine imposed is not paid. The remedies directly against tenants tend to be less effective. Therefore, the board must discipline the owner rather than the tenant, and make the owner responsible for the tenant's behavior.

It is not necessary to treat tenants differently from owners. Tenants may be invited to serve on committees, and can be provided with copies of bulletins, newsletters and minutes. Tenants can also be invited to participate in meetings, even though they may not be eligible to vote (unless they have been given a proxy by their owner/landlord).

49.3 Lease Requirements. As part of the association's rules and regulations or as part of the recorded restrictions, the board can require that copies of all leases be in writing and that a copy of a written lease for each tenant be given to the board. The board may require that certain provisions be contained in the lease; for example, provisions requiring the tenant to acknowledge his or her awareness of and agreement to be bound by the CC&R provisions to the same extent as if they were an owner instead of a tenant. Association rules and regulations may also require that all leases be in writing and that the terms of the leases be reviewed and approved by the board, at least as to the inclusion of certain provisions.

49.4 Fees. May an association charge fees to tenants that are not also charged to owner occupants? So long as such fees are not prohibited by state statutes or local ordinances, and are specifically provided for in the legal documents, they should be legally enforceable. However, there should be some legitimate connection between the nature and amount of the fee and the existence of the tenancy. There should be support for the fee as reimbursement for an added cost or expense of the association as the result of having a tenant or an absentee owner to deal with.

49.5 Disciplining Tenants. At times the board of directors of a project may become frustrated by their inability to control the behavior of tenants who may feel they can violate the rules of conduct of the association with impunity, since they are not subject to fines by the board. It is true that while the board can adopt and enforce rules of conduct, it may lack any direct authority to discipline tenants. The board can, however, bring pressure to bear on a tenant indirectly by disciplining his or her landlord who is the owner of the unit. The accepted procedure where a tenant repeatedly violates rules of conduct is for the board to call the owner before a disciplinary committee, or before the board itself, for a hearing. The owner, who will have previously been instructed to require his/her tenant to conform to the rules and regulations, will be shown evidence of the repeated violations of his/her tenant, and will be disciplined in some form or another. The usual method is to establish a fine that can be either a one-time fine or it can be a fine consisting of a certain amount to be paid for each continuing violation by the tenant. If the fine remains unpaid, the board can use its lien powers to collect it. *See Chapter 27.5.*

49.6 Rental Management Agreement. In very large projects, it may be advisable to enter into a rental management agreement with a professional management company. Such agreements are common in the resort rental management field. The agreement is entered into between the professional management company and each of the unit owners.

Under the agreement, each owner would appoint the management company as its agent to manage its unit, sign agreements with tenants for the use of the unit, coordinate the management and operation of the unit, and act as attorney-in-fact or agent for the owner, having full power to do everything necessary to manage and rent the unit for the duration of the agreement.

CHAPTER 50
Fire Safety

50.1 Fire Alarm Systems. Many different fire detection, prevention, safety and alarm systems are now available and are common in newly constructed residential projects. Smoke detectors and heat sensors, either battery-operated or hard-wired, are available everywhere and are relatively inexpensive. Such devices are required by local ordinances and state laws in most jurisdictions wherever new housing is constructed and, in many states, when title to existing dwellings is conveyed. In some cases, fire sprinklers may be required in newly constructed or remodeled residential projects.

Manager's Note: *How many smoke detectors should each home have? According to fire prevention and safety experts, a smoke detector should be located on every floor of a home and in each bedroom. Surprisingly, according to recent surveys conducted by national fire experts, as many as 60 percent of all installed smoke detectors do not have functioning batteries.*

Smoke detectors should be tested as often as once each quarter—a good rule of thumb is to test the detector whenever you change a light bulb. Smoke detectors should also be periodically vacuumed to prevent the accumulation of dust and debris that can reduce their efficiency.

50.2 Legal Requirements. Where ordinances or laws have been adopted, they typically provide that the required device, such as a smoke detector, be installed by a certain date. New owners and tenants must be notified of the requirements of the ordinance. Owners who are selling their units are also required to state that a smoke detector or other required equipment is installed and is in operating condition. In some cases, the ordinances are very specific as to where and how the devices shall be mounted, and how many of them are required for a dwelling of a certain size.

Maintenance requirements may also be included, and there may be provisions requiring periodic testing of the devices. There may also be a disclaimer provision that states that none of the provisions of the ordinance shall require any agency of the local government to conduct any inspections. Some ordinances provide for a civil action against an owner by a buyer or renter or other aggrieved party who is damaged because of the failure to install the required equipment or failure of the equipment to operate due to improper maintenance.

The project legal documents may also contain certain provisions requiring the installation, periodic inspection and maintenance of smoke detectors or other fire detection or suppression equipment. They may also impose certain obligations on the association to maintain such devices, or they may impose obligations upon the owners of the units in the project to maintain the equipment within their respective units. The association and the board of directors should be well aware of fire safety device requirements applicable to the project, and should be prepared to carry out any duties and responsibilities that are placed upon the association and the board. If the board fails to adequately perform the duty of inspection or maintenance of fire detection devices located in the common area, the association and possibly the individual members of the board of directors could be held liable for injuries or damages resulting from the failure of those devices to properly operate. The same would be true of smoke detectors located within privately owned units, if the board has the obligation to inspect and maintain smoke detectors within those units. If a fire breaks out, spreading to other units or the common area, individual owners can also be held personally responsible if the legal documents require each owner to maintain smoke detectors within the unit.

50.3 Maintenance Contract. If a board is charged with the responsibility for maintaining fire detection or suppression equipment, it should discharge its responsibility by hiring an experienced and reputable maintenance company to handle the periodic inspection and maintenance of the fire safety equipment.

50.4 Fire Safety Rules. A multi-story or high-rise condominium or stock cooperative project should have well-established and current fire safety rules. Such rules should be in writing and should be distributed to all members and tenants. They should also be posted in appropriate places throughout the project. Some high-rise condominium or stock cooperative projects conduct periodic fire safety drills.

50.5 Insurance. With rising insurance rates, it is important that the board of directors initiate policies and procedures to minimize rate increases for the fire insurance. The board should meet periodically with the association's insurance broker to discuss ways to lower the premiums. Having a good fire detection and prevention system should be valuable in keeping increases in the association's insurance premiums to a minimum.

CHAPTER 51
Toxic Materials

51.1 Asbestos. Asbestos was a common fireproof insulation material used in construction of buildings from the 1920's through the 1960's and was still widely used up until the mid 1970's. Asbestos has proven to have severe side effects, causing disability and death to a number of people who inhaled asbestos fibers. Asbestosis and lung cancer have been found in a significant number of people who were employed in asbestos manufacturing and installation industries.

Many buildings, both residential and commercial, are known to have substantial quantities of material containing asbestos. Typically, asbestos may be a component of vinyl floor tiles and flooring, patching compound, textured paints, ceilings, stoves and furnaces, and walls and pipes. In the mid-1970's the Environmental Protection Agency banned spray-on asbestos in mid-walls and on pipes. Since that date, very few materials containing asbestos have been used in new construction. There is, however, a residual problem of what to do about the existing asbestos materials.

At the present time there are no federal regulations which require the removal of asbestos from private buildings. Environmental protection regulations focus on control strategies if a building is demolished or substantially renovated. Occupational Safety and Health Agency (OSHA) regulations established standards for protection of workers. While it is possible to test the air in a building to determine its content of asbestos fibers, there are no requirements that such testing be done, nor are there any legislative requirements that materials containing asbestos be encapsulated so as to become harmless, or that they be removed.

Some states have taken action in this area by adopting regulations which require property owners to determine if asbestos is present in buildings, and if so, to keep the asbestos from becoming dangerous to the health of occupants. In most cases, the materials containing asbestos are harmless unless something happens to cause the asbestos to become friable.

To determine whether or not asbestos is present, one should inspect the vinyl floors, insulation inside the walls, insulation in attics or crawl spaces, the material used to wrap furnace air ducts or hot water pipes, and any sprayed-on textured ceilings or walls. In most areas, testing companies exist that are capable of doing a field test on a residential project to determine the extent of asbestos within the project, and to estimate the degree of relative danger to inhabitants based upon the present condition of the materials containing asbestos.

51.2 Proposed Legislation. Federal legislation has been proposed that would establish asbestos standards for privately owned buildings. If and when passed, such legislation will probably require the Environmental

Protection Agency to promulgate standards requiring inspection and abatement of asbestos. The legislation will probably apply to federally owned buildings, and may or may not apply to state- or privately-owned property.

51.3 Legal Issues. To date, almost all litigation involving manufacturers of products containing asbestos has been brought by employees who were exposed to the manufacturers' asbestos products at their place of employment or by the owners of buildings into which asbestos products were introduced, such as schools and other public buildings. There have been very few cases involving suits by the owners or occupants of multi-family residential projects against manufacturers of products with asbestos or against the builders, contractors or architects responsible for the presence of asbestos.

It is clear in the case of personal injuries suffered by individuals who have contracted asbestosis that a cause of action for the personal injuries lies against those responsible for the presence of the product under certain conditions. There are statutes of limitation that apply; in some states, the statute does not begin to run until the person who has been injured discovers that (s)he has been injured by exposure to asbestos. Legal rights and liabilities arising from the presence of asbestos-containing materials within buildings have not yet been clearly established.

There are a number of different theories of recovery, including negligence, breach of warranty, misrepresentation (where there was a failure to disclose the presence of asbestos), unfair trade practices, and strict liability in tort. Until legislation is adopted, reliance will be placed on common law principles. To give an example, in order for a contractor, builder or architect to be liable to a homeowners association for damages because of the presence of asbestos, the homeowners association would have to prove that those responsible for the existence of the asbestos were negligent. To be negligent, they would have had to conduct themselves in a manner that falls beneath the standard of reasonably prudent contractors, architects or engineers. If asbestos-containing materials were specified by the architect, and were installed by the builder or contractor at a time when these materials were very widely used and there was no knowledge that the materials were potentially dangerous, it would be difficult, if not impossible, to prove negligence.

If the theory were based upon strict liability, it would require a state court in the jurisdiction where the matter would be tried to hold builders, architects and contractors to that standard, which means that no negligence must be proved. Strict liability has been imposed upon merchant builders who are in the business of mass-producing and selling homes, at least in certain states. *See Chapter 37.* So far, these cases have been limited to construction defects, and have not yet involved the use of dangerous or toxic materials. It is predictable that a court will at some point extend strict liability to a builder, architect, engineer or contractor as well as the manufacturer of materials containing asbestos. Because of the widespread existence of asbestos, such a decision would have very far-reaching consequences. A national survey conducted by the Environmental Protection Agency concluded that there are approximately 733,000 buildings in the United States that are government buildings, private non-residential buildings, or multi-unit residential buildings which include friable asbestos-containing materials. Asbestos-containing materials were used widely between 1900 and 1980, with most of the asbestos-containing material having been used between 1950 and 1980. Asbestos was often used to strengthen vinyl floor tiles; the fibers can be released if the tiles are sanded or seriously damaged. Some wear and tear may also cause fiber release.

In 1977, the United States Consumer Products Safety Commission banned patching compounds and textured paints containing asbestos. Some wall and ceiling joints were patched with asbestos-containing material manufactured before 1977. Sanding or scraping old material can release asbestos fibers. Homes built or remodeled between 1945 and 1978 may contain friable asbestos materials that have either been sprayed or troweled onto the ceiling or walls. Some ceiling tiles also contain asbestos.

Cement sheets, millboard and paper containing asbestos were frequently used as thermal insulation to protect the floor and walls around wood-burning stoves. Oil, coal or wood furnaces with asbestos-containing insulation and cement are generally found in older homes. Updating the system can result in removal of or damage to the old insulation.

Hot water and steam pipes in some older homes and buildings may be covered with an asbestos-containing material used primarily to reduce heat loss and prevent accidental contact. Pipes may also be wrapped in asbestos blankets or asbestos paper tape manufactured from 1920 to 1972.

Homes constructed between 1930 and 1950 often used wall and ceiling insulation that contained asbestos. Renovation and home improvements frequently expose and disturb these materials.

Asbestos was also used as a binding agent with Portland Cement in some roofing materials, shingles, and siding.

51.4 Removal of Asbestos. If the presence of asbestos is known, the parties undertaking a remodeling contract should specify how and by whom the materials are to be removed, how the environment is to be protected, and who shall bear the cost. There are specially licensed companies that detect and can safely remove asbestos. Generally, the personnel are equipped with safety suits, self-contained breathing devices, special vacuum equipment, and plastic bags that are used to seal in the materials so they can be safely removed from the premises. Special disposal sites have to be used to dispose of friable asbestos materials that have been removed from the job. It may be necessary to seal off a job site in order to prevent entry by persons who do not have the proper breathing equipment. It is extremely important that in any remodeling program of an older building, accurate information be obtained about the presence of asbestos. The health of the residents of the building could be catastrophically affected if asbestos fibers are released during a retrofit and upgrade of a multi-residential forced-air HVAC system, that causes erosion and rapid decay of sprayed-on asbestos fireproofing material hidden behind the dropped ceiling or the plenum areas. No doubt such situations have occurred and, despite precautions, will occur in the future.

Insurance is practically unavailable to cover losses due to asbestos abatement programs. Owners and occupants of older condominium and stock cooperative buildings who are contemplating renovating those buildings must give serious consideration as to how they want to handle the asbestos problem, considering the expense and potential liability involved. In many cases, encapsulation of potentially friable asbestos-containing materials is less expensive and less dangerous than removing and replacing the material.

51.5 Other Toxic Substances.
Urea formaldehyde foam insulation (UFFI) was used to insulate homes during the 1970's. It was subsequently found to be toxic and was banned in the late 1970's. Where it is known to exist, disclosure laws require that buyers and tenants be notified of its presence. No legislation yet exists which requires the removal of such materials.

Paint or plaster that contains lead has also been found to be dangerous to human health, particularly to children. Some statutes require owners of residential property to remove or cover paint or plaster that contains specified levels of lead, and some states now require disclosure of the presence of lead to new owners.

Radon gas is a radioactive gas that occurs under natural conditions, and has been shown to be carcinogenic. Radon may come from a contaminated landfill or from a natural occurrence such as granite, which tends to emit high levels of radon gas that seeps through the ground and becomes trapped in homes, especially in the northeastern United States. Recent building and construction design techniques have been developed to dissipate naturally seeping radon gas so that it does not become trapped inside a house. Small, affordable test units are available to test for the presence of radon gas. It is also possible to modify construction by the use of ventilation and ventilating equipment to reduce the level of naturally occurring radon gas within a building in an area where radon gas is naturally present.

In situations where prior owners have placed toxic substances on the land upon which a project is built, there may be a cause of action for damages and/or personal injury against the prior owners and perhaps against the builder/developer, under certain circumstances. This is a developing area of the law, and anyone who either resides in or owns property in a project which is discovered to be located on land containing toxic substances should consult with a lawyer who specializes in such matters to explain their options and remedies.

In some cases, an owners association that finds that the project is located in an area containing toxic substances, or that the building contains toxic or hazardous materials such as asbestos or formaldehyde, have made agreements for relief with developers and contractors. One example would be an agreement entered into between the owners association, on behalf of all of its members, and the builder/developer who built and sold the project. Under the terms of the agreement, the builder/developer would bear either all or some portion of the cost of removing toxic materials from the project. It may be necessary to wait for enabling legislation to be adopted or for studies to be completed before the respective obligations of the parties can be established, and before methods can be adopted for the safe treatment and removal of toxic materials from the premises. The board of directors of an owners association has a responsibility to be aware of, investigate, and act on such matters.

If there is any suspicion that the project may contain asbestos or formaldehyde, or if the land contains toxic materials, the board should investigate and take appropriate action. The failure to conduct a reasonable investigation and to take reasonable action in light of evidence that such materials are present could constitute a breach of the fiduciary obligation of the directors, and might subject them to personal liability for failure to act as reasonably prudent directors.

Chapter 52
PEST CONTROL

52.1 Pest Control Responsibility. When a question arises about responsibility for pest control within a project, the board must first look to the project legal documents to determine whether the matter is addressed. If included, the provisions in the document control. If the project documents are silent, the board will have to determine how to proceed. In a common-interest subdivision, it would seem prudent that the board of directors should centrally control the inspection and preventative measures that relate to termites and other pests. When termites or ants or other pests invade a project, they do not infest one unit alone, nor do they respect distinctions between common areas and private areas. It is not practical for each owner to take care of his or her own termite problem without other owners being involved. While an owner can theoretically stop the invasion of termites at the borders of his or her unit, termites cannot be prevented from continuing to infest the area as long as neighbors have not taken similar measures to rid their units of the pests. Therefore, if the project legal documents are silent about responsibility for pest control, they should be amended to provide that the board of directors has the duty and the authority to conduct periodic inspections for termites or other wood-destroying organisms and to take appropriate remedial measures.

52.2 Repairs. If termites have invaded a building, causing damage, and if there is fungus and dry rot damage, termite tubes, and an active termite colony, the work required will involve removing and replacing the affected materials and treating affected areas and soil with spray, chemicals, or other means. Who should bear the expense of this work? In a condominium project, the affected areas will be located almost entirely within the common area, where only the association has the authority to undertake the work. In that case, even if the legal documents are silent on the subject, it seems obvious that the association has to undertake the work and pay the expenses.

In a planned development where each owner owns the unit and the underlying land, the project legal documents may provide that the association only has the responsibility for exterior maintenance of roofs and siding. In such a case, who pays for the termite repairs? Where the project legal documents do not authorize the board to make such repairs, the typical response is to make each owner pay for his or her share of the expenses involved. This, of course, leads to problems if one owner refuses to pay his/her share and refuses to allow the work to be done on his/her premises. Where such a situation exists, the legal documents should be amended to provide that the board has the authority to make the repairs, and that it is the obligation of each member of the association to pay a pro rata share of the cost. Termite and other pest damage threatens the entire residential community, and is a risk that should be shared by all. No one can predict where the pests will strike and, like fire, the risks of damage should be spread among all of the owners.

What happens when, during a sale transaction, a termite inspection shows that there is substantial damage, with significant costs of correcting the deficiencies and undertaking preventative measures? In such a case, the owner of the unit should notify the board as soon as (s)he finds out about the conditions contained in the report. Under such circumstances, if the board does not yet have a policy, and if the legal documents are silent on the matter, it would be appropriate for the board to adopt a policy and, if necessary, amend the legal documents. The policy should require the association to pay for the termite damage and the repair and preventative measures, and to assess all of the members fairly for the costs thereof. However, if the owner of a property proceeded to make repairs without notifying the board and then submits a request for reimbursement to the board, there is no obligation on the part of the association or board to pay that bill in the absence of specific legal document provisions.

CHAPTER 53
Architectural Control

53.1 Establishment of Architectural Controls.
In order to preserve and protect the property values of a project, it is important to control future construction. The accepted or customary method is to provide architectural standards in the project legal documents that provide a mechanism for regulating structures that may be built in the future. The recorded declaration of restrictions for the project would contain the architectural provisions, and would require plans and specifications for any future construction, alteration, or modification to be reviewed and approved by a specified body. The body may be a group of individuals who are appointed by the original developer and named in the recorded declaration. Alternatively, it may consist of a committee that is to be appointed by the association or the board of directors of the association.

The architectural committee is charged with the responsibility of reviewing and approving plans that are submitted by persons who desire to add to or modify existing construction or construct some new improvements within the project. If the existing legal documents do not contain a provision for architectural control, they can be amended to provide for the establishment of a committee to examine proposals for construction, alteration, addition, or change of any building or structure within a project.

53.2 Architectural Control Committee.
A typical architectural committee consists of three or five individuals appointed by the board of directors to serve for a term of one year. The committee should consist of individuals that can read plans, understand specifications, and have some background in building, contracting, or architectural design. In most cases, the members of the committee will be owners of subdivision interests within the project. It is possible, particularly in a large project, that the bylaws will permit the appointment of members to the architectural committee who are not owners. For example, it may be advisable in some instances to appoint an architect to the committee and to compensate him or her for acting as a committee member. This may require an amendment to the project legal documents.

The committee serves a very important function: to protect and preserve and even enhance the property values by ensuring that nothing is permitted to be built within the project that will detract from property values. The committee must discharge its duties in an efficient and knowledgeable manner. It must be able to tell from reviewing plans what a structure will look like when it is completed, and whether or not it will be compatible with the existing and surrounding architecture.

The committee must review the plans and specifications, responding to the owner within the time limit required, which is usually 30 days from the date of submission to the committee. The legal documents may provide that if the committee does not act within a certain time period, the plans will be deemed approved. As a practical matter, if the committee did not get back to the owner until 24 hours after the deadline had expired, the owner would probably not be able to go ahead and build according to those plans unless (s)he had already committed himself/herself in some way. On the other hand, if the committee waited until two weeks after the deadline and then notified the owner of the plan's disapproval, it would probably be too late to stop construction, especially if the owner had incurred substantial obligations in preparing to build or had even started construction.

53.3 Procedures for Architectural Control Committee. The committee may prescribe certain rules for submission of plans and specifications. It may require that plans be submitted in a certain format, with a minimum number of copies. A reasonable filing fee may also be required. The committee may either hold regular meetings which are open to members of the association, or it may conduct its meetings at a time and place convenient to the committee members and announce its decisions either verbally or in writing. Unless the legal documents specify these details, the committee is free to establish its own procedures. The one overriding principle is that the committee must follow the rules it adopts, and the rules must be reasonable. There cannot be arbitrary or whimsical decisions or procedures, and the procedures and decisions must be consistent so that each owner receives equal treatment.

53.4 Guidelines. It may be helpful for a committee to establish certain written construction or architectural guidelines, which should be made available to any owner. The guidelines should indicate what types of structures will be favorably received and what will not normally be permitted. For example, the guidelines might specify the materials or colors that can be used. They might also specify the percentage of lot coverage, heights, setback restrictions, total square footage to be allowed and, in some cases, the architectural style that will be allowed. Thus, if the buildings are designed in a Victorian theme, the guidelines might indicate that any additions must also be Victorian style or another compatible type of architecture. By creating guidelines, the association will ensure that owners and their architects will know in advance what styles and types of structures will be acceptable.

__Manager's Note:__ Unless the association has the assistance of qualified volunteers with construction or building expertise, creating a set of guidelines can be a particularly difficult task for the typical "lay person." It may be necessary to obtain the assistance of an architect to create the guidelines for an association.

Acceptable paint colors can be chosen from the palette of colors currently used in the project. Typically, the first sets of proposed architectural improvements may set the "tone" for specific types of structures, such as awnings, trellises, and arbors or gazebos. For example, an especially well-designed trellis may become the guideline that other homeowners will follow in designing their trellis structures. Guidelines may incorporate the successful designs of owner's structures as "standards" to provide guidance for other owners wishing to build similar structures.

53.5 Enforcement. Part of the enforcement process consists of early prevention of violations. The committee should ensure that all members of the association, and particularly all new members, are informed about the requirements and procedures and are provided with copies of the most current version of the guidelines, if available. The committee should function in a business-like, fair and efficient manner. Applications should be processed expeditiously and with a consistently applied policy.

Any violations of the architectural policy as established by the committee should be dealt with promptly. It is not appropriate for the committee or the board to permit a violation to occur and to exist for a period of time and then suddenly announce that the architectural control provisions have been violated and enforcement will occur. As soon as a violation is noted, immediate action should be taken to notify the owner of the violation and to request that the violation be removed and/or the matter be corrected. If a violation occurs in the form of an unapproved building alteration, the committee should notify the board, and the board should take immediate action to provide a written notice to the owner to appear before the board and explain the violation. The notice should also require him to cease and desist from further construction activities that are in violation of the project restrictions and of the architectural guidelines. When the member appears before the board, evidence of the violation, which can be photographs or eyewitness testimony, should be presented. The owner or the owner's representative should also present the owner's defense of his/her position. The board can then take appropriate action, which may include ordering the violation to cease and requesting the removal of the offending structure. If the owner refuses to cooperate, the board can assess fines to the owner or can go to court to seek an injunction. If the board chooses to fine the owner, it can file a lien against the property, if the owner refuses to pay the fine. However, because fining an owner is not likely to produce the desired result, which is the removal of the offending addition, the preferable remedy in this case is for the association to get an attorney and seek an injunction against the owner who has violated the architectural restrictions. If the restrictions are properly drafted and the procedures that were followed have been reasonable and fair, the court will order the offending structure removed at the expense of the owner, and, if the legal documents so provide, may order the owner to reimburse the association for its attorneys' fees.

Manager's Note: *Not all states or communities allow a lien to be placed on the owner's property for unpaid fines. When in doubt, check with the association's attorney to determine what enforcement actions are available to collect unpaid fines.*

53.6 Landscaping. Many project legal documents contain provisions regulating landscaping. These documents may provide that no landscaping be added by any owner either to the lot or the common area without the advance approval of the board or of a committee appointed by the board. The provision may also prevent any owner from cutting trees on the property without the permission of the board, whether the trees are in the common area or within a private lot. One example provides a good illustration of the importance of clearly establishing rules and then conscientiously following those rules. In this case, the owners of a lot in a planned development planted eight palm trees by their unit without having submitted their plans to the architectural committee for approval. The association's legal documents provided that no improvements could be placed on any lot until the committee had approved the plans. The association filed a complaint seeking an injunction, which the trial court granted, compelling the removal of the trees. The appellate court reversed the trial court's decision because there was nothing in the record to show that the governing body of the association, the board of directors or the architectural committee, ever met to consider whether or not the palm trees violated the standards set forth in the project legal documents. In the records, there was some indication that the association discussed the matter at several meetings and that at least two polls were taken of the membership to determine community opinion concerning the trees. However, there was no record that either the board or the committee had made a formal investigation and had adopted findings that the trees were in violation of some provision of the standards. The court said that because the association had failed to establish that the duties, procedures and standards prescribed in the legal documents had been fully and fairly followed, the association was not entitled to an injunction. This decision is a reminder that when faced with a violation of the project legal documents, the appropriate committee or the board should take immediate action, documenting all of its enforcement actions and procedures in writing, and be able to demonstrate that its standards and procedures were followed.

53.7 Solar Panels. Solar panels and solar easements have become the subject of dispute in a number of cases. In some states, enabling legislation has been adopted which encourages the use of solar energy systems and encourages the use of architectural design intended to take advantage of passive solar opportunities. In those jurisdictions where the legislature has indicated that there is public interest in encouraging solar energy systems, provisions in project documents that effectively prohibit the installation or use of solar energy systems have been held by courts to be void and unenforceable. Reasonable restrictions on solar energy systems that do not significantly increase the cost of the system or significantly decrease its efficiency are usually permissible and, in some cases, have been made so either by statutory enactment or by legal decision.

Easements for light and air, and, particularly, easements to collect sunlight to energize solar collector panels may or may not exist. In some states, legislation has been adopted that prohibits planting trees or constructing buildings that will shade active solar collectors during certain hours. Those statutory enactments have in some cases been held to apply to active solar collectors as distinguished from passive solar homes. Thus, such legislation may protect the right to have access to sunlight for an active solar collector system, but may not protect the right of access to sunlight for an exclusively passive solar home. An example of an exclusively passive solar home would be one where the windows were oriented in such a way as to admit sunlight which would warm some mass such as a concrete, brick or rock wall that would then radiate heat slowly during the evening. In some cases, courts have distinguished between that type of passive solar system, holding that it is not entitled to protection, and an active solar system, where the sunlight is needed to energize heating panels to heat domestic water or the house itself. In the absence of statutes or local ordinances creating easements for light and air applicable to passive solar homes or active solar systems, homeowners who want to establish sunlight easements will have to rely upon recorded restrictions applicable to the property.

CHAPTER 54
Security

54.1 Security in General. An owners association does not necessarily have an obligation to provide security for the benefit of the owners. The project legal documents may be silent on the subject, in which case there is no obligation unless the board of directors assumes such an obligation. The project documents may provide that the board has the authority but not the responsibility to provide for security. In that case, the board would be authorized to spend money or to take action to promote security for the project, but would not be bound to do so. If the board is inclined to adopt some security measures and the project legal documents are silent on the matter, the question should probably be submitted to the membership for approval and, if necessary, amendment of the legal documents, before the board adopts security measures. Security measures are likely to involve considerable expense, and will doubtless require restructuring of the budget and increased assessments.

Under certain conditions, the board may be exposed to liability for failure to provide security even if the association is not charged by its legal documents with the responsibility to provide security. In one case, the board of directors of an owners association required a member who had placed exterior lighting outside of her condominium unit to remove the lighting because it had not been approved by the architectural committee. The member refused to remove the lighting, so the board had it removed. When the member was assaulted and robbed shortly thereafter, she brought suit against the board and succeeded in obtaining a judgment against the directors personally. The theory of the case was that the board had exposed her to a foreseeable risk of harm by removing the lighting that she had installed there for the very purpose of preventing the harm from occurring. Therefore, even though the board was not responsible for providing security, when it acted to deprive an owner of a measure designed to enhance her security, it exposed itself to liability for that action. The board was in a difficult position, because if it failed to remove the lights that had not been approved, it would have failed in its responsibility to enforce the architectural restrictions that required any exterior lighting to be approved in advance. By removing the lights as it did, it exposed the members of the board to personal liability for their actions. Clearly, the board should act with extreme caution in this area. In retrospect, the board should determine what kind of exterior lighting would be acceptable and notify the owner that her lights would have to be replaced, but in the meantime they could remain on a temporary basis. In this way, the board would not have jeopardized the owner's safety, nor would it have defaulted on its obligation to maintain architectural standards.

Personal security is extremely important to homeowners, and is frequently one of the significant selling points in a condominium or planned development project. One problem that often arises is that builders or developers will advertise a project as having "24-hour security," "guarded gates," or "security patrols." The guards or patrols or 24-hour security provisions are paid and provided by the developer in the beginning of the project in order to enhance its image and facilitate sales. However, when a substantial number of units have been sold and the developer seeks to transfer the costs of maintaining the security to the new buyers, they decide that the cost of continuing such security is more than they care to pay. At that point, the security will be curtailed or perhaps eliminated altogether. Some buyers, who bought their homes based on the representation that the security would be provided, may have assumed that it would be provided permanently or at least for a somewhat longer period of time. At that point, there may or may not be a right of action on behalf of the owners against the developer for misrepresentation about the nature and the extent of the security. If the developer's advertising and the developer's sales representatives have led people to believe that the developer would continue to pay the cost of that security until the project is sold out and the project is not yet sold out, the developer may have some continuing liability to provide that security as long as its advertising or the representations of its agents led the buyers to reasonably believe that it would be provided.

54.2 Alarm Systems. If a common-interest development contains an alarm system, it will require a central control unit. The project legal documents should provide for maintenance, inspection and repair of that system by the association, and not by the individual unit owners. The budget should include the estimated cost of maintenance, repair and replacement of the alarm system. The project legal documents should prohibit any owner from tampering with the system or from shutting it off within any particular unit. It is also possible to have an alarm system without a central station, so that each unit has its own self-sufficient alarm system. In that case, the legal documents may provide that each owner is responsible for the maintenance, repair and replacement of his or her own alarm system.

54.3 Guards and Patrols. If the association elects to continue a guard service or patrol service started by the developer or to initiate such a service, it should solicit bids from companies offering private guards or private security patrols. Before such a contract is entered into, the membership should be advised and should approve the cost thereof, unless it is clear from the legal documents or from the minutes of prior membership meetings that the board has the authority to enter into such a contract. It is even more important that before security service is curtailed or eliminated, the membership be notified, in order to avoid surprises. There could be some potential personal liability involved for a board of directors that suddenly terminates or curtails guard service or patrol service without notifying the members in advance.

54.4 Cooperative Security Systems. Any association should have its own internal security procedures, and owners should be aware of those procedures. The procedures should be standardized throughout the project. For example, owners who are going to be away on vacation should let the management organization responsible for maintenance of the property know when they are leaving and when they will return. The board of directors should also have this information, and neighbors on each side should be notified. If the project does not have an alarm system and the owner who is leaving does not have an alarm system in his/her unit, there should be a uniform policy which provides that when owners are leaving town they will arrange for some lights to be turned on and off or for some radios to be turned on and off, as an indicator to anyone that someone is probably home. Bushes and shrubs should be trimmed away from windows and doors so that windows and doors can easily be seen. Mail and newspapers should be picked up daily. Draperies and blinds on the first floor should be closed.

54.5 Security Committee. The board of directors should appoint a security committee consisting of members of the association. A security committee should work out an overall security policy for the association. The policy should be written and a copy of a directive should be sent to all owners informing them of the security precautions to be taken, so that a uniform plan can be adopted to cover the entire project.

The committee should cooperate with the local police department. The police can be very helpful in providing information to create a secure environment. Most police departments will send out an officer to answer questions about security and to give advice, and even to inspect homes to find out what can be done to make them more secure.

CHAPTER 55
Resales

55.1 Rights of First Refusal. In some projects the legal documents create rights of first refusal, which require that anyone who wants to sell his or her unit must offer it either to the association or to the other members before it can be sold to a third party. Consult your legal documents to see whether such provisions are included. If they are, the provisions may not be enforceable in certain jurisdictions, but otherwise are enforceable and must be followed. In order to avoid charges of discrimination, it is important that uniform procedures be followed in every case. If the purpose of the right of first refusal is for the other members to be able to evaluate the prospective purchaser and decide whether they would like to have him or her as a neighbor and a fellow member of the association, the criteria used to determine whether or not to exercise a right of first refusal must not be based upon race, religion, sex, sexual preference, age, or disability. Decisions based on character references, bank references, and other pertinent information may be supportable.

55.2 Signs. A project may have restrictions on signs that include the size and number of signs used to advertise a unit for rent or for sale. Such restrictions or regulations are enforceable, provided they do not totally prohibit signs. An owner has a right to post at least one sign advertising the unit for sale. The restrictions may prescribe the size and location of the sign, but may not prohibit it altogether in most jurisdictions without violating either specific statutory provisions or violating first amendment or other constitutional rights.

55.3 Transfer Fees. Some projects impose transfer fees upon the sale or resale of the units. Such fees are legitimate if they are reasonably calculated to reimburse the association for costs that it incurs as a result of a transfer. Such costs may include changing the records of the association, issuing new membership certificates and card keys, changing names on lobby sign boards, etc. *See Chapter 4.3.*

55.4 Notices to New Members. Whenever a sale occurs, it is important that the new owner receive copies of the project legal documents, including the latest rules and regulations. In some states there are legal requirements that a new owner be provided with copies of all the relevant project legal documents. Many associations adopt a policy of welcoming new members into the community, providing copies of all the rules and procedures and documents for which the new owners will be responsible.

55.5 Assessments. Whenever a unit changes hands, the assessments should be paid to the date of transfer. Normally this is handled in the escrow; however, occasionally a transfer occurs where the prior owner is delinquent in his or her assessments and the new owner is unaware of the delinquency. The board is then faced with the choice of having to try to collect delinquent assessments from an owner who has sold and departed, or asking the new owner, who did not know anything about the delinquency, to pay for the previous owner's assessments.

Some states have adopted legislation that requires the homeowners association to provide a statement of assessments to the escrow company, and requires that all delinquent assessments be paid at the time the escrow is closed. Where such laws are not in effect, it is extremely important that the association keep its assessment collection records up-to-date. If it has any advance notice about a pending sale, a lien is filed against the unit that is to be transferred in order to protect the association against the possibility that the unit will be sold and escrow closed before the assessments can be collected. By filing a lien, the prospective purchaser is put on notice that assessments are delinquent and (s)he is thereby prevented from closing escrow and taking title to the unit without those assessments being paid. *See Chapter 25.*

55.6 Statement from Association. As part of any escrow and the transfer of a unit or lot, the purchaser can and should demand from the association a statement of assessments regarding that unit or lot. When asked for such a statement, the association should respond promptly and indicate whether the assessments on that home have been paid up-to-date, and if not, it should indicate the total amount of the arrearages, including interest and penalties. Such a statement provided by the association is sometimes referred to as an "estoppel statement." The purchaser is entitled to rely upon that statement, and if (s)he closes escrow in reliance upon it, the association will not be able to demand payment of fees in addition to those set forth in the estoppel statement.

CHAPTER 56
Loans & Lenders

56.1 Authority to Borrow. Occasionally, an association needs to borrow money. For example, large unscheduled expenses, such as unfunded emergency building repairs, may cause a need for a loan. Can the association borrow money to pay the expense until a special assessment is collected? The legal documents, including the articles of incorporation, may specifically provide that the corporation has the authority to borrow funds. State statutes may also give powers to nonprofit homeowners associations that are broad enough to permit borrowing funds. If the legal documents are silent about the power to borrow funds and the state law provides no assistance, the association may not have the necessary authority to borrow funds unless it amends its documents.

56.2 Corporate Resolution. Lenders may require a corporate resolution from the owners association authorizing the borrowing of money, even though the project legal documents give the association the power to borrow money, and even though state statutes may vest non-profit corporations with the power to borrow money. In such cases, the board of directors will have to adopt a resolution in a form acceptable to the lender that officially authorizes the borrowing of funds and authorizes the execution of the loan documents. If the board of directors has some doubt about whether or not it has the authority to borrow funds, it should put a question to the membership for majority approval. In a real emergency, such as for unscheduled, unfunded building repairs, the board may have to act without membership approval if there is insufficient time to seek and obtain membership approval.

CHAPTER 57
Title and Title Insurance

57.1 Title Problems in Common-Interest Projects. The board of directors may discover that the project had an inadequate boundary survey, or even worse, that the title documents that created the project were faulty in some way. One example is the inaccurate computation of square footage of units, which computations were used as the basis for assigning undivided interests in the project. Another example is the failure to properly identify restricted common areas such as parking or storage spaces. When such defects come to light, it may be necessary to take action to have the legal documents, declarations, maps or plans re-formed. In such a case, the board should turn to the professionals who were responsible for the documents and who may have made the errors. If these persons are still available, they should be asked to take whatever remedial action is required. If they are not available, or are available but refuse to cooperate, the association should consult its attorney about means to make them cooperate. The other alternative is for the association to hire its own experts to correct the deficiencies and to make sure that title to restricted common area interests or association property has been properly conveyed.

57.2 Title to Association Property. In a planned unit development, where title to common area property has been conveyed to the association, the title should be free and clear of any liens or encumbrances at the time it is conveyed. It would not do to have a lender foreclose on the common area when the developer defaults on its loan, and have the common area taken away from the association because the lender had not subordinated its deed of trust to the condominium or planned unit development declaration. *See Chapter 26.8.* One way that the association can be sure that it has clear and unencumbered title is to request a title insurance policy. If it does so at the time property is conveyed to it by the developer, the association may be able to get the developer to pay for cost of the title insurance.

57.3 Title to Restricted Common Area Easements. The project legal documents may have established certain restricted common area exclusive easement rights. *See Chapter 45.1.* Occasionally, the exclusive common area easement rights become confused. A situation may arise where the board of directors discovers that the parking place assigned to a particular unit is different from the parking place that the unit owner has been using. In another case, one unit owner may have been assigned a storage space that can only be reached through another owner's property or exclusive-use area. In such cases, the problem needs to be resolved. The board can ask the developer and the title company to cooperate in straightening matters out, and should consult its attorney to see what its options are. It may be that owners can execute reciprocal grants of easement, conveying to each other their respective rights to use certain restricted common area parking spaces so that each owner will end up with the proper parking space.

CHAPTER 58
Multi-Phased Developments

58.1 Assessments in Phased Developments. In a multi-phased development, there will be a change in assessments each time that a new phase is annexed to the project. The addition of more lots or units to the project will result in the receipt of more assessments to pay for the additional expenses incurred for operating the common area facilities in the added phase. If the majority of the recreational facilities were included in the initial phase, each subsequent phase added to the project should reduce the amount of the assessments per unit or lot. Usually the sale of a unit or lot in an annexed phase will initiate the assessments in the subsequent phase. In some jurisdictions, the declaration may provide the developer with a partial exemption from assessments during the period dwellings in the annexed phase are being constructed.

58.2 Phased Budgets. In a multi-phased project, the budget will undergo a change every time a new phase is added. In some jurisdictions, the developer is required to prepare in advance a budget for each phase, which is then approved by the state body regulating the sale of real estate projects to the public. Where control of the owners association has been assumed by members of the association who have purchased their homes from the developer, the board may have revised the original budget prepared by the developer. As soon as a new phase is annexed, the board will make further revisions to its budget to cover the maintenance and reserve costs of the newly annexed homes and common areas.

58.3 Subsidization During Phasing. In a multi-phased project where there are extensive recreational facilities placed into operation in the early stages of the project, the developer may elect to subsidize the association in order to charge a reasonable level of assessments to the buyers. In such case, the association's budget and assessments will be structured around the subsidy contract between the developer and the association. If the subdivider defaults in payment of the monthly subsidies, the association can pursue its rights under the subsidization contract, which can include an action on any bond that has been posted by the subdivider to secure subsidy contract performance and payment. When the developer provides a subsidy, the assessments will normally remain at a certain level for a specified time period as provided in the subsidization contract. However, assessments may change immediately upon termination of the subsidization contract.

Manager's Note: Here is an example of how a subsidy might be structured. Let's assume that a project has three phases, each with 20 homes per phase. The recreational facilities, consisting of a pool, spa, a small clubhouse, and a large landscaped area are constructed in and annexed to the first phase of the project. Suppose the cost to maintain the recreational facility and surrounding landscaping is $2,000 per month.

Obviously, these maintenance costs alone, spread among the first 20 owners, will be quite burdensome at $100 monthly per home. When the second phase is added, however, this same maintenance cost would be distributed among 40 owners, at a more manageable cost of $50 per unit. In this case, the developer may choose to pay for or "subsidize" the difference between the higher assessments of the first phase owners and that of the second phase units. Thus, a subsidization contract can be written that allows each owner in the first phase to pay only $50 per month for the recreational facilities, while the developer pays the other $50 per home until the second phase is annexed.

58.4 Additional Amenities in Phased Projects.

Recreational facilities are often included in the first phase of a multi-phased project. When additional phases are annexed, the project costs, including the operation of the recreational facilities, will be spread among a larger number of owners, decreasing the assessments upon the addition of each phase. If additional recreational facilities are added in subsequent phases, the increased costs of operation of the existing and new recreational facilities may cause an increase in the individual assessments when the total costs are distributed among all of the owners. Where all of this has been pre-arranged and full disclosure has been made, there should be no problem. However, if a developer desires to annex very expensive recreational facilities in an additional phase, resulting in increased assessments beyond both budget constraints and what was previously represented to the owners, it may be possible to persuade the developer to either subsidize the additional phases or to require reduction in the scale of the amenities.

58.5 Shared Use of Recreational Facilities.

In some common-interest projects, the use of recreational facilities will be shared by owners in the initial phase or phases with tenants in subsequent phases that have yet to be annexed. In large projects, this can occur in a number of different ways. In a conversion project, the condominium converter may phase the project in order to meet the lender's requirements. The part of the project that has not yet been annexed will continue to be occupied by renters who will share the use of the recreational facilities with the buyers of units in the first phase. In a similar situation, a developer may build a condominium project, but elect to operate it as a rental project for a period of years. When permission is obtained from the state agency to offer units for sale to the public under a phased program, both renters and new owners may share the recreational facilities.

In these cases, the recreational facilities will be used by the rental tenants in the project when escrow closes on the sale of the first unit. The recreational facilities will then be turned over to the association at or prior to the close of escrow on the sale of the first unit or lot. Tenants in the units that have not yet been annexed will continue to use those facilities that are now under the ownership and control of the association. An agreement between the association and the owner of the rental units is needed. The agreement will normally provide that the association will operate, manage and insure the recreational facilities, and the owner of the rental apartment units will pay a monthly fee to the association for the tenants' use of the recreational facilities. Where such an arrangement is under the jurisdiction of a state agency, the subdivider may be required to have a bond or other security to guarantee performance of its agreement to pay the association for the use of the recreational facilities. If the developer defaults on its obligation to pay a portion of the recreational facilities operating expenses, the association should be able to proceed against the developer's bond or other security.

58.6 Insurance on Phased Projects. In a phased project, as soon as a phase is annexed, the association must increase its public liability coverage to include all of the common areas in the annexed phase. In a condominium project or other project where the association carries its master policy covering the dwellings as well as the common areas, the insurance coverage will also have to be increased when the subsequent phase is annexed. Coordination between the association and the developer is required to ensure that there is no lapse of coverage. The association needs the advice of a knowledgeable insurance broker who is experienced in handling insurance on phased common-interest subdivision projects.

58.7 Architectural Control of Phased Projects. The project legal documents will normally provide for architectural review of any new construction or any alterations to be made in a project. *See Chapter 53.1.* Usually, a committee will be appointed by the board to review and approve plans for any construction within the project. *See Chapter 53.2.* The declaration will generally provide that any structures designed and built by the developer are excluded from the requirement of architectural review until all units or lots in all phases have been sold. In addition, the developer will usually retain control over the architectural committee in order to protect the architectural integrity of the project until the sales program for the entire project is completed. The board of directors should be familiar with the architectural control provisions of the declaration in a phased project, and should be alert to an opportunity to appoint the members of the committee or to appoint a majority of the members of the committee. Even though the developer has retained control over the architectural committee, the discretion of the developer in approving plans for new structures must be exercised in good faith. When the developer acts as the architectural committee for the association, it has a fiduciary obligation to the association and its members. If that duty is discharged in a way that is beneficial to the developer and adverse to the interests of the association and its members, the developer may be potentially liable for a breach of fiduciary obligation. For example, a project is originally designed in one particular style, and to boost sales, the developer decides to redesign the rest of the project in an architectural style that is incompatible with the initial phase of the project. If the owners in the initial phase object to the radical change in architectural style proposed for the subsequent phases, they may be able to obtain the help of the court in preventing the developer from making such a radical change in architectural style. If the developer has reserved the right to change the unit design by appropriate provisions in the legal documents, (s)he may be able to do so despite the objections of the members.

Usually the state regulatory agency will require assurances that changes in the unit mix or design will not result in a material increase in assessments, adverse parking ratios, or overburdening of recreational facilities. The local governmental body may also prevent the developer from changing the unit mix or design of a project where permits, plan approvals or other discretionary governmental approvals are required. The buyers of units or lots in the preceding phases may be able to prevent the developer from making changes in unit mix or design that adversely and materially affect the project's economics. For example, if the owners of homes in the previous phases could prove that unit changes would materially increase density, causing recreational facilities and/or parking to become overburdened, the owners may be able to prevent the developer's proposed unit mix or design changes. If the proposed new design is so radical as to be clearly inharmonious with existing units, the existing owners may be able to enlist the aid of the court in precluding the design changes desired by the developer. Even if the developer controls the architectural review committee, members may be able to show that approval of the radical design would be an abuse of the committee's responsibilities. If the members who object prevail and the court stops the annexation, the developer would have to choose between a less radical design and not annexing the subsequent phase. However, if the developer were required to annex the phase (that is, if annexation was not discretionary), the new phase may need to be designed to be harmonious with existing structures.

58.8 Promises and Representations by Developer. Promises contained in recorded documents and made by a developer will be binding upon successor developers to the extent that the promises "touch and concern" the land, and benefit the owners of lots or units in the property subject to the recorded covenants. Thus, a developer who sold a project based on a map or overall site plan showing a certain area as "reserved," could not sell the reserved property for construction of a church when sales personnel had told buyers that the parcel was reserved for a park.

CHAPTER 59
Master Association

59.1 Master Associations in General. In some projects, a master or umbrella association will be created to manage and control certain aspects of the development. An umbrella association may be required to serve as a vehicle for accepting title to various parcels of open-space land throughout a large project. In such a case, the association would own and maintain those properties. The umbrella association may also be charged with enforcing use restrictions which govern the project as a whole, and may be responsible for maintaining private streets and utilities, including storm and sanitary sewers.

The membership of the master or umbrella association could consist of individual unit or lot owners, each having one vote, or its membership could consist of a number of sub-associations that control a particular project within the overall development. Owners of individual lots or units may pay assessments directly to the master association in addition to assessments paid to their own sub-association, or the owner may pay only the sub-association, which in turn pays an assessment to the master association.

Master or umbrella associations are useful for very large projects that are developed over a period of years. Where such master associations exist, the board of directors of a sub-association needs to be aware of its obligations to the master association and its obligations and responsibilities under the master set of covenants, conditions and restrictions.

59.2 Membership in Master Association. Where membership in a master association is representational, the board of a sub-association may be charged with the responsibility of either electing or appointing a representative of the sub-association to attend the master association meetings and to cast the votes on behalf of the sub-association and its members.

59.3 Interaction Between Associations. In a project where a number of separate sub-associations are joined together under one umbrella association, questions may arise as to whether the umbrella association may amend its declaration in a manner that affects the rights of the individual owners of units or lots within each of the sub-associations. For example, could the master association amend its declaration to provide that in the future there will be one central budget which will be prepared by the master association, and the individual sub-associations will no longer prepare their own budgets and will no longer assess their members? Such an amendment could not take place unless it had approval of the requisite majority of the members of the umbrella association and the requisite majorities of each of the sub-associations. Each sub-association would then have to amend its declaration to be consistent with the amendment to the master declaration.

59.4 Use Restrictions. If the use restrictions imposed by the master declaration differ from those imposed by the declaration of a sub-association, the sub-association restrictions may be more restrictive in nature than the restrictions imposed by the umbrella association. The sub-association could not relax its restrictions so that they are less severe than those of the umbrella association. Thus, if the umbrella association allows one pet per household, a sub-association could not adopt a more flexible restriction allowing two pets per household.

Form 1   Annual Meeting Notice

NOTICE OF ANNUAL MEETING
OF
_____ HOMEOWNERS ASSOCIATION

NOTICE IS HEREBY GIVEN of the annual meeting of the members of _____ HOMEOWNERS ASSOCIATION, to be held on the _____ day of (*month*), (*year*) at _____ a.m./p.m. at __(*location*)__.

The purpose of the meeting is to elect a Board of Directors to serve for a term of __(#)__ year(s), and to conduct such other business as may come before the membership.

Issues to be discussed at the meeting will include: _____. There will be a vote of the membership on the following issues: _____.

Following the membership meeting, the newly elected Board of Directors will hold a short meeting to elect officers and to appoint committees.

For those who are unable to attend, a proxy is enclosed. If you cannot attend the meeting, please sign the enclosed proxy and return it to the undersigned secretary of the Association in the envelope provided.

Dated: ___(*month*)___, _(*year*)_   _____
                                            Secretary

Form 2   Reminder Notice of Annual Meeting

REMINDER

NOTICE OF MEETING OF MEMBERS
OF THE _____ HOMEOWNERS ASSOCIATION

(*Time and Date*)
(*Location*)

AGENDA:

1. **Proposed Amendment to _____ Association Bylaws.**

Article IV, Section 1 of the Bylaws provides that the Annual Meeting of Owners be held on January 15 of each year at 8:00 p.m.

It has been proposed that the date of the Annual Meeting of Owners be changed to November 16 each year at 8:00 p.m. The change would be effective in (*year*), and the next Annual Meeting would therefore be held on (*month*), (*year*). There would also be minor changes in Article V, Section 2 to conform to the terms of the Directors with the change in the date of the Annual Meeting.

Reasons for the proposed change:
A. To consolidate the current finance and budget meetings held in November with the election meeting held in January.
B. Savings to the Association in time, postage, paper, notices, etc.
C. Two meetings scheduled at holiday time are inconvenient for many people and may affect attendance at the meetings.
D. All items of regular business (budget, assessments, annual report, election, etc.) would be handled at one meeting.

The Board of Directors is neither for nor against the proposed amendment, and feels this decision should be made by you, the owners. If the amendment is approved, the terms of the current Directors and those elected at this meeting would expire on November 16 of the appropriate years.

2. **Election of Three Directors to Three-Year Terms of Office.** Terms are subject to adjustment if the Bylaws are amended. The Nominations and Elections Committee has nominated the following:

   _____
   _____
   _____

Nominations may also be made from the floor at the meeting.

3. Beyond the above, the Board of Directors is not aware of any other business to be transacted at the meeting.

CUMULATIVE VOTING: *(This paragraph is written assuming three directors and three votes per home.)*

Our Association has cumulative voting in the election of Directors. We are electing three Directors. Therefore, each unit or lot has three votes. You may cast three votes for one nominee, OR two votes for one nominee and one vote for another, OR you may cast one vote for each of three nominees. The number of votes cast for Directors by any one unit or lot may NOT exceed three votes.

PROXIES:

If you are unable to attend the meeting, you may vote by proxy. You may instruct your proxy holder as to how you wish your votes to be cast. If you do not instruct your proxy holder, he or she may cast your votes as he or she sees fit. A proxy form and an addressed return envelope are enclosed with this notice.

The proxy form must be fully completed—fill in all blank spaces—and signed by one owner of the unit or lot. Proxies should be received before the commencement of the meeting and should be sent or delivered to:

_____
_____
_____

VOTING ELIGIBILITY:

Unit or lot owners are entitled to one vote for each unit or lot owned (one vote for each Director to be elected). If more than one person owns a unit or lot, the vote(s) may be exercised as they determine, but in no event shall more votes be cast with respect to any unit or lot than that unit or lot is entitled to cast. *Monthly assessments and any interest or costs must be paid through (month), (year) in order to be eligible to vote.*

QUORUM:

The presence at the meeting of members entitled to cast, or of proxies entitled to cast, 50 percent [*or enter the percentage amount required by documents*] of the total votes is required for a quorum.

WE NEED ____ OWNERS PRESENT IN PERSON OR BY PROXY IN ORDER FOR THE MEETING TO BE "OFFICIAL"

Please try to attend this meeting in person. If you just cannot attend, please complete and mail or deliver your proxy to the secretary before the meeting.

Form 3 — Sample Agenda

_____ HOMEOWNERS ASSOCIATION
ANNUAL MEMBERSHIP MEETING

(*Location*)
(*Date and Time*)

AGENDA

1.0 Call to Order/Establishment of Quorum

2.0 Welcome Message by Board President

3.0 Association Report by Board of Directors

4.0 Approval of Minutes of Previous Annual Membership Meeting

5.0 Election of New Board of Directors

     5.1 Slate Presentation/Introduction of Candidates
     5.2 Nominations from Floor
     5.3 Motion to Close Nominations

6.0 Questions and Answers/Homeowner Forum (During Tabulation of Ballots)

7.0 Announcement of Election Results

8.0 Adjournment

Form 4   Sample Proxy

PROXY

> If you cannot attend the Annual General Membership meeting, please fill out and return this proxy in the enclosed envelope to (*address of association secretary or manager*). Any proxy may be reclaimed at the meeting if the owner attends. Your right to vote may be given to another homeowner or family member or agent by signing this proxy and giving it to your designated representative. Only one signature is required.

_____ HOMEOWNERS ASSOCIATION
ANNUAL GENERAL MEMBERSHIP MEETING

(*Date and Time*)

I/We, owner(s) of Unit/Lot____, hereby give my (our) proxy to:

- ❏ The Board of Directors, and direct that my vote be cast in manner as they would vote (*if this box is checked, do NOT check any other boxes*)

- ❏ The Board of Directors, and direct that my vote be cast as follows (please check boxes in Sections A-B as applicable)

    A. Election of Officers: (Please vote for no more than ___ members)

    - ❏ Name of Candidate   ❏ Name of Candidate
    - ❏ Name of Candidate   ❏ Name of Candidate

    B. IRS Rev. Ruling 70-604 approval to defer income against assessments in next fiscal year

    - ❏ Approve IRS Ruling 70-604   ❏ Disapprove IRS Ruling 70-604

    C. With respect to Bylaws amendment, I/We are:

    - ❏ For   ❏ Against   ❏ Abstain

- ❏ Another Member (please print name) _____

- ❏ This proxy to be used to establish a quorum only.

This proxy revokes all proxies heretofore granted by the undersigned. Unless sooner revoked, this proxy shall remain in effect until the final adjournment of the membership meeting, or any subsequent date to which and at which the meeting is finally adjourned.

Date: _____   Signed: _____

Form 5   Sign-In Sheet

_____ HOMEOWNERS ASSOCIATION
ANNUAL MEETING OF OWNERS

(*Date and Time*)

SIGN-IN SHEET

Unit/ Lot #	Name	Address	In Person	By Proxy	Signature

Manager's Note: Names, lot numbers and addresses should be printed on this form prior to the commencement of the meeting. Homeowners will then be able to find their names and sign in, rather than taking time to fill in all the above information.

Form 6   Sample Ballot

Manager's Note: *This ballot assumes three nominees and cumulative voting for three directors.*

_____ HOMEOWNERS ASSOCIATION
ANNUAL OWNERS MEETING

(*Date and Time*)

BALLOT

Nominees for Election – Three Directors to be Elected to ___ Year Terms

Nominee	(1)	(2)	(3)
____(Name of Nominee)____	☐	☐	☐
____(Name of Nominee)____	☐	☐	☐
____(Name of Nominee)____	☐	☐	☐

Cumulative Voting: Each eligible unit/lot owner may cast three votes. You may cast three votes for one nominee, or two votes for one nominee and one for another, or one vote for each of the three nominees. Put the number of checkmarks (☑) behind the name of the nominee(s) that will indicate your vote for the nominee(s). ***If there are more than three checkmarks on this ballot, the ballot will be considered invalid and will not be counted.*** No more than three votes total may be cast per unit/lot.

Nominations may also be made from the floor.

(Optional)

Name: _____   Address: _____

                                                         _____

Form 7   Run-Off Ballot

Manager's Note: *This ballot will only be used in the event of a run-off between candidates with tied votes.*

_____ HOMEOWNERS ASSOCIATION
ANNUAL OWNERS MEETING

(*Date and Time*)

BALLOT

**To be Used Only In the Event of a Tied Vote
When a "Run-Off" Election is Necessary**

Write in the Name of the Nominee(s) for whom you wish to vote:

_____

_____

*THIS BALLOT WILL ONLY BE USED FOR A RUN-OFF ELECTION:
PLEASE DO NOT USE UNLESS INSTRUCTED TO DO SO BY
THE ELECTION PROCTORS*

Form 8   Minutes of First Meeting

_____ HOMEOWNERS ASSOCIATION
MINUTES OF THE FIRST MEETING OF THE BOARD OF DIRECTORS

(*Date*)

The initial Directors of _____ HOMEOWNERS ASSOCIATION, a (*state*) nonprofit [mutual benefit] corporation, held their first meeting at (*location address, city and county*), on (*month*), (*year*) at _____ a.m./p.m. Present at the meeting were _____. [The resignations of _____ and _____ were tendered, and upon motion duly made, seconded, and unanimously carried, were accepted. _____ and _____ were then appointed as Directors by _____, the remaining Director. The new directors accepted their appointments.]

On motion made, seconded, and unanimously carried, _____ was elected temporary Chairman and _____ was elected temporary Secretary of the meeting.

The Chairman reported that the meeting was being held pursuant to a written waiver of notice and consent to meeting signed by all of the Directors. The Secretary was directed to place the waiver and consent in the Minute Book of the corporation following the minutes of this meeting.

It was reported that the Articles of Incorporation have been filed in the Office of the Secretary of State on (*date and year*). A certified copy of the Articles of Incorporation was submitted, and the Secretary was directed to insert the copy into the Minute Book of the corporation.

The matter of the adoption of the Bylaws for the regulation of the corporation's affairs was next considered. The Secretary presented a form of Bylaws, which were duly considered and discussed. Upon motion duly made, seconded, and unanimously carried, the following resolution was adopted:

> **RESOLVED**, that the Bylaws presented to this meeting be and the same are hereby adopted as and for the Bylaws of this corporation, and the Secretary of this corporation be and is hereby authorized and directed to execute a Certificate of Adoption of said Bylaws and to insert said Bylaws as certified in the Minute Book of this corporation, and to see that a copy of said Bylaws similarly certified is kept in the principal office for the transaction of business of the corporation, and that by adoption of said Bylaws the principal office of this corporation is established and shall be maintained at _____, _____ [until the construction of the _____ project has been completed and a majority of the residences have been sold, at which time the principal office shall be moved to the site of the project in the City of _____], and shall remain there until said location is changed by the corporate resolution of the Directors of the corporation.

The meeting then proceeded to the election of officers, and the following were duly elected to the office indicated after their names:

Name	Office
_____	President
_____	Vice President
_____	Chief Financial Officer
_____	Secretary

_____ recommended action on fiscal matters of the corporation and, after discussion, the following resolutions were adopted:

> **RESOLVED,** that this corporation shall conduct its affairs on the basis of a calendar year [fiscal year, starting _____ and ending _____].

> **RESOLVED, FURTHER,** that this corporation shall conduct its affairs and maintain its accounting records on a cash basis.

The necessity of establishing bank accounts was next discussed, and it was agreed that the corporation shall provide for a depository for the funds of the corporation for operating funds. For this purpose and to authorize certain officers to deal with corporate funds, the following resolution was adopted:

> **RESOLVED,** that all funds of this corporation be deposited with _____ in _____, or such other branch as the officers shall hereafter select, and that withdrawals from said account shall be authorized upon the signatures of any two (2) officers of the corporation.

To facilitate maintenance of the Minute Book and corporate records, the Secretary proposed the following resolution, which was unanimously adopted:

> **RESOLVED,** that the Secretary of this corporation be and is hereby authorized in [his][her] discretion, to establish and to maintain under [his][her] supervision and control, a file or files entitled "Exhibits to the Minutes of the Meetings of the Directors of _____ Homeowners Association" and to place therein a copy of each document referred to and incorporated by reference in the minutes of any meeting of the Directors, or in minutes of proceedings of the Directors without a meeting. The Secretary shall include appropriate identification marks on each such document relating to appropriate references in the minutes, to the end that the minutes of the meetings of the Directors shall not be required to have a copy of any such document attached thereto to comprise a record of the action of the Directors, but that copies of such documents shall be maintained in said file appropriately identified for reference purposes as a part of such minutes.

There being no further business, upon motion duly made, seconded and carried, the meeting was adjourned.

_____, Secretary

Form 9   Minutes of Special Meeting

Manager's Note: *Occasionally, the board of directors may hold a special meeting. In this case, these sample minutes assume that the secretary of the association resigned and a new member fills the position.*

_____ HOMEOWNERS ASSOCIATION
MINUTES OF SPECIAL MEETING OF THE BOARD OF DIRECTORS

(*Date*)

The Directors of _____ Homeowners Association, a (*state*) nonprofit [mutual benefit] corporation, held a special meeting *at (location address, city and county*), on (*date and year*), at _____ a.m./p.m. Present at the meeting were _____, _____, _____, and _____. The resignation of _____ as Secretary was tendered, and upon motion duly made, seconded, and unanimously carried, was accepted. _____ was then elected as Secretary to complete the term vacated by _____.

The Chairman reported that the meeting was being held pursuant to a written waiver of notice and consent to meeting signed by all of the Directors. The Secretary was directed to place the waiver and consent in the Minute Book of the corporation following the minutes of this meeting.

There being no further business, upon motion duly made, seconded and carried, the meeting was adjourned.

_____
_____, Secretary

Form 10 Waiver of Notice and Consent

_____ HOMEOWNERS ASSOCIATION
WAIVER OF NOTICE AND CONSENT TO BOARD MEETING

The undersigned, being all of the Directors of _____ Homeowners Association, a (*state*) corporation, do hereby waive notice and consent to the holding of the meeting of the Board of Directors of said corporation on (*date and year*), and approve the foregoing as full, true, and correct minutes of said meeting.

This waiver of notice and approval of minutes is made in compliance with the terms of the appropriate provisions of the Corporations Code of the State of _____, and the undersigned hereby consent that the same may be made a part of the records of said meeting, and that any business transacted thereat shall be as valid as if had at a meeting regularly called or noticed.

Dated: (*month and date*), (*year*), at _____(*city*)_____, _____(*state*)_____.

_____
Director

_____
Director

_____
Director

Form 11 — Resolution of Board

_____ HOMEOWNERS ASSOCIATION
RESOLUTION OF THE BOARD OF DIRECTORS

NO. ____

RECITALS

WHEREAS, on (*state the date and time of the meeting*);

WHEREAS, (*state the facts upon which the resolution is based*);

WHEREAS, (*state any additional facts, as necessary to support the resolution*);

RESOLUTION

It is hereby resolved by the Board of Directors for the Association that (*state the substance of the resolution*) _____.

Executed this _____ day of (*month*), (*year*).

By: _____
_____, Secretary

Form 12   Sample Letter of Resignation

LETTER OF RESIGNATION

Date: _____

To: Board of Directors of _____ Homeowners Association

Ladies and Gentlemen:

Please accept my resignation as (*state officer position—director, secretary, etc.*) effective this _____ day of (*month*), (*year*).

                                        Sincerely,

                                        _____

Form 13   Amendment of Articles

CERTIFICATE OF AMENDMENT
OF ARTICLES OF INCORPORATION

_____ HOMEOWNERS ASSOCIATION

_____ and _____ certify [_____ certifies]:

    1. That they are the President and Secretary, respectively, of _____ Association, a _____ nonprofit _____ corporation.

    [1. That he/she is the sole incorporator of _____ Association, a _____ nonprofit [mutual benefit] _____ corporation.]

ALTERNATIVES:

    2. By unanimous vote of the membership, and approval by the Board of Directors, the following resolution was adopted to amend the Articles of Incorporation:

    2. By unanimous written consent of the membership and approval by the Board of Directors, the following resolution to amend the Articles of Incorporation was adopted:

    2. By affirmative vote of members representing a majority of the voting power of the Association, including a majority of the votes of members other than the Declarant, and approval by the Board of Directors, the following resolution amending the Articles of Incorporation was adopted:

    2. By written consent of members representing a majority of the voting power of the Association, including a majority of the votes of members other than the Declarant, and approval by the Board of Directors, the following resolution amending the Articles of Incorporation was adopted:

    2. By affirmative vote of members representing a majority of the voting power of the Association, including a majority of each class of membership, and approval by the Board of Directors, the following resolution amending the Articles of Incorporation was adopted:

    2. By written consent of members representing a majority of each class of membership, and approval by the Board of Directors, the following resolution amending the Articles of Incorporation was adopted:

2. The corporation having been incorporated by a sole incorporator, and no Directors having been named in the original Articles, and no Directors having yet been elected, and the corporation at this time having no members; pursuant to Corporations Code § _____, the following amendment to the Articles of Incorporation was adopted by a writing signed by the undersigned as the sole incorporator:

RESOLVED, that so much of Article III as presently reads: _____,
is hereby amended to read as follows: _____.
[*INSERT ARTICLE III*]

ALTERNATIVE:

RESOLVED, that the Articles of Incorporation shall be amended to read as herein set forth in full:
[*INSERT COMPLETE NEW ARTICLES*]

ALTERNATIVE:

RESOLVED, that the following provisions set forth herein shall be added to the articles:
[*INSERT COMPLETE NEW ARTICLES*]

ALTERNATIVE:

RESOLVED, that Article ____ shall be amended to read as follows:
[*INSERT AMENDED ARTICLE*]

3. The total number of members is ___; the total number of authorized votes is ___; the total number of members other than Declarant is ___; the total number of [votes for] [written consents to] adoption of the resolution was ___; the total number of its votes or written consents of members other than Declarant for adoption of the resolution was ___. [The resolution was adopted by the required vote of members as provided in Corporations Code § _____.]

[3. The above amendment was adopted by the undersigned as sole incorporator as provided in Corporations Code § _____.]

[Each of] the undersigned further declares, under penalty of perjury under the laws of the State of _____, that the matters set forth in this Certificate are true and correct of [our][my] own knowledge. Executed at _____, _____, on (*month*), (*year*).

_____
President

_____
Secretary

Form 14 Sample First Amendment

When Recorded Return To:

(*Name*)
(*Address*)
(*City, state and zip*)

FIRST AMENDMENT TO
(*Declaration Title*)

This Amendment to the "(*name of the CC&Rs or Declaration*)," which was recorded on (*date*), (*year*), Book _____, page(s)_____, Instrument/Serial Number _____, (*name of County where document was recorded*) County Official Records, is amended by the undersigned, as follows:

1. Section _____ is hereby amended to read as follows:

   "(*insert wording for section in this area*) _____."

IN WITNESS WHEREOF, this First Amendment to the Declaration is executed by the undersigned president and secretary of the association, who certify that the foregoing amendment has been approved by the required percentage of owners as specified in the _____ Declaration.

                        _____ Homeowners Assoc.
                        A _____ nonprofit [mutual benefit] corporation

                        By: _____
                                 _____, President

                        By: _____
                                 _____, Secretary

(*Add appropriate acknowledgement for notary signature and stamp*)

Form 15   First Amendment to Bylaws

FIRST AMENDMENT TO
_____ HOMEOWNERS ASSOCIATION BYLAWS

The _____ Homeowners Association Bylaws are hereby amended pursuant to the written consent of the members representing a majority of [the total voting power of the Association] [a quorum of the Association].

Section _____ is amended to read as follows:

"_____."

IN WITNESS WHEREOF, this Amendment to said Bylaws has been executed and effected this _____ day of (month), (year), by the undersigned officers of the _____ Homeowners Association, each of whom hereby certifies that the foregoing Amendment has been approved by the consent of a majority of [the total voting power] [a quorum] of the _____ Homeowners Association.

                                       _____ Homeowners Association
                                       A _____ nonprofit _____ corporation

                                       By: _____
                                                  _____, President

                                       By: _____
                                                  _____, Secretary

| Form 16 | Sample Association Rules |

Manager's Note: *The following rules and regulations are selected sample provisions that can be used as guidelines in drafting the association's rules and regulations. Such rules and regulations are usually best drafted by the unit or lot owners after they have taken over control of the association. The developer can function fairly well just using the provisions of the Declaration, Articles and Bylaws. Since the rules may be expected to change, and are seldom drafted by an attorney, no standard form has emerged. There has been no attempt to include every possible provision in these sample rules. Instead, the more common types of rules and regulations have been suggested.*

_____ HOMEOWNERS ASSOCIATION
RULES AND REGULATIONS

1. Use of Common Area. Halls, entrances, stairways, or sidewalks shall not be obstructed, and children shall not play in lobbies, elevators, halls, stairways, garages, storage areas, etc. There shall not be any storage of goods or materials in any common area except as expressly permitted.

2. Use of Recreational Facilities.

    A. Pool. Children under ____ years of age shall not use the pool unless accompanied at all times by a parent. The pool shall not be used before the hour of _____ or after the hour of _____. Food or beverages shall not be permitted within ____ feet of the pool. Use of the pool shall be restricted to Owners, their tenants, and their guests. Entrance to the pool shall be by use of keys, which shall not be given or loaned by members of the association to nonmembers other than tenants.

    B. Tennis Courts. _____.
[*Rules should regulate proper attire, hours of play, reservations, priorities, duration of play while other players are waiting, guest privileges, restrictions on equipment, etc.*]

    C. Putting Green, Golf Course, Etc. _____.
[*Rules should be similar to the standard golf club or golf course rules.*]

    D. Gymnasium, Spa, Sauna, Etc. _____.
[*Rules should regulate hours of use, numbers of persons allowed, guest privileges, age limitations, etc.*]

    E. Recreation Room. _____.
[*Rules should regulate hours of use, responsibility for cleaning up, reservations for special events, etc.*]

3. Decoration of Units. _____.
[*Restrictions on use of color or material in drapes, window coverings, etc., which are visible from other units or from the common area are sometimes regulated.*]

4. **Elevators.** _____.
[*Typical elevator restrictions might include regulations concerning clothing or attire to be worn in elevators; restriction of certain elevators for use by persons in swimming suits, workers, delivery personnel; prohibition against children playing in elevators; or the decorating or display of signs, posters, etc., in elevators.*]

5. **Garage and Parking Facilities.** _____.
[*Typical rules include restrictions on parking, decals on automobiles, and prohibition against storage or repair of vehicles in the garage, driveways, parking areas, etc.*]

6. **Storage.** The Board of Directors or manager of the project may assign and reassign storage spaces. The association assumes no liability for damage or theft of any items stored in common area storage space. [*These or similar regulations might be applied to storage space which is not specifically allocated by the Declaration or the Condominium Diagram to particular units.*]

7. **Refuse.** _____.
[*Regulations might cover time and manner of delivery of refuse from apartment units to basement or ground floor, use of garbage chutes, requirements for wrapping or depositing garbage, and regulations on use of garbage cans or other means of garbage disposal.*]

8. **Maintenance.** All unit owners are required to keep their units and those portions of the restricted common area over which they have exclusive easements in a good state of cleanliness and repair at all times. [*Other provisions could be included, such as prohibiting sweeping or throwing debris from windows, doors, terraces, balconies, etc.*]

9. **Air Conditioning Systems.** _____. [*If air conditioning has not been provided during initial construction, consideration should be given to whether the rules and regulations or the Declaration itself should put some restrictions on installation of air conditioning devices. The visual impact of such devices, the noise level generated, and the use of electrical current in the event units are not separately metered should all be considered.*]

10. **Electrical Equipment.** Unit owners shall not be permitted to install any electrical equipment, including shop machinery, radio or television equipment, heavy-duty office equipment, etc., which may overload the electrical circuits of the project or of the unit, or violate local fire rules and regulations, or cause an increase in the insurance premiums charged to the association.

11. **Vehicles.** _____.
[*Regulations should include use and storage of bicycles, tricycles, motorcycles, etc. The provisions of the Declaration relating to motor vehicles could be adapted so as to be compatible with the wishes of the unit owners.*]

12. **Noise.** Unit owners shall not cause or permit any noise to be made in their unit or in the common area which might tend to interfere unreasonably with the peace and quiet of other unit owners. [*Some rules and regulations include restrictions on the hours during which or the number of hours each day that*

musical instruments can be practiced, and restrict playing of televisions, radios, stereos, etc., during certain hours of the late evening and early morning.]

13. Pets. _____.
[*The condominium owners might wish to expand upon the restrictions on pets contained in the Declaration. Such restrictions would include use of particular stairways or elevators for escorting pets to and from the premises, excluding pets from the lobby, etc.*]

14. Solicitors and Domestic Help. _____.
[*Some projects, particularly those containing expensive units in high-rise buildings, sometimes include restrictions on which elevators and entrances may be used by domestic help, salesmen, delivery persons, messengers, etc.*]

15. Deliveries. _____.
[*Rules and regulations might include provisions on the delivery of merchandise, baggage, etc.*]

16. Plumbing. _____.
[*Since plumbing malfunctions caused by the misuse of facilities may require repairs within the common area, it is not unusual to have restrictions about misuse of plumbing facilities, such as dumping anything down a toilet which may cause backups, etc.*]

17. Condominium Employees. _____.
[*If a condominium project has one or more full-time employees, it is customary to establish rules concerning the duties of such persons, to prevent any attempts by unit owners to make use of such personnel for personal errands or tasks, etc.*]

18. Pest Control. The Board of Directors may authorize any licensed pest control operator or his/her employees to enter any condominium unit at any reasonable hour of the day for the purpose of inspecting such unit for the presence of any undesirable insects or vermin, and to take preventative or protective measures to control or exterminate the same.

19. Terraces, Patios, and Balconies. _____.
[*Regulations might include prohibitions against cooking outdoors, or other uses of terraces, patios, or balconies which might be annoying to adjoining unit owners.*]

20. Pass Keys. _____.
[*Regulations might permit the Board or the manager to have a passkey to each unit, and might prohibit unit owners from installing new locks without providing the Board with a new key.*]

21. Utility Room. _____.
[*In projects having a utility room or laundry room, the association might want to establish regulations for the use of such facilities.*]

22. Roof. _____.
[*It might be desirable to restrict members from climbing on the roof of the project at any time.*]

23. Tipping. _____.
[*The association might wish to prohibit tipping of condominium employees, but may wish to provide for an annual gratuity for each employee payable at the end of the year.*]

24. Parties. _____.
[*Rules should be established for the use of the recreation room, swimming pool, etc., by large parties, providing for a reservation system. A provision might be included requiring owners who plan to entertain large groups in their unit to notify management in advance so that arrangements can be made to admit people coming to the party, to provide for parking, etc.*]

25. Moving Expense Fees. The Board of Directors is authorized to assess a "moving fee," reasonably related to the cost of supplies, labor, services, maintenance, and repairs related to moving activities, against the owner of a unit, assessed at the time anyone moves into a unit (other than the initial move-in following the original purchase of the unit).

| Form 17 | Procedures for Enforcement of Association Rules |

Manager's Note: *The enforcement of rules by the association can sometimes be a trying experience, particularly in a large project. The board of directors is normally charged with the responsibility for adopting rules and regulations for the conduct of the owners, members, tenants, guests, etc. The following form illustrates one method of approach. This is a fairly detailed and specific form, which attempts to spell out most of the rules and procedures required to investigate complaints, conduct hearings, and impose discipline.*

_____ HOMEOWNERS ASSOCIATION
POLICY RESOLUTION NO. _____
RULES ENFORCEMENT

WHEREAS, Article _____, Section _____, of the CC&Rs (Bylaws) grants the BOARD powers for the conduct of the affairs of the ASSOCIATION which are granted by law and the Project Legal Documents ("DOCUMENTS"); and

WHEREAS, for the benefit and protection of the ASSOCIATION and of the individual MEMBERS, the BOARD deems it desirable to establish and operate a procedure to assure due process in cases where there is a question of compliance by a MEMBER, his/her family, and/or his/her guests or tenants with the provisions of the DOCUMENTS or adopted RESOLUTIONS, thereby attempting to minimize the necessity of seeking action in or through a court of law; and

WHEREAS, it is the intent of the BOARD to establish procedures for the BOARD and RULES COMMITTEE where they must take action relative to questions of compliance by an individual with the provisions of the DOCUMENTS or adopted RESOLUTIONS;

NOW, THEREFORE, BE IT RESOLVED THAT SPECIAL RESOLUTIONS shall be adopted in accordance with the following procedures:

I.   VIOLATIONS OF THE DOCUMENTS OR ADOPTED RESOLUTIONS.

Section 1. Actions Prior to Initiation of Formal SPECIAL RESOLUTION Process.

Any MEMBER or agent of the ASSOCIATION has the authority to request that a MEMBER or resident cease or correct any act or omission which appears to be in violation of the DOCUMENTS. Such informal requests must be made before the final process is initiated.

Section 2. Written Complaint. If the actions described in Section 1 prove unsuccessful, the SPECIAL RESOLUTIONS PROCESS shall be initiated upon the filing of a written complaint by any MEMBER, or by any officer or member of the BOARD, with the RULES COMMITTEE. The complaint shall constitute a written statement of charges, which shall set forth in ordinary and concise language the acts or omissions with which the respondent is charged, to the end that the respondent will be able to prepare a defense. The complaint shall specify the specific provisions of the DOCUMENTS or adopted RESOLUTIONS which the respondent is alleged to have violated, but shall not consist merely of charges phrased in the language of such provisions without supporting facts. Further, the written complaint must contain as many specifics as are available as to time, date, location, persons involved, etc., so that the complaint may be investigated by the RULES COMMITTEE.

Section 3. Service of Complaint. Upon the filing of the complaint, the RULES COMMITTEE shall assign the complaint a Special Resolutions number and serve a copy of the complaint on the respondent by either of the following means: (1) personal delivery, or (2) by registered or certified mail, return receipt requested, and addressed to respondent at the address appearing on the Books of the ASSOCIATION. Service by mailing shall be deemed delivered and effective two (2) days after such mailing in a regular depository of the United States mail. The complaint shall be accompanied with a postcard or other written form entitled "Notice of Defense" which, when signed by the respondent, or on behalf of the respondent, will constitute a Notice of Defense hereunder. No order adversely affecting the rights of the respondent shall be made in any case unless the respondent shall have been served as provided herein.

Section 4. Notice of Hearing. Along with service of complaint, the BOARD shall serve a notice of hearing as provided herein on all parties at least ten (10) days prior to the hearing. The notice to the respondent shall be substantially in the following form but may include other information:

"You are hereby notified that a hearing will be held before the RULES COMMITTEE at (____location____) on the (_date_) day of (___month___), (_year_), at the hour of _____, upon the charges made in the complaint served upon you. You may, but need not, be present at the hearing; may, but need not, be represented by counsel; may present any relevant evidence; and you will be given full opportunity to cross-examine all witnesses testifying against you. You are entitled to compel the attendance of witnesses and the production of books, documents, or other items by applying to the BOARD."

If any of the parties can within twenty-four (24) hours show good cause as to why they cannot attend the hearing on the set date, and indicate times and dates on which they would be available, the RULES COMMITTEE may reset the time and date of hearing and promptly deliver notice of the new hearing date.

Section 5. Notice of Defense. Service of complaint and notice of hearing shall be accompanied by a Notice of Defense. The Notice of Defense shall state that the respondent may:

(1) Attend a hearing before the RULES COMMITTEE as hereinafter provided;
(2) Object to a complaint upon the ground that it does not state the acts or omissions upon which the RULES COMMITTEE may proceed;
(3) Object to the form of the complaint on the ground that it is so indefinite or uncertain that the respondent cannot identify the violating behavior or prepare his/her defense; or
(4) Admit to the complaint in whole or in part. In such event, the RULES COMMITTEE may make a determination as to whether it will waive hearing and simply impose penalty, if any, or conduct a hearing to determine the appropriate penalty.

Any objections to the form or substance of the complaint must be received by the RULES COMMITTEE within ten (10) days of its receipt by the respondent. The RULES COMMITTEE shall make its determination and notify all parties within ten (10) days of receipt of an objection. If the complaint is insufficient, the complaining party shall have seven (7) days within which to amend the complaint to make it sufficient. The same procedure as set forth above shall be followed with respect to any amended or supplemental complaint. If it is determined by the RULES COMMITTEE that the complaint is still insufficient, then the matter shall be dismissed by the RULES COMMITTEE.

Section 6. Amended or Supplemental Complaint Before Submission. At any time prior to the hearing date, the RULES COMMITTEE may file or permit the filing of an amended or supplemental complaint. All parties shall be notified thereof in the manner herein provided. If the amended or supplemental complaint presents new charges, the

RULES COMMITTEE shall afford the respondent a reasonable opportunity to prepare his/her defense thereto.

Section 7. Discovery. Upon written request to the other party made prior to the hearing and within fifteen (15) days after service of the complaint by the RULES COMMITTEE, or within ten (10) days after service of any amended or supplemental complaint, either party is entitled to (1) obtain the names and addresses of witnesses to the extent known to the other party, and (2) inspect and make a copy of any statements, writing(s) and investigative reports relevant to the subject matter of the hearing. Nothing in this Section, however, shall authorize the inspection or copying of any writing or thing which is privileged from disclosure by law or otherwise made confidential or protected as the attorney's work product. Any party claiming that his/her request of discovery has not been complied with shall submit a written petition to compel discovery to the BOARD. The BOARD shall make a determination and issue a written order setting forth the matters or parts thereof which the petitioner is entitled to discover.

Section 8. Constraints on the RULES COMMITTEE. It shall be incumbent upon each member of the RULES COMMITTEE to make a determination as to whether he or she is able to function in a disinterested and objective manner in consideration of the case before the RULES COMMITTEE. Any member incapable of objective consideration of the case shall disclose such to the RULES COMMITTEE and recuse himself/herself from the proceedings, and have it so recorded in the minutes.

In any event, the respondent may challenge any member of the RULES COMMITTEE for cause, where a fair and impartial hearing cannot be afforded at any time prior to the taking of evidence and testimony at the hearing. In the event of such a challenge, the BOARD shall meet to determine the sufficiency of the challenge. If a majority of the BOARD sustains the challenge, the President shall appoint another owner to replace the challenged member of the RULES COMMITTEE. All decisions of the Board in this regard shall be final.

Section 9. Hearing.

(a) Whenever the RULES COMMITTEE has commenced to hear the matter and a member of the RULES COMMITTEE is forced to withdraw prior to a final determination, the remaining members shall continue to hear the case and the President of the ASSOCIATION shall replace the withdrawing member. Oral evidence shall be taken only on oath or affirmation administered by an officer of the ASSOCIATION.

(b) Each party shall have these rights: to call and examine witnesses; to introduce exhibits; to cross-examine opposing witnesses; and to rebut the evidence against him/her. Even if the respondent does not testify in his or her own behalf, (s)he may be called and examined as if under cross-examination.

(c) The hearing need not be conducted according to technical rules relating to evidence and witnesses. Generally, any relevant evidence shall be admitted if it is the sort of evidence upon which responsible persons are accustomed to rely in the conduct of serious affairs, regardless of the existence of any common law or statutory rule which might make improper the admission of such evidence over the objection in civil actions. Hearsay evidence shall not be sufficient in itself to support a finding.

(d) Neither the accusing party nor the allegedly defaulting party must be in attendance at the hearing. At the request of any principal, the hearing shall be conducted in executive session.

(e) At the beginning of the hearing, a member of the RULES COMMITTEE shall explain the rules and procedures by which the hearing is to be conducted. Generally, each principal is entitled to make an opening statement, starting with the complainant. Then each party is entitled to produce evidence, witnesses, and testimony and to cross-examine the witnesses and opposing party. Each party is then entitled to make a closing statement. Any party may waive the right to exercise any part of this process, and the RULES COMMITTEE is entitled to exercise its discretion as to the specific manner in which the hearing will be conducted.

Section 10. Decision. After all the testimony and documentary evidence has been presented to the RULES COMMITTEE, the RULES COMMITTEE shall vote upon the matter, with a majority of the entire RULES COMMITTEE controlling. The RULES COMMITTEE shall make its determination only in accordance with this resolution. The decision may be made at the conclusion of the hearing or may be postponed to no later than ten (10) days hence. The RULES COMMITTEE will prepare written findings of fact. A copy of the findings and recommendations of the RULES COMMITTEE, including majority and minority opinions, if any, shall be served by the RULES COMMITTEE on each party in the matter and his or her attorney, if any. A summary of the decision, excluding names of persons involved and addressing only the issue and the RULES COMMITTEE's decision with respect to the issue, shall be included in the MINUTE BOOK. Disciplinary action, if any, shall become effective ten (10) days after it is served upon the respondent, unless otherwise ordered in writing by the RULES COMMITTEE.

II. FINE STRUCTURE.

First Offense; Warning
Second Offense; $_____ Fine
Third Offense; $_____ Fine
Fourth Offense (and each additional occurrence) will be $_____ more than the previous fine imposed.
Offenses for separate rules will each start at the warning stage.

III. APPEALS.

Section 1. Rules Committee. Any MEMBER may appeal a decision of the Rules Committee to the Board, provided that all subordinate avenues of resolution have been pursued, and further provided that all parties involved comply with the decision of the RULES COMMITTEE until such time, if any, as the BOARD amends or reverses the RULES COMMITTEE's decision.

Section 2. Appeals Petitions. Appeals petitions must be legibly written and be submitted to: _____ HOMEOWNERS ASSOCIATION, in substantially the following form:

"(I)(We), _____, hereby petition the BOARD to hear an appeal of Special Resolution No. _____."

"(I)(We), _____, further understand that within the ASSOCIATION a decision of the BOARD on this issue is final, and that if further action is initiated by the ASSOCIATION, another OWNER, or [myself] [ourselves], it will be through legal proceedings in a court of law."

Signed: _____
Address: _____
_____
Dated: _____

Section 3. Notice of Hearing on Appeal. Notice of hearing shall be as in Section I.4 of this Resolution.

Section 4. Action of Board of Appeal. Through a vote of the majority of the BOARD, the BOARD may uphold the RULES COMMITTEE's decision in its entirety, may amend such decision, or may overturn such decision.

Section 5. Further Action. Any individual MEMBER shall exhaust all available remedies of the ASSOCIATION prescribed by this resolution before that MEMBER may resort to a court of law for relief with respect to any alleged violation by another MEMBER of any provision of the founding documents or adopted RESOLUTIONS. The foregoing limitation pertaining to exhausting administrative remedies shall not necessarily apply to the BOARD or to any MEMBER where the complaint alleges non-payment of assessments.

Form 18   Sample Notice of Hearing

_____ HOMEOWNERS ASSOCIATION
NOTICE OF HEARING

Date: _____

Dear Homeowner:

Attached you will find a written complaint which has been filed with the Rules Committee and assigned Special Resolution Number _____.

You are hereby notified that a hearing will be held before the Rules Committee at _____ on the _____ day of (*month*), (*year*), at the hour of _____ a.m./p.m., upon the charges made in the complaint served upon you. You may, but need not, be present at the hearing; may, but need not, be represented by counsel; may present any relevant evidence; and you will be given full opportunity to cross-examine all witnesses testifying against you. You are entitled to compel the attendance of witnesses and the production of books, documents, or other items by applying to the Board of Directors.

If you can show good cause as to why you cannot attend the hearing on the date and time set, indicate the time and date on which you would be available; the Rules Committee may reset the time and date of the hearing and will promptly deliver notice of the new hearing date.

The Rules Committee may be contacted by writing at: *(address of chairperson for Rules Committee)*.

Thank you.

_____, Rules Committee

Form 19	Sample Letter to New Owners

Manager's Note: *Upon learning of a sale of a home, the president of the association's board or the manager should mail a letter of introduction to the new owner. This letter welcomes the new owner as a new member of the association and outlines the responsibilities of the new owner, including payment of the assessments. The letter may accompany copies of the Articles of Incorporation, Bylaws, Declaration and/or the association's rules and regulations.*

_____ **HOMEOWNERS ASSOCIATION**
(*Mailing address for association*)
(*Telephone and fax numbers*)

Date: _____

Dear _____:

Welcome to _____ Homeowners Association. We are the Board of Directors of the Association, and it is our responsibility to maintain the Common Areas. However, it is your responsibility to participate in the Association, by volunteering to serve either on the Board of Directors or a committee of the Board. If at any time you have any questions, suggestions, or problems, please make note of our telephone number and call us.

Your Association's annual assessment is $ _____, payable monthly, and has been paid through escrow to (*date*), (*year*). You will receive monthly billings directly from our office or from the Association Manager.

The operation of your Association is administered by the Board of Directors. If you require Association action on something, you can contact the Association at the address shown above. If you wish to inspect your Association records, they are maintained in our office at the address shown above, and you are always welcome during normal business hours.

Enclosed is a copy of the Articles of Incorporation and Bylaws of the Association, together with a copy of the recorded Declaration of Restrictions affecting the Project. Use and enjoyment of your unit/lot is subject to compliance with the restrictions contained in the Declaration. You should familiarize yourself thoroughly with these restrictions.

Your Association manager is _____, who is available to talk with you during office hours (*insert office hours*) by calling (*telephone number*).

Sincerely,

_____ HOMEOWNERS ASSOCIATION

_____, Board President

Form 20 — Notice of Assessment Increase

_____ HOMEOWNERS ASSOCIATION
NOTICE OF INCREASE IN ASSESSMENTS

Date: _____

To All Owners/Members, _____ **Homeowners Association:**

Pursuant to the provisions of Section ____, Article ____, of the Declaration of Covenants, Conditions and Restrictions of the _____ Homeowners Association, dated _____, (*year*), the annual assessment per unit/lot is being *increased* to $_____ effective January 1, (*year*) [*or use date when fiscal year begins*]. This is an increase of ____ % over the previous year's assessment.

The assessment is payable monthly at $_____ per month, starting January 1, (*year*). You will soon receive a supply of [coupons] [payment cards] [statements] and envelopes for use in paying your monthly assessments.

The monthly assessment is due and payable not later than the ____ of the month for which payment is due. A late charge will be added if payment is not received by the ____ of the month.

A copy of the (*year*) budget was previously furnished to all Owners.

                                                Sincerely,

                                                Board of Directors, _____ HOA

                                                _____
                                                _____ Treasurer/CFO

Form 21   Sample Budget Summary

_____ HOMEOWNERS ASSOCIATION
BUDGET SUMMARY

Acct No.	Expense Item	Current Budget	Total Annual	Total Monthly	Per Unit/Lot Per Month
100	**Fixed Costs**				
101	Federal Taxes				
102	Corporation Franchise Taxes				
103	Insurance				
104	License and Inspection Fees				
	TOTAL FIXED COSTS				
200	**Administration**				
201	Local Management				
202	Legal Services				
203	Accounting				
204	Miscellaneous Office Expense				
205	Printing and Postage				
	TOTAL ADMIN. COSTS				
300	**Maintenance**				
301	Laundry Rooms				
302	Custodial Area, Restrooms				
303	Landscape Area				
304	Elevators				
305	Private Streets and Driveways				
306	Heating and Air Conditioning Maint.				
307	Swimming Pool and Spa				
308	Tennis Court				
309	Security Guard/Motorized Gate				
310	Miscellaneous Maintenance				
311	Pest Control				
312	Minor General Repairs				
313	Lakes and Waterways				
314	Intercoms				
315	Snow Removal				
316	Lighting Repairs				
	TOTAL MAINTENANCE COST				
400	**Utilities**				
401	Electricity				
402	Gas				
403	Water				
404	Sewer				
405	Refuse Collection				
406	Cable TV				
	TOTAL UTILITIES				
500	Allocation to Reserves				
501	Contingency				

TOTAL BUDGET

Form 22　　　　　　　　　　　　　　　　　　　　　Resolution on Exempt Status

_____ HOMEOWNERS ASSOCIATION
RESOLUTION ON EXEMPT STATUS
RESOLUTION NO. _____

The President commenced a discussion of the tax status of the Association, including available exemptions and special tax treatment under federal and state tax laws. On motion duly made, seconded and unanimously carried, the following resolution was adopted:

RESOLVED, that the (*title of officer*) consult with the Association's tax advisors to ascertain the availability and advisability of tax exemptions or other special tax treatment under the federal and state tax laws, and, if such exemptions or special tax treatment are available and advisable, *the* (*title of officer*) is authorized and directed to execute and file all necessary applications with the appropriate state and federal authorities in order to qualify for the exemptions or special tax treatment.

Executed this _____ day of _____, (*year*).

By: _____
　　　Secretary

Form 23   Reminder to Member of Unpaid Assessment

_____ HOMEOWNERS ASSOCIATION
(*Association address*)
(*Telephone number*)

Date: _____

Dear _____:

Our records indicate that you have not paid your monthly assessment(s) to the Association for the period _____, which total(s) $_____. If payment of this amount is not made by (*date*), a late charge of $_____ will be assessed.

It is important that you give this matter your personal attention at this time. Your obligation to promptly pay assessments to the Association is reflected in your deed restrictions. These regulations require that we collect membership assessments from each owner, and take collection action and legal steps against those who are delinquent.

However, it has been our experience that most people who are behind in their payments have not given this matter the attention it requires. The purpose of this letter is to impress upon you the importance of sending us a check at this time.

Please send your check today, or contact the undersigned regarding payment arrangements.

Sincerely,

_____, Treasurer

Form 24 Notice of Delinquent Assessment (Condo)

When Recorded Return to:

(*Name*) _____
(*Address*)
(*City, state and zip*)

NOTICE OF DELINQUENT ASSESSMENT

NOTICE IS HEREBY GIVEN that condominium unit number ____ as described in _____ [the condominium plan entitled _____ or the combined Map and Condominium Plan] recorded on the ___ day of _____, (*year*), in Book ____ of [Maps], page ____, [Official] Records of _____ County, has been assessed by the Board of Directors of the _____ Owners Association pursuant to its authority under Article ____, Section ____ of the Enabling Declaration Establishing a Plan for a Condominium, executed on the ____ day of _____, (*year*), and recorded on the ____ day of _____, (*year*), in the Official Records of the County of _____, State of _____, in Book ____, at page ____.

The record owner of said condominium unit is _____.

The amount of the assessment is $_____. The amount of additional charges is:

      Interest - $_____
      Collection Costs - $_____
      Attorneys' Fees - $_____
      Late Charges - $_____

      Total - $_____

The name and address of the Trustee authorized by the Association to enforce the lien by sale is:

_____
_____
_____

Dated: _____, (*year*)   _____ ASSOCIATION

                        By: _____
                            _____, President

[*Add appropriate acknowledgement*]

Form 25 Notice of Delinquent Assessment (PD)

When Recorded Return to:

(*Name of association*)
(*Address*)
(*City, state and zip*)

NOTICE OF DELINQUENT ASSESSMENT

NOTICE IS HEREBY GIVEN that lot number _____, as described in _____ [the subdivision map entitled _____] recorded on the ___ day of _____, (*year*), in Book ____ of [Maps], page ____, [Official] Records of _____ County, has been assessed by the Board of Directors of the _____ Owners Association pursuant to its authority under Article ____, Section ____ of the Declaration of Covenants, Conditions and Restrictions, executed on the ____ day of _____, (*year*), and recorded on the ____ day of _____, (*year*), in the Official Records of the County of _____, State of _____, in Book ____, at page ____.

The record owner of said lot is _____.

The amount of the assessment is $_____. The amount of additional charges is:

    Interest - $_____
    Collection Costs - $_____
    Attorneys' Fees - $_____
    Late Charges - $_____

    Total - $_____

The name and address of the Trustee authorized by the Association to enforce the lien by sale is:

    _____
    _____
    _____

Dated: _____, (*year*)　　　　_____ ASSOCIATION

                                                 By: _____
                                                      _____, President

[*Add appropriate acknowledgement*]

Form 26   Notice of Default

When Recorded Return to:

(*Name of association*)
(*Address*)
(*City, state and zip*) __

NOTICE OF DEFAULT IN PAYMENT OF ASSESSMENT LIEN

IMPORTANT NOTICE: IF YOUR PROPERTY IS IN FORECLOSURE BECAUSE YOU HAVE NOT PAID YOUR ASSESSMENTS, IT MAY BE SOLD WITHOUT ANY COURT ACTION. You may have the legal right to cure the default by paying all of your past-due assessments plus permitted costs and expenses within _____ months from the date this Notice of Default was recorded. **REMEMBER, YOU MAY LOSE LEGAL RIGHTS IF YOU DO NOT TAKE PROMPT ACTION.**

Name of Owner of Unit/Lot: _____
                                                                 _____

NOTICE IS HEREBY GIVEN that a breach of obligation has occurred in connection with the Assessment Lien recorded on the ____ day of _____, (*year*) in Volume ___, page ____, Official Records, _____ County, by the _____ Association. Said obligation consists of the failure to pay an assessment lien in the amount of $_____. By reason of said breach and default, it is hereby declared that the entire amount of $_____ is immediately due and payable, and notice is hereby given of the election of the undersigned to sell or cause to be sold the property known as Unit/Lot ____, and the accompanying interest in the common area appurtenant thereto as described on the [condominium plan] [subdivision map] recorded on the ____ day of _____, (*year*), in pages ____ through ____, Official Records, _____ County. The obligation, default of which has resulted in this Notice of Default, includes payment of the principal sum of $_____, together with interest thereon at _____% per annum from and after _____, attorneys' fees in the amount of $_____, costs in the amount of $_____, and late charges in the amount of $_____.

Dated: _____, (*year*)   _____ ASSOCIATION

                                            By: _____
                                                          President

                                            By: _____
                                                          Secretary

[Add appropriate acknowledgement]

Form 27   Satisfaction and Release of Lien

When Recorded Return to:

(*Name of association*)
(*Address*)
(*City, state and zip*)

SATISFACTION AND RELEASE OF LIEN

      This is to certify that a certain lien owned and held by the undersigned, bearing the date of _____ [*date of lien*], was executed by _____ [*as stated on lien*], as authorized agent of _____ Association, against Unit/Lot _____, owned by _____, and recorded in the County Clerk's Office, County of _____, on the _____ day of _____, (*year*), in Book ____, Page ____, is fully paid and has been satisfied. The undersigned therefore consents that the aforesaid lien may be discharged on the records thereof, according to the statutes in such case provided.

      IN WITNESS WHEREOF, _____, authorized agent by the Board of Directors, hereby sets his/her hand this _____ day of _____, (*year*).

Dated: _____, (*year*)   _____ ASSOCIATION

                                              By: _____
                                                  _____ [*name*]
                                                  (Authorized agent of Board of Directors)

[*Add appropriate acknowledgement*]

Form 28   Sample Management Agreement

Manager's Note: *Most management companies have and require clients to use their firm's management contracts. However, most will agree to modify contracts slightly to meet the needs of their clients. The management contract used by the association's manager may contain slightly different information than in this template.*

OWNERS ASSOCIATION MANAGEMENT AGREEMENT

This Management Agreement is made this _____ day of _____, (*year*), by and between the _____, hereinafter referred to as "Association," and _____, hereinafter referred to as "Manager" [or "Management"].

RECITALS

This Management Agreement is made with reference to the following facts:

A. The Manager shall mean and refer to _____, whose address is _____.

B. The Association shall mean and refer to the _____, a Community Association under the laws of the State of _____.

C. The Project shall mean and refer to the following: The property which the Association is charged with the obligations and duties to manage and operate is that real estate development known as _____ (the "Project"). The Project is a [condominium] [planned development] project situated at: _____.
The Project consists of _____ (___) [condominium units] [residential lots] and Common Area.

D. The Project Management Documents include the _____ Declaration and Covenants, Conditions and Restrictions, the Articles of Incorporation, and the Bylaws of the Association, and the rules and regulations adopted by the Association, as such instruments may be amended from time to time.

AGREEMENT

The Association hereby contracts with Manager to operate and manage the Project, and provide certain specified services to the Association, on the terms and conditions hereinafter set forth.

ARTICLE I
General Conditions

1.1 Retention of Manager. The Association hereby retains Manager to manage the operations of the Association and provide certain services to the Association on the terms and conditions set forth in this Agreement for a term of _____ (___) months commencing on the ___ day of _____, (*year*). Thereafter, this Agreement shall continue for successive one-year periods unless on or before sixty (60) days prior to the date last above mentioned, or on or before thirty (30) days prior to the expiration of any such renewal period, either party hereto shall notify the other in writing of an intention to terminate this Management Agreement, in which case this Agreement may be terminated prior to the last-mentioned date.

1.2 **Status of Manager.** Manager shall be an agent on behalf of the Association as a disclosed principal with respect to the matters covered by this Agreement; provided, however, Manager shall have no authority to execute or enter into contracts on behalf of the Association unless specifically directed to do so by Board resolution.

1.3 **Role of Manager.** Manager shall assist the Board in the management, operation, and administration of the Association. Manager shall use its reasonable efforts and diligence to perform its duties under this Agreement in accordance with the Association's governing documents, including its Declaration of Covenants ("Declaration"), Bylaws, rules and regulations, and other duly enacted policies and procedures (collectively referred to as the "Project Documents"). Manager shall be available at reasonable times to confer with the Board and its representative regarding the performance of the services set forth herein.

1.4 **Delivery of Association Records.** As soon as reasonably practical after the date of commencement of this Agreement, the Association shall deliver to Manager all documents and records relating to the management of the Project, including, without limitation: budgets, financial statements, and bank statements; a list of assessment balances for each owner; maintenance records; outstanding bills; copies of service contracts, certifications, and licenses held by the Association; copies of the Association's insurance policies and income tax returns; a list of all employees and contractors; copies of the Project Documents; a list of the names and addresses and telephone numbers of the Owners; the plans and specifications for the project; an inventory of the equipment and personal property of the Association; and guarantees and/or warranties affecting Association property. If the above records are not available, or if available records are incomplete or inaccurate, Manager will evaluate and report the status of such condition to the Board.

1.5 **Authorized Representatives of Association.** Manager shall only act upon instructions from the Board of the Association or officers of the Association or other representatives of the Association expressly delegated authority by the Board to work directly with Manager.

1.6 **Experience as Manager.** Manager represents and warrants to the Association that Manager is skilled and experienced as a property manager of community associations for common interest developments, and that Manager will provide skilled and experienced personnel for undertaking its responsibilities hereunder.

ARTICLE II
General Administration

2.1 **Scope of Article.** Manager shall perform the following routine general administration services:

2.1.1 **Attend Board Meetings.** Attend [up to] [one (1)] regular Board meeting[s] per month as may be directed by the Board. Manager has no obligation to attend regular Board meetings on holidays or for more than three (3) hours in any single meeting. The Board shall give Manager reasonable advance notice of such meetings and make an effort to accommodate any conflict in the Manager's schedule.

2.1.2 Attend Annual/Committee Meetings. Manager shall attend one (1) regular annual membership meeting and three (3) committee meetings per year, or such lesser number as the Board may direct. Manager shall not be obligated to attend meetings on weekends or holidays, or for more than three (3) hours for annual meetings or for more than two (2) hours for any other meeting.

2.1.3 Minutes. Manager shall take minutes and prepare a record of actions taken at Board and general membership meetings attended pursuant to this Agreement, and shall maintain a chronological file of all duly adopted minutes and resolutions.

2.1.4 Meeting Notices, Agendas, and Coordination. Manager shall schedule, notice, and coordinate the Board and general membership meetings, and shall prepare necessary materials such as notices, agendas, reports, ballots, proxies, and similar items. Manager shall prepare and distribute Board and membership meeting agendas and supplementary materials at least three (3) days prior to a meeting.

2.1.5 Owner Roster. Manager shall maintain a current roster of the names, addresses, and, to the extent readily available, telephone numbers of all unit/lot Owners.

2.1.6 Correspondence. Manager shall receive and review Association correspondence, and shall prepare and send such correspondence as may be appropriate.

2.1.7 Record and File Maintenance. Manager shall maintain the records and files relating to the operation and management of the Association with respect to the sale or transfer of each condominium unit/lot.

2.1.8 Sale/Resale Information. Manager shall prepare, distribute, and process information required of the Association with respect to the sale or transfer of a unit/lot.

2.1.9 Resident Information Pamphlet. Manager shall assist in the preparation and distribution of informational materials to the Owners regarding the rules and policies of the Association.

2.1.10 Communication to Association Members. Manager shall provide information and expertise to develop methods of communication to Association members, if so authorized by the Association's Board of Directors. The costs and expenses of preparation, printing, and mailing of any newsletter shall be reimbursed to Manager.

2.1.11 Emergency Services. Manager shall provide after-hour answering and/or emergency assistance service as may be necessary for the health, safety, and well-being of the occupants of the Property.

2.1.12 Rule Enforcement. Manager shall assist the Board in enforcing the Project Documents.

2.1.13 Insurance Liaison. Manager shall obtain and submit an insurance program for Board review, and provide liaison services with Association's insurance brokers and/or agents.

2.1.14 Office Hours. Manager shall maintain normal office hours Monday through Friday (except holidays) for communications related to Association business, and shall provide a 24-hour emergency telephone number and/or answering service.

2.1.15 Documents to Prospective Purchaser. Upon written request of a unit/lot Owner who has contracted to sell his or her community association interest, Manager shall, as soon as practical, but in any event within 10 days of the mailing or delivery of the request, provide such owner with such information or documentation as the owner may be entitled under the Project documents and applicable laws.

ARTICLE III
Duties of Manager; Property Management

3.1 Scope of Article. Manager shall assist the Board in the creation, implementation, and administration of a maintenance program covering those areas for which the Association has responsibility under the Project documents and applicable state laws, and, as part of that program, shall perform the following routine property management services:

3.1.1 Ordinary Maintenance/Repair of Common Area. Manager shall schedule and monitor maintenance and repair of the common area, including the following: common area structures, streets, walks, and gutters; pool(s), spa(s), sauna(s), and related equipment; painting, plumbing, janitorial services; trash collection; garages/carports; and landscaped areas.

3.1.2 Major Repairs/Alterations of Common Area. Any repairs, structural changes, alterations, or additions to the common area, or any portion thereof, that require an expenditure of more than $_____ shall be deemed major repairs/alterations and require specific Board authorization.

3.1.3 Specification/Bid Preparation. Manager, at the request of the Board, shall obtain competitive bids for the work for major repairs/alterations and submit them to the Board. The Board shall then decide which company or professional to hire to do major repairs. Manager shall coordinate and monitor the work in progress, but shall not supervise or be responsible for the satisfactory completion of the work. The Board shall hire a construction supervisor, if appropriate, and that party shall supervise and ensure satisfactory completion of the work.

3.1.4 Property Inventory. Manager shall maintain an inventory of all Association property, with complete records regarding the acquisition and disposition of such property.

3.1.5 Work Order Processing. Manager shall prepare and implement a system to receive and respond to work order requests from Owners, and shall report to the Board in writing on a periodic basis on the status of the request and work in progress.

3.1.6 Site Inspections. Manager shall make two (2) routine site inspections per month, covering the entire common area.

3.1.7 Periodic Building/Amenity Inspection Report. Manager shall prepare and present for Board review on a periodic basis a written building/amenity inspection report noting recommended maintenance and repairs.

3.1.8 Government Requirements. Following receipt of notification of approval by the Board of Directors of the Association, Manager shall take such action as may be necessary to comply promptly with any and all orders or requirements affecting the Project imposed by federal, state, county, or municipal authorities having jurisdiction thereover.

3.1.9 Relations With the Owners. Manager shall maintain business-like relations with the Owners, and respond in a systematic, professional fashion to inquiries or complaints. No services shall be provided to individual units/lots or Owners without prior written consent of Board of Directors. Complaints regarding Association affairs and operations shall, after thorough investigation, be reported to the Board of Directors of the Association with the appropriate recommendations.

3.1.10 Legal Assistance and Enforcement. Where legal assistance is needed for matters, that assistance shall be obtained through legal counsel designated by the Board of the Association. With the prior approval of the Board, Manager shall offer counsel and assistance in the interpretation of the regulations of the Association and enforcement of same, including specifically the regulations and requirements for architectural review and control by the Architectural Control Committee.

3.2 Scope of Authority. The Manager's authority does not include management of any separate interests or units/lots in the Project, but solely pertains to the Association's duties and responsibilities for maintenance and operation of the Common Area of the Project and overall management of the Project under the Project Management Documents.

3.3 Compliance With Laws. Manager shall manage the Project under this Agreement in full compliance with the requirements of all applicable state or federal legislation governing discrimination or fairness in housing, and shall take action considered appropriate to carry out the purpose of any such legislation.

3.4 Use of Equipment. The Manager shall use its best efforts to obtain maximum use of existing maintenance equipment of the Association in the performance of its duties. Additional or replacement equipment necessary for the reasonable performance of the Manager's duties under this Agreement shall be provided by the Association at the Association's expense, provided that the Board of the Association consents to such expenditure. All equipment used in the performance of the Manager's duties under this Agreement shall be operated and maintained at the expense of the Association, whether owned by the Manager or the Association, and the Manager shall exercise reasonable and customary efforts to preserve and protect all such equipment.

ARTICLE IV
Duties of Manager; Financial Management

4.1 Scope of Article. Manager shall cause to be performed the following routine financial services:

4.1.1 Assessment Collection. Manager shall cause assessment billing coupons to be prepared and mailed to the membership as the Board may direct, and shall bill the owners, as necessary, for other assessments, fees, and charges levied by the Association. Manager shall cause to be undertaken the collection and, as necessary, receive payment of all assessments, fees, charges, or other income received by the Association.

4.1.2 Deposit of Collections. Manager shall deposit all monies collected by Manager into the appropriate Association account(s) within one (1) business day of receipt. Manager shall also maintain the records of the Association's interest-bearing reserve accounts pursuant to a reserve schedule to be provided by Association, along with such other funds as Board may direct.

4.1.3 Disbursements. Manager shall cause regular disbursement from Association's operating accounts covering all expenses and obligations authorized to be paid by and on behalf of the Association as set forth in this Agreement. Manager shall have no authority to sign checks or authorize withdrawals or authorize transfers from Association's reserve accounts.

4.1.4 Delinquency Follow-Up. Manager shall be responsible for collecting delinquent assessments and other charges in accordance with the policies and procedures of the Association. Manager shall cause to be maintained delinquent assessment records, and shall submit to the Board a monthly aged delinquent assessment list at each regular Board meeting or as otherwise directed by the Board. Manager shall act as liaison between the Board and retained counsel and/or a collection service to provide the information and records necessary to pursue collection of delinquent accounts. Manager may charge an additional fee for filing and releasing liens, and for costs associated with participating in any collection action as provided in Paragraph 7.2 of Article VII, below.

4.1.5 Invoice Approval. Manager shall review and approve all invoices for budgeted items and other approved expenditures, and shall promptly report to the Board all apparent discrepancies or irregularities in invoices or Association expenditures that come to Manager's attention. Manager shall submit all invoices for unbudgeted items and other unapproved expenditures to the Board for review and approval prior to payment.

4.1.6 Invoice Payment. Manager shall not make any unapproved expenditure during any one month exceeding $_____, nor incur any obligation, either singly or in the aggregate, without prior Board approval, except in case of an emergency threatening life or property or suspension of necessary utility or public services. In such an emergency, Manager shall attempt to contact a member of the Board for expenditure approval, but if unsuccessful, Manager is authorized to act in any reasonable manner to address the emergency situation.

4.1.7 Payroll Accounting for Employees. Manager shall not be responsible for payroll and payroll accounting for Association employees except by separate written agreement.

4.1.8 Financial and Report Preparation. Manager shall maintain, or cause to be maintained by an outside service, complete and accurate financial books and records for the Association in accordance with generally accepted accounting practices, including a balance sheet, a general ledger, and subsidiary journals utilizing a double-entry method of accounting, separate and apart from those of any other entity. Manager shall prepare and submit to the Board on a periodic basis such financial reports as the Board may reasonably request.

4.1.8.1 Manager agrees to prepare and submit to the Board monthly a detailed operating statement of receipts, expenses, and charges with respect to the Manager services provided pursuant to this Agreement. Said report shall be due on the 15th of the month directly following the reporting month. Said report shall include the original invoices for all services and contracts paid by Manager for the reporting month.

4.1.8.2 Budget sheets and a cumulative comparison of income and expenses to budget with respect to such Manager services shall be prepared by Manager and furnished annually to the Association. This service does not include the preparation of the Association's tax returns or annual audit. However, Manager shall assist Association with preparation of tax returns and audits. All books and records maintained by Manager in connection with the Association shall be made available at the request of the Board of Directors to any accounting firm employed by the Board of Directors.

4.1.9 Tax Return and Audit Preparation. Manager shall assist the Association and its bookkeeper, certified public accountant, or other financial consultant in preparing tax returns, audits, and financial reviews. Manager shall distribute copies of year-end financial reviews to the membership within 120 days after the close of the Association's fiscal year or otherwise required by law.

4.1.10 Budget Preparation. Manager shall assist in the preparation of a pro forma operating budget so that it is available to the Board not less than sixty (60) days prior to the beginning of the Association's fiscal year, unless the Board elects to distribute a summary of the pro forma operating budget. If the Board elects to distribute a summary and any member requests a copy of the full financial statements to be mailed to the member, Manager shall send a copy by first-class mail within five (5) days of the request.

4.1.11 Lien Enforcement Policy and Practices. Manager shall assist in the preparation of a statement describing the Association's policies and practices in enforcing lien rights or other legal remedies for the collection of delinquent assessments against Association members, and distribute the statement to the membership during the 60-day period immediately prior to the beginning of the Association's fiscal year.

4.1.12 Reserve Study. Manager shall schedule and coordinate preparation of a periodic reserve study, if an outside service is utilized.

4.1.13 Fiscal Affairs. Manager shall manage the Association's fiscal affairs in accordance with the Project Manager Documents and applicable state laws and within the guidelines of the adopted annual budget, except when specifically authorized by the Association's Board of Directors to exceed any portion of the annual budget.

4.2 Liability for Use of Financial Statements. The Association shall have exclusive responsibility for the content and use of all approved financial statements, budgets, and other financial documents prepared by or at the direction of the Association. The Association hereby agrees to indemnify and hold Manager harmless from all claims, expenses, actions, liabilities, and damages (including attorneys' fees and litigation costs) arising out of the content or use of all such documents. Any draft financial statements, proposed budgets draft reserve studies, and/or other financial documents prepared shall be marked "DRAFT" until approved by the Board.

4.3 Manager to Be Bonded. Manager and all employees who handle or are responsible for handling funds belonging to the Association shall (without expense to the Association) be bonded by a fidelity and surety bond(s) acceptable to the Association.

ARTICLE V
Contracting Policies

5.1 Administration of Contracts. The Board shall select all contractors, vendors, and service providers, unless Manager is instructed by the Board to make the selection. After selection and retention, Manager shall schedule and monitor the activities of the contractor, vendor, or service provider, including, without limitation, the obtaining of contract documents, certificates of insurance, copies of bonds, warranties, releases of liens, and other necessary or prudent documentation. Manager shall monitor the work in progress, keep the board apprised of its status, and process warranty claims. Manager also shall cooperate and assist professional consultants retained by the Board for specialized functions such as legal, accounting, and other services.

ARTICLE VI
Complaint/Service Request Procedures

6.1 Complaint/Service Request Procedures. Manager shall develop and maintain a program to respond to all reasonable complaints and all reasonable requests for maintenance, repairs, and minor alterations in accordance with the procedures and guidelines adopted by the Board. Manager shall report monthly to the Board on all such complaints and requests. Manager shall prepare and distribute to the members a guide outlining complaint and service request procedures.

ARTICLE VII
Compensation of Manager and Bookkeeper

7.1 Scope of Article. Unless otherwise specifically agreed to in writing, Manager shall be compensated under this Agreement exclusively as provided in this Article.

7.2 Routine Services. The Association shall pay Manager a flat monthly fee of $_____ for those routine services specified in Articles II, III, IV, V, and VI. In addition, the Association shall pay Manager additional compensation in accordance with Exhibit "A" (Additional Compensation) attached hereto.

7.3 Non-Routine Services. Manager may, at the request of the Board, perform certain non-routine services for additional compensation at the rate of $_____ per hour, plus travel time at one-half (½) such hourly rate and travel expenses actually incurred, or at such other rate of compensation as may be agreed upon in writing by Manager and Association. Non-routine services include, but are not limited to, the following:

7.3.1 Participating in any type of lawsuit, dispute resolution proceeding, or administrative proceeding, including, without limitation, lawsuits or proceedings involving the Association or any of its members, officers, directors, employees, agents, or contractors, or in any way related to Association business, Association property, collection of delinquent assessments, and/or enforcement of the Project Documents.

7.3.2 Providing assistance in the investigation, evaluation, and presentation of claims arising from defective workmanship, defective materials and/or substandard services in the development or construction of the Project.

7.3.3 Processing insurance claims involving bodily injury and/or property damage, beyond preparation and submission of the original claim. Any such charges by Manager shall be submitted to the insurance company as part of the claim.

7.3.4 Pursuing and prosecuting claims for delinquent assessments or other receivables.

7.3.5 Attending more meetings of the Board, Committees, or general membership than required under Paragraph 2.1 of Article II above.

7.3.6 Preparing or causing to be prepared architectural or landscape specifications, schematics, construction estimates, construction drawings, and contracts for major renovation or repair of the common area.

7.3.7 Providing assistance in emergency situations or responding to resident complaints at times other than normal working hours (8:30 a.m. to 5:30 p.m., Monday through Friday, except holidays). Emergency calls during non-working hours requiring Manager to travel to the Project will be billed at 1.5 times the rate for non-routine services, with a minimum 2 hours charge per site visit.

        7.3.8   Revision of the project Declaration, Articles of Incorporation, and Bylaws, but excluding revision of rules, regulations, and policies of the Association, which shall be included in routine services.

        7.3.9   Negotiation and management of contracts with outside contractors that involve a contract price in excess of $5,000.

        7.3.10   Organizing, participating in, and documenting common area acceptance and/or the release of bonds or other financial assurances which guarantee completion of the common area.

        7.3.11   Organizing, participating in, and documenting incorporation of the Association.

        7.3.12   Maintaining any type of roster or other information on non-owner residents.

        7.3.13   Participating in the initial sale, resale, financing, or refinancing of a unit/lot, other than to provide information and documentation set forth in Paragraph 2.1.15 of Article II above or as otherwise required of the Association by law.

    7.4   **Documentation of Non-Routine Services.** All compensation for non-routine services shall be supported by a statement itemizing the time and activity on a daily basis and recorded in increments of one-tenth (1/10) of an hour.

    7.5   **When Compensation is Due.** The Association shall pay Manager the basic fee for routine service monthly, in advance, on or before the 10th day of the month during which such services are to be performed, and for non-routine services on or before the 10th day of the month following submission of a statement for items of additional compensation as provided in this Article. Delinquent invoices will be charged a late fee of 18% per annum or 1.5% per month, compounding monthly on the unpaid balance.

    7.6   **No Rebates, Discounts, or Commissions.** Manager shall not collect or charge any undisclosed fee, rebate, discount, or commission in connection with any business of the Association. Any such fee, rebate, discount, or commission, if received, shall be the property of the Association, shall be immediately credited to the Association's account, and shall be made an agenda item by the Manager for the next Board meeting.

ARTICLE VIII
Special One-Time Services

    8.1   **Special Services.** At the request of the Board, Manager may, at Manager's option, provide special one-time services at additional compensation as provided in Paragraph 7.3 of Article VII above, which may include, without limitation, the following:

        8.1.1   **Resident Orientation and Participation Program.** Prepare a program for resident orientation, leadership recruitment, and training for the purpose of achieving community participation in the Association.

        8.1.2   **Governance Manual.** Prepare a governance manual to inform the general membership of the Association's operations, its organizational structure, the manner of conducting meetings and adopting policies and procedures, and setting forth the policies and procedures already in effect.

8.1.3 Plan of Management. Prepare a plan of management that sets forth the long-range financial goals and objectives of the Association.

8.1.4 Employee Policy Manual. Prepare an employee policy manual, which should include job descriptions, benefits program, hiring and firing procedures, and compensation policies.

ARTICLE IX
Books and Records Inspection

9.1 Books and Records. Manager shall maintain a comprehensive system of books and records in a manner satisfactory to the Board and/or set forth in this Agreement. Copies of contracts, filings with public agencies, and financial books and records shall be maintained at the principal office of the Manager. Originals of all books and records may be maintained in the custody of the Manager; however, they shall be the property of the Association and shall be provided to the Association or its representative immediately upon demand.

9.2 Inspection. Except for materials designated as confidential by the Board, all books and records maintained at the Association's office shall be made available for inspection by any and all unit/lot owners or their authorized representatives, upon reasonable notice, during normal business hours. Access to confidential materials shall be allowed only as authorized by the Board.

9.3 Records and Correspondence. All records and correspondence regarding the Association are and shall remain the sole property of the Association, and upon termination of this Agreement, Manager shall forthwith return all cash, records, and correspondence to the Association.

ARTICLE X
Insurance

10.1 Maintenance of Insurance by Association. The Association agrees to purchase and maintain a policy of comprehensive general liability insurance with a limit of no less than $1,000,000 per occurrence in coverage for bodily injury (including death), property damage and contractual liability, which shall name Manager as an additional insured for all loss liability and expenses, including costs of defense, arising out of or in any way connected with the maintenance, repair, or condition of the managed premises. Such insurance shall be primary and non-contributory to any insurance maintained by Manager, and shall include a cross-liability endorsement. The Association shall deliver to Manager a certificate of insurance evidencing such policy within ten (10) days of execution of the Agreement, and such certificate shall provide that Manager be given thirty (30) days' notice of cancellation or diminution in coverage.

10.2 Maintenance of Insurance by Manager. Regardless of the provisions of indemnification set forth herein, Manager shall maintain in force, during the term of this Agreement, comprehensive general liability insurance and such other forms of insurance, in such amounts as may be reasonably required in writing by the Association. Manager shall deliver to the Association a certificate of insurance evidencing such policy within ten (10) days of execution of this Agreement, and such certificate shall provide that the Association be given thirty (30) days' notice of cancellation or diminution in coverage.

ARTICLE XI
Termination and Transition

11.1   Notice of Termination. This Agreement may be terminated for failure to comply with the scope of work as per the "Management Bid Specification," or for any other reason by either party on not less than fifteen (15) days' written notice, which notice may be given at any time during a month, provided that in any event the termination shall be effective at the end of the first calendar month following the month during which notice is given. Upon termination of this Agreement, Manager shall, within five (5) working days, deliver to the President or other duly authorized Board member all books, papers, records, documents, funds, passbooks, checks, and other Association property in the control of the Manager.

11.2   Cooperation in Transition. Manager shall continue to perform all its duties and responsibilities under this Agreement after notice of termination until the termination date. Manger and Association agree to cooperate fully with one another to transfer Association property, to execute whatever documents and to take whatever other action may be necessary prior to termination to cause an orderly transition of Association management to a new manager. After termination, Association shall compensate Manager at the rate set forth in Paragraph 7.3 of Article VII above for additional services requested by Association in assisting in such transition.

ARTICLE XII
Miscellaneous

12.1   Modification and Status. This writing is intended by the parties as a full expression of their Agreement and all negotiations and representations between the parties having been incorporated herein. No variation, modification, or changes of the Agreement shall be binding unless it is made in writing and executed by both parties.

12.2   Applicable Law. This Agreement shall be construed in accordance with the laws of the State of _____ and the Project documents.

12.3   Conflict of Interest. Manager shall not accept from any party providing goods and services to the Association, including vendors and independent contractors, any remuneration or consideration in any manner or form as consideration for or inducement to the Manager for using the party's goods or retaining their services on behalf of the Association; all such benefits shall be the property of the Association.

12.4   Affiliated Interest. Manager shall not enter into any agreement to provide goods or services to the Association with any party, partnership, corporation, or other entity related to or affiliated with Manager, its directors, officers, and employees without prior written disclosure to the Board.

12.5   Bankruptcy/Insolvency. This Agreement may be terminated at the option of the Association: if the Manager shall be adjudicated as bankrupt or insolvent and such adjudication is not vacated within thirty (30) days; or if a receiver or trustee shall be appointed and it shall not be vacated within thirty (30) days; or if a corporate reorganization of Manager or any arrangement by statute shall be filed; or if Manager shall make an assignment for the benefit of creditors.

12.6   Attorneys' Fees. If any legal action is necessary to enforce the terms of this Agreement, the prevailing party shall be entitled to reasonable attorneys' fees in addition to any other relief to which he/she/it may be entitled.

12.7   Dispute Resolution. The parties agree that all claims or controversies or disputes, whether based on contract, tort, other legal or equitable theories or upon statute, arising out of or related to this Agreement or in connection with or in relation to the interpretation, performance, or breach of this Agreement, or any subsequent agreement among the parties concerning the subject matter of this Agreement ("Dispute"), shall be resolved in the manner herein provided, unless any such subsequent agreement expressly disclaims the application of the contract provision.

12.7.1   Mediation. If the Dispute cannot be resolved by negotiations among the parties involved, or in the judgment of any party involved therewith that efforts at negotiations have not yielded sufficient progress to encourage further and continued negotiations, the parties to the Dispute shall submit the Dispute to mediation by a mediator mutually selected by the parties involved with the Dispute. If the parties are unable to agree upon a mediator within thirty (30) days from the date of service by any party upon the other parties of a notice to mediate, then the mediator shall be appointed under the procedure stipulated in the Rules of Commercial Mediation of the American Arbitration Association ("AAA"), unless the parties agree to some other mediation service.

12.7.1.1   The parties shall reserve no more than five (5) business days for the mediation process. If the dispute is not resolved within the reserved time period, the parties shall be required to resolve such Dispute by arbitration as set forth below.

12.7.2   Arbitration. All claims, disputes, and other matters in question between the Association and Manager that arise out of or relate to this Agreement or performance of services under the Agreement, whether arising in contract or tort (hereinafter referred to collectively as "Arbitrable Matter"), which are not resolved by negotiations or mediation, shall be decided by binding arbitration in accordance with the then-obtaining seven-step Rules of Practice and Procedure (Rules of Practice and Procedure for Arbitration of Commercial Disputes) of Judicial Arbitration and Mediation Services, Inc. ("JAMS"), as set forth below, unless the Manager and the Association each elect not to participate in arbitration.

12.7.3   Notice of the demand for arbitration shall be filed in writing with the other party to this contract and with JAMS. The demand shall be made within a reasonable time after the Arbitrable Matter in question has arisen. In no event shall the demand for arbitration be made after the date when institution of legal or equitable proceedings based on such claim, dispute, or other matter in question would be barred by the applicable statute of limitations.

12.7.4   The arbitrator shall decide whether the dispute is an Arbitrable Matter. In addition, the arbitrator shall award to the prevailing party its costs and attorneys' fees actually incurred.

12.7.5   Either party shall, within fifteen (15) days of receipt of the date that the hearing time and date is set, have the right to demand in writing, served personally or by facsimile, that the other party provide a list of witnesses it intends to call, designating which witness will be called as an expert witness and a list of documents it intends to introduce at the hearing. A copy of such demand shall be served on the arbitrator. Such lists shall be mutually exchanged and served personally or by facsimile on the opposing party within fifteen (15) days thereafter. Copies thereof shall be served on the arbitrator. Listed documents shall be made available for inspection and copying at reasonable times prior to the hearing.

12.7.6   Depositions for discovery shall not be taken unless leave to do so is first granted by the arbitrator, and in no event is any party entitled to more than four (4) depositions, two percipient witnesses, and two experts.

12.7.7 Neither party shall be entitled to serve any form of written discovery request (interrogatories, requests for admission, requests for authentication, requests for document production, or written depositions) on any other party in the arbitration. The only document production allowed shall be done pursuant to the demand above.

12.8 Access. In order to perform the duties hereunder, Manager shall have access to Association property and to other properties to the extent afforded the Association pursuant to the Project documents.

12.9 Notices. All notices to the Association shall be in writing and mailed postage prepaid to the designated address of the Association President. All notices to Manager shall be in writing and mailed postage prepaid to the current or last known business address of Manager.

12.10 Attorneys' Fees. In the event of any litigation or arbitration between the parties hereto with respect to the subject matter hereof, subject to Paragraph 12.7.4 above, the losing party agrees to pay to the prevailing party all costs and expenses, including, without limitation, attorneys' fees, consultants' fees, and expert fees incurred therein by such prevailing party.

12.11 Binding. This agreement shall be binding on the parties hereto, their heirs, executors, administrators, successors, and assigns, and may not be changed orally, but may be changed, amended, or altered only by a written agreement signed by the parties.

Date: _____   _____ ASSOCIATION

                                           By: _____
                                           _____ [print name]

Date: _____   Manager [Management]

                                           By: _____
                                           _____ [print name]

EXHIBIT "A"
Additional Compensation

1. Lien Actions:
   Preparing notification of intent to lien (for each letter) $_____
   Preparing and recording assessment lien (for each lien recorded) $_____
   Preparing notification of intent to foreclose (for each letter) $_____
   Coordination of foreclosure (for each foreclosure) $_____
   Preparing and recording release of lien (for each lien release) $_____

2. Providing Documents for Sale of Unit/Lot:
   Articles of Incorporation (each)* $_____
   Bylaws (each)* $_____
   Budget, current year (each)* $_____
   Covenants, Conditions and Restrictions (each)* $_____
   Fidelity Bond (each)* $_____
   Rules and Regulations (each)* $_____
   Transfer Fee (each)* $_____
   Demand Fee (each)* $_____
   Rush Fee (within 48 hours) $_____

3. Compilation of Financial Forecast (per hour) $_____
4. Mailing of Registered/Certified Letters (per letter) $_____

5. Processing Returned Checks or Generating
   Out-of-Cycle Checks (per check) $_____

6. Association Mailings (per hour) $_____
7. Responding to Government Agency Requests
   or Filings Request (each) – IRS/FTB/FHA $_____

8. Word Processing for Documents Over Four
   Pages or Newsletter (per hour) $_____

9. Providing Owner Payment History (per request) $_____
10. Providing mailing lists (per hour) $_____

11. Materials and Supplies Expense:
    Mailing labels (each) $_____
    Envelopes – standard (each) $_____
    Envelopes - large manila (each) $_____
    Photocopies (each) $_____
    Postage (each at cost) $_____
    Long-distance telephone calls (each at cost) $_____
    Fax transmission (each at cost) $_____
    Binders/archives boxes/files (each at cost) $_____

* Items that may be charged to an owner's account, if appropriate, provided authority exists under the Project documents.

APPROVAL AND ADOPTION OF MANAGEMENT CONTRACT
RESOLUTION NO. _____

The President presented to the board a proposed management agreement between the Association and _____ [*name of management entity*], and described the material facts of the transaction.

[Include, if applicable]
_____ [*name(s) of Director(s)*] disclosed that _____ [*he/she/they*] _____ [*has/have*] a material financial interest in the management entity as follows: _____
[*describe interest*].

[Continue]
After discussion, and upon motion duly made, seconded, and unanimously carried,

[Include, if applicable]
by vote of Directors other than _____ [*name(s) of Director(s) with material financial interest*],

[Continue]
the following resolution was adopted:

RESOLVED, that the Board of Directors has reviewed the proposed management agreement between the Association and _____ [*name of management entity*], and has determined that the agreement is

[Include, if any Director has a material financial interest in the entity]
just, reasonable, and

[Continue]
in the best interests of the Association, and therefore approves and adopts the agreement on behalf of the Association and authorizes and directs _____ _____ [*name(s) of officer(s)*] to take the necessary steps to execute the agreement on behalf of the Association.

_____
Secretary

LANDSCAPE MAINTENANCE AGREEMENT FOR

_____
[Name of Project]

_____, _____   _____, (*year*)
    [City]   *[State]*

_____, hereinafter called "Contractor," agrees to perform the following services under the terms and conditions provided herein for the benefit of _____ Homeowners Association, hereinafter called "Association."

REQUIREMENTS: In addition to work outlined in attached Schedule "A," it is further agreed that:

    1. Equipment, Tools, and Supplies. Contractor shall provide all labor, materials, grounds equipment, and tools, including mowers, edgers, spreaders, sprayers, hoses, shears, picks, hoes, shovels, etc., for the care of lawns, trees, shrubs, and ground cover as specified below to maintain the existing landscape plan. Any changes require approval of the Association.

    Walkways, driveways, streets, gutters, and surrounding areas shall be swept or vacuumed immediately following each mowing or edging. Parking areas shall be swept or vacuumed every month. All debris created by Contractor will be removed from property on same day of accumulation.

    2. Irrigation. Contractor shall maintain and repair the sprinkling system to ensure adequate and proper functioning at all times. Parts shall be paid for by the Association at cost, except for any sprinklers, pipes, or structures broken or damaged in the process of maintenance, which will be repaired or replaced by Contractor at no extra cost. Time clocks shall be set by Contractor to provide watering as frequently as necessary to maintain planted areas and lawn in a green and healthy condition. Normal watering will be done during the early morning hours except when sprinkler testing is being done during working hours.

    Continual inspection, adjustment, or repair and trimming around the sprinkler heads for "full coverage" to allow for complete watering of all planted areas shall be provided at no additional cost to the Association for labor.

    Any major extraordinary items to be repaired or replaced shall be paid for by the Association.

    3. Mowing and Edging. Lawns shall be mowed and edged weekly April through October, twice monthly in December, January, and February, and three times monthly in March and November. (See Schedule "A.")

    Edging of ground cover will be done as needed for attractive area appearance.

4. **Weeding.** In addition to pre- and post-emergent weed control by herbicides, hand removal of weeds will be done as necessary. Contractor shall remove monthly, on a planned rotation schedule, all weeds from the common area, and promptly dispose of same.

Contractor will keep streets, sidewalks, and driveways free of growing weeds or grass in cracks.

5. **Insecticide and Pesticide Spraying.** Trees, shrubs, lawns, and planted areas shall be kept reasonably free of pests at all times. Contractor shall contract with an independent company for commercial application of pest control sprays at Association's expense according to Schedule "A" after approval by the manager of the Association.

6. **Aeration.** Aerate lawn and area twice a year. (See Schedule "A.")

7. **Tennis Courts.** Once every month; blow off, hose down, and squeegee debris and dust from tennis courts.

8. **Trimming and Pruning.** Contractor shall pinch, prune, thin, and trim all ground covers, shrubs, and trees on site to maintain normal and healthy plant growth, removing all suckers, cross branches, and dead wood. Contractor shall re-stake, prune, and re-tie trees as needed.

9. **Fertilization.** Fertilizer shall be applied to lawns every six (6) weeks from February through November (total of eight times). Trees, shrubs, and ground cover shall be fertilized twice a year. (See Schedule "A.")

Fertilizer and chemicals are to be paid for by the Association. Types and amounts to be applied will be approved by the manager representing the Association.

10. **Cleaning of Common Area.** Contractor shall inspect all areas for superfluous materials and trash and remove same on a continuing basis.

11. **Replacing Plants and Extra Work.** During the course of normal maintenance, it may become necessary to remove and/or replace dead or missing plant or lawn material.

All removals and/or replacements shall be done at the recommendation of the Association, and all work shall be subject to the approval and acceptance of the Association.

All replacement lawn and plant material shall be extra and paid for by the Association. Contractor shall replace at its own cost all lawn and plant materials that die due to its negligence.

Contractor shall furnish the Association with an itemized estimate for any additional planting or extra work that may be required or requested. In no event shall work begin until it has been authorized by the Association.

12. **Payment of Contractor.** Contractor shall be paid _____ _____ Dollars ($_____) monthly by the Association for services rendered.

13. **General Provisions.** The above requirements are minimum duties, and the Contractor shall provide more frequent servicing as necessary to maintain landscaping in a neat and healthy appearance.

Contractor shall be responsible for any damage caused by negligence on its part, or that of its employees, and shall at all times have in effect Workers' Compensation and

Contractor's Liability Insurance of at least _____ Dollars ($_____) property and _____ Dollars ($_____) personal, holding _____ Association, its Board of Directors and manager, harmless from any claims or lawsuits arising from activities of Contractor, and shall provide a Certificate of same.

Contractor agrees to keep property free of liens and encumbrances which may arise from its activities.

If required work is not performed by forty-eight (48) hours after written notice by the President of _____ Association or the management company, then other workers may be hired to perform the work, and the cost will be charged back against the Contractor's latest billing.

Contractor's Federal Employers Identification No.: _____.

Contractor's State/County Business License No.: _____.

Invoicing shall be made monthly and will be paid within ten (10) days.

This Contract is for a period of one (1) year beginning _____, (*year*) and ending _____, (*year*). It may be terminated by either party upon serving thirty (30) days' written notice.

This contract includes provisions of Schedule "A."

This Agreement is entered into this ____ day of _____, (*year*), by:

ASSOCIATION: _____ Homeowners Association

By: _____
President

CONTRACTOR: By: _____

(Attach a schedule detailing any additional provisions to the landscape contract)

Form 31   Maintenance Agreement

Manager's Note: *Any schedule of additional fees should be attached to this contract.*

MAINTENANCE AGREEMENT
FOR RECREATIONAL FACILITIES

_____ HOMEOWNERS ASSOCIATION

THIS AGREEMENT is entered into this ____ day of _____, (*year*), by and between the _____ HOMEOWNERS ASSOCIATION, hereinafter referred to as "Association," and _____, hereinafter referred to as "Agent." Association desires to hire Agent to manage the condominium project commonly known as _____, located at _____, in the City of _____, County of _____, State of _____. Agent desires to manage said condominium project, and the parties therefore agree as follows:

ARTICLE I
DEFINITIONS

1. The definitions contained in the Declaration are incorporated by reference herein.

2. "Declaration" shall mean and refer to the _____ Enabling Declaration Establishing a Plan for Condominium Ownership applicable to the property recorded on the ____ day of _____, (*year*), in Book ____, pages _____, Official Records, _____ County.

ARTICLE II
TERM

This Agreement commences on the ____ day of _____, (*year*), and unless earlier terminated in accordance with subsequent provisions of this Agreement, it shall remain in effect for a term of _____ [*one (1) year, or as case may be*] and shall automatically expire on the ____ day of _____, (*year*), unless renewed, in writing, for an additional term of _____, prior to the expiration date, by mutual consent of both parties. This Agreement may be terminated immediately, at the option of Association, in the event of the filing of a petition in bankruptcy for or against Agent, an assignment for the benefit of creditors made by Agent, a levy of execution on the assets of Agent pursuant to judgment, or initiation of receivership proceedings for or against Agent, or the termination or substantial destruction of the project. This Agreement may be terminated by Association, for cause, on _____ days' written notice, or without cause and without payment of a termination fee or penalty, on _____ days' written notice.

ARTICLE III
COMPENSATION

As full compensation for the services which Agent is to perform under this Agreement, Agent shall receive a fee computed and payable monthly in an amount equal to _____ Dollars ($_____) for each unit in the project which is subject to the Declaration and whose owner is a member of the Association.

ARTICLE IV
DUTIES OF AGENT

1. Maintenance of Recreational Facilities. Agent shall provide for complete maintenance of the recreational facilities in the project which are described in Exhibit "A" attached hereto and incorporated by reference herein.

2. Maintenance shall include maintenance in good condition of all structures, structural elements, machinery, and equipment constituting the recreational facilities described in Exhibit "A."

ARTICLE V
DURATION AND TERMINATION OF AGREEMENT

This Agreement shall remain in force and effect during the period of time that any of the recreational facilities described in Exhibit "A" are not owned by the Association. This Agreement shall terminate automatically upon such date as the Association acquires title to all the recreational facilities described in Exhibit "A." It is Agent's obligation to maintain said recreational facilities in good operating condition until such time as title thereto is transferred to the Association as provided above.

ARTICLE VI
GENERAL PROVISIONS

1. Entire Agreement. This Agreement constitutes the entire Agreement between Association and Agent, and no modification thereof shall be permitted except by written agreement executed by both parties.

2. Non-Waiver. The waiver by either party of any provision of this Agreement shall not constitute a waiver by that party of any other provision of this Agreement.

3. Use of Pronouns. The use of the masculine, feminine, and neuter, and singular or plural, shall each be deemed to include the other, whenever the context so permits.

4. Assignment. This Agreement shall inure to the benefit of and be binding upon the successors and assigns of the respective parties hereto. Agent may not assign its interests under this Agreement without the consent of Association.

5. Arbitration. In the event of any dispute between the parties to this Agreement, the matter shall be submitted to arbitration in accordance with the Rules of the American Arbitration Association.

6. Attorneys' Fees. In the event any party brings an action to enforce arbitration under this Agreement, or in the event of an arbitration proceeding, the prevailing party shall be entitled to reasonable attorneys' fees.

IN WITNESS WHEREOF, the parties hereto have executed this Agreement the day and year set forth above.

_____ **ASSOCIATION**

By: _____

AGENT

By: _____

Form 32 Lease of Facilities

AGREEMENT FOR LEASE OF FACILITIES

This Agreement is entered into this _____ day of _____ , (*year*) , by and between _____ , a _____ corporation, hereinafter referred to as "Developer," and _____ HOMEOWNERS ASSOCIATION, a _____ nonprofit mutual benefit corporation, hereinafter referred to as "Association."

Developer is the owner and developer of a _____-unit condominium (PUD) project described on the Subdivision Map of Tract _____, known as _____ Condominiums, located in the City of _____, County of _____, State of _____ , hereinafter referred to as "the Project."

Developer [has constructed] [*or*] [will construct] upon the property a residential project including certain recreational facilities, which contain, among other things, a recreation room. Developer is in the process of selling units in the project and desires to make use of [the meeting room] [a portion of the meeting room] as a display center and sales office. The Association has agreed to lease said facilities to the Developer, and the parties therefore agree as follows:

1. **Description of Leased Premises.** The Association hereby agrees to lease to the Developer, upon the terms and conditions herein contained, part of the recreational facilities of the _____ project described as follows: Meeting room (approximately ___ square feet).

2. **Term.** The term of this lease shall be for a period of one (1) year [three (3) years] commencing on _____, plus an option to renew for one (1) additional year, exercisable any time within sixty (60) days before or after expiration of the first year by Developer.

3. **Rental.** Developer agrees to pay to Association, as rental for the use of the above-described premises, the sum of _____ ($_____) per month, payable on or before the 10th of each month during the term of the lease.

4. **Uses.** Developer shall use the leased premises for the purposes of display of models, sales materials, brochures, optional items, and for a sales office. [The use shall be shared, with the Developer having the use during normal sales (business) hours, and the Association having use during evening hours.]

5. **Cleaning and Repairs.** Association is to be responsible for normal cleaning and maintenance of [the recreational facilities including] the meeting room. Developer agrees to maintain the leased premises in a neat and clean condition at all times, and shall either provide its own janitorial service for that purpose, or shall reimburse Association for the reasonable cost of periodic janitorial service provided by the Association or its agent or employee.

6. **Insurance.** The Association carries a master policy insuring the facilities and including public liability insurance. Developer shall carry its own insurance on its personal property and its own public liability insurance.

7. **Utilities.** Heat, electricity, [telephone,] and water are included in the monthly rental.

8. Termination. The lease shall terminate at the end of the term, or earlier upon completion of all sales, or upon thirty (30) days' notice by Developer of its intention to terminate the lease. Upon termination, Developer shall remove all of its personal property and equipment from the premises, and shall, at its expense, restore the premises to its original condition.

IN WITNESS WHEREOF, the parties have executed this Agreement on the date set forth above.

Date: _____

_____
A _____ Corporation

By: _____
Its _____

Date: _____

_____ ASSOCIATION
A _____ Nonprofit Corporation

By: _____
_____
Board President

Glossary

ADA – acronym for the "Americans with Disabilities Act," which is federal legislation requiring equal access in public places for handicapped people. The provisions of the ADA will affect many public spaces within a common-interest development.

Airspace – the cube of space that constitutes a condominium unit.

Annexation – the addition of a subsequent phase to an existing project.

Appurtenant – attached to and connected with the use and enjoyment of land or other real estate interest; by right, used with the land for its benefit.

Association – an entity formed by a number of persons united or being united together; a nonprofit corporation or unincorporated entity created for the purpose of managing a common-interest development.

Attorney's Opinion Letter – a letter drafted by an attorney in response to a client's request for a legal opinion. A lender, for example, may request that an attorney give a written opinion confirming that a condominium project has been formed in accordance with all legal requirements.

Balance Sheet – a written financial statement summarizing the assets, liabilities and net worth of a person or an association at a specific date.

Business Judgment – in the context of an officer or director of an association, the process of analyzing and examining the relevant facts and circumstances in order to make a decision or recommend an action to be taken by or on behalf of the association.

Common Area – the portion of a project that is owned in common by the owners of individual units or lots in the project. The homeowners association to which all the owners belong may also own part or all of the common area.

Common-Interest Subdivision, Common-Interest Development – a condominium, planned development, stock cooperative or community apartment development in which there are individual owners of units or lots who also own, in common, some portion of the project that is referred to as the common area.

Common Law – that body of law that was formulated and developed in England, derived from judgments and decrees of courts, and which has been adopted by courts in the United States.

Condemnation – the process by which real property of a private owner is taken for public use without the owner's consent upon payment of a fair compensation.

Condition – a clause in a deed or a declaration that affects title by imposing restrictions upon use and/or obligations upon ownership.

Condominium – an estate in real property that consists of an undivided interest in a portion of real property held in common with other owners, coupled with a separate interest in space called a unit, the boundaries of which are described on a recorded map or condominium plan.

Conversion – the process by which or the manner by which title held to real property is changed; as, for example, changing a stock cooperative or a rental apartment project into a condominium.

Covenant – a promise in writing to perform or to refrain from performing a specific action.

Covenant Running with the Land – a promise in writing that has been recorded, stating on its face that it is appurtenant to a particular parcel of real property. The covenant is said to "run with the land" because it remains with the property whenever the property is conveyed from one owner to the next.

Declaration – a recorded document that applies to a real estate development project, containing covenants, conditions and restrictions.

Declaratory Relief – the order or judgment of a court that resolves a dispute over the meaning and intent of a legal document, or an ambiguous clause in a legal document.

Due Process – the shortened version of "due process of law," meaning notice, opportunity to be heard, to defend, to examine witnesses, to be represented by counsel, and to have a fair hearing; proceeding according to the rules and regulations to which an association is subject.

Eminent Domain – the condemnation or the exercise of the power of government to condemn property for the benefit of the public interest.

Equitable Servitudes – covenants that burden real property, creating obligations for property owners and creating rights in others with respect to that property.

Express Warranty – a written warranty or guarantee pertaining to a product, such as an appliance or to a home or other improvements to real property, that includes a promise that the warranted items will perform adequately and/or be fit for the purpose for which intended for a certain minimum time period.

FHA – acronym for "Federal Housing Administration," a branch of the U.S. Government charged with promoting affordable housing.

FHLMC – acronym for the "Federal Home Loan Mortgage Corporation," also known as "Freddie Mac."

FNMA – acronym for "Federal National Mortgage Association," also known as "Fannie Mae." The FNMA publishes the "Seller and Servicer's Guide."

Fiduciary Duty – the obligation of a person to act not for his or her own benefit, but primarily for the benefit of another or others.

Foreclosure – the exercise of a power of sale contained in an instrument such as a deed of trust without court action.

HUD – acronym for the "Department of Housing and Urban Development," a department of the U.S. Government.

Implied Warranty – an unwritten promise that something such as an appliance or other improvement to real property is fit for the purpose for which it is intended.

Income or "Profit and Loss" Statement – a financial statement of a person, corporation or association, summarizing the income received and expenses paid during a certain period of time.

Master Association – in a large multi-phased residential development consisting of a number of subdivisions containing diverse communities, each of which is governed by its own sub-association, the single association to which all owners of lots or units in the larger project belong, and which has jurisdiction and control over some aspects of the entire project, is called the master association, and sometimes referred to as an "umbrella association," meaning that a number of subassociations are beneath its "umbrella."

Merchant Builder/Developer – a tract builder; a home builder that routinely builds and sells significant numbers of homes (as distinguished from a contractor or custom home builder who builds one or two homes at a time, but seldom exceeds that number). In some states, merchant builders are held to a higher standard; that is, a standard of strict liability for any construction defects.

PD – acronym for "Planned Development" (see below).

PUD – acronym for "Planned Unit Development" (see below).

Partition – the division of real property by order of a court. The property may be partitioned physically—divided into two or more parcels—or it may be partitioned by sale with the proceeds being divided among two or more owners.

Phase – a group of lots or units within a project composed of multiple phases.

Planned Development, Planned Unit Development – a real property development that involves clustering. It may also refer to zoning for a cluster development.

Pro-ration – division or allocation of an assessment among lots or units in a common-interest project.

Prudent Person ("Man") Rule – in deciding whether or not action taken or a decision made meets the legally required standard, the test to be applied is to ask what a reasonably prudent person ("man") would have done in a similar circumstance.

Quorum – a majority of the entire body; the number of members of a body as is competent to transact business in the absence of the other members.

Real Property – land or land including improvements; an interest in land.

Restrictive Covenant – a recorded covenant or promise that affects real property, such as a covenant not to sell liquor, or a covenant to build a certain kind or type of housing development.

Sister Association – in a large project with more than one homeowners association, the reference to one of two similar homeowners associations.

Stock Cooperative – a project in which a corporation holds title to improved real property and the members of the corporation own a right of exclusive occupancy in a portion of the real property.

Sub-Association – in a large project with multiple associations, any one of the associations which are subordinate to the master or "umbrella" association.

Tax Exemption – A special statutory exemption given to homeowners associations, the effect of which is to exempt the income received by the association in the form of assessments paid by its members from income tax.

Time-Share – a project where property is or may be owned collectively by a large group of people, each of whom has the right to use the property for a certain period of time or during certain dates each year.

Townhouse – an architectural style that describes a home with generally two or more stories in a planned development or condominium, depending upon the legal organization.

Unincorporated Association – a homeowners association that has been organized as an association, but has not been incorporated.

Unit – generally, a single condominium. Also a description of a dwelling in a project, whether it is a condominium or not.

VA – acronym for the "Veteran's Administration," a department of the U.S. Government providing specific benefits to veterans of the armed services.

Warranty – a promise either express (written) or implied (unwritten) that something shall be as stated and will perform as reasonably expected.

Warranty Work or Pick-up Work – action by a builder/developer after close of escrow (completion of a sale) to repair defects in design or construction in order to comply with a warranty.

Index

A

Absentee ballots, 82
Accountant, 98, 112-113, 218
Accounting, 148-151
    Accrual vs. cash basis, 149
    Audits, 150-151, 222
Accrual basis accounting, 149
Address, change of, 100
Adjournment
    (Of) board meetings, 40, 64
    (Of) general membership meetings, 64, 71-72
Administration/operation, 94-103
    Adoption of budget, 94-96
    Attorney, 98-99
    Bank account, 96
    Central filing system, 99
    Checklist of initial organization, 100-102
    Computers, 96-97
    Initial organization, 97-98, 100-102
    Loans, 99, 264
    Review of legal documents and procedures, 94
    Rules and regulations, 94, 233-234, 291-294
    Security, 97, 259-261
Age restrictions, 22, 235-236
Agenda
    (For) annual meeting, 276
    (For) board meeting, 38-41
    (For) general membership meeting, 62
Agreements (see **Contracts**)
Airspace, defined, 332
Alarm systems
    Fire, 101, 121, 245-246
    Security, 97, 101, 260
All-risk insurance coverage, 134
Alterations or additions, and use restrictions, 236
Amending documents, 13-19
    Certified vs. verified, 19
    Consent needed for, 15
    Procedures for, 16-19
    Recording of, 17
    (As) source of legal authority, 2
Amendments
    (Of) articles of incorporation, 287-288
    (To) bylaws, 290
    (To) declaration, 289
    Forms for, 287-290
    Proposing, 68
Annexation, defined, 332
Annual membership meetings, 57, 101
    Agenda for, 276
    Notice of, 273
Annual report, 149

Annual statement of policies, 149
Antennas, 236
Appeals
    Due process and, 173
    Procedures for, 298-299
    Robert's Rules for, 65
Appliances, warranties on, 201
Architectural committee, 52, 236-237, 254-255
Architectural control, 254-258
    Committee for, 254-258
    Enforcement of, 256
    Guidelines for, 255-256
    Landscaping, 256-257
    (Of) phased projects, 270
    Solar panels, 257-258
Articles of Incorporation
    Amendment of, 287-288
    Defined, 8-9
    (As) source of legal authority, 1
Asbestos, 247-250
Assessments(s), 154-158
    Accelerating, 158
    Billing for, 158
    Challenging, 157-158
    Collection of, 159-163
    (Against) custodian unit, 207
    Delinquent, 160, 164-166, 305-308
    Exemption from, 157, 163
    Increases or decreases in, 145, 156, 302
    Insurance for, 132
    Notice of, 156
    Notice of delinquency, 306-307
    Notice of increase in, 302
    Organizational start-up and, 100
    Original, 154
    Payment of, 157
    Phased, 156-157
    (In) phased developments, 267
    Pro-rated, 157
    Reminder of unpaid, 305
    Resales and, 262-263
    Setting, 154
    Special, 95, 155-156
    Utility, 225
Assessment liens, 160-161, 164-166
    Authority for, 164
    "Blanket," 164
    Foreclosure of, 165
    Notice of default in payment of, 308
    Notice of Delinquent Assessment, 164, 306-307
    Removal of, 165
    Satisfaction and release of, 309
    Subordination of, 161-162
    Use of to collect fines, 165-166

Assets, distribution of, 215
Assets and liabilities, statement of, 148
Assistant officers, 48
Association
    Authority to borrow money, 3-4, 99, 264
    Duties of, 5-7
    Enforcement powers of, 2, 168, 295
    Formation of, 12
    Incorporated vs. unincorporated, 23, 223
    Interaction between associations, 271
    Lawsuits against, 175-176
    Lawsuits by, 177-178
    Legal authority of, 1-4
    Liability of, 175-176
    Limits on authority, 4
    Master, 11, 271-272
    Master, defined, 333
    Mixed-use, 221, 224-5
    Sister, 11
    Sister, defined, 334
Association personal property insurance, 136
Association records (see **Records**)
Attorney
    Amending legal documents and, 16
    Contact with, 110-112
    Due process and, 172
    Litigation and, 191-192
    Need for, 98-99
    Selection of, 110-112
    Tax, 98
Attorneys' fees
    (In) collection of assessments, 163
    (In) lawsuit, 177-178
Attorney's opinion letter, 332
Audits, 150-151, 222
Automobile insurance, 135
Auxiliary structures, insurance coverage for, 136

B

Bad faith, of insurance company, 176
Balconies, maintenance of, 129
Ballots, 58, 77, 81-82
    Absentee, 82
    Form for, 279
    Secret, 77
    Spoiled, 80
    (See also **Elections, Voting**)
Bank account, 96, 100
    (See also **Reserves**)
Board meetings, 38-41
    Action without, 46
    Adjournment, 40, 64
    Equipment for, 41
    Executive session, 46
    First, 43-44, 94
    Location of, 38
    Minutes of, 39, 41-42, 62-63, 96, 281-283
    Notice of, 38, 46-47, 274
    Open vs. closed, 61-62
    Quorum for, 42-43
    Secret, 46
    (By) telephone, 46
    Timing of, 57
Board of Directors
    Architectural control and, 256, 269
    Budget and, 94-96
    Developer's obligations as member of, 197
    Developer's representation on, 85-86
    Eligibility for, 26
    Enforcement of developer's obligations, 35-36, 44-46
    Management by, 103-104
    Operations of, 41-42
    Role of, 41
    Security and, 259
    Size of, 26, 82-83
    Tenants and, 243
    Toxic substances and, 251
    (See also **Board meetings; Directors**)
Boiler and machinery insurance coverage, 136
Boilerplate provisions
    Committees and, 52, 55
    Defined, 13
Bonding
    (Of) developer, 44-46, 195-197, 269
    (Of) officers and directors, 37
Budget
    Adoption of, 94-96
    Estimating expenses for, 147
    First by new board, 145
    Items in, 144
    Organizational startup and, 100
    Original, 144-145
    (In) phased developments, 267
    Sample, 303
Builder (see **Developer**)
Business judgment, defined, 332
Business judgment rule, 33
Bylaws
    Amendments to, 290
    Defined, 9
    (As) source of legal authority, 1

C

Cable television contract, 118
Calling for the question, 67
Capital improvements, contracts for, 120
Carport maintenance, 130
Cash basis in accounting, 149
Casualty insurance, 133
Certificate of correction, 229
Certified document, 19
Certified public accountant (CPA), 98, 112-113, 218
Chairperson
    (Of) board meeting, 39
    (Of) general membership meetings, 58, 62
Checks, signatures on, 96
Chief financial officer (treasurer), 50
    Management and, 103-104
    Reports of, 39-40

*(See also **Officers**)*
Children, discrimination against, 235
Chimney sweeping, 125
Civil rights
    (In) amending legal documents, 16
    Discrimination and, 22
Civil Rights Act, 22
"Claims made" insurance coverage, 137
Closed board meetings, 46
Clotheslines, 236
Co-insurance, 138-139
Committees, 51-55
    (For) amending legal documents, 16
    Architectural, 52, 236-237, 254-256
    Delegation of duties to, 51-52
    (In) due process, 173
    Fiscal, 53
    Grievance, 226
    Landscaping, 54-55
    (In) legal documents, 11
    Maintenance, grounds and equipment, 53-54
    Membership in, 51
    Nominating, 52-53, 78
    Owner relations, 54
    Personnel, 53
    Public relations and, 226
    Purpose of, 51
    Reports of, 38-40, 55
    Rules, 55
    Security, 97
    Social/recreational, 54
Common Area
    (In) condominium plan, 9
    Defined, 332
    Exclusive-use rights, 122, 228-230
    Maintenance of, 122
    Record of assignments, 91
    Restricted, 122, 228-229, 265-266
    Title to, 265-266
Common area office
    Reconversion of, 210
    Rental to developer, 209
Common-interest ownership
    (In) legal documents, 11-12
    Title problems in, 265-266
Common-interest subdivision or development
    (In) declaration, 8
    Defined, 332
    Membership in, 10
Common law
    Defined, 332
    Developer's obligation under, 194-195
    Duties of association and, 6-7
    (As) source of legal authority, 3
Communications, 226-227
Community Associations Institute, 17-18, 101, 110, 227
Compensation
    (Of) in-house manager, 104
    (Of) officers and directors, 34-35

Complaint(s)
    Amended, 296
    (About) construction and design defects, 187
    Grievance committee and, 226-227
    Management and, 109
    Procedures for, 187
Complaint register, 109
Completion bond, 196
Comprehensive insurance coverage, 134
Computers, 96
Condemnation, 179-183
    (Of) condominium, 182
    Defined, 332
    Eminent domain and, 179-180
    Partial, 179
    (Of) planned development project, 182
    (Of) stock cooperative project, 182-183
Condominium
    Condemnation of, 182
    Defined, 332
Condominium conversions, and warranties, 199
Condominium plan
    Defined, 9
    (As) permanent record, 91
Conflicts of interest
    (Of) directors, 34
    (Of) officers, 48-49
Consent, written
    (In) amending legal documents, 14
    Voting by, 15, 77
Construction, completion of, 195, 202
Construction/design defects, 187-193
    Complaints about, 187
    Developer's responsibility for, 188, 199
    Directors' responsibility for, 188-189
    Latent defects, 192, 200
    Litigation concerning, 191-192, 202-203
    Plans and specifications and, 187-188
    Statutes of limitation and, 192-193
    Types of, 190-191
    Warranties and, 198-199
Consultants, 110-114
    Attorney (*see **Attorney***)
    Certified public accountant, 112-113, 218
    Contracts for (*see **Contracts***)
    Insurance broker, 113-114
Consumer protection laws, 152, 194
Contracts, 115-120
    Cable television, 118
    Capital improvements, 120
    Consultant, 120
    Form of, 115-116, 310-331
    Garage maintenance, 118
    Garbage and trash disposal, 119-120
    Janitorial/window cleaning service, 118
    Landscape, 116-117, 325-327
    Laundry operations, 117
    Lease, 330-331
    Management, 107-108, 116, 310-324
    Organizational start-up and, 100

Painting, 118-119
Pest control, 117-118
Recreational facility maintenance, 328-329
Resolution approving adoption of, 324
Remodeling, 120
Security, 118
Snow removal, 119
Street repair, 119
Termination of management, 108
Contractors
    Bids and proposals from, 116-120
    Notification of, 101
Contractual authority, 115
Contractual duties of association, 5-6
Contractual liability, 185
    (Of) association, 175-176
    (Of) members, 22
    (Of) officers and directors, 36
Contractual obligations, of developer, 194
Corporate records, 152-153
Corporate resolution, 264
Corporate seal, 93
Correcting deed, 229
Counsel *(see **Attorney**)*
Courts
    Choice of, 177
    Collection of assessments and, 162
    Due process and, 172
    Enforcement of restrictions and, 170
    Interpretation of documents by, 20
    Reformation of documents and, 20
Covenant
    Defined, 332
    Restrictive, 8, 205-206, 334
Covenant running with the land, 8, 332
Cross-liability endorsement, 139
Cumulative voting, 76, 86
Custodian unit, 207-208

D

Debate, limiting, 67
Decks, maintenance of, 129
Declaration
    Amendment to, 289
    Defined, 8, 332
    (As) source of legal authority, 1
Declaration of restrictions, 8
Declaratory relief, 170
Decorum, at meetings, 70
Deed
    Correcting, 229
    Use in creating condominium project or PD, 9
Delegation of duties, 34, 51-52, 109
Delinquent assessments, 160-163
    Liens and, 160-163, 164-167
    Notice of, 159-162, 164-167, 305-308
Deposition, defined, 178
Design changes, developer's responsibility for, 203
Design defects *(see **Construction/design defects**)*

Destruction, of project, 211-215
Developer
    Actions against, 204-205
    Bonding of, 44-45
    Collecting assessments from, 159-160
    Documents to obtain from, 63
    Enforcement of restrictions by, 169
    Liability of, 44, 202
    (Of) phased projects, 270
    Product liability insurance and, 205
    Promises and representations, 203-204, 270
    Rental of common area office to, 209-210
    Responsibility for construction/design defects, 188, 202-204
    Responsibility for design changes, 203
    Restrictive covenants and, 205-206
    Voting privilege of, 61, 73, 77-78, 86
    Warranties and, 198-201, 204
Developer's obligations, 194-197
    (As) board member, 197
    Bonded, 195-197
    Common law imposed, 194-195
    Consumer protection laws, 194
    Contractual, 194
    Disclosure as, 197
    Enforcement of, 36, 44-46
    Statutory, 194
Directors, 26-47
    Bonding of, 37
    Business judgment of, 33
    Compensation of, 34-35
    Conflicts of interest of, 34
    Defense costs for, 37
    Delegating duties of, 34, 51-52, 109
    Duties of, 31-33
    Election of, 28-29
    Enforcement of restrictions by, 168-169
    Indemnifying, 37-38
    Initial, 27
    Insurance protection for, 37, 135-136
    (In) legal documents, 10
    Liability of, 35-36
    Nomination of, 27-28
    Number of, 26, 82-83
    Prudent person rule and, 33-34, 333-334
    Quorum of, 42-43
    Removal of, 30-31, 83
    Replacement of, 31
    Resignation of, 29-30
    Responsibility for construction/design defects, 202-203
    Term of office of, 26-27
    *(See also **Board meetings, Board of Directors**)*
Disciplinary actions, 169-170, 296-299
Disclosure requirements, 152, 197
Discovery, 178
Discrimination
    Age, 235-236
    (In) sale or lease, 22
    (In) use restrictions, 241

Documents, to obtain from developer, 63-64
 (See also Legal documents)
Dram shop insurance coverage, 136
Due process, 172-174
 (In) amending legal documents, 15-16
 Court test of, 172-173
 Hearings, 172-174

E

Earthquake insurance, 134
Easements, 231-232, 265-266
Elections, 73-84
 Ballots for, 58-59, 78-82
 Checklist for, 80, 81
 Contesting, 84
 (Of) directors, 28-29
 Forms for, 277-280
 Notice of, 84
 Preparation for, 58, 78-82
 Procedures for, 58-59
 Record-keeping for, 84
 (See also Nominations; Voting)
Elevator maintenance, 124-125
Eminent domain
 Condemnation and, 179-180
 Defined, 333
Enforcement of association rules, procedures for, 295-299
Enforcement of restrictions, 168-170, 241
 Authority for, 168
 (By) developer, 169
 Directors and, 169
 Disciplinary actions, 169-170
 Fines, 243-244, 298
 Obligations for, 168
 Officers and, 169
 (By) owners, 169-170
 Prerequisites to, 168-169
 Remedies and defenses, 170
 Waivers and, 169
Equipment
 Instructions for, 101
 Landscaping, 53-54, 123-124
 Laundry, 117
 Maintenance of, 53-54, 124
 Warranties on, 201
Equitable servitudes, defined, 333
Estoppel certificates, 163, 263
Exclusive-use (restricted) common area rights, 122, 228-230
Executive Council of Homeowners (ECHO), 17, 101, 110, 227
Executive session, 46
Expenses, estimating, 147
Expert witness, 191
Express warranties, 198, 204, 333
Extension, of projects, 216
Extra majority, 77

F

Fannie Mae *(see Federal National Mortgage Association)*
Federal Home Loan Mortgage Corporation (FHLMC), 333
 Condemnation and, 181
 Delegation of duties and, 51-52, 109
 Destruction of project and, 214
 Insurance and, 134
 Lease/occupancy and, 242
 Legal authority of associations and, 1
 Professional management and, 105
 Voting and, 77
Federal Housing Administration (FHA), 333
 Delegation of duties and, 109
 Legal authority of associations and, 1
Federal income taxes, 218-219
Federal National Mortgage Association (FNMA), 333
 Bonded obligations of builder/developer and, 196-197
 Delegation of duties and, 51-52, 109
 Insurance and, 134
 Lease/occupancy and, 242
 Legal authority of associations and, 1
 Professional management and, 105
 Voting and, 77
Federal statutes
 (On) asbestos, 247-249
 Duties of the association and, 6
 (As) source of legal authority, 1-2
Federal Trade Commission, 2
Fees
 Attorneys', 163, 177-178
 (For) collecting assessments, 161, 162-163
 (For) recording amended documents, 17
 (For) review of plans and specifications, 256
 (For) tenants, 243
 Transfer, 24, 262
Fences, maintenance of, 129-130
FHA *(see Federal Housing Administration)*
FHLMC *(see Federal Home Loan Mortgage Corp.)*
Fiduciary duty, of directors, 32-33
Filing system, 99-100
Financial management, 144-147
 Assessments, 100, 145
 Bank account, 96, 100
 Budget, 94-96, 144-147, 267
 Estimating expenses, 147
 Investing funds, 146-147
 (Of) phased development, 267-268
 Professional services, 98, 104-105, 112-114
 Reserve fund, 95-96, 148-149
 Start-up funds, 144
 (See also Chief financial officer; Fiscal Committee)
Financial Reports, 148-149
 Sample of, 303
Fines
 Architectural control and, 256
 (To) enforce restrictions, 169

Structure for, 298
(Against) tenants, 243-244
Use of liens to collect, 165-166
Fire insurance, 246
Fire safety, 245-246
   Alarm systems, 101, 121-122, 245-246
   Rules for, 246
First meetings, 43, 56
First refusal, right of, 25, 262
Fiscal committee, 53
Flood insurance, 134
Floor, obtaining, 67
FNMA *(see **Federal National Mortgage Assoc.**)*
Foreclosure, 159, 160, 162, 163, 165
Formaldehyde foam insulation, 250
Foundations
   Common, 130-131, 232
   Defects in, 189-190
   Maintenance of, 130-131
Freddie Mac *(see **Federal Home Loan Mortgage Corporation**)*
Funds, investment of, 113, 146-147

G

Garage maintenance, 130
   Contract for, 118
Garbage disposal contract, 119-120
General membership meeting, notice of, 57, 274
   *(See also **Meetings**)*
Glass coverage rider, 136
Grandfather clause, 15
Grievance committee, 226
Guards and patrols, 260
Guests, 233

H

Handicapped regulations, 238-239
Hearings, 173-174
   Notice of, 300
   Procedures for, 296-299
   Record of, 173
HO-6 insurance policy, 132-133
Hobbies, and use restrictions, 239
Homeowners association groups, 101-102, 110, 227
Homeowner Rules and Regulations, 94, 233-234
   Example of, 291-294
   Procedures for enforcement of, 295-299
   *(See also **Use Restrictions**)*
HUD *(see **U.S. Department of Housing and Urban Development**)*

I

Implied warranties, 198-199, 204, 333
Income tax
   Federal, 218-219
   State, 219
Incorporation
   Incorporated vs. unincorporated association, 23, 223
   Limited liability and, 185-186
   *(See also **Articles of Incorporation**)*
Indemnity, 37-38
Independent contractors, 108
Inflation guard endorsements, 137
Information, request for, 69
Inspections, 109
Insulation
   Asbestos, 247-251
   Formaldehyde foam, 250
Insurance, 132-143
   Automobile, 135
   (On) auxiliary structures, 136
   Casualty, 133
   "Claims made," 137
   Co-insurance, 138-139
   Comprehensive, 134
   Coverage checklist, 139-140
   Cross-liability endorsement, 139
   (On) custodian unit, 207
   Deductible, 141
   Destruction of project and, 213-215
   Distribution of proceeds, 215
   Dram shop coverage, 136
   Earthquake, 134
   (For) exclusive-use common areas, 230
   Failure to obtain, 36
   Fire, 246
   Flood, 134
   Glass coverage, 136
   Individual policy, 132-133
   Inflation guard endorsement, 137
   Liability, 133-134
   Master policy, 132, 140-143
   Non-conforming building endorsement, 138
   (For) officers and directors, 37, 135-136
   Organizational startup and, 100-101
   Over-insurance, 141
   (In) phased projects, 269
   Personal property, 136
   Policy exclusions, 138
   Product liability, 137, 205
   Property damage, 137
   Purchase of, 139
   Rain damage, 136
   Recommendations on, 142-143
   Replacement cost endorsement, 137
   Special multi-peril policy, 142
   Umbrella coverage, 136-137
   Title, 137, 265
Insurance broker, 113-114
Insurance company
   Bad faith of, 176
   Defense by, in lawsuit, 176
Internal Revenue Code, 2
   Changes in legal documents and, 14
   Condemnation and, 181

(On) incorporation, 222
(On) stock cooperatives, 218-219
Tax exemption and, 219-220
(See also Taxes)
Interrogatories, defined, 178
Interstate Land Sales Registration Act, 2
Investment management, 113, 146-147
Irrigation system, defects in, 189

J

Janitorial service, 53, 118
    Contract for, 118
Joint and several liability, 185
Judicial foreclosure, 162

L

Landscape contract, 116-117, 325-327
Landscaping
    Control of, 256-257
    Defects in, 189-190
    Maintenance of, 123-124, 129
Landscaping committee, 54-55
Latent defects, 192, 200-201
Laundry operations contract, 117
Lawsuits, 175-178
    Asbestos and, 248-249
    (Against) association, 175-176
    (By) association, 177-178
    Avoiding, 190-191
    (For) collection of assessment, 162
    (For) construction/design defects, 191-192, 204
    Statutes of limitation and, 192-193
Lawyer *(see Attorney)*
Laying (motion) on the table, 69-70
Lead, 250
Lease agreement, sample, 330-331
Lease/occupancy, 243
Legal authority of association, 1-4
    (To) borrow money, 3-4, 99, 264
    Contractual, 115-116
    Limits on, 3
    (To) rent common area office to developer, 209-210
    Sources of, 1-3
    Standard of reasonableness and, 4
Legal counsel *(see Attorney)*
Legal defense
    Enforcement of restrictions, 170
    (By) insurance company, 176
    (For) officers and directors, 37
Legal documents, 8-20
    Amending, 13-20
    Basic, 8-10
    Certified vs. verified, 19-20
    Grandfather clause in, 15
    Interpretation of, 2
    Judicial review and interpretation of, 20
    Reformation by court order, 20
    Review of, 94-95
    (See also Contracts)
Letters
    (To) new owners, 301
    (Of) resignation, 286
Liability, 184-186
    (In) amending legal documents, 16
    (Of) association, 175-176
    Contractual, 22, 35, 175-176, 185
    (Of) developer, 44, 202
    (For) exclusive-use common areas, 230
    (Of) individuals, 22
    Joint and several, 185
    Limited, 36-37, 185-186
    (Of) officers and directors, 35-37
    (For) payment of assessments, 162
    Personal, 35
    Tort, 22, 35-36, 175, 184-185
Liability insurance, 133-134
Liens, 164-167
    Assessment, 160, 164-166, 308-309
    Authority for, 164
    "Blanket," 164
    Foreclosure of, 165
    Mechanics', 166-167
    Notice of default in payment of, 308
    Notice of delinquent assessment and, 164-165, 306-307
    Removal of, 165
    Satisfaction and release of, 165, 309
    Subordination of, 161-162
    Use to collect fines, 165-166
Lighting, 101
Loans, association's power to borrow, 3-4, 99, 264
Local ordinances
    Duties of association and, 6
    (As) source of legal authority, 1
Local taxes, 219
Loss assessment coverage, 132

M

Mail, voting, 77
Maintenance, 121-131
    (Of) carports and garages, 130
    (Of) chimneys, 125
    (Of) common areas, 122, 229-230
    (Of) common foundations, walls and roofs, 130-131
    (Of) decks, balconies and patios, 129-130
    (Of) elevators, 124-125
    (Of) equipment, 53-54, 124
    (Of) exclusive-use common areas, 229-230
    (Of) fences, 129-130
    Janitorial service for, 130
    (Of) landscaping, 123-124, 129
    (Of) private areas, 122-123
    Responsibility for, 121
    (Of) roofs, 130-131
    (Of) shingles, 131
    Standards of, 129

(Of) storm and sanitary sewers, 130
(Of) streets and driveways, 125-128
(Of) stucco, 131
(Of) swimming pool, 123
(Of) windows, 130
Maintenance, property and equipment committee, 53
Majority vote, 77
    Extra majority, 77
Management, 103-109
    (By) board of directors, 103
    Complaints, 109, 226-227, 295-297
    Consultant, 105
    Contract, 107-108, 116
    Delegation of management duties, 109-110
    In-house, 104
    Inspections, 109
    (In) legal documents, 10-11
    Professional, 104-105
Management Consultant, 105
Management Contract, 107-108, 116
    Resolution approving adoption of, 324
    Sample, 310-323
    Termination of, 108-109
Management reports, 40
Manager
    Duties and responsibilities of, 310-323
    Resident, 104
    Selection of, 105-106
Master association, 271-272
    Defined, 11, 333,
    Membership in, 271
    Use restrictions and, 272
Master insurance policy, 132, 140-143
Materials and equipment warranties, 201
Mechanics' liens, 166-167
Meetings, 56-64
    Adjournment of, 64, 71-72
    Agenda of, 38-41, 62, 276
    Annual, 57, 101, 274-275, 276-280
    Attendance at, 57
    Board (see **Board meetings**)
    Calling, 57
    Conduct of, 58-59, 65-72
    Decorum at, 70
    First general membership, 56
    Location of, 58
    Minutes of (see **Minutes**)
    Notices of, 45, 46-47, 57, 273-275
    Quorum for, 60-61
    Rules for conducting, 58-59
    Secret, 46
    Special, 57
Membership, 21-23
    Age and, 22, 235-236
    Classes of, 10
    (Of) committees, 51
    Exclusion from, 22
    Incorporated vs. unincorporated association, 23
    (In) legal documents, 10
    Liability of, 22

    Qualifications for, 21
    Suspension of, 21-22
    Transfer of, 10, 24-25, 74-75, 262-263
Membership certificates, 21
Membership roster or membership roll, 21, 59-60, 91-92
Merchant builders, 195, 333
*(See also **Developer**)*
Meters, for utilities, 224-225
Minority interests, protection of, 83-84
Minutes book, 62, 63, 89, 90, 153
Minutes, 62-63, 87-89
    (Of) action without meeting, 88
    (Of) board meetings, 38-41, 62-63, 87-88, 281-283
    Forms for, 281-283
    (Of) general membership meetings, 62-63, 87-88
    Resolutions in, 88-89
    (Of) telephone meetings, 88
Mixed-use association
    Destruction of, 212-213
    Taxes and, 221
    Utilities in, 224-225
MLB-29 policy, 142
Motions
    (In) board meetings, 39
    Defined, 65
    (In) general membership meetings, 63
    Laying on the table, 69-70
    (For) nominations, 67-68
    Privileged, 68-69
    Reconsidering, 70
    Seconding, 66
    Substitute, 68

N

National Environmental Policy Act, 2
New Owners
    Sample letter to, 301
    Statement from association to, 263
    *(See also **Resales, Transfer of Membership**)*
Newsletter, 227
Noise levels, 239-240
Nominating committee, 52-53, 78
Nominations
    (Of) directors, 27-28
    Motions for, 67-68
    Procedure for, 27-28, 84
Nonconforming building endorsement, 138
Non-owned automobiles, insurance on, 135
Notice(s)
    (Of) annual meeting, 273-275
    (Of) assessments, 156
    (Of) board meetings, 38, 46-47
    (Of) default in payment of assessment lien, 308
    (Of) delinquency, 160, 164-166, 306-307
    (Of) elections, 76, 84
    (Of) general membership meetings, 57

(Of) hearings, 296-299, 300
(Of) increase in assessment, 302
Organizational start-up and, 100
(Of) owners' meeting, 273-275
Pertaining to enforcement of rules, 295-300
Waiver of, 47, 57, 284

O

Obsolescence, 211
Obtaining the floor, 67
"Occurrence" insurance coverage, 137
Office, rental of, 209-210
Officers, 48-50
    Assistant, 48
    Bonding of, 37
    Compensation of, 34-35
    Conflicts of interest of, 34, 48-49
    Contractual authority of, 115
    Defense costs, 37
    Eligibility of, 48
    Enforcement of restrictions by, 168-169
    Indemnifying, 37-38
    Insurance for, 37, 135-136
    (In) legal documents, 10
    Liability of, 35-37
    Selection of, 27-28, 31
    (See also Directors)
One form of action only rule, 161
Open meetings, 61-62
Operation *(see Administration/operation)*
Orders of the day, 69
Ordinances *(see Local Ordinances)*
Organization startup, 100-102
    Checklist for, 100-102
Owner relations committee, 54
Owners association *(see Association)*
Owners' meeting, notice of, 272-275
    (See also Meetings)

P

PD *(see Planned Development)*
Painting contract, 118-119
Parking
    Assigned, 91, 237-238
    Exclusive-use rights and, 228-230
    Use restrictions and, 237-238
    (See also Garage maintenance)
Parliamentary procedure, 39-43, 62
    Table of, 71, 72
    (See also Robert's Rules of Order)
Partial condemnation, 179
Partition, defined, 333
Party walls,
    Defined, 231
    Fire safety and, 121
    Maintenance of, 130-131, 231
Patios, maintenance of, 129
Perpetuities, rule against, 25
Personal liability

(Of) members, 22
(Of) officers and directors, 35-37
Personal property taxes, 219
Personnel committee, 53
Pest control, 252-253
    (As) administrative task, 101
    Contract for, 117-118
    Repairs and, 252-253
    Responsibility for, 252
Pet(s)
    Changes in rules concerning, 15, 240
    Use restrictions on, 241
Pet amortization rule, 240
Phased assessments, 156-157
Phased development, 267-270
    Annexation of phases and, 86
    Architectural control of, 269-270
    Assessments in, 267
    Budgets in, 267
    Defined, 12-13
    Developer's obligations in, 44-46
    Insurance on, 269
    Promises and representations by developer, 270
    Recreational facilities in, 268-269
    Subsidization and, 267
Pick-up work (warranty), 199-201
Plandominium, 180
Planned development (PD)
    Condemnation of, 182
    Defined, 333
Planned unit development (PUD)
    Defined, 333
    Local ordinances and, 6
    Subdivision map of, 9
Plans and specifications
    Architectural control and, 254
    Construction/design defects and, 187-188
    (As) permanent records, 91
Point of information, 69
Point of order, 66-67
Pool maintenance, 101, 123
Population density restrictions, 235
President, 49
    (See also Officers)
Privileged motions, 68-69
Product liability insurance, 137, 205
Profit and loss statement, 148
Project
    Destruction of, 211-215
    Extension of, 216
    Obsolescence of, 211
    Termination of, 216-217
Property damage insurance, 137
Property rights, in amending legal documents, 16
Property taxes, 219
Proxies, 58, 59, 60, 75-76, 82
    Form for, 277
Prudent person rule, 33-340 334
Public relations, 226-227
PUD *(see Planned unit development)*

Q

Question of order, 66
Quorum
    Defined, 334
    (Of) directors, 42-43
    (For) general membership meeting, 60-61

R

Radon gas, 250
Rain damage, insurance coverage for, 136
Readers, for elections, 80
Real estate broker, rental of common area office to, 209
Real Estate Settlement Procedures Act, 2
Real property taxes, 219
Reasonableness
    Standard of, 4
    Test of, 3
Rebuilding, 211-215
Recess, of meeting, 71
Records, 90-92
    Checklist of, 90
    Filing system for, 99-100
    (Of) hearings, 173
    Minutes *(see Minutes)*
    Organizational start-up and, 100-101
Recreational facilities
    Maintenance agreement for, 328-329
    (In) phased projects, 268-269
Reminder of unpaid assessments, 305
Remodeling, contract for, 120
Rental management agreement, 210, 330-331
Replacement cost endorsement, 137
Reports
    Annual, 149
    Committee, 39-40, 55
    Corporate, 152-153
    Financial, 148-149
    Management, 40
    Statutory, 152
Request for information, 69
Resales, 262-263
Rescission, purchaser's right of, 197, 204-205
"Reservation of rights," defense under, 176
Reserves, 96, 148
    Investment of, 146
    Sample reserve account sheet, 303
    Statement of, 148
Resident manager, 104
Resignation(s)
    (Of) directors, 29-30
    Sample letter of, 286
Resolutions, 63, 65-66, 88-89
    Corporate, 264
    (On) exempt status, 304
    Sample, 285
Restraints on alienation, rule against, 25
Restricted common area, 122, 228-229, 229, 265-266

Restrictions
    Enforcement of, 168-169, 241
    Waiver of, 169
    (See also Use restrictions)
Restrictive covenant
    Defined, 334
    Failure to enforce, 205
    "Running with the land," 8, 332
Road maintenance, 125-128
    Contract for, 119
Robert's Rules of Order, 65-72
    Adjournment, 71
    Amendments, 68
    Appeals, 67
    Calling for the question, 67
    Decorum, 70
    Laying motion on the table, 69-70
    Motions, 65, 66, 67-71
    Nominations, 67-68
    Obtaining the floor, 67
    Orders of the day, 69
    Point of order, 66-67
    Privileged motions, 68-69
    Recess, 71
    Reconsidering motions, 70
    Request for information, 69
    Resolutions, 63, 65-66, 88-89
    Seconding motions, 66
    Substitute motions, 68
    Suspension of rules, 69
    Table of parliamentary rules, 71-72
    Voting, 70-71
Roofs
    Common, 130-131, 232
    Defects in, 188-189
    Maintenance of, 130-131
Rules, suspension of, 69
Rules and regulations *(see Homeowner rules and regulations)*
Rules committee, 55
Rules of order *(see Robert's Rules of Order)*

S

Seal, corporate, 93
Seconding motions, 66
Secret ballot, 77
Secret meetings, 46
Secretary, 49-50
    Management and, 103
    Membership roster and, 21, 59-60
    Voting register and, 74
    (See also Minutes; Officers)
Securities and Exchange Commission (SEC), 2
Security, 259-261
    Committee for, 97, 261
    Contract for, 118
    Fire safety, 245-246
    Systems for, 97, 101, 260

Senior citizens' projects, 235-236
Sewers, maintenance of, 130
Shingles, maintenance of, 131
Sign(s), 236, 262
Sign-in sheet, 58, 278
Sister association, defined, 11, 334
Smoke detectors, 121, 245
Snow removal contract, 119
Social/recreational committee, 54
Soil problems, 189
Solar panels, 257-258
Special assessments, 95, 155-156
Special meetings, 57
Special multi-peril (SMP) policy, 142
Sprinkler system, 101, 123-124
Square footage, as basis of percentage interests, 12
State income taxes, 219
State regulatory agencies, and changes in legal documents, 13-14
State statutes
   (On) amending legal documents, 14
   Consumer protection laws, 152, 194
   (On) destruction of projects, 213
   Duties of association and, 5
   Proxy votes and, 75-76
Statement of Assets and Liabilities, 148
Statement of reserves, 148
Statutes *(see **Federal statutes, State statutes**)*
Statutes of limitation, 192-193
Statutory duties of association, 5
Statutory obligations of developer, 194
Statutory reports, 152
Stock cooperative project
   Condemnation of, 182-183
   Liability in, 186
   Taxes and, 218-219
Storm drains, maintenance of, 130
Street maintenance, 125-128
   Contract for, 119
Stucco, maintenance of, 131
Subdivision maps, 9-10, 91
Subordination of liens, 161-162
Subpoenas, 178
Subrogation, waiver of, 138-139
Subsidy, 267
Subsidy bond, 196-197, 267
Substitute motions, 68
Suits *(see **Lawsuits**)*
Summons, 178
Suspension of membership, 21-22
Suspension of the rules, 69
Swimming pool maintenance, 101, 123

T
Tabling a motion, 69-70
Tally clerks, 80, 81
Tally sheets, 79-80
Tax(es), 218-223
   Destruction of project and, 215
   Federal, 218
   Local, 219
   Minimizing, 221
   Personal property, 219
   Real property, 219
   State, 219
Tax exempt status, resolution on, 304
Tax exemptions, 219-220
Tax identification number, 223
Tax laws, changes in legal documents and, 14
Tax lawyer, 98
Tax Reform Act of 1976, 222
Tax returns, 100, 112, 113, 222
Telephone meetings, 46, 88
Television
   Antennas, 236
   Cable, 118
Tenants, 242-244
   Discipline of, 243-244
   Fees for, 243
   Restrictions on, 242-243
Termination of project, 216-217
Termites, 252-253
Time-share, defined, 334
Title, 265-266
Title insurance, 137, 265
Tort liability, 184-185
   (Of) association, 175
   (Of) members, 22
   (Of) officers and directors, 35-36
Townhouse, defined, 334
Toxic materials, 247-251
Transfer fees, 24, 262
Transfer of membership, 24
   First refusal right and, 24, 262
   Resales and, 262
   Restrictions on, 24-25
   Voting and, 74-75
Trash disposal contract, 119-120
Treasurer *(see **Chief financial officer**)*
Two-class voting, 14, 73-74

U
Umbrella association *(see **Master association**)*
Umbrella insurance policy, 136-137
Uniform Condominium Act, 198
Unincorporated association
   Contractual authority and, 115
   Defined, 334
   Incorporated association vs., 23, 223
   Proxy rights in, 60
Unit, defined, 334
Urea formaldehyde foam insulation (UFFI), 250
U.S. Consumer Products Safety Commission, 249
U.S. Department of Housing and Urban Development (HUD), 333
U.S. Environmental Protection Agency, 247-248

Use restrictions, 235-241
    Age, 235-236
    Alterations or additions, 236
    Antennas, 236
    Clotheslines, 236
    Discriminatory, 241
    Enforcement of, 168-170, 242
    Hobbies, 239
    Master association and, 272
    Noise, 239-240
    Parties, 240-241
    Pets, 240
    Population density, 235
    Signs, 236
    Unreasonable, 241
    Vehicles and parking, 237-238
    Violations of, 241
    Waiver of, 169
    Window coverings, 236
Use rights *(see Exclusive-use common area rights)*
Utilities, 224-225

V

VA *(see Veterans Administration)*
Vandalism, 124
Vehicles, 237-238
    (See also Parking)
Verified document, 19
Veterans Administration (VA), 1, 334
Vice-president, 49
    (See also Officers)
Voting, 73-74, 83-84
    (On) amending legal documents, 14-15
    Ballots for, 58, 80, 81-82, 279
    Calling for the question, 67
    Cumulative, 76-77
    Custodian unit and, 207
    (By) developer, 61, 73, 77, 85
    (By) mail, 77
    Majority, 77
    Nominating committee and, 52-53, 78
    Procedures for, 28-29, 58-59
    (By) proxy, 58, 59, 60, 81-82, 277
    (For) removal of director, 30-31
    Robert's Rules on, 65, 70
    (By) secret ballot, 77
    Suspension of voting rights, 84
    Transfer of membership and, 74-75
    Two-class, 14, 73-74
    Weighted, 73
    Written consent and, 15
    (See also Elections)
Voting register, 74
Voting rights, suspension of, 84

W

Waiver of notice, 47, 57, 284
Waiver of restrictions, 169
Waiver of subrogation, 138
Walls
    Maintenance of, 130-131
    Party, 130-131, 231
Warranties, 194, 198-199
    Actions against developer and, 204
    (On) appliances, 201
    (On) condominium conversions, 199
    Express, 198, 204
    Implied, 195, 198-199, 204
    (On) materials and equipment, 201
    Pick-up work and, 199-201
Warranty work, 199-201
Water leakage, 189
Weighted voting, 73
Window Cleaning, 130
    Contract for, 118
Window coverings, 236
Worker's Compensation Insurance, 135

Z

Zero lot lines, 231-232

Order Form

Hanna Press
525 University Avenue, Suite 705
Palo Alto, CA 94301-1921

(650) 321-5700
Fax (650) 321-5639

Please send me the following book by John Paul Hanna and Grace Morioka:

_____ copy(ies) of <u>Homeowners Associations</u>
at $35.00 each - $_____

California residents add applicable sales tax -   _____

Shipping: _____

- Priority mail - $4.30 for one book (3 lbs.)
- Standard/bound and printed matter - $1.60 to $2.60 for one book, depending on zone

Total Order - $_____

I understand that I may return any book within ten (10) days for a full refund if not satisfied.

Name: _____

Address: _____

_____

City/State/Zip: _____

Telephone: _____